DICKENS STUDIES ANNUAL
Essays on Victorian Fiction

DICKENS STUDIES ANNUAL
Essays on Victorian Fiction

EDITORS

Michael Timko
Fred Kaplan
Edward Guiliano

DICKENS STUDIES ANNUAL

Essays on Victorian Fiction

VOLUME
10

Edited by

Michael Timko, Fred Kaplan,
and Edward Guiliano

AMS PRESS, INC.
NEW YORK, N.Y.

DICKENS STUDIES ANNUAL

ISSN 0084-9812

International Standard Book Number
Series: 0-404-18520-7
Vol. 10: 0-404-18530-4

Dickens Studies Annual: Essays on Victorian Fiction welcomes essay and monograph-length contributions on Dickens as well as on other Victorian novelists and on the history or aesthetics of Victorian fiction. All manuscripts should be double-spaced, including footnotes, which should be grouped at the end of the submission, and should be prepared according to current MLA style. An editorial decision can usually be reached more quickly if two copies are submitted. The preferred editions for citations from Dickens' works are the Clarendon and the Norton Critical when available, otherwise the Oxford Illustrated Dickens or the Penguin.

Please send submissions to the Editors, *Dickens Studies Annual*, Room 1522, Graduate School and University Center, City University of New York, 33 West 42nd Street, New York, N.Y. 10036; please send subscription inquiries to AMS Press, 56 East 13th Street, New York, N.Y. 10003.

Contents

Preface

This is the third consecutive volume of *DSA* in which we are fortunate to print a previously unpublished or unattributed work by a major Victorian author, in this instance William Morris's *The Novel on Blue Paper*. Once again the *Annual* contains a range of scholarship and criticism on Dickens and on other Victorian authors, and we continue to cover selectively the field of Victorian fiction with research guides/review essays. This volume, as has also previously been the case, contains several essays considerably longer than standard journal length. The Morris novel and the long essays explain why this number contains fewer essays than the previous two, although it is approximately the same length.

Looking ahead, we are pleased to say that *DSA 11* will follow this volume in just a few months, and that it will contain a generous allotment of essays on Dickens. By publishing two volumes of *DSA* within a year's time, we are making up for the year lost in the transfer of the *Annual* from Southern Illinois University and are clearing our files of accepted essays so that we can continue to give new submissions our full and uninhibited attention, and to offer timely publication of work we believe merits the attention of our readers.

We wish to thank Saul Novack, Dean of the Arts Division, Queens College, City University of New York; Deans Norma Rees and Sydel Silverman, Graduate Center, CUNY; Professor Lillian Feder, Executive Officier, Ph.D. Program in English, CUNY; Professor Lois Hughson, Chairperson of English, Queens College, CUNY; William B. Long, Editor, and Gabriel Hornstein, President, AMS Press, Inc.

We are especially grateful to Mr. F. H. Thompson, General

Secretary of the Society of Antiquaries of London for obtaining us permission to publish the Morris manuscript.

We are pleased to announce that beginning with this volume Donald Stone has joined our Editorial Board. Once again Jon Katz has contributed significantly to *DSA* through his excellent work as our editorial assistant. And once more we wish to express our gratitude to all the readers and advisors whose generous efforts serve us all.

THE EDITORS

Notes on Contributors

RICHARD D. ALTICK has recently retired as Regent's Professor of English at the Ohio State University. His next book, a study of the treatment of subjects from English literature in British art, 1760–1900, is on the way.

KATHLEEN BLAKE received her Ph.D. from the University of California, San Diego and is Associate Professor of English at the University of Washington. Author of *Play, Games, and Sport, The Literary Works of Lewis Carroll* (Ithaca and London: Cornell University Press, 1974) and articles on De Quincey, Jean-Paul Richter, George Eliot, Hardy, Olive Schreiner, Stevenson, and Barrie, she currently is writing about love and the woman question in Victorian literature and the role of women in ballet.

PENELOPE FITZGERALD is a novelist, biographer, and a committee member of the William Morris Society. Among numerous other works, she is the author of *Edward Burne-Jones: a Biography* (London: Michael Joseph, 1975). It was while working on this life that she became interested in Morris's *The Novel on Blue Paper*.

MARILYN GEORGAS is Professor of English at Lamar University in Beaumont, Texas. She has published articles on Sir Philip Sidney, on James Hogg and on *Blackwood's Edinburgh Magazine*. She is working currently on the relationship of *The Old Curiosity Shop* to the *ars moriendi* tradition.

EDWARD GUILIANO has written on numerous Victorian authors and topics but cites his work on Victorian comedy and especially on Lewis Carroll's nonsense as fundamental to his labors as an editor of *DSA*. His previous publications on Carroll include *Lewis Carroll*

Observed, ed. (1976); *Lewis Carroll: An Annotated International Bibliography* (1980); *Lewis Carroll: A Celebration*, ed. (1982); *The Complete Illustrated Works of Lewis Carroll*, ed. (1982); and *Soaring with the Dodo*, ed. with James Kincaid (1982). A bibliophile with a fine Dickens collection, he is currenting working on a critical edition of Dickens' major novels.

BARBARA FASS LEAVY, Associate Professor of English at Queens College, brings together many of her interests in her essay on Collins's *The Woman in White*. She is the author of *La Belle Dame sans Merci and the Aesthetics of Romanticism* (1974) and is presently working on a companion volume on the Demon Lover motif. Her works on demonology in the fairy tale and also on the history of British psychology during the Victorian age have been presented at the Research Seminars of the History of Psychiatry Section of the New York Hospital-Cornell Medical College at which she is a participating member.

DWIGHT N. LINDLEY is Hamilton B. Tompkins Professor of English Literature at Hamilton College. He co-edited, with Francis E. Mineka, *The Later Letters of John Stuart Mill*, Volumes XIV, XV, XVI, XVII, of the *Collected Works*.

ROGER D. LUND, Associate Professor of English at Le Moyne College, Syracuse, N.Y., compiled *Restoration and Early Eighteenth-Century English Literature, 1660–1740: A Selected Bibliography of Resource Materials* (MLA, 1980). His interest in satire had led to "*Res et Verba*; Scriblerian Satire and the Fate of Language," forthcoming in the *Bucknell Review*, and he is working on a study of Alexander Pope and his nineteenth-century critics.

SYLVIA MANNING is Chairperson of the English Department at the University of Southern California and Secretary-Treasurer of the Dickens Society. Her publications include *Dickens as Satirist* (1971).

BARBARA WEISS received her doctorate from Columbia University in 1981 and has taught at Fairleigh Dickinson University and Columbia University. She is currently teaching at Manhattanville College and finds solace during a grim economy by working on a study of bankruptcy in the Victorian novel.

Victorians on the Move; Or, 'Tis Forty Years Since

Richard D. Altick

In the dim, dear, distant days when academic paperwork got done perfectly well without the aid of computer printouts, course enrollments were tallied on a row of blackboards in the college gym, where registration, cafeteria-style, was held every term. It was at one such college, on one such occasion in September 1941, that somebody discovered that, for reasons not immediately clear, an announced course in Victorian poetry had attracted enough students to warrant its being given, and nobody had been assigned to teach it.

The task fell to the newest and lowest occupant of the departmental totem pole, a young instructor who was grateful, as any freshly fledged Ph.D. would be, for the chance to teach an advanced literature course. His qualifications to undertake a survey of Victorian poetry, however, hovered between the minimal and the non-existent. Such information as he had acquired in graduate school was mostly about eighteenth-century English literature and Romanticism. As an undergraduate at the same college, he had once taken a course in Victorian prose, but the intervening three or four years had sufficed to erase the memory of most of what he had read then, and, apart from the usual extracurricular indulgence in Dickens and possibly a few glimpses of other writers, that was the extent of his acquaintance with Victorian literature.

Of necessity, therefore, he had to learn as he taught. As it happened, the fact that his knowledge of Victorian matters was, at the

1

outset, a *tabula rasa* proved to be not so much a disadvantage as a stroke of luck, because it represented the general state of affairs as of 1941. If he was not actually present at the creation, he was certainly on hand in the very earliest stage of the scholarly study of Victorian literature and life. For if the appearance of an annual bibliography of publications can be said to mark the moment a scholarly discipline is officially recognized, this one was just eight years old, the first issue of the Victorian Bibliography, covering the publications of 1932, having been published in the May 1933 issue of *Modern Philology*. One who joined the nascent discipline in the early 1940s was privileged to watch it grow with what seems in retrospect to have been dramatic speed, to learn along with everybody else as Victorian studies passed, as it were, from the dark ages into the light of its own Renaissance. The development amounted to a textbook case, a paradigm, a microcosm of the way scholarly disciplines burgeoned in English and American culture after the Second World War.

Few specialists who joined the profession in, say, the 1960s can fully appreciate how recently, and from how low a starting point, this particular branch of English literary study rose. Medieval studies had long been established as a lofty and fertile field of humane learning. Decades earlier, scholars had found the English Renaissance colorful, intellectually and aesthetically exciting; the English eighteenth century had been discovered to be full of Palladian dignity as well as Hogarthian animation; the Romantic age had its own well established claims to attention, despite the demotion its poets had suffered at the hands of Paul Elmer More and the New Humanists and, more recently, the critical school of T. S. Eliot. And, thanks largely to the surge of nationalism in the fermenting 1930s—the rediscovery of America's unique past as well as a renewal of faith in its promise—the study of American literature had begun to generate its own excitement.

But *the Victorians*——! The very word was ineffaceably and banefully associated with Lytton Strachey and, even worse, his tinhorn imitators. In 1941, the twenty-three-year-old shadow of *Eminent Victorians* cast a retrospective pall, as well, over the whole long era that bore the name. Most of the popular writing that had been done on the Victorians since the First World War was wearisomely jokey, simply because the Stracheyan image of the age required it to be. Practically nobody under the age of fifty took the Victorians seriously. Yet Victorianism survived: people over fifty in the 1940s were Victorians by birth and often in spirit too, which rendered them fair targets for the iconoclasm of the new age. The Victorian era was still too close to the present to have any chance of being viewed with reasonable objectivity. Moreover, in the academic study of literature the unwritten criterion of a writer's suitability for serious consideration was that he be comfortably dead, preferably for a century or so. No one then envisaged that by the 1950s academic dissertations were to be devoted to authors who were not only alive but had hardly had time to acquire a reputation. To be sure, the Germans had never had any such ground rules: they had unapologetically prepared "philological" dissertations on Victorian authors while those authors were still alive, and were continuing to do so. But who, not least in the aftermath of the First World War and in the first years of the Second, cared what pedantic German scholars did? In the United States as well as in Britain, it was hard to justify studying Carlyle or Tennyson when so many older English authors still demanded attention.

The Victorians' fine arts likewise were so little valued that in 1935 John Martin's last apocalyptic canvases, a trilogy so sensationally popular in the 1850s that they had been toured in Britain and America as a profit-making exhibition, had brought at auction a total of seven pounds. The nadir, however, was reached about the same time when a London dealer offered to give a customer one of John William Waterhouse's paintings, which was taking up space in his showroom. The customer, who was broadminded and had nothing to lose, would have removed it, except that he found he could not get it inside a taxi. The routine destruction of Victorian buildings in the interests of "modernization" called forth no protests. On the contrary, people cheered as the wrecker's ball demolished the ornate Ruskinian facades. In music, only the continuing popularity of the Savoy operas reflected appreciation of the Victorians' achievement; their oratorios were as little esteemed by the discerning as the moral maxims of Martin Tupper.

Given such an atmosphere, it is no wonder that when a few academics began to take a serious interest in Victorian literature, they suffered a collective inferiority complex (a term that was outliving its vogue even then). The low opinion entertained of Victorianism in general lent, so it seems as one looks back, an air of embarrassment to their cottage industry. There was some encouragement to be found in the fact that they had nowhere to go but up. The trouble was that the basic materials for scholarship in their field still were lacking. Medievalists had their Wells *Manual* for bibliographical help, their long row of *EETS* texts, and Karl Young and E. K.

Chambers to provide a firm foundation for the study of the early drama. The eight volumes of Manly and Rickert's *The Text of the Canterbury Tales* were fresh from the press in 1940. Shakespeare scholarship could draw on the riches of the New Variorum, obsolescent as some of the volumes were, and on the first fruits of McKerrow, Greg, and Pollard's "New Bibliography." Miltonists had in hand Masson's seven-volume *Life*, and in 1940 the last volume of the Columbia *Milton* had been published. In eighteenth-century studies the letters of Addison, Steele, Sterne, Gray, Goldsmith, and Burns had been edited according to modern principles; R. K. Root and George Sherburn had laid the basis for the intensified study of Pope; and the eighteen-volume set of *The Private Papers of James Boswell from Malahide Castle* energized Johnsonian scholarship, though the Yale editions of Boswell and Johnson were still in the future and only a handful of people knew how large and rich a body of documents remained unpublished. Specialists in the Romantic period had the De Selincourt edition of Wordsworth's letters, Buxton Forman's of Keats's, and Grierson's of Scott's; they had Newman White's newly published life of Shelley, Howe's *Complete Works of Hazlitt*—and *The Road to Xanadu*.

No such array of bibliographies, editions, and biographies was available to the pioneering Victorian scholar. The only bibliography of earlier commentary which attempted comprehensiveness (it actually fell far short of that), Ehrsam, Deily, and Smith's *Bibliographies of Twelve Victorian Authors*, had appeared in 1936. A mere glance through it today would reveal how thin and superficial was the existing body of printed scholarship and criticism down to that time. The collected annual bibliographies for 1932–44 and C. F. Harrold's methodical survey of "Recent Trends in Victorian Studies, 1932–1939" in a 1940 issue of *Studies in Philology* are chiefly remarkable today for their demonstration of how few of the newly published books and articles they cite remain unsuperseded, and of how by far the greater part of our present knowledge has been acquired since then. The quantum leap that occurred in scientific knowledge after the Second World War had its counterpart in literary studies generally, but in Victorian studies especially.

Among collected editions of Victorian authors, the vast Cook and Wedderburn *Ruskin* stood out in lonely grandeur. Although, as Helen Gill Viljoen was to show, it was not without flaws, its comprehensiveness, minuteness of apparatus, and incredibly detailed index made it a model, for the time, of what a "definitive" edition should be like. There were no other models. Quite the contrary: the received texts of Victorian authors, if not always object lessons in How Not To Do it, were products of a pre-scientific age when texts were not sacrosanct and corruptions multiplied from edition to edition. The Bonchurch edition of Swinburne was unfortunately typical of most textual sources that Victorian scholars had to be content with unless they had access to the original printings.

There were then no biographies of Victorian writers to equal Wilbur Cross's lives of Fielding and Sterne. One read about Tennyson in his son's two-volume "memoir," a notorious masterpiece of suppression, evasion, and filial devotion, or in Harold Nicolson's shorter book, which was considerably livelier but identifiably a product of its time (1923). For Carlyle, there were David Alec Wilson's six heavily prejudiced volumes, more a compilation than a coherent, interpretive narrative. For Browning, there was the totally undistinguished Griffin and Minchin; for Rossetti, Mégroz and, of all people, Evelyn Waugh; for Morris, J. W. Mackail; for Charlotte Brontë, Mrs. Gaskell, still "standard" after over eighty years; for Dickens, Forster, considerably more informative than most biographies of great Victorians but by no means even-handed or well proportioned. In addition, there were the readable but slick and trendy biographies by such popularizers as "Hugh Kingsmill" and Hesketh Pearson; and the best that could be found on several lesser figures were the slim volumes in the English Men of Letters series, none of which provided a firm basis for intensive scholarly work.

Apart from Hugh Walker's severely dated *Literature of the Victorian Era* (1910), the only general history was Oliver Elton's belletristic two-volume *Survey of English Literature 1830–1880* (1920). Holbrook Jackson's *The Nineties* (1913) did a better job with the *fin de siècle* than anybody had succeeded in doing with the preceding fifty years. Whatever their deficiencies, these works nevertheless were more useful, except as a source of lively anecdotes to spice lectures, than such vulgarizations as "Frances Winwar's" best-selling biographical extravaganza starring the Pre-Raphaelites, *Poor Splendid Wings*.

The fund of criticism that could help a novice in 1941 get his bearings is best described by reciting a few names. The essayists—one shrinks from invoking the word "critics" in this context—who had written on the Victorians since the beginning of the century included Stopford Brooke, A. C. Benson, Arthur Symons, and F. L. Lucas. Between-the-wars commentators, who typically were belated Edwardians like Edmund Gosse or Georgians like J. C. Squire, either were candidly hostile to the Victorians or, in a dutiful but plainly unenthusiastic attempt to make the best case for them, succeeded only in showing that the best case they could make was not very convincing. Most of the wisdom on Dickens was concentrated in the volumes, still respected today of course, by Gissing and Chesterton.

For social background, one had Esmé Wingfield-Stratford's Stracheyesque three-volume kaleidoscope of many colors, characteristically titled *Those Earnest Victorians, The Victorian Sunset,* and *The Victorian Aftermath.* There were, as yet, few serious studies of ideas as embodied in Victorian literature, nothing comparable to A. O. Lovejoy's *The Great Chain of Being*; among those few was Joseph Warren Beach's *The Concept of Nature in Nineteenth-Century English Poetry.*

Like their colleagues in American literature, then, Victorian specialists had to build the systematic foundations of their knowledge—the materials of biography, text, social and intellectual milieu—at the same time that they were erecting the superstructure of informed interpretation and criticism.

By 1941 there were enough straws in the wind to permit one to believe that something was up. Now, at last, the once-over-lightly causeries, long on grace and short on substance, were starting to give ground to the products of hard-headed research. Perhaps it could be said that the skeptical investigatory spirit which is indispensable to scholarship was first notably introduced into Victorian studies by Carter and Pollard's exposé of Thomas J. Wise's forgeries in 1934, which encouraged every thoughtful student of books, not least Victorian books, to distrust appearances and received "truths" wherever found, and whomever they might concern. (Fannie Ratchford's efforts to implicate the elder Buxton Forman and, less successfully, Gosse in the Wise fraud were still in the germinal stage in 1941.) In 1935 the first edition of DeVane's *Browning Handbook* efficiently organized the existing body of information on the individual poems, with the overdue and salutary effect of relegating Mrs. Sutherland Orr's *Handbook* (1885) and E. P. Berdoe's *Cyclopaedia* (1892) to the back shelves. In 1937, Harrold's edition of *Sartor Resartus* set a standard for annotated editions of individual texts that was seldom to be matched.

The next year appeared Harrold and Templeman's massive anthology of prose (1,743 double-columned pages, printed on the secular equivalent of Oxford Bible paper), a prime instance of a textbook, in some respects in advance of its time, which stimulated rather than merely reflected scholarship in its field. Its magisterial 67-page introduction provided teachers and students alike with a well-informed, panoramic survey of the Victorian social and intellectual background. In 1939, Lionel Trilling's *Matthew Arnold*, a revision of his Columbia dissertation, offered a model for prospective explicators of an author's leading ideas. Nobody could have foreseen it at the time, but two almost successive items in the Victorian Bibliography for 1940, Orwell's essay on Dickens in *Inside the Whale* and Edmund Wilson's "Dickens: The Two Scrooges" in the *New Republic*, marked the beginning of what was arguably the most momentous development of all in post-war Victorian scholarship and criticism, the discovery of Dickens as a towering and complex artist. In the same year was published the *Cambridge Bibliography of English Literature*, whose third volume, notwithstanding its many errors and omissions, supplied Victorian scholarship with its single most frequently consulted tool.[1]

Contemplating the sheer magnitude of the Victorians' printed output (one estimate was to place the number of novels published in Britain during the nineteenth century at roughly 40,000), no ground-breaking researcher had cause to fear that his resources would be exhausted. In addition to the countless books and files of periodicals from the era, untold quantities of manuscript material in both institutional and private hands awaited discovery and examination. Some known caches, to be sure, were inaccessible. Rossetti's letters to Jane Morris, possibly containing secrets of their love affair, were kept under lock and key at the British Museum, not to be opened until 1964. The collection of Tennyson literary manuscripts in the library of Trinity College, Cambridge, including drafts of *In Memoriam*, was under the "perpetual interdict" ordered in Hallam Tennyson's will; to the exquisite frustration of scholars, the papers could be looked at but not quoted from. "Never" promised to be a long time.

Now, in the 1940s, literary study began to be institutionalized, and nowhere was the tendency more evident than in the Victorian field. Far from being, as it had been in large part, the domain of literary journalists and enthusiastic but unsystematic and uncritical amateurs, it became the province of professionals. Organized with what British onlookers regarded as a fearsome efficiency of which only Americans, fortunately, were capable, subsidized with imposing (but never quite sufficient) amounts of money for research and publication, equipped with all the machinery the post-war world of

learning devised to speed the process—societies, periodicals, bibliographies and research guides—literary scholarship flourished as
never before.

It was fitting that of all the fields of literary study, Victorian
scholarship became one of the most thoroughly organized. Firm be-
lievers as they were in the efficacy of the printed word in spreading
information and ideas, the Victorians themselves had had equal
faith in the power of mass effort to achieve ends that were beyond
individual capability. Like F. J. Furnivall, in this respect the Victorian prototype of the modern scholar, they delighted in setting up a
new society whenever one seemed desirable. Modern students of
Victorian literature piously followed their example. In the elaborate
structure of the Modern Language Association they had, and of
course still have, their own section, which sponsored not only pa-
per-reading programs and overpriced luncheons at the annual
meetings but, more valuably, the preparation of convenient reviews
of published research in Victorian poetry, fiction, prose, and periodicals. From the parent organization, regional Victorian studies
associations hived off, to multiply the benefits of communal discussion by holding annual meetings of their own. Beyond these, numerous special-interest groups, chiefly devoted to the study of individual authors, sprang up, with varying life expectancies.

In further but no doubt unintentional emulation of Victorian
practice, alongside the organizations appeared journals for the publication of research. Dominating the Victorian field since 1957 has
been the august *Victorian Studies*. Originally conceiving it as a
journal whose contents would exemplify and stimulate the cross-
fertilization of disciplines, its editors found that articles that genuinely reached across two or more fields were hard to come by, so
that they had to settle for a good quarterly mix of articles addressed
to separate portions of its constituency, social, economic, political,
and cultural historians as well as students of literature.

Alongside *Victorian Studies* have flourished (in most cases) several specialized periodicals, the venerable prototypes of which were
the *Transactions of the Brontë Society*, founded in 1898, and *The
Dickensian*, dating from 1905. Until after the Second World War,
the latter was the organ of an amiable cult in harmony with the
mental set and activities of the Pickwick Club. Then, in response to
the temper of the times and the advent of a new, tough-minded generation of Bozolators, it was gradually converted into a scholarly
periodical of some importance. The first post-war journal to be devoted to a Victorian novelist was *The Trollopian*, which soon found

that the wartime enthusiasm for Trollope's novels did not leave enough momentum to propel a quarterly periodical exclusively concerned with him, and therefore transformed itself into the highly respected, broad-gauge *Nineteenth-Century Fiction.* Another American journal, *Victorian Poetry*, has been somewhat more uneven in quality, but it has always printed the best essays submitted to it.

In the foothills sprang up numerous publications of more specialized interest. Like their sponsoring organizations they had varied life expectancies, some not surviving their editor's loss of dedication and/or financial and moral support, and the successful ones tending to turn themselves from modest news letters into fairly pretentious "reviews." Thus there were, and in some cases still are, informal information-exchanges or quarterly journals devoted to Browning, Gissing, Kipling, Mill, Disraeli, Morris, Shaw, Samuel Butler, Hopkins, Arnold, the Pre-Raphaelites, Lewis Carroll (*Jabberwocky*, the organ of the Lewis Carroll Society), even John Forster. Some of the interests represented in this array were specialized indeed. One wonders how many subscribers the *William Carleton Newsletter* attracted during its brief lifetime in the mid-1970s.

Even the abnormally energetic Furnivall did not think of founding "research centers" for the coordinated study of Chaucer, Wycliff, Shakespeare, Shelley, or Browning. But these proved to be a natural outgrowth of the post-war societies for the study of individual authors as well as of the establishment in American universities of "factories" devoted to preparing definitive critical editions of Hawthorne, Melville, Thoreau, and William Gilmore Simms, projects of such scope and complexity as to require a staff of textual and research specialists and the support of rich related library collections. Some such enterprises, like the Tennyson Research Centre at Lincoln and the Disraeli Project at Queens University, Canada, contented themselves with "researching" the life and works of single writers; others, like the Victorian Studies Centre at Leicester University and the nameless *de facto* one at Indiana University, took all (Victorian) learning as their province.

As a natural accompaniment and consequence of this organized activity, the major British and American research libraries themselves became informal headquarters for Victorian scholarship. Masses of letters and literary manuscripts, some of which they had owned for generations, were brought to light, studied, and published for the first time, and into the British Museum Library, the Berg Collection, the Morgan Library, the Huntington

Library, and the special collections rooms at such American universities as Harvard, Yale, Princeton, and Texas flowed a golden stream of newly acquired manuscripts.

And so Victorian scholars possessed not only the will but the way to catch up with their colleagues in other fields. Gradually they remedied their lack of dependable working tools. One of their most urgent needs was for reliable critical texts. This was met more slowly than could be wished, but the results, when they came, were worth the wait: the Clarendon Press *Dickens*, for example, though regrettably unannotated, and the Michigan edition of Arnold's prose. The ambitious critical edition of Browning unfortunately was beclouded by an acrimonious dispute over the choice of copy text, and another much-needed edition, that of Newman, was abandoned by its publishers after the untimely death of its editor.

The study of some authors was handicapped by the sheer unavailability of some of their works, which had long been out of print and were to be found in few libraries. Efforts to restore them to print, in unedited form, were not uniformly successful. The Oxford University Press launched a complete edition of Trollope's novels only to drop it, for lack of sufficient sales, after several volumes had been published. The various facsimile reprint series which flourished in the period when the libraries of newly established institutions of higher learning were being built from scratch did not make much of a dent in the list of Victorian titles of which no modern editions were available.

The appearance of scholarly editions of authors' letters had proved to be of great assistance to workers in other periods. Now it was the Victorians' turn. The Pilgrim edition of Dickens' letters, with its formidable apparatus of explanatory notes; the Edinburgh–Duke edition of the Carlyles' correspondence; the letters of Thackeray, Macaulay, George Eliot, Newman, Merdith, Pater, Swinburne, FitzGerald, Carroll . . . a brave company. Not that they were all without blemish. The Doughty-Wahl edition of Rossetti's letters, besides lacking an index, was so incomplete and unreliable that a completely new edition had to be undertaken, and such even useful editions as Booth's of Trollope will eventually be superseded.

By the 1950s an awareness grew of the commanding importance of contemporary periodicals in the study of Victorian literature and life. Several volumes had been published on the history of individual magazines and reviews, but these paid scant attention to their contents as a mirror of the culture of the time. The *Wellesley Index to Victorian Periodicals*, as it proceeded from its first volume in 1966, effectively displayed the contents of some fifty influential journals, and, thanks to its editors' dazzling feats of tenacious investigation, succeeded in identifying nearly ninety percent of the authors of unsigned articles. The Research Society for Victorian Periodicals applied itself to bringing further order out of that particular realm of chaos, but except for the severely criticized "Phase I" of the *Waterloo Directory of Victorian Periodicals*, its record of sponsorship so far has been longer on major projects envisaged than major projects accomplished.

The growing number of scholars who prospected for ore in library files of bound periodicals found themselves assisting, however unwillingly, at a process already under way, the inexorable physical disintegration of those irreplaceable volumes. In many libraries, the sad condition of much-used periodicals like *Punch*, the *Athenaeum*, and the *Illustrated London News* testified alike to their value as source material for a wide variety of literary and cultural studies and to the impermanence of woodpulp (a proud Victorian invention). Ironically, with the substitution of microfilm copies, supposedly an emblem of technological progress, scholars found themselves no better off than medieval bureaucrats had been when they were obliged to unwind long, sewed-together and rolled-up parchments to get to a single document.

A substantial number of library-stack explorers, though their ID cards identified them as members of English faculties, reached into areas outside literature and contributed toward the achievement of what may well be regarded as the supreme goal of Victorian scholarship, the weaving of a seamless web of historical knowledge that embraces all aspects of the age's life and expression. No previous century in any country, said Kitson Clark, had left behind so staggering a mass of documentary and graphic evidence, and, even as literary scholars were widening their knowledge of what Victorian poets, novelists, and essayists had written, historians were examining the whole social-cultural-intellectual condition of Victorian life. There were, in fact, two simultaneous and related "knowledge explosions," with the result that Victorian writers, as conceived by a new generation of scholars, took shape against a steadily more detailed and authentic historical background. Such seminal books as Walter Houghton's *The Victorian Frame of Mind* dissipated the parochialism which in effect had separated literature from the history of Victorian social, philosophical, moral, and religious attitudes. The rediscovery of Henry Mayhew's *London Labour and the London Poor*, first by way of Peter Quennell's three volumes of selections and then through the Dover facsimile reprint of the entire work, performed a like service at the opposite end of the social and cultural scale.

As a consequence of all this activity, among those in the know, at least, the former summary dismissal of Victorianism as a lengthy aberration of the cultural process was recanted, and in its place developed an almost excessive regard for the age's literary and artistic products. The indifference with which wartime Londoners had watched the destruction of Victorian warehouses and office blocks while they lamented the disappearance of Wren churches gave way to a new version of Morris' "Anti-Scrape" crusade, the purpose this time being the rescue not of Gothic churches imperiled by self-styled "restorers" but of Victorian structures threatened by "developers." This did not, in the end, prevent the destruction of the Euston Arch or the Coal Exchange, but the preservationists gave the speculators a harder fight for their money.

In the realm of the fine arts, however, the most spectacular development was the rehabilitation of Victorian painting. One of the three Martin canvases which had fetched a total of seven pounds in 1935, *The Great Day of His Wrath*, was hung in a prominent location in the Tate Gallery, its worth being estimated at an amount befitting its huge size. As auction prices soared, public galleries in London and the provinces put on exhibition after exhibition of the work of such artists, celebrated in their own time and now revalued, as Etty, Dyce, Maclise, Mulready, and Frith; there were at least a dozen shows given over to the Pre-Raphaelites alone. The Tate and the Victoria and Albert Museum both installed the cream of their collections in newly appointed rooms. In literary studies, this release of long-suppressed interest in Victorian art generated a thorough re-examination of the Pre-Raphaelites' dual role in poetry and painting, the intellectual and emotional connotations of nature in poetry and landscape art, Ruskin's art criticism generally, and typology and iconology in poetry and painting. Especially suggestive was the demonstration, by several scholars, that the illustrations in Dickens' novels were considered by both novelist and artist to be integral extensions and amplifications of the fictional text.

The Victorian book was also studied as an artifact and commodity, the product of such extra-literary forces as publishing economics, technological innovations, and popular reading taste. Michael Sadleir's *XIX Century Fiction*, a bibliographical record of a collector's passion for the popular literature of the epoch, laid out the colorful background of three-deckers, shilling shockers, and railway novels against which the more permanent heritage of Victorian literature might profitably be studied. Although sadly reduced during the war, when such unexplored archives as those of Cassells and Longmans perished in the Blitz, the surviving stock of Victorian publishers' records, some still in the firms' hands, some in libraries, became available to students of the publishing practices that determined how much an author was paid to write and what the public was offered to read.

As is true also of other periods of literary history, the precise degree to which contextual research illuminated the literary document is open to debate. There are those (certainly including the formerly young instructor) who would argue that forty years of intensive biographical and historical scholarship have profoundly affected the way Victorian texts should be read if they are taken to be more than autonomous linguistic events occurring independently of author and milieu. The various formalist schools of criticism were to have a delayed and rather uneven impact on the reading of Victorian literature. In 1940, as Theodore Morrison suggested in a gently satirical piece in *Harper's Magazine* called "Dover Beach Revisited," there were four academically respectable ways a poem could be read: as a poetic expression of the age's sensibility; as a "criticism of life"; as a mirror of the poet's psychic condition; and as an index of whether he was a Marxist or not. Noticeably absent from these alternatives was the perspective of the New Criticism, which at that moment was beginning its ascent to the peak of influence it would reach in the 1950s. If Morrison meant to imply that "Dover Beach" was not considered to be amenable to New Critical analysis, he was right—for the moment, at least. The ironies, paradoxes, tensions, and ambiguities that were being discovered in Donne and Pope seemed in short supply in Tennyson, Browning, and Arnold, with the result that the methods of the New Criticism were applied in Victorian studies much less often than they were in, say, the study of seventeenth- and eighteenth-century poetry. The only poet who benefited substantially in those early years from the modernist mode of criticism was Hopkins, whose reputation steadily rose as his poems were examined, thanks largely to his great influence on contemporary poets, with an inspired minuteness not then lavished on any other Victorian poet's canon.

Eventually, of course, few approaches to literature that were devised in those yeasty years went unrepresented in the criticism of

Victorian authors. With Lewis Carroll, these approaches ranged from psychoanalysis and the anatomy of nonsense to game theory, symbolic logic, and the theory of comedy. Nobody evidently tried to present Carroll as a Marxist, though that feat would seem to have required no more ingenuity than the attempts that were made to identify Dickens as a proto-existentialist. It was, in fact, Dickens' seeming ability to accommodate almost every current variety of fiction criticism that was responsible for his becoming the most written-about of all Victorian authors. In the earlier years, when he was given a break between sessions on the couch he was signed up as a Marxist, even though the closest he ever came in life to that beatific allegiance was his theoretically possible encounter with Karl Marx as a fellow-reader at the British Museum. In the course of time, all fashionable critical instruments were tried out on him, with predictable results: illumination in the case of those that were genuinely applicable, fiasco in the case of those that were not.

So far as quantity was concerned, the high water mark of Dickens scholarship and criticism was reached in the years 1970–72, when some eighteen double-columned pages of the Victorian Bibliography were needed to record the output. The reason for this great additional burst of interest was the centenary of his death in 1870. The first such celebration to stimulate the flow of scholarly and critical articles in Victorian studies was the hundredth anniversary of Hardy's birth. Hardy studies were already thriving then, thanks to the indefatigable sponsorship of Carl J. Weber, but the extra momentum picked up in 1940 was sustained without interruption in the years that followed. Four later centenaries, including Dickens', were responsible for similar outpourings: in 1944, that of Hopkins' birth, when nearly one hundred articles appeared, some of them in special Hopkins issues of the *Kenyon Review*; in 1945, that of Newman's conversion to Rome; and in 1959, that of the first publication of *On the Origin of Species*, which touched off four years of commentary on Darwin before the tide ebbed. The year 1959 is also memorable for the example it afforded of the way current events sometimes play into the teacher's hands, for it witnessed the famous re-match between Science and Culture in the persons of C. P. Snow and F. R. Leavis respectively. Even before the Age of Obligatory Relevance, a purgatorial term of years which no teacher of pre-1950 literature looks back upon with nostalgia, it was always expedient to prove, if one could, the Victorians' inveterate timeliness.

Events like the centenary observances naturally gave a healthy boost to the critical stock market, where, despite the fluctuations in individual prices that were inevitable when so mixed a list of stocks was involved and the critical atmosphere was so volatile, the Dow-Jones index of shares in Victorian reputations moved steadily upward. George Eliot was the combined IBM and Xerox stock of the post-war era. In the seven years 1942–48 the annual bibliography listed a total of only twenty-six items about her, ten of which were mere scraps in *Notes and Queries*; in 1949 not a single new item on Eliot was published, in 1950 only three, and in 1951, one. Eliot's critical standing at that moment was not unfairly represented by Samuel Chew's unenthusiastic account in the Baugh *Literary History of England* (1948):

> No other Victorian novelist of major rank is so little read today. The effort to lift fiction to a higher plane than that upon which her predecessors and contemporaries were satisfied to work, though it brought her temporary prestige, has ultimately been responsible for this decline. . . . [I]n George Eliot's hands the novel was not primarily for entertainment but for the serious discussion of moral issues. If these issues are no longer felt to be vital, as the Victorians felt them, and if the solutions proposed now seem unsatisfactory, the *raison d'être* of the stories which are but vehicles for these ideas is enfeebled, if, indeed, it does not vanish altogether.

There is not a little irony in the fact that this evaluation was published in the same year that Leavis's *The Great Tradition* appeared.

A few blue chip stocks, mainly those of poets—Tennyson, Browning, Arnold, Hardy, Hopkins—were equitably priced at the outset of the period and rose steadily in value; they were notably exempt from the vicissitudes of the market. Stock in Thackeray, grossly undervalued in the 1940s, would have returned good profits to a farsighted speculator. Little scholarship was devoted to him before the mid-forties (the 1944 bibliography cited but a single item, again in *Notes and Queries*), and despite the publication of Gordon Ray's edition of Thackeray's letters and Stevenson's and Ray's biographies, it was not until the sixties that he achieved his present place in the hierarchy of novelists. Trollope would have been an equally profitable investment, though one would have had to wait longer, until the past decade in fact, to realize the maximum return. Two lesser-known stocks that were underpriced forty years ago have performed well—Gissing and Mrs. Gaskell. A third, that of Arthur

Hugh Clough, enjoyed much activity in the sixties but seems in retrospect to have been somewhat overvalued. From time to time there were signs that an over-the-counter stock might qualify for a higher rating—Landor and "Mark Rutherford" come to mind—but the flurry of interest in them proved short-lived.

On the other hand, two stocks that have always been on the big board have had indifferent records. George Meredith never appealed to more than a few investors, and despite a small boom in the seventies, trading in him has generally been light. In 1959 a writer in the *Manchester Guardian* remarked, "It looks as though Macaulay were in for a revival. His life and his work are part of that nineteenth-century tradition of liberal thought to which we are increasingly turning." But nothing much happened, despite the appearance of the first volumes of his collected letters and the first volume of John Clive's biography. Instead, the revival of interest in Victorian liberal thought chiefly benefited John Stuart Mill, the rise in whose stock was signalized by the early volumes of a collected edition.

Two stocks have had an erratic record and their prospects are, at this moment, uncertain. During the early part of the period there was a continual output of Stevensoniana, much of it of no great critical importance. By the mid-fifties the production of both criticism and research was dwindling, and by the early seventies surprisingly little was being written about him. A similarly curious phenomenon was the variable fortunes of Kipling. In 1942 *Scrutiny* greeted T. S. Eliot's *A Choice of Kipling's Verse* by observing that "certainly Mr. Eliot should never have lowered himself to advocating a revival of interest in such a writer." But the imprimatur by Eliot counted for more than the Leavisites' fastidious dismay, and Kipling enjoyed a modest revival, though most of the commentary on him, to be sure, did appear in the *Kipling Journal*.

The recent brisk activity in Rossetti and Morris scholarship is attributable in part to non-literary circumstances. One poet has benefited from the resurgence of interest in Victorian painting, the other from the concurrent rediscovery of the arts and crafts movement. Morris, in addition, bears political credentials which have served him well in a time when Victorian radical Socialism became a lively subject of study.

The rise and fall of critical reputations could be discerned only in long perspective. But Victorian scholarship produced plenty of spot news, the printed chitchat and scandal of the marketplace—misguided or overambitious enterprises, controversies, squibs that failed to go off, revelations. The first and (as it proved) only volume of a massive projected life of Ruskin barely managed to get his parents off on their honeymoon. Helen Rossetti Angeli denounced Violet Hunt for her culpable misrepresentation of the story of Elizabeth Siddal Rossetti's suicide. A scholar tried unsuccessfully to convince the community that Christina Rossetti had been secretly in love with William Bell Scott. Sir Charles Tennyson drew aside the curtain that had concealed for so long the terrible truth about home conditions at Somersby as well as rattling some other skeletons in the family's well furnished closet, a process recently carried further by Robert B. Martin's relentlessly but tactfully candid biography of the poet. It became common knowledge that the official biography of Hardy, nominally by his second wife, was in fact the work of the novelist himself. There was a protracted squabble over the issue of whether Hardy had or had not had an affair with Tryphena Sparks, and whether the child she bore, if she bore one, was Hardy's.

It was to be expected that this, the side of their lives that the Victorians most resolutely kept from public view, was responsible for the greatest furor when hidden aspects did come to light in a less reticent age. The sensation was all the greater in the case of the Victorians because it involved the destruction of conceptions—"images" was the new term—sedulously cultivated by the people in question and perpetuated by their descendants. During these same years, the revelation, in his *London Journal*, of Boswell's invincible raunchiness came as no surprise to those acquainted with the sexual libertinism of his time, however hard it may have been for them to accept the dim hint, from other evidence, that Dr. Johnson once craved the touch of the whip. F. W. Bateson's controversial argument that there was an incestuous element in the relations of William and Dorothy Wordsworth was received with relative calm by a scholarly public long since accustomed to the presence of Annette Vallon in Wordsworthian biography, to say nothing of their even longer-standing acceptance of Shelley's and Byron's sexual irregularities. But once again: *the Victorians——?*

Some hint that Dickens, the genial Boz, the welcome guest at every fireside where *Pickwick Papers* was read aloud, had had a mistress had surfaced as early as 1934. But it was not until the 1950s that the fuller documentation of the Ellen Ternan affair, by Ada Nisbet and others, stirred the most vehement rear-guard resistance by Dickensians for Conjugal Fidelity. The most furious controversy, however, occurred when Admiral Sir William James,

grandson of Effie (Ruskin) Millais, published documents relating to
the intimate facts of Ruskin's unconsummated marriage which reflected favorably on his grandmother, and J. H. Whitehouse
countered with another document (Ruskin's own statement) which
presented the other side of the story. Most interested spectators denounced this well publicized display of the family laundry as grossly unedifying and irrelevant, but they overlooked the greatest irrel-
evancy of all, the fact that Effie's fierce octogenarian defender had
many years earlier, even prior to being dressed in his first sailor suit,
modeled for Millais's picture of Bubbles, world-famous from its appearance in Pears' soap advertisements. By the time the Ruskin sensation had run its course in the scholarly headlines, people were prepared to accept with equanimity Phyllis Grosskurth's frank treatment of John Addington Symonds' homosexuality and even the dis-
closure that the Reverend Charles Kingsley had enjoyed making
highly explicit erotic drawings for the delectation of self and, presumably, spouse.

Now the forbidden caches of papers were opened, one by one.
Cecil Lang was able to print in his edition of Swinburne's letters the
account of the poet's sexual proclivities which Edmund Gosse had
prepared but, not daring to publish it in his life of the poet (1917),
had deposited in the British Museum against the day when such
revelations would not shake the foundations of society. Markedly
less interesting when they were opened were the long-embargoed
letters from Rossetti to Jane Morris; they proved to contain little
that was not already known. And, though here no personal gossip
was involved, the Tennyson manuscripts at Cambridge were
thrown open for unrestricted scholarly use, just too late for
Christopher Ricks to use them in his critical edition of Tennyson's
poems.

It must not be inferred from the foregoing pages that the history
of Victorian studies lacks instances of inefficiency and waste. Unlike
other busy industries, academic ones have no safeguards against the
squandering of energies and no reliable means of quality control.
Repetition of effort and overemphasis of the trivial are prices that
seemingly must be paid for the freedom of activity that every
scholar and critic enjoys. Complaint can justly be made of what
David DeLaura has called "the endless circling around the same
questions" that has distinguished the criticism of Victorian literature in recent years. So much remains to be learned that the talents
of the profession need not—should not—be deflected to re-doing
what has already been done, re-stating with an air of discovery

what has already been adequately canvassed. For despite the deple-
tion of forty years, the reservoir of provocative subjects for initial or
justifiably renewed investigation and discussion remains well supplied. Some are minor questions, on the order of "Who, if anyone,
was George Eliot's model for Casaubon?" Larger issues cannot, by
their very nature, always be settled for good, requiring, as most do,
fresh attention from each passing generation. What *was* the genetic
relationship between the Romantic and Victorian periods: was
there a severe disjunction, or were the continuities of thought and
sensibility more significant than the divergences?

One pressing need is for a synthesis of the best that scholars and
critics have discovered and proposed, in the form of a reasonably
large-scale history of Victorian literature. (There seems to be no
sign that the long-promised volume covering the period in the Oxford History of English Literature is imminent.) None of the short
treatments, such as that in the Penguin Guide to English Literature,
is very satisfactory. Despite the consensus that a great deal of what
is most important to learn about the Victorians is embodied in their
periodical literature, no scholarly or even semi-scholarly history of
Victorian periodicals exists. Nor is there a well informed over-all
account of Victorian publishing. Formal large-scale primary bibliographies of most of the major authors, on the model of Richard
Purdy's bibliography of Hardy, should be priority projects. A large
mass of important prose demands annotation in an age when most
of the topical as well as the literary references baffle the imperfectly
educated: who, for example, will undertake to footnote the five volumes of Carlyle's "Critical and Miscellaneous Essays" in the
Centenary edition?

There should be full-length studies of the "higher journalists"
who figure in John Gross's *The Rise and Fall of the Man of Letters*
and, more extensively, in the author lists of the *Wellesley Index*, for
these were the influential people who had the ear of the public
throughout the Victorian era. The shelves devoted to scholarly editions of authors' letters still have some gaps. There is no collection
of Arnold's letters, nor, apart from volumes confined to individual
correspondences, is there any of Browning's, preferably unbur-
dened of the countless social notes and other trivia which make an
exhaustive edition both impractical and undesirable. Some fiction
writers of the second rank or below would reward attention if our
understanding of the total literary and cultural environment of Victorian literature is to be expanded. Robert Wolff's large book on
Mary Elizabeth Braddon exemplifies what might be done for a

number of popular writers about whom ample information might be accumulated with sufficient determination and a bit of luck: Surtees is a prime example. . . . The list, needless to say, could continue. The more we possess, the more we quite reasonably think we need.

It has been an engrossing spectacle to watch, this academic industry which, after a late start, has taken its place among the most fruitful of its kind, enabling us, as it has, to know with ever-increasing intimacy the Victorians as they lived and their literature as they wrote it. Thousands of men and women have joined to dispel the ignorance and pervasive misapprehension in which notions of the Victorian age were still wrapped in 1941. Knowledge, understanding, and tempered sympathy have replaced condescension or—worse—facetious disdain. And yet, as this cursory reckoning nears the bottom line, the chilling thought occurs: Has all this bustle been only machinery, in the Arnoldian sense of the word? What end, apart from the enlightenment of an infinitesimally tiny fraction of society—practicing students of Victorianism, talking to each other—has it accomplished? Have Victorian studies passed one test by which the fruits of historical research are judged, their effect on the public understanding of a past society? Are the major Victorian writers now read more widely, and more intelligently, than they were forty years ago? Is the popular conception of Victorianism—all the images and associations the word now conjures up—significantly different from what it was then? The spirit of Furnivall's Browning Society, after all, still broods over a shrine in Texas, and in today's argumentative vocabulary the epithet "Victorian" remains loaded with derogation.

Furthermore, for whatever it may be worth, one longtime Victorian-watcher must reluctantly testify, from the depths of his consciousness, that a few of the crude stereotypes he already entertained that bright September day in 1941 have stubbornly resisted the corrective action of forty years. But this is witness only of the durability of impressions acquired in receptive youth, and it is inadmissible evidence when the larger issue is confronted—as neither space nor inclination permits here. Unless academics do, in fact, work in the ivy-covered, hermetically sealed tower attributed to them in the laity's hoary myth, the processes of scholarship and criticism must, in subtle, mysterious, unmeasurable osmotic fashion, influence the attitudes society holds towards the object of their study. And the advancement of learning, in any case, is not "machinery"; its value is not contingent on some clear demonstration of its social utility. So let the chilling thought be withdrawn and the account finally balanced to this effect: The success of the great Victorian-studies enterprise, stretching from the innocent days of the New Criticism to the brave new world of post-deconstructionism, is beyond question. To end a backward glance like this in a warm Macaulayan glow would seem alien to the modern spirit, a shameful reversion to the Victorians' own complacency. But Progress, in this connection, is neither illusion nor cant. It is a matter of abundant record.

NOTE

1. It is worth noting, in confirmation of the tenor of the present essay, that when the *CBEL* came to be revised, the third volume was the first to be published (1969), because it was the one that had most urgently required updating. As the editor remarked, "In the 1930s Victorian literature, and especially the Victorian novel, had with rare exceptions barely entered into the accepted range of scholarly activity. . . . The study of the eighteenth century, and of the Middle Ages and Renaissance, has swollen in extent over the last generation; but it has not transformed the subject as recent studies of romantic and Victorian literature have done."

Dickens, Defoe, the Devil and the Dedlocks: The "Faust Motif" in *Bleak House*

Marilyn Georgas

While Dickens' *Bleak House* is greatly admired, the character of Mr. Tulkinghorn has posed a serious problem for most readers. Studies of *Bleak House* have focused rather exclusively on Chancery and the law as the novel's symbolic center, and on the story of Jarndyce and Jarndyce as its significant plot. Such studies may regard Mr. Tulkinghorn as one of the more notably characterized lawyers in the novel, but since he is not related to Jarndyce and Jarndyce, he and his pursuit of Lady Dedlock are regarded as irrelevant to the main business of the novel. Moreover, his persecution of Lady Dedlock is seen as insufficiently motivated for the Tulkinghorn-Dedlock plot to be credible as an entity. Tulkinghorn's so-called "purposeless malignance"[1] becomes a major weakness of the novel. There are, of course, successful characters in literature who may be described as figures of motiveless evil, most notably Iago; but as Grahame Smith sees it, Iago is a "poetic presentation of absolute evil, and as such is imbued with a more than personal force," while Tulkinghorn is simply "a realistic figure whose delineation is impaired by his lack of motivation." Smith thinks that there can be no "saving explanation" for the story of Lady Dedlock and Mr. Tulkinghorn.[2]

A few critics have found explanations for Tulkinghorn which leave them satisfied with his role. Eugene Quirk, for example, finds Tulkinghorn sufficiently motivated to be fully effective as a literal, realistic character. Though he does not deal with the Tulkinghorn-Dedlock plot in relation to the novel as a whole, Quirk argues con-

23

vincingly that the desire for revenge on the fashionable world, to whom he is a mere retainer, is Tulkinghorn's driving motive, a motive sufficient to make his role in the novel credible.[3] Joseph I. Fradin, on the other hand, disregards the significance of motivation entirely. He likens Tulkinghorn's role to that of a witch in a fairy tale, and says simply that a witch with credible, human motivation would cease to be a witch. Fradin is exceptional and illuminating in arguing a super-personal identity for Tulkinghorn—Tulkinghorn is, finally a "monstrous embodiment of the will to power,"[4] yet his interpretation denies any effectiveness to Tulkinghorn at the literal level.

Tulkinghorn is, I think, believable enough as a proud, resentful, crafty, malicious old man who hounds Lady Dedlock because in getting at her he is getting at the aristocratic circle of whom he is subtly but viciously resentful. But he is much more than this. It is the purpose of this study to make clear that Tulkinghorn is imbued with a "more than personal force," that he is not just a malicious old lawyer, credible or otherwise, but that he is a vision of absolute evil, and as such, is drawn deliberately and carefully as a devil figure. He is, therefore, more than flat embodiment of a single form of evil; he subsumes all the forms that evil may take. In recognizing Tulkinghorn's super-personal identity, we shall gain a new concept of his pursuit of Lady Dedlock and shall come to recognize the central importance to the novel of that pursuit.

It will be necessary first to demonstrate that Tulkinghorn is drawn as a fully-developed archetypal devil figure, and then to define the Tulkinghorn-Dedlock relationship in terms of the patterns which that identity dictates. This will enable us in turn to recognize the artistic implications and intentions of this relationship. Various literary and folklore materials with which Dickens was familiar will be the main sources by which my arguments are established. In addition, a few secondary works will be cited.

I

First it is necessary to show that Tulkinghorn is a devil figure. Most helpful in doing so is Defoe's *Political History of the Devil*. While this book was largely a repository of familiar ideas about the devil and probably provided Dickens with little actual devil lore that he did not already know about,[5] its organization, its intense and opinionated style, and its lively digressions made it a unique reading experience. Dickens' enthusiasm for the work is revealed in a letter written to Forster on November 3, 1837, in which he exclaimed of it, "What a capital thing it is! I bought it for a couple of shillings yesterday morning, and have been quite absorbed in it ever since."[6] The work is helpful for the purposes of this study in defining a specific quantity of material with which we can be sure Dickens was familiar. Another encyclopedic source of concepts about the devil and his workings among mankind with which Dickens, along with most literate Victorians, was familiar, was, of course, *Paradise Lost*. These two works, along with Maximilian Rudwin's *The Devil in Legend and Literature*, will be the main sources used in this section.

In his first appearance in the novel, Tulkinghorn is three times in notably close succession called by the epithet "the old gentleman," which is one of the more than fifty traditional epithets for the devil incorporating the adjective "old" listed by Maximilian Rudwin.[7] Throughout the novel Tulkinghorn is called by this and other such epithets—"the old scholar,"[8] for example, and "the old man" (xxxiii, 416). The name "Tulkinghorn" echoes another common tag, "Old Horny," as well as evoking an image of the devil's traditional hornedness. Also it echoes the Scottish epithet "muckled-horned Dee'l," mentioned by Defoe.[9] Late in the novel, he is more often called the "enemy" (as in lv, 666), another familiar epithet.

The "old gentleman" Tulkinghorn's black clothing calls to mind the traditional folklore devil, who always wore black, but the emphasis on the dullness of Tulkinghorn's clothes (as in xxix, 358), their constant description as "irresponsive to any glancing light" (ii, 13-14), suggests the Miltonic Satan, whose "luster" is "visibly impaired"; who along with his horde, has "lost all transcendent brightness," and has now only a "faded splendor wan."[10]

Defoe tells of the devil's unusual powers and liberties of moving about both "upon the surface of this earth, as well as in the compass of the atmosphere" (200). Tulkinghorn is imaged in this tradition. He seems simply to "melt" from one place to another (xlii, 514), to "drop into" his room at Chesney Wold, to "appear" ten minutes before dinner (xii, 146). As for habitat, he seems happy only when he goes to his wine-cellar, a dark underground location analogous to the "bowels of the earth" where the prince of darkness reigns. In his conferences with Lady Dedlock he usually seeks the proximity of the fireplace (as xii, 149), and the vicinity of his apartment in Lincoln's Inn Fields is described as an "oven made by the hot pavements and hot buildings" (xlii, 514).

The dominant description of Tulkinghorn, as an old gentleman always in a black suit and a knotted necktie and accepted into the

best drawing rooms, suggests a figure in total contrast to the commonplace medieval devil. The medieval devil was thought of as
cloven-hoofed, deformed, or otherwise malignant-looking. He was
thought to change himself into animal forms as a principal means
of deluding and capturing souls, and was thought also to work particularly through jugglers, puppet shows, magicians and the like,
since occasions for the activities of these groups were sure to draw
crowds. The devil, therefore, was connected particularly with the
atmosphere of the fair. But Defoe says that as the world grew wiser,
the devil had to become subtle and sophisticated. He was "obliged
to lay by his puppet shows and his tumblers . . . his mountebanking and quacking," and to take on the "grand manner" (355). In
Bleak House, the Smallweed family are drawn pointedly from the
older tradition, being imaged frequently as a family of spiders and
monkeys, and stylized much like figures from a puppet show at a
fair. In fact, Bartholomew's Fair is directly suggested by the grandson's name, Bart, and the granddaughter is named Judy. Grandfather Smallweed is like Punch in his abuse of his wife and offspring, though he has none of Punch's charm.

Tulkinghorn, on the other hand, is drawn largely from the image
of the latter-day Satan, with his dignity and his courtly manners,
his proper black suit and necktie. There are details, however, which
link him to the older tradition, or to the "old school," a relationship
which Dickens frequently enforces by calling Tulkinghorn a gentleman "of the old school" (as in ii, 14, xi, 129). Several images relate
Tulkinghorn to conjuring, such as the one in which Sir Leicester is
described as being to Tulkinghorn as "the coin of the conjuror's
trick" (ii, 13). Tulkinghorn's name is close to being "tusk" and
"horn," both of which words link him to the predatory animal. A
few times he is imaged directly with animal images—likened to "a
larger species of rook" (xii, 146) at one time, for example, and
called "an Oyster of the old school" (x, 119) at another. And incongrously, his bow is always "clumsy" (xlviii, 575). In such ways as
these, the "old gentleman's" alter ego is kept before us.

Just as description identifies Tulkinghorn with the devil-figure of
folklore and literature, so also do his dominant character traits. No
trait is more frequently referred to than his identity as a repository
of secrets, which he carries "in every limb of his body, and every
crease of his dress" (xii, 147). The love of secrets is regarded by
Defoe as a major characteristic of the devil, who exercises "indefatigable vigilance" (154) in his task of discovering frauds and
revealing secrets (260). He excells at finding the one weak place at

which even the best man is susceptible (157). Once he possesses a
victim, he proceeds to reveal his victim's secret sins.[11] This, of
course, is an accurate description of Tulkinghorn's relationship to
Lady Dedlock.

Hatred and suspicion of women in general is a trait universally
attributed to the devil,[12] and is one of the most overtly-drawn traits
of Tulkinghorn. This trait helps to account for his pursuit of Lady
Dedlock, but, as Quirk demonstrates, his desire for control over
Lady Dedlock finally grows out of his bitter resentment of the fashionable world in which Lady Dedlock reigns supreme. He despises
this "splendour of which he is a distant beam" (xxix, 357). His malignance toward Lady Dedlock is a means to reach and gain power
over Sir Leicester, the real seat of the power to which he must be
subservient.[13]

Here Tulkinghorn is in a position much like Milton's Satan in
relationship to heaven. He is in an eternally secondary position and
knows that he is doomed to be so, yet will neither accept his position
nor change his ways, but instead responds with envy, hatred and
defiance. From Satan's hatred springs "So deep a malice, to con-
found the race / Of mankind in one root" (*PL*, ii, 382-383), and in
going after Sir Leicester, Tulkinghorn is exhibiting the same plan.
But he is in no position to wage open war; like Satan, Tulkinghorn
must work "in close design, by fraud or guile" (*PL*, i, 645-646).
Thus the obsessive love of secrets, and thus the "imperturbable"
countenance so frequently noted (xxxiv, 429; xl, 494). Satan, too,
"each perturbation smoothed with outward calm" (*PL*, iv, 120).

Tulkinghorn's pitiless pursuit of Lady Dedlock as a means of
revenging himself upon her circle, especially upon Sir Leicester, its
center, projects a situation and motivation similar to Satan's
relationship to Adam and Eve. Through Adam and Eve, Satan
would injure God. Sir Leicester stands, however, both as Adam, the
husband to be injured, and as God, in this microcosmic universe
which, in turn, stands as Paradise or as a heavenly firmament to
Tulkinghorn. While the story of Adam and Eve is the prototypical
account of Satan's ensnaring man by the use of woman as his agent,
this propensity for making relentless and pitiless use of women as
tools for effecting a larger evil is a standard part of devil lore.[14]

Tulkinghorn is marked by one other essential diabolical trait—he
is the victim of despair. This trait is revealed mainly in one extended
passage. One evening when Tulkinghorn, alone as always in his
apartment, is drinking some of his fine old wine and pondering his
secrets, he spares a thought to "that one bachelor friend of his, a

man of the same mould and a lawyer too, who lived the same kind of life until he was seventy-five years old, and then, suddenly conceiving (as it is supposed) an impression that it was too monotonous, gave his gold watch to his hairdresser one summer evening and walked leisurely home to the Temple, and hanged himself" (xxii, 273). This friend is, of course, a mirror image of Tulkinghorn, whose old-fashioned necktie, always "loosely twisted" about his neck (xlviii, 572), suddenly takes on a special significance with its suggestion of suicide. Tulkinghorn is cut off from love, has no sympathy for women and marriage, does not even have a hairdresser as far as we know; and he is forever cut off from full status in the class which he moves in and envies since one can only enter it by birth or marriage. Such ultimate despair is, of course, Satan's destiny.

Defoe explains that Satan is filled with "horrible resolutions of revenge" against mankind, and that the impossibility of executing those resolutions creates "a hell in his own breast" (188) and leaves despair "the reigning passion of his mind" (192). Milton too draws at length the despair of Satan, who knows that he cannot defeat God, yet despairs of peace, "For who can think submission?" (*PL*, i, 661). Tulkinghorn, then, is not just another lawyer in this novel. He is a devil-figure.

Tulkinghorn's role in the novel consists solely of his pursuit of Lady Dedlock and the activities necessary for entrapping her, and, as has been pointed out, to question his role is to question hers, as well as to question the point of their presence in the novel. When Tulkinghorn is recognized as a devil-figure, and Lady Dedlock identified as the object of a stylized diabolical pursuit, we have a new perspective from which to examine her role.

II

In order to understand Lady Dedlock's role, we need first to review a bit further Dickens' frame of reference in relation to literary and folklore versions of the devil. Dickens was, of course, familair with the Faust legend. This story, fixed in English tradition by Marlowe's version, enjoyed fresh vitality in Dickens' day as a result of Goethe's treatment, with its new "redeemable" Faust, popularized in England largely through Abraham Hayward's prose translation, published first in 1833, and reprinted in 1847 and 1855, and through P. J. Bailey's extravagant verse recreation *Festus*, first published in 1839, and by 1854, in its fifth edition.[15] The Faust story is itself a version of the basic medieval and

Renaissance morality plot, familiar to Dickens from many sources—from morality plays such as "Infans et Mundus," for example, which, in his edition of *Dodsley's Old Plays* as "Child and the World," he owned at least as early as 1844; and from the plight of the Red Cross Knight in Book One of Spenser's *Faerie Queene*, and of Christian in Bunyan's *Pilgrim's Progress*, two further works which were among his books by 1844.[16] Each of these three works had its prideful sinner, each its devil figure, and each, of course, its good angel.

In the configuration of characters that we considered in the discussion of Tulkinghorn above, Lady Dedlock was shown to be related in some respects to Eve. In general, she is understandable in terms of immediate Victorian religious concepts—she is proud and worldly, she harbors an unrepented sin, suffers terrors of conscience and has few or no redeeming "signs of election" (xxxvi, 450–452). But Lady Dedlock is imaged most fully in terms and patterns which relate her to medieval and Renaissance literary works in which the protagonist suffers from the deadly sin of sloth. Sloth, it should be recalled, presupposed pride. It was pride, the substitution of one's own will for God's will, which made one susceptible to sloth, which in turn caused one to become susceptible to the other deadly sins. Sloth amounted to the loss of joy in the things of the spirit, and was regarded as the inevitable gateway to worldliness; for the slothful sinner, losing joy in the things of the spirit, sought compensation in the only other source available to him, the pleasures of the world, and he took increasing pride in worldly triumphs as he left spiritual aspirations behind. But he gradually came to realize the hollowness of his worldly triumph yet was so stricken with guilt that he felt himself past all hope of salvation. From here came the tendency to despair. Early literary treatments of this cycle are characterized by a climactic episode in which the protagonist meets his adversary, the devil or a devil figure, in personified form. For the Infans in "Child and the World," for example, the adversary is Wanhope; for the Red Cross Knight and Bunyan's Christian, it is a personification of despair.

The cycle that I have just sketched will be referred to as the morality plot in the discussion below. The Faust story will be regarded as a specialized version of the morality plot which is distinguished by most or all of the following characteristics: (1) a deliberate pact with the devil made within the action or clearly implied as antecedent action; (2) a second pact made within the action; (3) the devil figure as a central character throughout the main action, as opposed to his appearance as an allegorical figure in a single climactic episode; (4) a time span of twenty to twenty-four years indicated as the length of the protagonist's wrong-doing before the devil comes for payment; (5) a configuration of characters that conspicuously duplicates the basic characters of the Faust legend.

Lady Dedlock is imaged from the beginning of *Bleak House* as "bored, frigid, and weary of soul." In her first major appearance in the novel, we are told that on the previous Sunday, in Paris, Lady Dedlock, "in the desolation of Boredom and the clutch of Giant Despair, almost hated her own maid for being in spirits" (xii, 139). The detail that this was her state on Sunday emphasizes the absence of comfort to her of spiritual practices, the basic symptom of sloth, and the reference to the Giant Despair provides clear linkage to *Pilgrim's Progress*. Sundays at Chesney Wold too, it should be noted, have already been singled out as joyless days (ii, 11).

Revelation of antecedent action lets us know that the young Honoria Barbary, now Lady Dedlock, had fallen in love with a Captain Hawdon in her youth, had borne his child out of wedlock while he was at sea, had been told by a bigoted sister that the child was dead, and had despaired of Hawdon's return, there having been a report that he had drowned. We are told nothing of her immediate reaction to these events, but are shown that without too much delay she went very deliberately after other stakes—wealth, position, and power, pursuing them with "beauty, pride, ambition, insolent resolve, and sense enough to portion out a legion of fine ladies" in the race for Sir Leicester Dedlock's favor (ii, 12). Honoria, then, had abandoned her commitment to her heart's honest desire for love, for physical fulfillment, for a child, and had gone after worldly values, values which she has pursued with dazzling success by the time that we meet her. This sketch suggests that Lady Dedlock had in a sense sold herself to the devil, and as the antecedent action is further revealed and the present played out, we see that Dickens definitely intended us to draw the parallel for he shaped the relationship of Tulkinghorn and Lady Dedlock with marked similarities to the traditional relationship of Mephistopheles and Faustus.

First of all, we should notice that the name "Mister Tulkinghorn" echoes precisely the syllabic cadence of "Mephistopheles" and duplicates the stressed consonants as well, giving a sound similarity that seems a deliberate suggestion of the parallel intended between the two characters. Not so conclusive in themselves perhaps, but certainly of significance in conjunction with "Mister Tulkinghorn" are the Dedlocks' names. "Honoria" is a close phonetic counterpart, perhaps as close as one could find among female names, for Goethe's Faust's first name in English, "Henry." And one can hardly avoid thinking of Mr. Tulkinghorn's patron Sir Leicester as Lucifer at times, a substitute which Dickens even suggests through Mr. Boythorn (ix, 108). (The sense in which Sir Leicester serves as Lucifer will be discussed further below.) Dating in the novel, moreover, can be worked out very specifically to indicate that exactly twenty-four years, the most typical length of time for a bond with the devil, and the time allowed in Marlowe's version of the legend, elapse between the time that Lady Dedlock dedicated herself to worldly pursuits and the time when the devil claims dominion (xlviii, 580–583). Esther was "almost fourteen" (iii, 20) when her godmother died, and it was immediately thereafter that she went to Greenleaf, where she passed "six happy, quiet years" (iii, 26) before Richard and Ada came into her life. When she first met Richard and Ada, then, she was twenty or very close to it, Richard "not more than nineteen, if quite so much," but two years older than Ada. This made Ada right at seventeen, Richard right at nineteen, and Esther right at twenty, establishing Esther as three years older than Ada. As Lady Dedlock nears exposure, we find Ada having her twenty-first birthday (i, 600), making Esther twenty-four. This is just after Tulkinghorn, shortly after claiming Lady Dedlock, has been killed and just as suspicion begins to go to Lady Dedlock, therefore just before she strips away all that she had sold herself for—sumptuous apparel, wealth, position, and power in society. Her powers are abandoned as ineffectual after a clearly-defined twenty-four year period of reign for which she has paid with an ever-increasing despair and frigidity.

The present action of the novel deals only with the climactic years of the protagonist's power, when the allotted time for her reign is running low and an agent of the devil is on hand to collect. Though Tulkinghorn, like Marlowe's Mephistopheles, abhors marriage and tells Lady Dedlock that he is as much against her marriage now as he was when it first occurred (xli, 512), he is not shown to have been a participant in the original diabolical efforts at procurement of Lady Dedlock's soul, but only as following his own nature, and in so doing operating in the larger scheme of destruction and malice as the agent who is now on hand to claim the devil's due.

We first meet Lady Dedlock at the time that Esther is about twenty and Lady Dedlock many years into her reign in the world of fashion. The reader knows of Lady Dedlock's weary enthrallment to the

Giant Despair, yet what the world sees is her constant movement about in England and abroad (ii, 11–12; xii, 139). When we first hear of her, she has just returned from her town house to Chesney Wold previous to going to Paris; and after the trip to Paris, which brought her no joy, we hear of her intensified movement in England and abroad (xvi, 195), a version of the terrestrial wanderings that typified Faustus's years of power, just as the secret conflict and discontent characterized him. A difference however is that Marlowe's Faustus really enjoyed his pleasure, at least at times when it "conquered sweet despair." Lady Dedlock enjoys nothing except for the rural girl Rosa, with whom she finds some moments of release. This redemptive interest in Rosa echoes the relationship of Goethe's Faustus to the rural girl Margaret, and is a point to which we shall return.

While despondent within, however, Lady Dedlock continues to reign over a shrine of followers who worship her beauty, title and wealth. The scenes of Lady Dedlock's continued reign, particularly the scene in chapter twelve, suggest in their pomp the Vanity Fair scene from *Pilgrim's Progress*, yet even more notably link Lady Dedlock to Lucifera and her reign in the House of Pride in Book One of *The Faerie Queene*. In these scenes, Sir Leicester is in a sense the devil to Lady Dedlock. His name reminds one of "Lucifer," and it is he who has the limp, from gout, that recalls the cloven foot of the devil. In his insensitivity to change and in his giving Lady Dedlock those prizes for which she sells her honest self, he is Lucifer. She is his Lady Lucifera, occupying a "gaudy platform" (xli, 512) where troops of visitors come into her presence as to a shrine (xii, 143–145).[17]

It is in chapter twelve, at the height of her power yet bored and despairing, that Lady Dedlock first notices the rural girl Rosa and asks her age (xii, 141). She ponders Rosa's answer, "nineteen," which the reader will subsequently realize is the approximate age of her own daughter. Lady Dedlock's relationship to Rosa will culminate in her breaking a "second pact" with the devil-figure Tulkinghorn. The motif of the "second pact" is common to Faust literature,[18] familiar to most of us from the last act of Marlowe's *Dr. Faustus*, where after the old man evokes a surge of repentance in Faustus, Faustus promptly rallies to Mephistopheles' threats and offers his blood again to reconfirm his former vows to Lucifer.

Throughout the novel, Lady Dedlock has felt increasingly Tulkinghorn's power over her. His menace culminates in chapter forty in his telling the story of her past, in a thinly-disguised form, to the entire fashionable circle gathered at Chesney Wold. In the next chapter it is later that same night. Lady Dedlock goes to Tulkinghorn's room and announces her plan to leave at once and her willingness to sign any sort of paper or release that Tulkinghorn wishes in order to spare her husband trouble "in obtaining his release" (xli, 509), presumably in achieving a legal separation which she assumes he would want when the truth came out. Tulkinghorn blocks her intention to leave by his demands for a new bargain, a second pact, if she is not to be exposed, and Sir Leicester, as a result, "driven out of his wits, or laid upon a death-bed," the family reputation and credit ruined (xli, 511–513). Tulkinghorn stipulates that as long as she continues her life exactly as before, "holding its pains at [his] pleasure, day by day" (xli, 512), she can be assured that he will forewarn her before he exposes her, should he decide to do so. Repeatedly he asserts that his only concern is for Sir Leicester. Even as he tortures Lady Dedlock in this scene, he is struck with admiration for her (xli, 508), reminding one of Satan's suspended admiration for Eve in the midst of his ruining her (*PL*, ix, 463-465).

Lady Dedlock is subdued by Tulkinghorn's casuistry. In Despaire's confrontation with the Red Cross Knight in the ninth canto of Book One of *The Faerie Queene*, Despaire uses "guilt" and "justice" as the loaded terms to bring the Knight to the point of final despair, at which time Una steps forth to remind him of love and mercy. In this scene, Lady Dedlock lacks the vision to challenge Tulkinghorn's sophistical arguments, which define Sir Leicester's good solely in terms of worldly values, "reputation" and "credit." She seems not to perceive that her lord the aged husband has sufficient love and mercy to render him forgiving, though there is reason to think that she has too much pride to accept a lesser position in his or any other eyes even it if were offered (xxxvi, 451).

The morality plot aspects of the scene—the desperation of the blind sinner and the bounteous mercy of her "lord," are emphasized when Dickens closes the chapter by describing Lady Dedlock's desperate frenzy after she returns to her room and then juxtaposing an account of Sir Leicester, close by in his own room, dreaming a dream which marks him as the very emblem of mercy. In the previous chapter he had expressed the utmost contempt and dread at the outcome of an election in which "his people" had elected an ironmaster to parliament, but at the end of this chapter, we are shown Sir Leicester "pardoning the repentant country in a magnificently condescending dream" (xli, 513).

In the confrontation scene between Lady Dedlock and Esther in chapter xxvi (450-452), Esther, in the role of "good angel," had urged her mother to take hope and to tell Mr. Jarndyce of the problem, that is, to confess and repent. Lady Dedlock was blind to the possibilities of hope and faith in that scene just as she was blind to the possibilities of mercy during the "second pact" scene just discussed. Yet in the final analysis, Lady Dedlock, unlike Marlowe's Faustus, who always backs down in his tentative defiance of the devil, breaks her agreement with Mr. Tulkinghorn. And it is not until the scene of that defiance and the confrontation with Tulkinghorn that follows it that the sounding out of Lady Dedlock's soul is complete.

In the defiance scene (xlviii, 567-582), Lady Dedlock announces in the presence of Sir Leicester and Tulkinghorn, as well as Rouncewell the ironmaster, that she wants Rosa put out because of her foolish attachment to Wat Rouncewell. Arrogantly, she indicates that if the girl may be so stupid as to let such an attachment intrude upon her advantages as a member of the house of Dedlock, she wants the girl out of her house. Sir Leicester's capacity for understanding and compassion are emphasized in this scene as he questions Lady Dedlock's ultimatum and defends Rosa. Tulkinghorn looms "bigger and blacker" than ever before Lady Dedlock throughout the scene, but he must repress his reaction in the presence of others. As for Lady Dedlock, only icy haughtiness is apparent, but the reader understands that Lady Dedlock dismisses Rosa from the household in order to protect the girl's chances for a good marriage from being spoiled if it is discovered that she lives under the patronage of a "ruined" woman. If Rosa separates herself from such a woman, her honor will be intact when that woman is exposed.

This dismissal of Rosa, of course, is an act not typical of Lady Dedlock's life as it has been and to which Tulkinghorn has constrained her. Thus she has broken the second pact. It is not long before Tulkinghorn finds opportunity to confront Lady Dedlock alone. There is a new "indefinable freedom" in Tulkinghorn's manner with Lady Dedlock now that she is, in his opinion, totally in his power (xlviii, 580). His manner suggests to the reader, however, an overreaching ambition, the flaw which led to his counterpart Satan's downfall. Tulkinghorn tells her that she can count on no warning from him now, that he will do as he pleases when he pleases; she simply must wait helplessly. In the very midst of his gloating torture of her—he even indulges in a "slight smile"—he continues to wonder at her control and composure, and to puzzle at her behavior. "*She* cannot be spared," he thinks, "Why should she spare others?" (xlviii, 581-82).

Though Tulkinghorn seems not to recognize that he has lost his prey, it has been made apparent to the reader that Lady Dedlock is not finally of the devil's party. The very fact that she has disobeyed the conditions of Tulkinghorn's agreement has shown us that she is throwing off the devil's rule over her life. And in breaking the agreement, she is sacrificing herself for Rosa and thereby performing a redemptive act, which allows us to assume that she dies in a state of grace, like Goethe's Faust. Her death occurs shortly after this last interview with Mr. Tulkinghorn. She has clad herself in poor apparel and headed for the burial place of Captain Hawdon. Pride and slothful passiveness are gone as she casts herself upon the gate of the cemetery in a final effort to reach his grave. Stripped of her sumptuous apparel, without regard for the world's opinion, she dies trying to reach all that remains of that which in her youth, as again now, evoked and defined her best, truest self.

Within the symbolic structure of the novel, the murder of Tulkinghorn after his triumphant interview with Lady Dedlock, hence at the moment of his highest presumption, seems appropriate. And there are various traditions which include the death of the devil, notable among which is the Punch and Judy story. This story invariably ends with the death of the devil, at which the crowd cheers, though they know full well that the devil will be alive and well for the next performance. Defoe summarizes the common conceptions that the devil acts through agents, of which there is a never-ending supply (207-208). The devil acting through Tulkinghorn as agent has been defeated in his efforts totally to secure Lady Dedlock and thereby torment and destroy Sir Leicester, but we know that the devil will find other agents and other prey. Lady Dedlock, however, dies reuinited with her original self and Sir Leicester's last coherent breaths express love for his lady and an impassioned hope for her return; his last days are comforted by honoring her memory and by other ties of affection reflected in George Rouncewell's devotion to him. Tulkinghorn did not destroy his spirit.

Like the typical medieval morality play, the morality plot of *Bleak House* indicates that it is never too late for redemption, that no person is steeped too deeply in pride and sin to reverse his course. Lady Dedlock's is not a very abundant or glorious redemption—she could have had so much more if she had only thrown herself upon her lord's gracious mercy. Yet she would have been violating her character just as surely as Marlowe's Faustus would have had he repented at the last hour. She was never as fully gratified by her sin as Faustus, and she was projected into it through a grievous experience, not merely through a spontaneous desire for power. For these reasons, the possibility of salvation remains present in her characterization to a greater extent than in Faustus'. But a full, melodramatic reconciliation with her husband and her long-lost daughter would require an unbelievable reversal of character on her part, and would give, I think, a falsified vision of human possibility and likelihood. Lady Dedlock dies a tortured spirit, barely resisting outright suicide, but she had hold of a sufficient shred of honesty, truth and repentance for one to feel that heaven can forgive her. No more; no less.

III

While Lady Dedlock's character and her relationship to Tulkinghorn have been defined largely in terms of medieval and Renaissance literature and of Goethe's version of the Faust legend, it is in Defoe that one finds a possible source. The most unusual feature of Dickens' use of the "Faust motif" is his use of a female figure in the Faust role. In E. M. Smeed's bibliography of literary treatments of the Faust theme, there is only one title indicating a female Faust figure, *Die Grafin Faustine*, by Ida Grafin Von Hahn-Hahn, a German work first published in 1841.[19] By 1845, two English translations had been published in London, but if Dickens had heard of or read this novel, he would have found only a romanticized character type, with none of the Faust legend's machinery. The book's heroine is a beautiful, gifted poetess who marries her ideal lover and has a beautiful and perfect little son, yet because of her craving for the infinite withdraws to a contemplative order of nuns and dies young.[20] Arnold's brief "To Fausta," published in 1849, makes no use of the legend. These works, could, however, have provided some suggestion for the female Faust figure. Certainly Dickens' own inventive powers were sufficient to suggest the possibility of the role reversal—he suggests the possibility of a female Othello through a comment by Bucket to Mrs. Snagsby when Mrs. Snagsby is in a jealous fit against Guster (lix, 708). But one finds in Defoe, a work with which we are sure that Dickens was familiar, a passage strongly suggestive of the possibility of a female

Faust figure, and of one drawn remarkably along the lines of Lady
Dedlock.

Heretofore in this study I have not claimed any influence by
Defoe, whose *History of the Devil*, as I have pointed out, was largely
a repository of familiar lore. In this instance there is no unique information. But Defoe's juxtaposition of traditional materials with
his own speculations and disgressions forms a possible source. As to
whether the passage struck a conscious creative response at
Dickens' first reading in 1837 or in a subsequent reading, I will not
conjecture. I simply wish to point out the fact that this passage,
with which we are sure that Dickens was familiar, provides marked
suggestion of the characterization and role that Dickens gives to
Lady Dedlock. The passage consists of chapter seven and the beginning of chapter eight in *The History of the Devil*.

In the seventh chapter (258-288), Defoe is largely discussing the
devil's methods. In pointing out that the devil works at recruiting
his agents and his victims, Defoe suggests one of those methods,
achieving intimacy with his intended object, as he comments, "No
doubt the Devil and Dr. Faustus were very intimate . . . ; no doubt
the Devil showed himself in the glass to that fair lady who looked in
it to see where to place her patches" (261). A bit farther along he
asserts that "hoop-petticoats" are one of the devil's favorite disguises (271), and spends the remainder of the chapter on the devil's
particular liking for the "fine lady" (277) and for ladies of "a fine
face, a divine shape and a heavenly aspect" (287) as means for his
disguise.

The next chapter, chapter eight (289-309), proceeds to the topic
of pacts with the devil. Defoe refers to Dr. Faustus's bargain as well
as to other folklore versions of such pacts as he dispenses the relevant lore. Toward the later part of the commentary, he remarks:

> I might, before I quit this point, seriously reflect here upon our *beau
> monde*, viz., the gay part of mankind especially those of the times we
> live in, who walk about in a composure and tranquility inexpres-
> sible, and yet, as we all know, must certainly have all sold them-
> selves to the Devil, for the power of acting the foolishest things with
> the greater applause. (304)

In the progression of Defoe's narrative that I have just sum-
marized, we have the juxtaposition of an image of the devil and
Faustus with an image of the devil and a fashionable woman in the
context of a discussion of the devil's methods of securing souls.

Then follows as extended discussion of a role that reverses conventional identities, the devil as a woman, rather than a man; then comes a discussion of the *beau monde* as participants in pacts with the devil. The possibility of a female figure from the *beau monde* bargaining with the devil is strongly suggested in this passage. The passage provides, I think, a likely source of Dickens' conception of the character of Lady Dedlock, reigning light of the "beau monde" (xii, 138), yet in bondage to the devil, to whom she has sold her soul for applause.

We have seen a rich synthesis of traditional literary and folklore materials in Dickens' creation of Tulkinghorn and Lady Dedlock and their relationship. Recognizing that this relationship was shaped with features which make it overtly parallel with the Faust legend adds greatly to our understanding of the meaning and intention of this plot. But the story exists as part of a much larger whole, and only in functioning significantly within the whole can it be judged as artistically effective in the final analysis. It is time now to consider what further meaning is given to the novel by the explication that has been provided in this study.

IV

After one recognizes the thorough development of the Tulkinghorn-Dedlock plot as a Faustian morality plot, one realizes that numerous other plots in the book share conspicuously some of the same characteristics. Nemo is referred to in his neighborhood as one who has "sold himself to the Enemy" (x, 124), and his story, revealed largely through a conversation between Mr. George and Smallweed (xxi, 269-270), reveals that he had definitely been an early candidate for despair, already in the clutches of gamblers and usurers when he went on the sea journey during which he went overboard, "whether intentionally or accidentally, I don't know," Mr. George reports. It becomes apparent in this conversation that Hawdon deliberately let the rumor of his drowning stand to avoid vicious creditors, presumably never even attempting to communicate with Honoria after his return. At one point in the novel, the omniscient narrator comments that the devil is "a more designing, callous, and intolerable devil when he sticks a pin in his shirt-front, calls himself a gentleman, backs a card or colour, plays a game or so of billiards, and knows a little about bills and promissory notes, than in any other form he wears" (xxvi, 324). It was to the devil in this guise that Captain Hawdon had sold himself, at the same time drawing the young Honoria Barbary into an intimacy that jeopardized her well being.[21] Some twenty years later, we find him as Nemo, a derelict opium addict, his only possibly redeeming features his kindness to Jo during this last phase of his life and his treasuring to the end of Honoria's letters. At the scene of his death is the devil figure Tulkinghorn, along with Krook and his cat, who suggest a folklore devil and his familiar.

Trooper George's approximately twenty years of vagrancy culminate in his being at the mercy of Smallweed's "friend in the city" whose name "begins with a D," and who will "have his bond" (xxi, 266-267). This "friend in the city," a "slow-torturing" kind of "old man" (xlvii, 566) and none other that Tulkinghorn himself, offers George a second pact of sorts which George is forced to accept (xxxiv, 429). George, after further suffering, is finally allowed full repentance and is restored as nearly as he can be to the family, friends and values of his youth.

It is Richard Carstone's story that provides the fullest and most significant parallel to the Tulkinghorn-Dedlock plot. This is a poignantly telescoped version of the plot, for Richard's whole life lasted little over twenty years. It is as if he was born into the devil's clutches. He never had any sense of purpose or "calling" in his entire life. In his plot, we have in Richard the errant sinner, in Esther, the good angel, in Ada, the redemptive love, and in Vholes, the devil figure on hand to snatch Richard's soul at the appropriate time.[22] Richard's suffering is portrayed physiologically, in passages that remind on of the Red Cross Knight's preliminary despondency and debility when he was imprisoned by the giant Orgoglio,[23] while Lady Dedlock's, as we have seen, is imaged psychologically, as is predominantly the case with the Red Cross Knight during his encounter with Despaire. Richard had not the strength to wage the battle required of an acceptable fictional protagonist. Lady Dedlock did. Richard is allowed repentance and reconciliation with family and friends before death. Lady Dedlock is not.

Gridley's case largely parallels Richard's, as does Miss Flite's. And there is more. But by now it has become apparent that the Faust motif and devil lore in general provide a unifying principle of the novel. In making the Faustian morality plot a virtual "master plot" of his novel, Dickens confirms his sense of this plot's authenticity as a basic pattern of human experience.

V

Having seen that the Tulkinghorn-Dedlock plot exists among numerous parallel plots, it remains for us to consider this plot's relationship to other principal motifs of the novel. As has been pointed out, most studies of *Bleak House* focus on the forces of Chancery and the law as the major symbolization of evil in the novel and as the major instrument for creating hell on earth—Richard Carstone's hell, for example, and the hell of Tom-all-Alone's and the hellish plight of Jo, all of which take place within the sanction of the law, not to mention the church. Yet Jarndyce and Jarndyce has no real significance in Lady Dedlock's life, and her pursuer is bent on personal revenge, not involved in a Chancery activity. Still, she as much as any victim of Chancery is in a hell, and Tulkinghorn is her chief tormentor. And he is a principal actor in a number of the novel's plots. Views regarding Chancery as the sole significant symbol of evil in the novel are, therefore, highly incomplete.

Chancery is surely one of the most potent and suggestive of artistic symbols of evil and its workings among mankind. The Lord Chancellor, his counterpart Krook, and all the descending ranks of lawyers convey a sense of the hopeless and stupid folly of the whole legal process and of the hopelessness of assigning blame within the network of a complex institution, perhaps within life itself. But Tulkinghorn defines evil as it works within the human personality and he defines it comprehensively. His characterization provides some significant contrasts with the other agents of evil in the novel. These agents, mostly the legal corps and their satellites, partake in varying degrees of Tulkinghorn's faults. They are guileful, secretive, and lacking in feeling or pity for others. But there are sharp differences. Even the Smallweeds, for example, have a family life, and a sort of give-and-take involvement with each other. And the repulsive Vholes has made some sort of personal contact in his life, for he has daughters as well as a father in the Vale of Taunton with whom he shares his life. This group is also motivated by greed; they enjoy the money they get, even if, as with Smallweed, only in a miserly way. Suddenly greed for money, which is tangible and can bring pleasure, seems healthy compared to the pure hatred and envy and spite that motivate Tulkinghorn. Tulkinghorn is a comprehensive personification of ultimate evil. Other characters are evil insofar as they partake of his nature. Lady Dedlock participates in his nature in her repression of her honest emotion and self and in her dedication to pursuits that give her position and power over others.

In Tulkinghorn and his pursuit of Lady Dedlock we are getting another view of evil, a view just as essential to the meaning of *Bleak House* as the more noted view symbolized by Chancery and its appendages. Lady Dedlock's suffering and vulnerability to the powers of evil are created not by legal problems, but by personal or spiritual problems—a sense of her own falseness, sinfulness and exemption from salvation. Given money, and power—all that Chancery supplicants yearn for and think would assure their happiness— Lady Dedlock is nevertheless the most miserable and desperate of souls. We see in Lady Dedlock that despair, waste, grief and misery are problems of the spirit; that evil and the susceptibility to evil are in the spirit, not in the external circumstances of life. Her story suggests that had Richard, Miss Flite, and Gridley achieved the wealth of which they dreamed, their spiritual peace and happiness might not have been any greater. The plot of Lady Dedlock insists on the tragic dimension of human suffering, its root within the human spirit, its final inevitability as a part of the human condition, as a result of human nature itself.

This vision is expressed in various ways in the novel; for example, in the contrast between Tom Jarndyce and John Jarndyce. Given the same circumstances, Tom was vulnerable to erosion of the spirit by the false promises of Chancery, as was Richard; John was not. Tom committed suicide and John survived as a productive, if limited, human being. But the central contrast is that between Lady Dedlock and Esther. Lady Dedlock was vulnerable to spiritual erosion in the face of personal and emotional deprivation. Esther was not. The novel, then, does not merely indict the presence of evil; it confronts and portrays the mystery of human susceptibility to evil.

In conclusion, I want to point out some implications of my reading in relation to the structure of the novel. Dickens' use of dual narrators has often been criticized, labelled a sign that Dickens was divided in artistic purpose or lacking in an adequate technique to encompass the breadth of his vision. And the character of Esther has been criticized as too much a personfication of self-sacrifice and devotion to duty to hold our serious attention. These criticisms have been variously made and variously answered. My reading provides a few further bases for rebuttal.

Recognizing Tulkinghorn as the personification of the evil that dominates in the omnisciently-narrated part of the novel provides a counterpart character to Esther as the personification of compassion, selflessness, and devotion to duty who dominates the parts of the book which she narrates. Chancery, an abstraction, does not appropriately balance with her in a good versus evil juxtaposition. Nor is Krook, a grotesque and in many ways pitiable emblem of evil, an appropriate counterpart. But Tulkinghorn is. He and Esther each function effectively at a literal level, but each also functions essentially as a symbolic extremity. Just as she is the touchstone for good in the novel, he is the touchstone for evil. Each is delineated by an image pattern that suggests his or her extremity as a character. Light imagery predominates in her world just as it is present in her name, while hellish imagery—fogs, mists, blackness, shadows and ominous animals—predominates in his, and is suggested in his name. In recognizing this organization into two worlds, each epitomized by a character who functions as the dominant principle of that world, we must recognize an organization related in concept to Milton's *Paradise Lost*. Like Milton, Dickens has given us two worlds, forever at war, both having to be traversed by every mortal in his earthly life, each taking its toll in various ways and to various extents. Lady Dedlock, I assert, is the protagonist of the novel; it is she who traverses most thoroughly before our eyes the landscapes of both worlds. It is she who is subject both to the good angel and the bad angel. Recognizing her plight as a treatment of the great epic struggle between good and evil brings into new focus the design of this remarkably complex novel and surely marks it as one of the most comprehensive of all such treatments.

NOTES

1. Edgar Johnson's phrase, *Charles Dickens: His Tragedy and Triumph*, 2 vols. (New York: Simon and Schuster, 1952), II, 765. Johnson's entire discussion, 762-782, especially 762 and 765, reflects the position being described. For earlier statements of the complaint, see E. B. Lupton, *Dickens the Immortal* (Kansas City: A. Fowler, 1923), p. 61, and David Cecil, *Early Victorian Novelists* (Indianapolis: Bobbs-Merrill, 1935), pp 48-49. For a recent statement see Michael Wilkins. "Dickens's Portrayal of the Dedlocks," *The Dickensian*, 72 (1976), 71.

2. Grahame Smith, *Dickens, Money and Society* (Berkeley and Los Angeles: University of California Press, 1968), pp. 125, 129. Two recent studies defend Lady Dedlock's story on the basis of its significance to Esther's story, but neither considers the role of Tulkinghorn in her story. These are Geoffrey Thurley in *Dickens' Mythology* (New York: St. Martin's Press, 1976), pp. 172-202, and H. M. Daleski in *Dickens and the Art of Analogy* (New York: Schocken Books, 1970), pp. 156-190. Thurley discusses Tulkinghorn briefly, pp. 193-195, but only as another of the novel's lawyers, and Daleski gives no attention directly to Tulkinghorn. Daleski does,

however, challenge the excessive attention to the Chancery plot and the "fog imagery" as the main clues to the novel's meaning, especially pp. 157, 159.

3. Eugene F. Quirk, "Tulkinghorn's Buried Life: A Study of Character in *Bleak House*," *JEGP*, 72 (1972), 526-535, Quirk also notices other studies that have attempted to define a significant role for Tulkinghorn and points out their shortcomings, 527 and note. See Fred Kaplan, *Dickens and Mesmerism* (Princeton: Princeton University Press, 1975), pp. 201-203, for an interesting defense of Tulkinghorn. Kaplan's discussion is largely theoretical, concerned with the ultimate causes of human commitment to good or evil more than with immediate, humanly perceptible causes.

4. Joseph I. Fradin, "Will and Society in *Bleak House*," *PMLA*, 81 (1966), pp. 102-104.

5. See Lauriat Lane, Jr., "The Devil in *Oliver Twist*," *The Dickensian*, 52 (1956), 132-136, on the commonplace nature of Defoe's devil lore. In this article, Lane challenges the argument of Marie Hamilton Law, "The Indebtedness of *Oliver Twist* to Defoe's *History of the Devil*," *PMLA*, 40 (1925), 892-897, that Defoe influenced Dickens' conception of Fagin as a devil figure. These two studies provide the only discussion of Defoe's relation to Dickens that I have seen.

6. *The Letters of Charles Dickens, 1820-1839*, ed. Madeline House and Graham Storey (Oxford: The Clarendon Press, 1969), I, 328. (Pilgrim Edition, referred to hereafter as Pilgrim *Letters*).

7. Maximilian Rudwin, *The Devil in Legend and Literature* (1931; rpt., LaSalle, Ill. : The Open Court Publishing Co., 1959), p. 32.

8. *Bleak House*, ed. George Ford and Sylvère Monod (New York: W. W. Norton and Co., Inc., 1977), ch. xi, p. 129. Subsequent references to this edition will be given parenthetically within the text, showing the chapter number followed by the page number.

9. *The Political History of the Devil*, Vol. X of *The Novels and Miscellaneous Works of Daniel Defoe* (1840; rpt., New York: AMS Press, 1973), p. 17. Subsequent references to this edition will be given parenthetically within the text, showing Defoe's name followed by the page number, unless otherwise indicated.

10. *Paradise Lost*, Book I, line 86 and Book IV, lines 850 and 870. All subsequent references to *Paradise Lost* will be given parenthetically within the text, showing the initial *PL* followed by the Book number and then the line number.

11. Rudwin, p. 138.

12. Rudwin, pp. 225-226.

13. Quirk, especially 531-532, demonstrates this motivation effectively.

14. Rudwin, pp. 266-269.

15. There were by mid-century various stage versions of the legend, both dramatic and musical. See *BMC*, "Faust (Johann), Dr.," subheading "Dramatization." See Pilgrim *Letters*, ed. Madeline House and Graham Storey (Oxford: The Clarendon Press, 1969), II, 334, and note, for Dickens' plans to see such a dramatization, William

Leman Rede's *The Devil and Dr. Faustus*. Rede's version (Cumberland's British Theater, No. 367) turns the legend into an undistinguished melodrama.

16. To identify Dickens' editions of these works as well as of Defoe's *Political History of the Devil* and of *Paradise Lost* owned in 1844, see the inventory of books made in 1844, in Pilgrim *Letters*, ed. Kathleen Tillotson, IV, 711-726. To identify editions of these works owned at the time of his death, see J. H. Stonehouse, ed., *Catologue of the Library of Dickens from Gadshill* (Picadilly: Fountain Press, 1935). These lists do not show an edition of Marlowe's or Goethe's drama. Both show an edition of R. H. Horne's verse drama *The Death of Marlowe* (n. p., 1839). *German Novelists*, edited by Thomas Roscoe (London: H. Colburn, 1826), included in both lists, contained in Vol. I a German folk version, "Doctor Faustus," translated by Roscoe.

17. See *The Faerie Queene*, Book one, Canto iv, especially stanzas 4 and 14, for similarities in imagery.

18. E. M. Butler, *The Fortunes of Faust* (Cambridge: Cambridge University Press, 1952), pp. 9, 20.

19. J. W. Smeed, *Faust in Literature* (New York: Oxford University Press, 1975), pp. 262-271.

20. One translation was by "A. E. I.," the other by "H. N. S." I used the latter (London: H. G. Clarke and Co., 1844).

21. Edgar Johnson, II, 765, assumes that Honoria had refused Hawdon because she was ambitious for aristocratic rank. I find no reason to assume this, while the passage that I am citing does give reason to assume his desertion of Honoria.

22. Thurley (note 2 above), p. 109, defines the quality of Richard's pride when he comments that it is "the refusal to take life as it is, without special privilege, that destroys Richard Carstone."

23. *The Faerie Queene*, Book One, Canto VIII. stanzas 38-43.

Genteel Fictions: Caricature and Satirical Design in *Little Dorrit*

Roger D. Lund

Lionel Trilling's observation that Little Dorrit is *"more* about society than any other of the novels" remains the most accurate and
concise characterization of Dickens' narrative intention in the
novel. "It is," Trilling writes, "about society in its very essence."[1]
Curiously, however, he defines this "essence" as the failure of the
"human Will," when as the text itself, and Dickens' "Monthly
Number Plans" clearly suggest, his own definition of the "essence"
of Society in *Little Dorrit* was apparently far more particular and
restrictive.[2] It is not society with a small "s," defined as a statistical
aggregate of human actions, manners, and institutions, which
Dickens seeks to anatomize in the novel, but *Society* in italics and
upper case letters, that abstract embodiment of the Victorian "will
to status" whose essence is the love of sham and the careful preser-
vation of a respectable surface.[3] This contemptutous view of Society
as an abstract and arbitrary creation, a kind of genteel fiction, motivates and focusses Dickens' satire in *Little Dorrit* and profoundly influences his creation and manipulation of satirical caricature in the
novel.[4]

I

Like *Hard Times, Little Dorrit*'s roots are anchored firmly in contemporary events. In the years preceding the composition of *Little
Dorrit,* and even as he was writing the novel, Dickens had grown in-

creasingly disgusted with the snobbery, the social climbing, and the sheer smugness which had consumed the interests of the aristocracy and the middle classes.[5] Writing to Forster, he complained, "I am hourly strengthened in my old belief that our political aristocracy and our tuft-hunting are the death of England. In all this business I don't see a gleam of hope."[6] The bureaucratic bungling of the Crimean War was for Dickens but a glaring evidence of a more fundamental national preoccupation with respectability and social status, accompanied as they were by an adamant refusal on the part of either public or Parliament to admit that anything could possibly be wrong in the "right little, tight little, island" (59).[7] In a letter to Captain Morgan, Dickens vents his frustration with the Crimean debacle, clearly indicating the connection between his disgust with Society and the progress of *Little Dorrit*: "You see what miserable humbugs we are. . . . we have got involved in meshes of aristocratic red tape to our unspeakable confusion, loss, and sorrow. . . . I am sick and sour to think of such things at this age of the world. . . . I am in the first stage of a new book, which consists in going round and round the idea."[8] In *Little Dorrit* itself we find the "idea" most trenchantly expressed by Young Ferdinand Barnacle, the unofficial spokesman for the Circumlocution Office: "We must have humbug, we all like humbug, we couldn't get on without humbug. A little humbug, and a groove, and everything goes on admirably, if you leave it alone" (718).

As Forster indicates, Dickens first conceived of *Little Dorrit* as a political satire with the working title, "Nobody's Fault," in which the central character would create a great deal of mischief, "lay it all on Providence, and say at each fresh calamity, "Well it's a mercy, however, nobody was to blame you know!'"[9] Although this was the premise of the novel up through the fourth number, as John Butt points out, there was no single character in the early chapters who even vaguely resembled the central figure described by Forster.[10] With the completion of Chapter Ten on the Circumlocution Office, however, it became clear that "Nobody's Fault" was developing into a less political, but more complex satirical anatomy of a Society where no individual could be blamed for its corruptions, but where everyone contributed to that atmosphere of deception and the evasion of responsibility seeping from politics into every area of English life. It is this satirical program which informs the satirical plot and which motivates Dickens' remark to Forster that in *Little Dorrit*, "Society, the Circumlocution Office, and Mr. Gowan, are of course three parts of one idea and design."[11] As the novel progressed, however, this satirical design was to be augmented by the introduction of a dramatic plot focusing on Amy Dorrit and her developing relationship with Arthur Clennam, complicated, of course, by the obligatory Dickensian mystery. This more optimistic plot line "sets in perspective" the social criticism of the "one idea and design," and according to John Butt, suggests "more subtly a leading idea of *Oliver Twist* and the *Old Curiosity Shop*; that of the strength and indestructability of natural innocent virtue."[12] In terms of its narrative design, therefore, *Little Dorrit* provides a double emphasis, almost a double plot of the kind described by Sylvia Bank Manning:

> The incidents of a Dickens novel, then, may be used simultaneously to tell a sentimental or romantic story and to plot a satiric vision of society. In much the same way the characters may serve a double purpose: they may be simultaneously dramatic (or novelistic) and rhetorical (satiric counters), or they may move from one mode to the other. More often the characters are divided into two groups, one dramatic and one rhetorical.[13]

This division between the dramatic (novelistic) and satirical (rhetorical) plots has significant implication for Dickens' development of character in the novel. Just as Arthur Clennam and Amy Dorrit are almost never treated satirically, so nearly all the other characters (Flora Finching is a notable exception) are conceived and bodied forth with reference to the satirical "idea and design." While Dickens relies upon the conventional devices of naturalistic characterization to display the actions and emotions of Amy Dorrit and Arthur Clennam, virtually every other figure in the novel is a caricature or "type" who contributes in some fashion to Dickens' satirical argument that form and convention, fiction and sham, social climbing and humbug had come to define that activity politely known as "moving in Society."

In no other Dickens novel is the Victorian preoccupation with respectability and social position made to seem so odious, so dangerous, or so grotesquely ridiculous, echoing Dickens' complaint to Forster that "mere form and conventionalities usurp, in English art, as in English government, and social relations, the place of living force and truth."[14] Perhaps no other writer has mined the lode of Victorian humbug and bogus gentility more successfully than Dickens, whose satirical imagination felt a peculiar affinity for the Pecksniffs, Podsnaps, Pumblechooks and Heeps of this world.[15] In

Little Dorrit, however, the humbugs and hypocrites have seemingly multiplied exponentially. Instead of encountering one or two notable poseurs like Pecksniff, a character who has virtually an independent life apart from his narrative role, we find an entire gallery of genteel humbugs less brilliantly but more systematically embodied. In Edmund Wilson's terms, Dickens creates a "novel of the social group,"[16] a fictional examination of an entire social edifice built upon the sands of hypocrisy, sham, and affectation, a narrative where the devices of caricature are strategically subordinated to the social criticism of the satirical plot.

Dickens' mastery of caricature has not always won critical praise. It has become a rather dubious commonplace of Dickensian criticism that "Dickens's people are nearly always flat,"[17] that he usually focuses on the externals of human behavior at the expense of a more complex psychological development. To quote Walter Allen, "always the emphasis is on the physical or sartorial oddity and idiosyncracy, and it is almost as though for Dickens these are themselves guarantees of the real."[18] Such a description seems accurate enough when applied to Dickens' use of caricature in earlier novels, but in *Little Dorrit*, Dickens' emphasis upon the external surfaces and idiosyncracies of character is far more sophisticated and self-conscious. While he certainly depends upon the convenient devices of caricature to provide a gallery of vivid and humorous characters, he also uses satirical caricature to explore those social interactions which are analogous to the creation of caricature itself. Dickens' satirical portraits in *Little Dorrit* consistently reflect that social process whereby men are seen, defined, and understood only in terms of their surface characteristics, only with reference to the public identities and masks they have carefully contrived for themselves. In his description of the slum-lord, Casby, whose patriarchal locks and serenely benevolent demeanor disguise a paragon of deceit, Dickens implicitly describes his own method of characterization in the satirical plot:

> It was said that his being town-agent to Lord Decimus Tite Barnacle was referrable, not to his having the least business capacity, but to his looking so supremely benignant that nobody could suppose the property screwed or jobbed under such a man; also, that for similar reasons he now got more money out of his own wretched lettings, unquestioned, than anybody with a less nobby and less shining crown could possibly have done. In a word, it was represented . . . that many people select their models, much as the painters . . . select theirs; and that, whereas in the Royal Academy some evil old ruffian

of a Dogstealer will annually be found embodying all the cardinal
virtues, on account of his eyelashes, or his chin, or his legs (thereby
planting thorns of confusion in the breast of the more observant
students of nature), so, in the great social Exhibition, accessories are
often accepted in lieu of internal character. (142)

As this description of Casby suggests, there is a good deal more to
Dickens' development of caricature here than the mere recapitula-
tion of idiosyncratic behavior and sartorial oddity. For he argues
that in the fictional world of the novel (clearly recognizable, nonetheless, as England in the 1850s) men purposely respond to each
other as though they were mere caricatures, nothing more than surfaces, or congeries of visible details, and he indicates that this
calculated, dehumanizing response is finally motivated by vanity
and greed. Society knows that Casby is rack-renting his tenants, and
it is precisely for that reason that they find his appearance so
perfectly suitable, willingly accepting him at face value, selecting
him as a "model" of benevolence because such an interpretation of
his surface allows Society to think the best of itself in the process.

In short, Dickens' description of the world of *Little Dorrit* as a
"great social Exhibition" where "accessories are often accepted in
lieu of internal character," emphasizes those qualities of self-aggrandizement and hypocritical respectability which the novel reveals to be the "essence" of Victorian Society. It also adumbrates a
strategy of satirical caricature to portray humbugs like Mrs. General, who has formed her own surface to "such perfection that it hid
whatever was below it (if anything)" (492), characters who have repressed or ignored genuine feelings and spontaneous behavior in
their pursuit of social prominence. It also serves to expose cheats
like Merdle and Casby who have manufactured socially acceptable
personae because their true acts and motives are too impolite to be
contemplated openly. Dickens' readers have observed that in his
novels, caricature frequently reveals the results of social pressure
which has "flattened" otherwise "rounded"characters. To quote
Barbara Hardy, "Dickens is from beginning to end interested in the
assumption of a social clothing, mask, habit, role, which may stifle
the inner life entirely, or still allow it a little inner breathing space."[19]
In this regard, one thinks of a character like Wemmick, whose personality and physical appearance alter radically between his home
and the office, as he gradually assumes his professional character,
and certainly this accidental warping of character is revealed in the
effects of imprisonment on Amy Dorrit and Arthur Clennam. But

with the possible exceptions of Pancks, the Bleeding Hearts, and of course, Amy and Arthur, the character portraits in *Little Dorrit* seem devoid of that residue of sympathy which attaches to a Wemmick, or even a Jaggers, characters who may be said to have been "flattened" or at least twisted into grotesque shapes by the terrible pressures of society. In *Little Dorrit* we sense only Dickens' indignation at characters whose social pressures are self-inflicted, characters who have *chosen* to deny their own best instincts, who have stifled their own vitality in favor of a sterile and lifeless gentility, characters who, in the words of Jonathan Swift, are in the "perpetual possession of being well deceived."[20] If in the dramatic plot, Dickens still seeks to examine the effects of environment on individual character, in the satirical plot the whole process becomes self-consciously parodic.[21] The actions and attitudes blamed on Society by the actors in the satirical plot are not even distantly related to nemesis or fate. For the members of the social exhibition Society is less an inexorable force than a convenient invention. It is in the nature of Dickens' satirical design, therefore, that the characters in *Little Dorrit* should strike us as "flattened" characters, for that is the way they see themselves.

II

In the satirical plot Dickens elaborates this vision of Society as a matrix of genteel fictions, focusing upon the inter-relations between a series of families from the aristocratic Barnacles to the impoverished Plornishes, all bound together by a web of deception and affectation.[22] At the center of this web sits Blandois. While critics have rightly emphasized the dexterity with which Dickens introduces the theme of imprisonment in the opening pages of the novel, they have paid far less attention to the thoroughness and skill with which he introduces the major satirical themes of the novel in the early soliloquies of Blandois. It must be seen as an index of Dickens' contempt for the whole notion of Society that he most fully embodies the Victorian craving for social acceptance and respectability in a character who has often been regarded as the embodiment of motiveless malignity in *Little Dorrit*, a devil-figure complete with red hair and comic-opera mustache.[23] While Blandois is certainly villainous (he does murder his wife and Gowan's dog), he displays none of the unalloyed brutishness of an Orlick or a Sikes, and fails to exhibit those purely atavistic impulses which are typical of the common criminal. Instead, like any social climber, Blandois seeks merely to conquer Society, to "subdue" it and make it "confess his merit" (347). It is significant that Dickens develops the character of Blandois in the same sociological terms and with the same metaphors that he applies to the other characters in the satirical plot.[24] Significant also is Blandois's conception of himself as a convincing mimic of the genteel behavior of Society: "You have a quick perception, you have humour, you have ease, you have insinuating manner, you have a good appearance; in effect, you are a gentleman" (347). While Blandois knows that he is a counterfeit, that his credentials for the social exhibition have been forged, he also understands that in a Society comprised of cheats and imposters, no one will hasten to expose him: "He had a certain air of being a handsome man—which he was not; and certain air of being a well-bred man— which he was not. It was mere swagger and challenge; but in this particular, as in many others, blustering assertion goes for proof, half over the world" (11). In every respect, Blandois presents a self-conscious "caricature" of gentility, in Henry Gowan's rather jaded opinion, "a humorous resource to have at hand for the ridiculing of numbers of people who necessarily did more or less of what Blandois over-did" (473).

The joke remains a private one, however, for Gowan alone regards Blandois as a "satire upon others who piqued themselves on personal graces" (473). Everyone else in the social exhibition accepts Blandois's caricature of gentility as though he were genuinely polite. To make certain that we recognize the significance of Society's blind acceptance of Blandois's charade, Dickens rather clumsily intrudes into the narrative in his own voice (one of a number of such occasions) to castigate the members of Society for so cheerfully ignoring the signs of danger revealed in Blandois's excessively polite demeanor: "On this man with his moustache going up and his nose coming down in that most evil of smiles . . . Nature, always true, and never working in vain, had set the mark, Beware! It was not her fault, if the warning were fruitless" (346). For all its melodramatic staginess (an excessive theatricality which is not a failure of characterization, but a consciously contrived tactic), Blandois's portrait suggests the extent to which Dickens was willing to manipulate caricature for the larger satirical purposes of the novel. There is certainly nothing in his later dealings with Miss Wade or Mrs. Clennam to require that we pay such close attention to Blandois's pretensions to gentility. Rather, as the first of those characters whose social success results from "blustering assertion" and a "certain air of being well-bred," Blandois draws our attention to the importance of interpreting caricature correctly (both for the members of the social exhibition and us as readers), of understanding it as a process whereby every participant in the social exhibition is in some fashion self-consciously engaged in creating his own genteel fictional identity.

The caricature of Blandois serves the satirical plot in another significant way, for like so many others in the social exhibition, he understands that gentility if finally only a game: "A gentleman you shall live, my small boy, and a gentleman you shall die. You shall win however the game goes" (347).[25] As a successful, if noticeably corrupt moral gamesman, Blandois outlines the analogies between his own pursuits (extortion and murder masquerading as gentility) and those games played out at the loftier levels of Society: "If you try to prejudice me, by making out that I have lived by my wits— how do your lawyers live—your politicians—your intriguers—your men of the Exchange?" (10). Blandois's actions, his very presence in the novel, remind us that extortion, rack-renting, and stock manipulation are finally the sordid foundations upon which the filigreed pavilions of Society have been laid. He merely "overdoes" what everyone does as a matter of course. He also establishes the connection between the demand for social conformity, Society's seemingly innocent pre-occupation with forms and conventions, and a much uglier kind of covert aggression. As Peter Christmas observes, "It is an important part of Dickens' view of Gentility in *Little Dorrit*, that it is a method of compelling others to accept one at one's own false evaluation."[26] As if foreshadowing the behavior of the Merdles, the Gowans, and the Dorrits, Blandois reveals himself as one, who having polished his own surface (to borrow a phrase from Mrs. General), cannot abide the hint of vulgarity in others, rationalizing the murder of his wife and his desire for her fortune as acts of social necessity: "Madame Rigaud was unfortunately a little vulgar, I sought to improve her manners and ameliorate her general tone" (49). Dickens implies that in the world of *Little Dorrit*, and by extension the world of Victorian England, the rigid enforcement of social conformity, like the murder of Blandois's wife, is often nothing less than a pretext for private brutality.

Finally, in Blandois's carefully cultivated rhetoric of gentility we are introduced to a kind of language which finds echoes in the speech of nearly every major character in the satirical plot. Consistently Dickens suggests that there are analogies between Blandois's cynical repetition of such terms as "manner" and "tone," his verbal signature "I am a gentleman," and the pseudo-genteel locu-

tions of a William Dorrit or Mrs. General, just as there are implicit
connections between the Circumlocution Office as a "school for
gentlemen" (358), and Mr. Merdle, who turns out to be "no gentleman" at all (774).[27] If Dickens exploits visual clues and emphasizes
behavioral oddity (Blandois's nose and mustache, Mrs. Merdle's
Bosom, Mrs. General's gloves, Merdle's habitual self-handcuffing)
to establish character quickly and economically, he also relies upon
linguistic tics and idiosyncratic verbal signatures to create a vivid
rhetorical world depending for its vitality upon the emphasis and
repetition of key words and phrases.[28] Certainly one encounters
idiosyncratic and bizarre patterns of speech in *Little Dorrit* which
are used for purely comic purposes: that blinding shower of verbal
nosegays and malapropisms which is the language of Flora Finching, for example. But Flora is an anomaly in this novel, a throw-
back to an earlier, less troubled vision of human behavior, and
Dickens' bemused tribute to lost love. What is new and significant
in Dickens' exploitation of the rhetorical possibilities of keyword
repetition in *Little Dorrit* is the care with which the seemingly
idiosyncratic speech patterns of individual characters are made to
reinforce and implicity evaluate one another. Such keywords as
"gentility," "tone," "surface," "position," and "Society" become
the common property of all the major characters in the satirical
plot, and their interchangeability suggests the degree to which
Dickens had crafted an appropriate rhetorical form to express the
idea first suggested in *Bleak House*, that the highest and lowest
members of society are knit together in a seamless web. This rhetorical continuity between the caricatures, their use to explore and
evaluate the meanings of terms like "gentility," and "Society" is but
one of the devices which serves to unify the satirical plot.

III

In the caricature of Blandois, then, we find an epitome of Society
and an index to the patterns of satirical argument which lie behind
Dickens' development of caricature: the acceptance of "accessories
in lieu of internal character," the exploitation of gentility as a weapon to maintain the status quo or to advance one's position in Society, and the careful crafting of a rhetoric of self-aggrandizement.
Nowhere are these patterns more readily observable than in the
characterization of Mrs. Merdle. A woman who "represent[s] and
express[es] Society so well" (383), Mrs. Merdle is a self-created artifact "not fresh from the hand of Nature, but . . . young and fresh

from the hand of her maid" (233), whose character is subsumed in her massive, if empty Bosom. For her, "heart" and "art" are "exactly the same thing" (580); and while this gorgeous "jewel stand" of a woman obviously caricatures the thoughtlessness and gaudy inconsequence of the rich, there is more to her character than mere affectation. The source of her power (aside from her wealth and knowledge of cosmetic improvement) is her tyrannical command of social decorum and propriety as instruments of personal influence. Like Mrs. General (another tissue of false hair and paint who "drove the proprieties four-in hand . . . over several people who came in the way") (435), Mrs. Merdle understands what one must do to succeed in Society; she understands its unwritten codes of behavior and is master of its euphemisms. Thus, when Mrs. Gowan seeks advice about the acceptability of her son's marriage to Pet Meagles, Mrs. Merdle knows instinctively that the woman does not require real counsel, but rather the imprimatur of Society on an act of fortune hunting which has already been accomplished:

> Perceiving the exact nature of the fiction to be nursed, she took it delicately in her arms, and put her required contribution of gloss upon it. . . . And Mrs. Gowan, who of course saw through her own threadbare blind perfectly, and who knew that Mrs. Merdle saw through it perfectly, and who knew that Society would see through it perfectly, came out of this form, notwithstanding, as she had gone into it, with immense complacency and gravity. (385-386)

This cynical, yet seemingly ingenuous *tete a tete* indicates that Dickens intends to investigate far more in *Little Dorrit* than the simple dichotomy (common enough in all satire) between appearance and reality.[29] Rather he takes careful aim at that elaborately stylized and maddeningly purposeful process of "varnishing" the truth, of "forming a surface" which Dickens found to be the heart and soul of Victorian respectability. To those initiates of Society, such behavior seems perfectly normal; it is what is "done." To the innocent and naive observer, however, the ritual seems utterly baffling. Thus Amy Dorrit feels completely nonplussed by the behavior of Mrs. Merdle who had dismissed Amy and Fanny from her door in London as poor creatures unfit to associate with Edmund Sparkler, and yet had greeted them in Italy as "young ladies of fortune in whose favour she was much prepossessed, and whom she had never had the gratification of seeing before" (450). What Amy cannot fathom is that in the eyes of Mrs. Merdle, she and Fanny are not real people; they are only caricatures, mere "abstraction[s] of

Society" (234). Amy's perplexity here is typical of her predicament throughout the novel: how to respond as a compassionate and spontaneous human being towards people who refuse to respond in kind, men and women who have trimmed their own characters to Society's pattern and who insist that a genteel surface is finally all that matters.

Just as other people are in some sense fictional creations to Mrs. Merdle, so her own identity is a kind of private fiction, perfectly exemplifying Walter Allen's observation that the language of Dickens' characters is often "the language of personal obsession, the expression of the character's permanent fantasies of themselves."[30] For Mrs. Merdle, the permanent fantasy takes the shape of pastoral innocence, as she consistently describes herself as a noble savage in disguise, "a child of nature if I could but show it" (235). Through Mrs. Merdle's rhetoric of affected pastoralism and bucolic simplicity, Dickens ridicules that pious pretension to benevolence and soft sentiment so dear to the public conscience of the Victorians. And in Mrs. Merdle's fantasy of her own innocent and impressionable nature compromised and thwarted by the constraints of a Society which "suppresses and dominates" (235), Dickens seems self-consciously to parody the notion, so familiar in earlier novels, that caricature, or the "flattening" of character, is the tragic but inevitable result of social pressure. Like the personal fictions of Mrs. General, William Dorrit, or Henry Gowan, Mrs. Merdle's rhetoric reinforces and perpetuates the self-serving myth of her goodness and grandeur, but like Blandois, she also reveals the depths of cynicism which lie beneath the surface of her sentimentality and bogus pastoralism:

> I wish Society was not so arbitrary, I wish it was not so exacting. . . . But . . . we must take it as we find it. We know that it is hollow and conventional and worldly and very shocking, but unless we are Savages in the Tropical Seas (I should have been charmed to be one myself—most delightful life and perfect climate I am told), we must consult it. (234)

Here, Mrs. Merdle expresses one of the guiding principles of the social exhibition; that as long as a fictional abstraction may be blamed for one's actions, questions of private moral responsibility need never be raised. Mrs. Merdle's assertion that callousness and greed are justified because we cannot all be savages in the tropical seas, echoes Dickens' original idea for *Little Dorrit*, that as long as Society is to blame, then whatever seems wrong is finally "Nobody's

Fault." Implied also in these remarks is Mrs. Merdle's recognition that Society and its demands provide a convenient prextext for polite violence. Thus she feels perfectly justified in her attempts to bludgeon her lumpish and inarticulate spouse into social conformity, arguing that "you really ought not to go into Society unless you can accommodate yourself to Society" (387), complaining bitterly that because Mr. Merdle's manner "is not the tone of Society . . . he ought to correct it" (389).

Merdle himself is incensed at his wife's failure to acknowledge his efforts on behalf of Society, pointedly observing that "if you were not an ornament to Society, and if I was not a benefactor to Society, you and I would never have come together. . . . You supply manner, and I supply money" (388). Yet, for all this seeming perspicacity, Merdle quite willingly nourishes his own fiction that he "was the most disinterested of men—did everything for Society, and got as little for himself out of all his gain and care as a man might" (341), arguing all the while that his wife, his goggle-eyed son-in-law, even his glorious Butler are sacrificial offerings on the altars of Society. Society, in its parasitic enthusiasm to attach itself to Merdle's millions, quite happily believes what it is told, and encourages Mr. Merdle in his delusions of philanthropy. Acting in the capacity of an estate agent, Bar suggests that Mr. Merdle owes it to Society to buy a small borough, while Bishop innocently asks if "Society might not unreasonably hope that one so blest in his undertakings, and whose example on his pedestal was so influential with it, should shed a little money in the direction of a mission or so to Africa" (245). Just as it overlooks Casby's abuse of his poor tenants because it is to its advantage to do so, Society quite willingly ignores Merdle's dull features, his social ineptitude, his air of being entirely out of place because "all people knew (or thought they knew) that he had made himself immensely rich; and, for that reason alone, prostrated themselves before him" (539). Despite clear evidence that Merdle is no deity, "the multitude worshipped on trust— though always distinctly knowing why" (539). Here Dickens ridicules Society's baffling but unquenchable desire to worship false idols, and in a passage bristling with indignation Dickens scarifies such representatives of Society as Bar, Horse Guards, and Bishop for their conspiracy of silence:

> There was a spectre always attendant on him saying to these high priests, 'Are these the signs you trust, and love to honor; this head, these eyes, this mode of speech, the tone and manner of this man?

You are the levers of the Circumlocution Office, and the rulers of
men. . . . Does your qualification lie in the superior knowledge of
men, which accepts, courts, and puffs this man? Or, if you are competent to judge aright the signs I never fail to show you when he appears among you, is your superior honesty your qualification?' Two
rather ugly questions these, always going about town with Mr. Merdle: and there was a tacit agreement that they must be stifled. (539)

The tone of Dickens' rhetoric indicates that he is not merely ridiculing his fictional creations, but attacking the movers and shakers of
his own society as well, reiterating in the bitterest terms one of the
central themes of the novel, that the failures of Society (both fictional and real) are in some sense failures to interpret the clues of character correctly. But insisting that "accessories" (in this case
Merdle's money) are an adequate substitute for internal character,
Society has, in effect, rejected the notion of true character altogether. All perception, all knowledge of other human beings has
been reduced to a trivial and self-serving form of social "recognition." Because the Gowans know the Merdles, William Dorrit feels
"It is quite right to know these people. It is a very proper thing. . . .
We will—ha—we will certainly notice them" (469). In the same
fashion "Society was aware of Mr. and Mrs. Merdle. Society had
said, 'Let us license them; let us know them'"(241). The success of
the great social exhibition depends upon the willingness of its participants to filter their perceptions, their knowledge, through the
lenses of popular and received opinion: "Nobody said what anything was, but everybody said what the Mrs. Generals, Mr. Eustace,
or somebody else said it was. . . . It had not a flaw of courage or
honest free speech in it" (498).

From beginning to end, *Little Dorrit* presents an indictment
of Society which is blind because it refuses to see. Nowhere is this
moral blindness more readily observable than at Merdle's elaborate
dinner parties which might be taken for pure farce were they not
metonymy for the English system of nepotism and jobbery which
according to Dickens had filled the Circumlocution Offices of
England with fools and scoundrels. The maneuverings of Bar,
Horse Guards, Bishop and the other Barnacles in Merdle's parlor
reproduce the actions of the government and bureaucracy in Westminster, each knowing what the others are after as they slyly jockey
Merdle and Lord Decimus toward an actual meeting to arrange a
post for Young Sparkler. Yet, the two great men stand at opposite
ends of the room "each with an absurd pretense of not having the
other on his mind, which could not have been more transparently

ridiculous though his real mind had been chalked on his back"
(549). Like these Barnacles in power, the Barnacles in retirement at
Hampton Court all maintain this same pretense that their disguises
are as grand and as impenetrable as they seem, hiding behind
"genteel blinds and makeshifts" (303) the fact that they are merely
gypsies camped at public expense. Fortified with this purblind sense
of genealogical favor, Mrs. Gowan, herself a Barnacle, sets out to
find a suitably lucrative match for her improvident son Henry.
Though she knows in her heart that the "Miggles people" (307) are
going to pay her son's debts and substantially underwrite his future
expenses, Mrs. Gowan also realizes that in order for Society to ap-
prove a marriage between a scion of the Barnacle clan and the child
of a banker, it must be publicly understood that "such people will
do anything for the honor of such an alliance" (309), even calling
upon Arthur Clennam to corroborate "this fable" (380). As expected, Society approves, and the marriage proceeds, all hard feelings varnished over by "the fiction that it was not Mr. Meagles who
had stood in the way, but that it was the Family greatness, and that
the Family greatness had made a concession, and there was now a
soothing unanimity" (397).

Mr. Meagles, meanwhile, is left to glean what comfort he can
from his connection with the Barnacles: "'It's very gratifying,' he
said, often repeating the remark in the course of the evening, 'Such
high company!'" (459). Dickens' caricature of Mr. Meagles as a
good-hearted snob who "had a weakness which none of us need to
go into the next street to find, and which no amount of Circumlocution experience could long subdue in him" (200), has a special place
in the satirical plot of the novel, for through him Dickens suggests
that even the middle classes could no longer be trusted as the repository of common sense and good faith. Meagles is precisely the
kind of no-nonsense, John Bull Englishman that Dickens would
have praised in earlier novels, and though he is likable enough here,
it seems clear that his old-fashioned English practicality provides
no protection against the infection of modern snobbery. As John
Lucas observes, "Dickens does not merely show that Meagles' type
of social fawning is a fact among 'good' men, but that it is an
important part of the social process by means of which the Barnacles are kept in positions of authority and because of which people suffer."[31]

When Dickens despaired of the upper and middle classes, he
moved down the social scale in search of sanity, benevolence, and
moral recitude.[32] But moving down the scale to the poor Dorrit fam-

ily, one finds an even more pernicious version of Meagles's social fawning: "If young John Chivery had had the inclination, and the power to write a satire on family pride, he would have had no need to go for an avenging illustration out of the family of his beloved" (225). First we encounter Tip, a walking testament to the debilitating influence of the pursuit of gentility, then Fanny, possessed from her youth by her "family assertion" (235), struggling always to enhance her position and to "shine most in Society" (675). But most devoted to dreams of social conquest is their father, William Dorrit, whose portrait is Dickens' most penetrating and pathetic examination of the corrosive effects of snobbery and social climbing. Blindly committed to "the family gentility—always the gentility,"[33] Dorrit steadfastly ignores Amy's sufferings, demanding that his children "preserve the genteel fiction that they were all idle beggars together" (72). Moving in Society as the patriarch of a family "more genteel than any lady" (446), he foolishly hopes to emerge "before the world—a-ha—gentleman unspoiled, unspotted" (464). Like Blandois and Mrs. Merdle, Dorrit has convinced himself that character is merely the product of conscious creation, nothing more than the acquisition of the proper mannerisms and the appropriate vocabulary. Feeling confident that he has formed his own character sufficiently, that he has burnished his own surface to a perfect gloss, Dorrit considers himself to be a "kind of example" (217), a perfect caricature of gentility. He discovers no irony in the pompous declaration to his brother that "you might be like me, my dear Frederick, you might be if you chose!" (217-8); and because he believes his own fictions, uncritically accepting his own assertions that he is a true gentleman, Dorrit assumes that every word he hears, every gesture he sees is somehow related to his own social position.

Thus he misinterprets Amy's artless and spontaneous gestures toward Pet Gowan and Old Nandy as calculated assaults on the family dignity, feeling insulted that she has not chosen to remake herself in his own image. In Dorrit's repeated demands that Amy "form a—hum—a surface" (465), Dickens finds an objective correlative for his argument that the preoccupation with gentility and social position invariably degenerates into some form of coercion and brutality. Even Dorrit's metaphors as he argues that "it is incumbent upon all people in an exalted position, but it is particularly so on this family . . . to make themselves respected" (442), reveal an undertone of aggression. One might argue that Dorrit intends to destroy Amy's "internal character" in order to replace it with more socially agreeable "accessories," insisting, in effect, that she become a mere caricature of the dutiful daughter, like her sister Fanny "a child brimful of duty and good principle, self-devoted to the family name" (578).

Like Bar, Horse Guards, and the Barnacles, Dorrit is yet another participant in the great social exhibition who wilfully fails to interpret the clues of character correctly. This blindness results in part from Dorrit's attempts to disguise the truth with a carefully crafted rhetoric of euphemism and self-aggrandizement. Even as a prisoner, Dorrit regards himself as a "moral Lord Chesterfield" (223), insisting that his gatherings of the idle and the impecunious constitute "quite a Levee—quite a Levee," and that the alms left by compassionate visitors are "testimonials" (80) to his position as Father of the Marshalsea. If Amy Dorrit perceives Society to be a superior form of imprisonment, her father sees the Marshalsea as merely an inferior version of Society, interpreting such small gestures as presiding over the evening's entertainment in the Snuggery as a "public duty," as one of the perquisites of his "position" in the "College" (371). Once freed from the Marshalsea, lodged safe in Italian anonymity, Dorrit is at liberty to recreate this past, to enrich and ornament his own caricature at will. Thus Amy's uncertain behavior is credited to the untimely loss her mother, and the fact that she has "lived with me as comparatively poor, though always proud, gentleman, in—ha—hum—retirement" (459). Preening his reputation in the presence of Mrs. General, he claims to have been "at the head of—ha—of a considerable community," insisting he is "not unaccustomed to—an influential position" (460-61). Every catch in Dorrit's voice, every pause indicates his uncertainty as to which euphemism to select, which fiction to express, so that the truth of his past may be completely varnished over. All the while, his life is plagued by domestics who seem to smile knowingly, and acquaintances from London, like the Gowans, who threaten to reveal his past. It is fitting, therefore, that his final speech before Mrs. Merdle's dinner guests, a speech swollen with euphemisms and convenient lies, should finally expose and humiliate the Father of the Marshalsea, as he collapses babbling of his "personal dignity" and his "humble endeavours to—hum—to uphold a Tone here—a Tone" (629).

IV

I have discussed the significance of Blandois's character as a pattern for the satirical caricature in *Little Dorrit* and as an ironic commentator on the behavior of the other members of the social exhibition. But of nearly equal importance to the satirical design of the novel are those other malcontents and misfits, Henry Gowan, whom Dickens indicated was part of the central "idea and design," and Miss Wade, through whose narrative was to flow the "blood" of the entire novel.[34] Although the "History of a Self Tormentor" was not entirely successful, as Dickens admitted, in at least one sense it is in perfect keeping with the satirical argument of *Little Dorrit*, for like the other characters in the satirical plot, Miss Wade's peculiar complaint (often mistakenly reduced to lesbianism) is shown to arise from a sense of her own social inferiority and a burning resentment of patronage real or imagined. Like William Dorrit, she has battled a life-long series of imagined slights in her struggle to establish her own dignity in the face of apparent social prejudice. From her childhood companions she received only "Fair words and fair pretences" (646), and their revelation of her illegitimacy left her with an interpretation of all human intercourse as a cruel exercise in patronage and condescension: "It showed me many new occasions on which people triumphed over me, when they made a pretence of treating me with consideration, or doing me a service" (646). Her love affair with the nephew of her employer is poisoned by her sense of her "dependent and inferior position" (649), but the cruellest blow of all is Henry Gowan's marriage to Pet Meagles, a woman whose "extraction" (324) and financial position enable her to marry the man Miss Wade once loved. This sense of awkwardness and social disadvantage is not the woman's only complaint, but it seems clear that Miss Wade's jaundiced view of the world is symptomatic of that disease which infects the rest of Society as well.

The epidemic of social disaffection and snobbery has certainly infected Henry Gowan. If Miss Wade's revenge upon a heartless Society manifests itself in the kidnapping of Tattycoram, Gowan's weapon against Society is his art, having become a "Painter; partly because he had always had an idle knack that way, and partly to grieve the souls of the Barnacles-in-chief who had not provided for him" (201). Angry that he has not been offered a sinecure like that purchased for Edmund Sparkler, Gowan affects a contempt for his family, never allowing anyone to forget that he is a "disappointed man" who has deserved better at the hands of Society. Ironically, however, Gowan knows that whatever success he has achieved derives from his connections, as he simultaneously vilifies and exploits them. As Blandois accurately observes, "He may, in effect, have repudiated his connections, proudly, impatiently, sarcastically . . . but he has them" (427). An artist without a vocation, Gowan confesses that at times the work of maintaining a surface is almost too great; he doubts that he can continue "to pass the bottle of smoke. To keep up the pretense as to labour, and study, and patience, and being devoted to my art" (393). Rather, painting for Gowan has become but one more form of humbug, of "hocus-pocus" (393) like the genteel fictions of Society or the obfuscations of the Circumlocution Office. For Gowan, artists, like everyone else in Society, are merely imposters: "Painters, writers, patriots, all the rest who have stands in the market. Give almost any man I know, ten pounds, and he will impose upon you to a corresponding extent" (302). The caricature of Henry Gowan completes that satirical "idea and design" which includes Society and the Circumlocution Office, for through him Dickens symbolizes his own disgust with the respectable timidity of contemporary art, and his conviction that art had become but another conventional but highly respectable fraud, an attitude he revealed in a letter to Forster: "It is of no use disguising the fact that what we know is wanting in the man is wanting in their works. . . . There is a horrid respectability about most of them—a little, finite, systematic routine in them, strangely expressive to me of the state of England herself."[35]

One measure of Dickens' pessimism in *Little Dorrit* is the degree to which his satirical spokesmen all seem to be villains. Gowan argues that one of the advantages of knowing a disappointed man is that "you hear the truth" (393), and the events of the novel bear out his indictment of Society as grand imposture. He is right in his belief that at every level of Society men invite deception. Even so minor a character as the solicitor, Rugg, is involved in the charade, insisting that Clennam allow himself to be arrested only by the superior courts because it "looks better" (697), and even Mrs. Chivery takes "notice that their John's prospects of the lock would certainly be strengthened by an alliance with Miss Dorrit" (206). Dazzled by the charms of the social exhibition, even the poor Bleeding Hearts are taken in by false appearances, believing that because Casby "looks" so patriarchal and benevolent, he must be unaware of the depradations of his rental agent: "For (said the Bleeding Hearts), if a gentleman with that head of hair and them eyes took his rents into his own hands, ma'am, there would be none of this worriting and wearing, and things would be very different" (272). Yet another measure of Dickens' anger and disgust with the deceptions and respectable humbug of his own society is the indication in *Little Dorrit* that even a good heart and simple innocence (powerful amulets against such deceptions in earlier novels) no longer provide an adequate defense against such a monstrous conspiracy, not for the Bleeding Hearts, not for Clennam, and not even for Little Dorrit.

It is in the nature of Dickens' dual plot that Amy Dorrit and Arthur Clennam are left to respond as best they can to Society and its fictions. While they both survive, they are left severely scarred. Despite recent praise of Little Dorrit's redemptive powers, the subdued and chastened conclusion of the novel suggests that Society has not finally been redeemed at all, that it may even be beyond redemption.[36] True enough, William Dorrit has been exposed, his past made public; Merdle has slashed his wrists, his financial empire in ruins; that "philanthropic sneak" (777) Casby has been shorn of his benevolent pretensions; Mrs. Clennam has suffered a retributive paralysis, and Blandois has been smashed to atoms beneath the house of Clennam: all powerful (if conventional) symbols of cleansing and unmasking. Yet Dickens suggests, I think, that in a Society so fervently dedicated to self-deception, such revelations, such gestures, are too little, too late.[37] In fact, we are offered no convincing indication that Society has been fundamentally altered. Reduced circumstances do not prevent Mrs. Merdle, Fanny, and Tip from playing the social game; the Gowans, mother and son, press on in their embittered pursuit of solvency and social eminence; the shoal of Barnacles still clings to the ship of state; while the Circumlocution Office with all its "forms" and its moral intransigence remains the most potent symbol of English Society, "not a wicked Giant to be charged at full tilt; but, only a windmill showing you, as it grinds immense quantities of chaff, which way the country wind blows" (717).

As Young Ferdinand Barnacle suggests, even Merdle "who must have been a master of Humbug. Knew people so well—got over them so completely—did so much with them" (718), was not an aberration, but a natural product of Society's desire to be deceived, its mania for opulent and genteel appearances, its willingness to accept "accessories" in lieu of internal character. "The next man who has a large capacity and as genuine a taste for swindling, will succeed as well. Pardon me, but I think you really have no idea how the human bees will swarm to the beating of any old tin kettle; in that fact lies the complete manual of governing them" (718). Clennam's response, "'If I could believe that . . . it would be a dismal prospect for all of us'" (718), sounds precisely the right note of anxiety and pessimism. For *Little Dorrit*, is, after all, Dickens' darkest novel, and in light of its pessimistic tone, its refusal to admit of easy or immediate solutions, one is reminded of the absurdity of Shaw's remark that the novel is a "more seditious book than *Das Kapital*."[38] The sounds we hear in this novel are not the cries of the revolutionary, but the indignant voice of the satirist and prophet. Although the novel was born of Dickens' disgust with politics and public administration, *Little Dorrit* is finally less a summons to the barricades than an embittered call for national repentence.

NOTES

1. Lionel Trilling, Introduction, *Little Dorrit*, New Oxford Illustrated Dickens (London: Oxford University Press, 1953); rpt. in *The Dickens Critics*, ed. George H. Ford and Lauriat Lane, Jr. (Ithaca: Cornell University Press, 1961), p. 280.
2. Trilling, p. 280.
3. While Trilling uses the phrase (p. 286), he does not explore the full range of its suggestions, turning away from its specific context to deal with the larger question of the human will in general. For the more particular applications of the term, see Paul D. Herring, "Dickens' Monthly Number Plans for Little Dorrit," *Modern Philology*, 64 (1966–67), 22-63, where the description of Mrs. Merdle suggests that Dickens is defining Society as an abstraction directly linked to his conception of caricature in the novel: "Mrs Merdle — Bosom—Society, Society, Society." (p. 34). See also, Harvey Peter Sucksmith, Introduction, *Little Dorrit* (Oxford: Clarendon, Press, 1979), p. xxvii.
4. See Janice M. Carlisle, "Little Dorrit: Necessary Fictions," *Studies in the Novel*, VII (1975), 195-212. Professor Carlisle argues that "Little Dorrit is an inquiry into the moral status of fiction" (p. 195), but she focuses on Amy Dorrit as a kind of surrogate novelist. Although Carlisles's definition of the term "fiction" is quite different from mine, her descriptions of the various kinds of "storytelling" that occur in the novel draw attention to the self-reflexiveness of the narrative in *Little Dorrit*, and the extent to which the characters in the novel see themselves as the creators of fictions.
5. Edgar Johnson, *Charles Dickens: His Tragedy and Triumph*, 2 vols. (New York: Simon and Schuster, 1952), II, 858.
6. *The Letters of Charles Dickens*, ed. Walter Dexter, 2 vols. (London: Nonesuch Press, 1938), II, 622.
7. *Little Dorrit*, ed. Harvey Peter Sucksmith (Oxford: Clarendon Press, 1979). All quotations from *Little Dorrit* are taken from this edition and cited by page number in the text.
8. *Letters*, II, 712.
9. John Forster, *The Life of Charles Dickens* (Boston: Estes and Lauriat, n. d.), III, 132.
10. John Butt and Kathleen Tillotson, *Dickens at Work* (London: Methuen & Co., 1957), pp. 222-233.

11. *Letters*, II, 766.
12. Butt and Tillotson, *Dickens at Work*, p. 230. On the development of the double emphasis in the narrative, see also Herring, pp. 24 ff., and Sucksmith, Introduction, *Little Dorrit*, xxi.
13. Sylvia Bank Manning, *Dickens as Satirist* (New Haven and London: Yale University Press, 1971), p. 9.
14. *Letters*, II, 700.
15. George Gissing, "Dickens Satiric Portraiture," rpt. in *The Dickens Critics*, pp. 76-108, still provides the best treatment of Dickens's penchant for satirizing humbug and hypocrisy, the "English vice *par excellence.*"
16. Edmund Wilson, "The Two Scrooges," in *The Wound and the Bow* (Cambridge, Mass.: Riverside Press, 1941). p. 34.
17. E. M. Forster, *Aspects of the Novel* (New York: Harcourt Brace and Company, 1954), p. 71. Even Forster admits that "part of the genius of Dickens is that he does use types and caricatures . . . and yet achieve effects that are not mechanical and a vision of humanity that is not shallow."
18. Walter Allen, "The Comedy of Dickens," in *Dickens 1970*, ed. Michael Slater (New York: Stein and Day, 1970), p. 8.
19. Barbara Hardy, "The Complexity of Dickens," in *Dickens 1970*, p. 39. See also John Holloway, Introduction, *Little Dorrit* (Harmondsworth: Penguin Books, 1967), p. 25, for another version of the argument that caricature "registers the distortion, the contortion of man by society."
20. Jonathan Swift, *A Tale of a Tub*, IX.
21. John Holloway argues that "necessity as a force in life . . . is an intrinsic part of his [Dickens'] vision" (pp. 16-17). While Dickens clearly indicates the importance of destiny in the novel, for example in the eventual reunion of all the travellers imprisoned in Marseilles, this kind of force of fate seems markedly different from the kinds of social pressures created and accepted by the characters in the satirical plot.
22. Peter Christmas, "*Little Dorrit*: The End of Good and Evil," in *Dickens Studies Annual*, 6, ed. Robert B. Partlow, Jr. (Carbondale and Edwardsville: Southern Illinois University Press, 1977), p. 135. Christmas argues that Dickens' interest in the Gowans, Meagleses, Clennams, and Dorrits derives from "the relationship that each family forms with Gentility." See also John Wain, "Little Dorrit," in *Dickens and the Twentieth Century*, ed. John Gross and Gabriel Pearson (Toronto: University of Toronto Press, 1962), pp. 179-180, on snobbery as a binding force in the book.
23. See Trilling, p. 285; "Blandois is wholly wicked, the embodiment of evil; he is, indeed a devil."
24. Barbara Hardy, *The Moral Art of Charles Dickens* (New York: Oxford University Press, 1970), p. 4, points out that Dickens had a "sociological imagination."
25. J. Hillis Miller observes that in *Little Dorrit* "Society is fictive, a game of false appearances." See *Charles Dickens: The World of His Novels* (Cambridge, Mass.: Harvard University Press, 1958), p. 226.

26. Christmas, p. 140. See also F. R. Leavis, and Q. D. Leavis, *Dickens the Novelist* (New York: Pantheon Books, 1970), p. 236, and John Lucas, *The Melancholy Man* (London: Methuen and Co., 1970), p. 267 on the parasitism and sheer aggressiveness of the characters in *Little Dorrit.*

27. George Gissing, p. 89, observes that "all Dickens's prominent creations say the same thing in the same way, over and over again."

28. David Lodge, *The Language of Fiction* (London: Routledge and Kegan Paul; New York: Columbia University Press, 1966), p. 152. See also Leavis, p. 225, on "focal words," and J. Hillis Miller, p. 229.

29. Numerous critics have discussed the dichotomy between appearance and reality in *Little Dorrit.* The best overview of this line of argument is Janice M. Carlisle's, pp. 197-198.

30. Allen, p. 15.

31. Lucas, p. 264.

32. Wilson, p. 33.

33. Herring, p. 32.

34. *Letters,* II, 776.

35. *Letters,* II, 700.

36. See Harvey Peter Sucksmith, *The Narrative Art of Charles Dickens* (Oxford: Clarendon Press, 1970), pp. 338-339. Trilling massively overstates the case calling Little Dorrit "the Paraclete in female form," p. 293. F. R. Leavis says of her that she is for "her father and brother and sister, the never-failing providence, the vital core of sincerity, the conscience, the courage of moral percipience, the saving realism, that preserves for them the necessary bare minimum of the real beneath the fantastic play of snobberies, pretences, and self-deceptions . . ." (p. 226). See also Ronald S. Librach, "The Burdens of Self and Society: Release and Redemption in *Little Dorrit,*" *Studies in the Novel,* VII No. 4, (Winter 1975), 538-551.

37. Holloway argues that "as the novel draws to its close, one character after another, in some decisive and self-renewing act, rejects the life of mannerism, surface and self-hallucinatory self-defence." He argues as well that the "imprisoning surfaces are broken through by the emancipating reality beneath" (p. 27). In a letter to Macready, Dickens indicates both his belief that the public *wishes* to be deceived, and his fear that no immediate reform is possible: "I do reluctantly believe that the English people are habitually consenting parties to the miserable imbecility into which we have fallen, and never will help themselves out of it" *Letters,* II, 695.

38. Quoted in Johnson, II, 883.

Secret Pockets and Secret Breasts: *Little Dorrit* and the Commercial Scandals of the Fifties

Barbara Weiss

It has often been claimed that the conception of Mr. Merdle in *Little Dorrit* originated in contemporary newspaper headlines about the fall of the Irish financier John Sadleir.[1] What has seldom been noted, however, is the larger issue of a widespread concern over commercial corruption; at the time Dickens was engaged in the writing of *Little Dorrit*, an epidemic of sordid financial scandals seemed to be shaking the confidence of the public. Sadleir was in fact only one of a series of con men and frauds whose well-publicized exposures in the fifies were the occasion of great indignation.[2] Indeed, this concern over what appeared to be the venal immorality of the commercial world seems to lie not only behind the creation of the financier Merdle, but seems in fact to be one of Dickens' pervasive themes in the novel.

The consciousness of this widespread corruption surfaces in ways which are likely to elude the present day reader of the novel. The modern reader may well be perplexed, for example, at the dramatically ominous atmosphere of the old Clennam house. The Clennam firm, while perhaps guilty of "sharp dealing" is certainly not a rival to the nefarious enterprises of Merdle, and the strong emphasis placed upon its criminal associations may indeed strike the reader as odd. The following passage is perhaps typical. Clennam approaches his mother's house with misgivings:

It always affected his imagination as wrathful, mysterious, and sad; and his imagination was sufficiently impressible to see the whole neighborhood under some tinge of its shadow. As he went along, upon a dreary night, the dim streets by which he went seemed all depositories of oppressive secrets. The deserted counting houses, with their secrets of books and papers locked up in chests and safes; the banking-houses, with their secrets of strong rooms and wells, the keys of which were in a very few secret pockets and a very few secret breasts; the secrets of all the dispersed grinders in the vast mill, among whom there were doubtless plunderers, forgers, and trust-betrayers of many sorts, whom the light of any day that dawned might reveal; he could have fancied that these things, in hiding, im-parted a heaviness to the air. The shadow, thickening as he ap-proached its source, he thought of the secrets of the lonely church-vaults, where the people who had hoarded and secreted in iron cof-fers were in their turn similarly hoarded, not yet at rest from doing harm; and then of the secrets of the river, as it rolled its turbid tide between two frowning wildernesses of secrets, extending thick and dense, for many miles, and warding off the free air and the free country swept by winds and wings of birds.[3]

Nothing that has been revealed about the Clennams thus far seems to justify this image of the crimes of the house contaminating the neighborhood, and by extension all of the city, with its dark crimi-nal shadow. And in fact the "crime" of Mrs. Clennam, when at last disclosed, proves to be an essentially private and domestic sin, and a rather anti-climactic one at that. However, to the readers of Dickens' own day, the dark references to banking houses with secret keys meant only for "a very few secret pockets and a very few secret breasts" would have instantly recalled current scandals of the fif-ties, and the widespread public concern over the apparent immoral-ity of the financial community.

It is impossible to doubt that Dickens had in mind the specific case of John Sadleir when he created the swindler Merdle; for one thing he hinted as much in the preface to the 1857 edition. "That extravagant conception, Mr. Merdle," Dickens declared, "originated after the Railroad-shares epoch, in the times of a certain Irish bank, and of one or two other equally laudable enterprises."[4] The similarities between the careers of Sadleir and Merdle are un-mistakable. John Sadleir, who started life in modest circumstances, rose to be the director of railroad and joint-stock companies and a member of Parliament. With his brother, Sadleir created the Tip-perary Joint Stock Bank in Ireland, and was chairman of the Lon-don and Country Bank. In 1853 he became a Junior Lord of the Treasury. He was being spoken of as future Chancellor of the Ex-

chequer when sinister reports began to circulate about his enterprises. Desperately Sadleir tried without success to raise money to
make good certain title-deeds he had forged and fictitious shares he
had manufactured. After writing letters expressing remorse for his
dishonest actions, he committed suicide. The news that Sadleir's
body had been discovered on Hampstead Heath broke upon an astonished public in February of 1856 as the first monthly numbers of
Little Dorrit were making their appearance. It was discovered
shortly thereafter that Sadleir had forged railway shares and embezzled money from the Tipperary Bank, which eventually went
bankrupt, ruining a large number of shareholders and depositors.[5]
The Times judged the affair to be "the greatest crash made by any
individual in recent times" (26 Feb. 1856, p. 9).

Although the parallels between Sadleir and the embezzler and
forger Merdle would seem to be convincing, it has been argued by
some that Dickens was at least as inspired by the notorious case of
George Hudson the Railway King, which had transpired a decade
earlier.[6] Like Sadleir, Hudson had risen from humble beginnings to
power and wealth as a promoter of railways. By 1845 he had
become a member of Parliament. Acquiring country estates and a
London mansion, he was soon considered among the pre-eminent
men of his age. The collapse of the railway shares, however, proved
to be his undoing, and subsequent investigations revealed that Hudson had been guilty of flagrant irregularities. Although he escaped
criminal prosecution, he lived out the rest of his life in relative
obscurity.[7]

The embezzlements of Hudson and Sadleir were the most spectacular of the mid-Victorian period. Throughout the fifties, however, there were constant scandals in which prominent businessmen
were exposed as swindlers, forgers, and thieves; those "other laudable enterprises" which Dickens mentions in the preface as his inspiration for Merdle were indeed well documented and known to
every reader of the daily newspaper. As flamboyant as either Hudson or Sadleir was Walter Watts, who appeared from nowhere in
1844 and gained great prominence in the theatrical world. Taking
a fashionable home in the West End, and a country home in
Brighton, Watts opened two theaters, laying out money for his theatrical productions on such a lavish scale that his theaters would
surely have been driven into bankruptcy had not Watts been exposed first as a thief. It was revealed that the theatrical entrepreneur was in reality a check clerk in the cashier's department of the
Globe Assurance Company, from which he had embezzled over

seven hundred thousand pounds to pay for his extravagances. By
1850, Watts had been sent to Newgate Prison, where he committed
suicide.[8] Even more shocking, because of the high rank of the offen-
ders, were revelations concerning the banking firm of Sir John Dean
Paul and his partners, Strahan and Bates, who were discovered to
have speculated with huge sums of money which had been entrusted to their bank, and to have made off with a large proportion of
the bank's assets as well.[9] The most galling aspect of the case of
Strahan, Bates, and Paul was the duplicity with which these gentlemen guarded their standing in respectable society. *The Times*
reported that

> while thus subsisting on wholesale plunder, these men assumed to be
> pious and charitable far beyond their neighbors—to be leaders in
> every subscription, the presiding and directing geniuses at every
> meeting for pious or eleemosynary purposes, the polished corners
> and the shining pillars of the temple. (29 October 1855, p.6)

The three were tried for fraud and sentenced to transportation in
1855.

The case of Joseph Windle Cole aptly illustrates the immense dangers of fraud in an economy largely dependent upon credit. Cole,
who set himself up in business in 1848 under the protection of a cer-
tificate of bankruptcy from his previous enterprise, obtained over
half a million pounds in loans from discount houses on the fraudulent security provided by forged dock-warrants for fictitious mer-
chandise in a fictitious warehouse. The case is doubly interesting
because of the involvement of Overend, Gurney and Co., the largest
money-discounting house in London, which apparently learned
about Cole's fraudulent warrants but refrained from exposing him
in hopes of recovering its money at the expense of his other creditors. Cole was finally exposed and tried in 1855 amidst much public controversy over the role played by Overend, Gurney and Co.[10]

Almost simultaneous with the scandal of John Sadleir, and also
alluded to by Dickens in the preface to *Little Dorrit*, was the scandal of the Royal British Bank. Established in 1850 as a joint-stock
banking company with branches all over London, the bank had several members of Parliament on its board. The revelations in the
Sadleir case led directly to allegations against the Royal British
Bank, and a subsequent run on the Bank forced it to close its doors
in September 1856. Upon investigation, it was discovered that the
directors had loaned money liberally and without security to themselves and their associates, the transactions being recorded only in a

secret ledger whose key was entrusted to only a few persons. According to *The Times*, "the directors had also a regular allowance of two thousand pounds a year among them, for what the Persians call "tooth money" for the wear and tear of their teeth in masticating and swallowing what they took" (23 September, 1856, p. 6.) The case of the Royal British Bank was dragged with great publicity through both Chancery and Bankruptcy Courts in 1856.[11] Two other notorious scandals of the fifties involved large-scale forgeries. William Robson was a clerk who forged huge amounts of Crystal Palace Shares, and proceeded to spend his money riotously, supporting a wife and two mistresses in extravagant style.[12] More circumspect was Leopold Redpath, a former bankrupt who became a clerk at the Great Northern Railway Company and forged transfers of shares. Redpath lived luxuriously but quite respectably on his embezzled fortune, contributing munificent sums to charity and serving conscientiously as a governor of Christ's Hospital before he was apprehended.[13]

To a public outraged by each new revelation of dishonesty, it must have seemed as if mercantile life in the mid-Victorian years had been overwhelmed with a corruption which threatened to poison the moral life of the whole community. In the wake of the disastrous Railway Panic of the forties, journals and periodicals were filled with outraged exposures of stock swindles and other dubious speculative ventures. As early as 1845, *Blackwood's Magazine* printed a satire on the railway schemes of the day, entitled "How We Got Up The Glenmutchkin Railway, And How We Got Out Of It," chronicling the promotion of a scheme for building a railroad in a part of Scotland inhabited primarily by sheep and goats.[14] Satire against phony stock speculation seems to have become a well-established genre at this time; by the fifties and sixties Dickens was regularly using the pages of *Household Words* and *All The Year Round* to satirize joint-stock speculation and other mercantile frauds in banking and insurance.[15] The fall of George Hudson had in fact been the occasion for national soul searching concerning the nature of speculative capitalism. Thomas Carlyle, for one, had pronounced the hero-worship of Hudson to be symptomatic of England's decadence.[16] Nor was Carlyle the only spokesman who found the morality of the mid-Victorian years abhorrent. Tennyson complained in *Maud* (1855) of an age "When who but a fool would have faith in a tradesman's wares or his word? . . . When only the ledger lives, and when only not all men lie."[17] The slogan of the times, Tennyson wrote despairingly, was "Cheat and be cheated, and die. . . ."[18] But it was not merely the poets and pro-

phets of the Victorian age who denounced the contemporary
climate of mercantile corruption and believed that it augured the
worst for English society. Members of Parliament denounced the
immorality of the times, and, during a bitter debate over the introduction of laws of limited liability, predicted an onslaught of
even greater corruption if corporate capitalism were allowed to
become the norm in conducting business.[19]

Many of the most widely read journals and papers of the day also
expressed despair and indignation at the revelations of corruption in
high places. As the daily columns of *The Times* chronicled each
new exposure and scandal, that worthy organ of public opinion edi-
torialized tirelessly thoughout the fifties about the sad condition of
commercial morality. Like Carlyle, *The Times* saw Hudson as the
true representative of his age ("Could there be a fitter prophet for
England and the year 1845?"[1 May 1849, p. 4]) and piously hoped
that the proper lesson would be drawn from his downfall. The scandal of Strahan, Bates and Sir John Dean Paul provoked another
prayerful comment from *The Times*:

> We trust that the fate of these three great delinquents will be a salu-
> tary lesson to the commercial community. From extravagance to
> fraud, from fraud to theft, from theft to transportation, is a law of
> progression which many a man trembling on the narrow verge be-
> tween right and wrong will do well to seriously consider. (29 Oc-
> tober 1856, p. 9)

The exposure of John Sadleir inspired *The Times* to new heights of
rhetoric in its outrage against the rapacious spirit of the fifties. Sadleir's suicide note is quoted to grim effect ("Oh! that I had resisted
the first attempt to launch me into speculation!") with an ominous
warning to those tempted to yield to the loose commercial morality
of the day: "There are many of the English public who would do
well to lay seriously to heart the dying words of John Sadleir" (26
February 1856, p. 9). As the final numbers of *Little Dorrit* were
making their appearance, *The Times* sadly surveyed the recent
scandals:

> The past two years have certainly been prolific of the most serious
> and saddening mercantile crimes. Men of the highest standing, of
> seemingly stainless character, have been found to have been for
> years in the practice of the most systematic and heartless fraud. We
> have had religious embezzlers, philanthropic connivers at forgery,
> felons of taste, education, and public spirit. . . . (16 February 1857,
> p. 6)

The *Economist*, too, deplored the "great commercial blots" of the day and stated that ". . . there have been brought to light, transactions . . . more unsound in character and more reckless and unscrupulous in practice than have been witnessed upon any former occasion" (2 January 1858, p. 1).

Other public voices were expressing alarm over the corruption which seemed to have engulfed the mercantile life of the nation. Throughout the fifties the respected editor of *The Banker's Magazine*, David Morier Evans, had been protesting in vain in the pages of his journal against the dubious financial morality of the day. In 1859, Evans finally published a complete account of the mercantile scandals his magazine had chronicled in the past decade. Entitled *Facts, Failures and Frauds: Revelations, Financial, Mercantile, Criminal*, it contained "a complete record of the astounding frauds and forgeries which have of late so frequently startled the commercial community from their propriety."[20] Evans emphatically deplored the "generally diffused rage for speculation" which he perceived as having produced "a bad moral atmosphere that has of late pervaded the whole of the commercial world."[21]

That Dickens was aware of the current scandals and the general indignation towards them is indisputable; for one thing it is well established that he was a faithful reader of *The Times*.[22] In *Little Dorrit*, easily "the most topical of Dickens' novels,"[23] it is hardly surprising that the latest financial scandals of the day should make their way into the pages of the novel quite apart from the creation of Merdle himself. One of the guests at Merdle's dinner party in Bk. I, ch. xxi, for example, is identified as "Brother Bellows who had been in the great Bank case," (p. 243) a reference either to Sadleir, or even more likely (as Sadleir's case had not yet been adjudicated when this chapter was composed) to the scandal of Strahan, Bates, and Sir John Dean Paul. A more striking allusion, however, lies in the description previously cited of the ominous shadow of crime and secrets hovering over the Clennam house. This passage was almost certainly composed between September and November of 1856.[24] The Royal British Bank was forced to close its doors early in September, and indignant articles featuring sordid revelations about the bank appeared in *The Times* almost daily throughout September. It seems quite likely, then, that the allusions to secret keys to records meant for only "a very few secret pockets and a very few secret breasts" refers clearly to the Royal British Bank, with its secret ledger for recording shady transactions. The entire passage, in fact, is clearly meant to evoke within the contemporary reader an indignant recollection of the many mercantile scandals of the fifties.

It has often been suggested that behind the pervasive metaphor of prison in *Little Dorrit* lies an uneasy consciousness of guilt; certainly the ominous description of the dark shadow over the Clennam home suggests a society haunted by universal economic guilt. London appears to be filled with dirty financial secrets, old monetary crimes which follow its inhabitants even to the grave. The corruption and scandals which glutted the columns of the newspapers in the fifties, the exposures of dishonest schemes, the revelations about secret ledgers with secret keys are seen here by Dickens as converging into a kind of oppressive shadow which darkens the city; all of London has become a "wilderness of secrets" banished by the weight of its guilt from the freer air of the country.

If Dickens was an avid reader of *The Times*, the editorial writers of that paper seem to have repaid the compliment by proving themselves fully aware of the current novel. Describing the rapacious behavior of the directors of the Royal British Bank, a *Times* editorial commented derisively, "Talk of public offices, the family of BARNACLES" (23 September 1856, p. 6). Although it would seem that Mr. Merdle would have provided the editors with a closer parallel to the case of the directors of the bank, the instinct of *The Times'* editors is essentially correct, in that the crimes of the Barnacles are similar in spirit to the crimes of Merdle. In this novel of interrelatedness, corruption has many forms: the same sordid motives that produce Merdle's frauds also operate in the Barnacles' grasping of office, in the machinations of Rigaud, in the greedy rent-squeezing of Casby, and in the economic marriages of Henry Gowan and Fanny Dorrit. Even Mrs. Clennam's crime when finally exposed, is part of this pattern of greed and deceit. In the interconnecting world of *Little Dorrit*, crimes of the heart are linked inseparably to economic crimes; those plagued with "secret breasts" are as guilt-ridden as those with "secret pockets" and all society has been contaminated by the dark shadow of mystery and crime.

In the metaphor of ecomonic corruption which underlies so much of the novel's imagery, downfall must inevitably result, as the real life scandals and exposures of the fifties had already proven. Like the many frauds and con men who had met exposure and ruin in contemporary scandals, Merdle is doomed to failure. His bankruptcy is a "thunderbolt" which appears to bring universal ruin in its wake; it is described in images of death, destruction, and apocalypse (Bk. II, ch. xxv and ccvi). Likewise, the sinister home of the Clennams is eventually rotted from within and collapses under the weight of the heavy shadow of guilty secrets it has harbored, amidst similarly apocalyptic images of storm and whirlwind (Bk. II ch. xxvi). The scandalous financial manipulations, deceits, and failures that had outraged the British public throughout the eighteen fifties had clearly provided Dickens with contemporary material to help dramatize his conviction that a guilt-ridden society must inevitably collapse under the weight of its own corruption.

NOTES

1. John Holloway, for example, says in his introduction to *Little Dorrit*, "Merdle's financial speculations reflect . . . the sensational case of John Sadleir." (Harmondsworth, England: Penguin, 1967), p. 17.

2. Whether in actual fact there was more commercial corruption in the late 1850s than in previous times is a complicated issue. Most standard economic histories hardly address the question of commercial dishonesty, but there seems to be some evidence that at least in the early years of corporate capitalism, the laws of limited liability led to a great deal of instability and corruption. R. A. Church speaks of the unsettling effects of joint-stock limited liability legislation of 1855–62 in *The Great Victorian Boom, 1850–73*, (London: Macmillan, 1971), p. 54. G. P. Pool and A. G. Pool discuss the "abuses which the *laissez-faire* spirit of the joint-stock acts almost invited" and attribute some of the corruption to the credulity of a general public of investors not yet prepared in the early years of corporate capitalism to read and comprehend prospectuses, balance sheets, and the financial press. (*A Hundred Years of Economic Development in Great Britain*, [London: Gerald Duckworth, 1940], pp. 134-135.) What is essential for the purposes of this study, however, is not to establish the exact extent of corruption in the 1850s, but to note the amount of publicity and public discussion accorded to prominent examples of such corruption. S. G. Checkland has noted in *The Rise of Industrial Society in England, 1815–1885* that joint-stock capitalism had by the eighties produced "a frightening array of scandals upon which journalists learned to play." (New York: St. Martin's Press, 1964), p. 210. W. W. Rostow notes that most periods of financial instability were followed by national "soul-searching" and cites as example a long article run in the *Economist* (1868, pp. 1-3) after the panic of 1866, entitled "Alleged Degeneration of England in Commercial Morality" (*British Economy of the Nineteenth Century* [Oxford: Clarendon Press, 1948; rpt. 1966], p. 172.) There is certainly evidence that the financial scandals of the mid-nineteenth century were accorded an enormous amount of publicity, and were the subject of editorial concern in such publications as *The Times*, the *Economist*, *Blackwood's*, *Punch* and Dickens' own *Household Words*, and that many Victorian leaders in the late 1850s were voicing grave doubts about the commercial morality of the times.

3. Charles Dickens, *Little Dorrit* (1857; rpt. Oxford: Clarendon Press, 1979, ed. Harvey Peter Sucksmith, The Clarendon Dickens), Bk. II, ch. x, pp. 525-526. Further references will appear in the text.
4. Preface, p. lix.
5. David Morier Evans, *Facts, Failures and Frauds: Revelations, Financial, Mercantile, and Criminal* (London: Groombridge and Sons, 1859), pp. 226-267.
6. See, for example, Grahame and Angela Smith, "Dickens As a Popular Artist, " *The Dickensian*, 67 (1971), 132.
7. Evans, pp. 6-73; Robert Lee Wolff, "The Way Things Were," *Harvard Magazine*, 77 (1975), 48; and "Mr. Hudson," *Fraser's Magazine*, 36 (August 1847), 215-222.
8. Evans, pp. 74-105.
9. Evans, pp. 106-153; and *The Times* (29 October 1855). p. 6.
10. Evans, pp. 154-225; and *The Times* (3 December 1855), p. 6.
11. Evans, pp. 268-390; and *The Times* (18 September 1856), p. 8, (23 September 1856), p. 6, (24 September 1856), p. 6, and (8 October 1856), p. 6.
12. Evans, pp. 391-431.
13. Evans, pp. 432-483.
14. W. E. Aytoun, *Blackwood's Magazine*, 58 (1845), 453-466.
15. Monroe Engels, *The Maturity of Dickens* (Cambridge, Mass.: Harvard University Press, 1959), pp. 57-67.
16. Thomas Carlyle, "Hudson's Statue," 1850; rpt. *Works*, Centenary Edition (London: Chapman and Hall, 1898; rpt. New York: AMS Press, 1969), *Latter Day Pamphlets*, Vol. XX, pp. 255-256.
17. Tennyson, Alfred Lord. *The Poems of Tennyson*, ed. Christopher Ricks, Annotated English Poets (London: Longmans, 1969), Part I, I, vii, 1. 25 and ix, 1. 35, p. 1042.
18. *Ibid.*, Part I, I, viii, 1. 31, p. 1042.
19. See *Hansard's Parliamentary Debates*, 3rd series, Vol. 114 (1851) 842; Vol. 134 (1854) 752; and Vol. 139 (1855) 1378.
20. P. iv. Evans's work has been an invaluable source of information concerning the scandals of the eighteen fifties.
21. Evans, p. 3 and p. 5.
22. Harvey Peter Sucksmith, "Dickens Among The Pre-Raphaelites: Mr. Merdle and Holman Hunt's 'The Light of the World'" *The Dickensian*, 72 (1976), 160 and 163, n. 4.
23. Sucksmith, Intro. to *Little Dorrit*, Clarendon Edition, p. xv.
24. Sucksmith believes that the twelfth number was probably composed in September of 1856. (See "Dickens Among the Pre-Raphaelites," p. 159.) The passage in question occurs in the next number, number thirteen, for which Dickens was still correcting proofs on November 24. (See Sucksmith, Intro. to *Little Dorrit*, Clarendon Edition, p. xxxiv.)

Clio and Three Historical Novels

Dwight N. Lindley

To the Victorians, as to us, the past must have seemed like an unknown land, to be explored with the same zest as J. H. Speke, David
Livingstone, and other Victorians explored Africa. Then and now
the past has often been evoked through the historical novel,[1] that
odd hybrid which attempts to recreate the past so that we as readers
believe that having visited the past, we can begin to understand it.
And if we can understand the past, perhaps we can understand the
present which briefly surrounds us and then recedes into and
becomes the past.

The historical novels[2] I am going to treat are Dickens' *A Tale of
Two Cities*, George Eliot's *Romola*, and Thackeray's *The History of
Henry Esmond*—surely the most important triumvirate gatherable
from amongst the Victorian novelists. Concerning historical novels
I shall make a series of statements and then comment briefly on the
applicability of each statement to the three novels. (The statements
may sound a bit like *ex cathedra* pronouncements; they are intended as points of definition rather than as commandments to believe.)
Thereafter, I shall treat each novel separately and in somewhat
more detail, though scarcely doing more than outlining the
possibilities of the topic.

First, historical novels should include within them important
events, should even, if possible, focus on such events. Of the three
novels the one which focusses on important events the most obviously is *A Tale of Two Cities*. The fall of the Bastille, the hanging

of the minister Foulon, the Terror, all of which occurred within the cataclysmic French Revolution, are major foci of that novel. Of the other two novels, *Romola* has also an impressive historical focus—the events being those of Florentine history between the death of Lorenzo de 'Medici, on April 8, 1492, through the execution of Savonarola, May 23, 1498. *Henry Esmond* covers important events—the campaigns of the War of Spanish Succession—and hints at the conspiracies in favor of the Old Pretender. Its most important historical comment, however, does not focus on an event, but rather is a reflection of what Henry Esmond learns: that the Hanoverian succession assures England of stability and that the Stuart cause, however romantic, is utterly lost.

Second, in the words of Georg Lukács, historical novels should include "world-historical figures,"[3] or at least reasonable facsimiles thereof. Around these, the events from history cluster. Both *Henry Esmond* and *Romola* include such figures, if we are willing to assume the forceful, historical influence of John Churchill, Duke of Marlborough, in the first novel and that of Savonarola in the second. As for *A Tale of Two Cities*, the closest to such a figure is Monseigneur, who is described as "one of the great lords in power at Court." He is to be taken as a symbol for all such lords, who are the principal means of oppression in pre-revolutionary France.

Third, and the most controversial of all such distinguishing features, historical novels should concern themselves with the "recovered," not the "felt" past.[4] For illustration of this distinction, *Vanity Fair*[5] is a novel of the "felt" past, Thackeray recalling in one passage the echoing effects of its great event, the battle of Waterloo. I quote from the end of Volume I, Chapter XXXII, just after Jos Sedley flees Brussels, and Amelia is left with Mrs. O'Dowd. "The tale is in every Englishman's mouth; and you and I, who were children when the great battle was won and lost, are never tired of hearing and recounting the history of that famous action. Its remembrance rankles still in the bosoms of millions of the countrymen of those brave men who lost the day." Notice the sense of the past conveyed through the narrator to contemporary readers, both English and French. The past of *Vanity Fair* has not been recovered through reading documents, looking at paintings and sculpture, or studyng old buildings; it has been evoked from the common feelings of those who lived through the period of the battle, feelings that surrounded Thackeray once he, a boy of six, arrived in England on June 15,1817, the eve of the second anniversary of Waterloo. (During the voyage home from India a stop at St. Helena permitted him a glimpse of Napoleon. "George the Third," *The Four Georges*.) Unlike novels which are set in the past close enough to be felt, the historical novels present their authors with a harder task—that of recovering the past through doing research.

The past has been recovered, more or less successfully, by all three novelists. Of that, as can be seen in the discussions below, there can be no doubt. Not one of the novelists, however, conveys a "felt" past in the same ways the Thackeray conveys it in *Vanity Fair*, or, for that matter, Dickens in *David Copperfield*, or George Eliot in *Middlemarch*. The pasts of these novels their authors experienced and "felt" rather than researched and recovered.

In conveying the recovered past in *A Tale of Two Cities*, Dickens was fortunate in having Carlyle as his mentor. From him Dickens absorbed an attitude towards the past and knowledge of the French Revolution,[6] as Dickens so admiringly makes clear in his "Preface" to the novel. Dickens was also writing of events which had not yet retreated into the distant past. The symbolic ending of the Revolution can be dated as November 9–10, 1799, the days of the *coup d'état* as a result of which Napoleon Bonaparte became First Consul—sixty years before the publication of *A Tale of Two Cities*. The French Revolution kept rippling through Europe and the Americas for generations. Close upon that first rippling effect Dickens was writing.

Thackeray's novel is set in a period more remote, the title of the last chapter, "August 1, 1714," being the date of Queen Anne's death and simultaneously the end of Henry Esmond's involvement with the Stuart cause. Thackeray diminishes the relative remoteness in time by his use of family history; for memoirs, as indeed letters, appear to be more immediate than other kinds of writing. The past seems familiar, if not "felt."

For herself George Eliot set a monumentally difficult task of recovery. She was not writing of a past just gone or of a family history inextricably mixed up with a national history. Rather she was writing about a mystical, exotic figure, Savonarola, who was caught up in complex and mystifying social forces in a foreign country at a relatively remote period of time. To recover that past, she tried to devour the period—its events, its politics, its everyday life, and its settings, both through careful reading of contemporaneous documents in the original langauges and by visits to Florence. Surely this passion for accuracy—for recovery of a myriad of facts—was one of the causes for the agony she felt as she struggled to write the novel.[7] No wonder she often conveyed the impression that she was not so much a novelist but an historian like Causabon,[8] carrying a dimly shining torch into a labyrinth, particularly in sections of the novel when she is attempting to convey a sense of place through detail, as in the scenes describing Tito Melema's arrival in Florence (Book I, Chapters I-IV).

Let us now turn from the three major requirements for historical novels—important events, "world-historical figures," and recovered pasts—to a consideration of how each of these novels views the historical events with which it is concerned. And let us try to answer the question—how does the perspective established by the author lead the reader to an understanding of the history, and what does that particular kind of understanding mean?

Let me begin with *A Tale of Two Cities*[9]—that is, with the novel which among the three deals with the most impressive historical crisis, the French Revolution. The narrator has at least three discernible voices—the comic, the ironic-prophetic, and the sentimental-melodramatic. It seems a pity not to linger over the comic, but Jerry Cruncher's attempts to prevent his wife Aggerawayter from praying or Miss Pross's deadly struggle with Madame Defarge have only a very little to do with the perspective on history. The ironic-prophetic voice and its counter voice, the sentimental-melodramatic, are the means through which the narrator and therefore Dickens tell us what to think of history.

The novel's opening chapter, and in fact its famous opening paragraph, are somewhat puzzling. Here, in the ironic voice, are a few of the well-known words: "It was the best of times, it was the worst of times, it was the age of wisdom, it was the age of foolishness, it was the epoch of belief, it was the epoch of incredulity. . . ." The balancing of opposites continues throughout the chapter, and the balancing not only concerns time—that is, all times may be considered good or all times may be considered evil, according to one's perspective—but the balancing also concerns space—that is, the spaces of both England and of France. And the two countries and their two cities are in ironically stated trouble, about as much of the brief chapter being given over to England's trouble as to France's. And therein lies the puzzle. Despite the balancing of the trial of Darnay in London with his two later trials in Paris, the rush of the narrative shifts the focus to France and the Revolution and away from England and its inhumane criminal court system. The puzzle is furthered by a shift away from the notion that all times are about equally good and about equally bad to the much more frequently stated notion—the seeds of destruction were planted long ago in

France; those seeds are now being harvested. In the course of the novel the possibilities of England's destruction simply disappear.

Let me cite two passages as illustrating the ironic-prophetic voice speaking the lesson of the Revolution, the first being from the assault on the Bastille: "The sea of black and threatening waters, and of destructive upheaving of wave against wave, whose depths were yet unfathomed and whose forces were yet unknown. The remorseless sea of turbulently swaying shapes, voices of vengeance, and faces hardened in the furnaces of suffering until the touch of pity could make no mark on them" (Book the Second, Chapter 21). In this description of the gathering of the people from the suburb Saint Antoine is the prophetic voice; the promise of upheaval can be seen and heard in the metaphor of the destructive waters.

And now a second passage, this one from the beginning of the final chapter of the novel, which is set during the Terror.

> Along the Paris streets, the death-carts rumble, hollow and harsh. Six tumbrils carry the day's wine to La Guillotine. All the devouring and insatiate Monsters imagined since imagination could record itself, are fused in the one realisation, Guillotine. And yet there is not in France, with its rich variety of soil and climate, a blade, a leaf, a root, a sprig, a peppercorn, which will grow to maturity under conditions more certain than those that have produced this horror. Crush humanity out of shape once more, under similar hammers, and it will twist itself into the same tortured forms. Sow the same seed of rapacious licence and oppression over again, and it will surely yield the same fruit according to its kind.

This remarkable passage carries within it much of the impact of the novel. Notice how Dickens has changed the ordinary freight of the tumbril, a name for a farm cart, from wine to the "day's wine," the blood of those to be guillotined. And the ordinary produce of "the rich variety of soil and climate" becomes the "seed of rapacious licence" which will "yield the same fruit according to its kind." Natural growth unnaturally crushed has become the fruits of the Revolution, and these fruits have become bloody.

The chapter and the novel end with the melodramatic-sentimental voice, as Sydney Carton gives his life for his good mirror image, Charles Darnay. After mentioning the evil characters and oppressors in France who condemned Darnay to death, Carton has these words to say, "I see a beautiful city and a brilliant people rising from this abyss, and, in their struggles to be truly free, in their triumphs and defeats, through long long years to come, I see the evil

of this time and of the previous time of which this is the natural
birth, gradually making expiation for itself and wearing out." Carton's final words then shift to a coda designed to draw tears from an
iron monster, in which Dr. Manette, Lucie Manette, her child, and
her descendents can look forward to telling Carton's story of self-
sacrifice. And, so, in the final words of Carton, the novel draws to a
close in a vision of a bright and happy future, both for the Manettes
and all French and all English.

Three different attitudes, then, towards the Revolution appear in
A *Tale of Two Cities*. The one of objective balancing concerning the
evils of the two countries, as seen in the opening, gives away in the
narrative to the one of impending doom. This sense of doom, in
turn, gives way to that of the happy future, as delivered in
Carton's last words.

At first, one is tempted to say that the sense of impending doom
has simply been contradicted by the vision of the happy future—a
contradiction which is all the more appealing because it guarantees
a happy ending. I believe there is another, more plausible explanation.

In absorbing Carlyle, Dickens absorbed at second hand Carlyle's
philosophy of history. This was a strange, heady mix of Calvinism
and Romantic transcendentalism, and echoes of Fichte, Kant,
Novalis, and Goethe.[10] Within the blend was a very strong strain of
Saint-Simonism, composed of the doctrines of the French social
philosophers who flourished as sectarian theorists just after the
French Revolution. From the Saint-Simonian society Carlyle had
received a packet of pamphlets and periodicals which he
acknowledged in a letter of August 9, 1830[11] to Gustave d'Eichthal,
who made a proselytizing trip to England in January, 1832. For a
time Carlyle was much taken with the Saint-Simonian philosophy
of history, and his *French Revolution* reflects that influence,
wherein the Revolution is looked upon as a necessary critical period
which precedes an organic one, when, once again, all will be under
the dominant control of a "spiritual power." (Carlyle regularly used
the word "disorganic" as a substitute for the French "critique.")
And following the Saint-Simonians, the period of the French
Revolution was the quintessential critical period, which would
precede a new organic one, Carlyle's *French Revolution* ending
with the most useful of all myths of rebirth, that of the phoenix bird
symbolizing the birth of a new period.

The ending of A *Tale of Two Cities* is reflective both of a critical
period, in the passage on the tumbrils going to the guillotine, and of

the movement towards a new organic period, in Dickens' vision as uttered by Sidney Carton.

Though the ending of *The History of Henry Esmond*[12] is a happy one, it is not the happiness called forth by a grand, historical scheme; rather it is the happiness of a private person, who has a private perspective and speaks in a private voice—the very title being suggestive of the privateness of the history. (To be sure, within that voice one hears, now and then, the ironic tones of Thackeray as he comments on the actions and characters in front of Henry.) The private voice is introduced by a preface, entitled "The Esmonds of Virginia," as written by Henry's daughter. From the beginning, then, the perspective is that of a family history, designed to let Henry Esmond's grandchildren in America know where and how Grandfather grew up, lived, fought, and loved in faraway England and Europe during the latter part of the seventeenth and the early part of the eighteenth century.

Within the perspective established by the preface and by the private voice of the narrator, there are at least five distinct modes of perception.[13] These I shall list and then comment briefly on, principally to demonstrate how complicated a single point of view can be. Much of the time, all the way through the novel but sounding a bit odd when Esmond describes his boyhood, the memoirs sound like an old man taking an objective, third person view of his young self. The person perceived becomes the character Henry Esmond, a being that appears to be independent of the speaker. Fairly often, however, the voice shifts from the third person, rather distanced mode to the first person; the old man becomes young again, at least as young, that is, as the age he would be during the episode being described. These two modes of voice are the principal ones in the novel, and the shift from one to another is easily discernible in the shift of person. Less important are two other modes, one of which is simply a device for filling in details Henry Esmond needs to know. In this, one of the other characters tells him what has occurred in his absence. The fourth mode is that of Henry's daughter, who not only introduces the memoirs, but makes brief points about them through footnotes. These lend further authenticity to the notion that we are reading family history.

The fifth mode, the ironic commentary of Thackeray, uttering forth out of Henry Esmond's persona, is the one that gives the sharpest sense of what Thackeray believes history, not simply that of the family, to be. In the Foreword to Book I, an account of what history is, appears the following passage; it is a comment on Charles

II, before the Restoration, to whom the main branch of the Esmond family, of Castlewood, is loyal:

> What spectacle is more august than that of a great king in exile? Who is more worthy of a respect than a brave man in misfortune? Mr. Addison has painted such a figure in his noble piece of "Cato." But suppose fugitive Cato fuddling himself at a tavern with a wench on each knee, a dozen faithful and tipsy companions of defeat, and a landlord calling out for his bill; and the dignity of misfortune is straightway lost. The Historical Muse turns away shamefaced from the vulgar scene, and closes the door—on which the exile's unpaid drink is scored up—upon him and his pots and his pipes, and the tavern-chorus which he and his friends are singing.

The passage moves from the opening rhetorical questions about king and exile, through the neatly contemporaneous allusion to Addison's "Cato," to a vivid, realistic picture of the exiled king wenching and drinking. The Historical Muse—Clio, pictured by the ancients with laurel symbolizing poets and a scroll for writing down prophetic truths—cannot stand the "vulgar scene," a scene that Thackeray thought to be the truth about human nature, kingly or otherwise.

And speaking of the plundering, raping conduct of the victorious allied troops, during the campaign of 1704, Esmond, once again with Thackeray behind him, remarks: "Why does the stately Muse of History, that delights in describing the valor of heroes and the grandeur of conquest, leave out these scenes, so brutal, mean, and degrading, that yet form by far the greater part of the drama of war?" (Book II, Chapter IX) The Muse should not, and therefore we should not, forget how men really act; they are often "brutal," "mean," and "degrading."

A private history interspersed with such comments, ironically realistic, is not one which develops a long view of history. In fact, *Henry Esmond* tells us not so much that history marches; rather time passes, and events occur. Esmond discovers that he loves Rachel, not Beatrice; he keeps his friendship for Dick Steele, and he resents Addison's false rendering of war in "The Campaign." He meets Swift and finds him to be a pompous fool. He supports General John Webb in his feuding with Marlborough. In short, *The History of Henry Esmond* is a novel which gives Henry Esmond's history; that takes place amongst exciting events and notable people from the past. And insofar as the novel catches the atmosphere of those years, it is an historical novel, and insofar as it is a study of

Marlborough as seen by the Tories, it includes an influential historical figure. But the view taken of history is that it is a series of events which occur. The important change, even progress, in the novel is the change in Esmond, who makes a decision: after finding out that he loves Rachel, he decides that he and Rachel should go to Virginia, where the two live in idyllic bliss—a bliss disrupted, to be sure, in the next generation, but that is another story. The private history ends in happiness ever after; the public history becomes events in the past—events which are described as those which men and women, not particularly endowed with virtue, participate in.

If *A Tale of Two Cities* has the sharpest focus on history as a grand event and *Henry Esmond* the most consistent view of history as being largely a matter of a private life caught up in the great doings of the times, *Romola*[14] is the novel which presents the most complicated and sophisticated view of history.

Its sophistication, which I shall return to later, is marred by a major flaw. The perspective on time often shifts, sometimes because time itself shifts in peculiar ways, and sometimes because the narrative voice itself is uncertain.

Time is not always the present of the novel's action, nor even the pastness to that present; it is often a time in the future—occasionally a future close to the time of the novel, as in the allusion to Giovanni de'Medici's papacy (1513–1521), or to artistic masterpieces of the Italian Renaissance not yet created, but also in allusions contemporaneous with George Eliot's life, as in one to the Benthamite happiness principle, or in others such as to scholars whose works George Eliot consulted.

A shifting perspective on time reflects also one of the problems in the "Proem," the most thoroughly puzzling section of the novel. The voice in the "Proem,"[15] a term which evokes the beginnings of the epics from antiquity, is sometimes that of an omniscient narrator, but also often that of a character called variously "Shade" or "Spirit"—the first name suggestive of classical, the second of Christian origins. The character is symbolic of a well-to-do citizen of Florence of the late fifteenth century,

> inheriting its strange web of belief and unbelief; of Epicurean laxity and fetichistic dread; of pedantic impossible ethics uttered by rote, and crude passions acted out with childish impulsiveness; of inclination towards self-indulgent paganism, and inevitable subjection to that human conscience which, in the unrest of new growth, was filling the air with strange prophecies and presentiments.

The "Shade" makes several observations on the differences between the Florence of his day and the one of the nineteenth century
and muses upon these differences. The device permits George Eliot,
among other matters, to warn the reader that the spire of Sante
Croce has not yet been built and that not all seventy of the city's
towers still stand. And the narrator tells the "Shade" that much of
the politics talked on the nineteenth-century streets would be
incomprehensible. But the main point conveyed is that there are
more similarities than differences between nineteenth-century and
fifteenth-century Florence, in the "outlines" of the city, in the
mountains surrounding the city, in the valley of the Arno, in the
children and their "chants" in the churches, and in the "ebb and
flow in human hearts."

Without a belief in the ultimate unchangeability of human
hearts, a reader cannot read an historical novel, nor can a novelist
write one, but the belief is very nearly lost in the "Shade's" two personae and in the shifting perspectives it takes on time.

The truth is that George Eliot attempted too much in the
"Proem." It opens with a description of dawn as if written for an
epic, with a fanciness to the language which is unbecoming and un-
natural. There follows too much of everything—an evocation of Ec-
clesiastes, remarks on Florence which sound touristy, movements
back and forth in time, both through the narrator and the "Shade,"
comments on Florentine politics, and obscure hints at the fate of
Savonarola—all within a few pages.

Though the perspective on time is sometimes disturbing, perhaps
even confusing, the treatment of narrative so that historical events
come into sharp focus is very well handled indeed. All of the following important events in Florentine history receive a kind of magisterial treatment: the entry of Charles VIII of France into Florence,
the preaching of Savonarola against Pope Alexander VI and for the
moral and political reform of Florence, the Burning of the Vani-
ties—that puritanical attack upon the art, literature, and luxury of
Florence—the aborted Trial by Fire between the Dominicans and
the Franciscans, and the riots consequent upon that event, including the attack upon San Marco.

As these events appear, they are carefully intertwined with the
lives of the fictional characters so that the fiction appears to be part
of the history. (In *Henry Esmond*, the history appears to be part of
the fiction.) One scene, from the preaching of Savonarola, will serve
as an example. Listening to Savonarola preach is Baldassare, Tito
Melema's foster father, whom Tito first abandoned and then repu-

diated. In Chapter XXIV, "Inside the Duomo," Baldassarre, seeth-
ing with anger towards Tito, hears the historically accurate words
of Savonarola, as he alternately threatens and prophesies concerning the reform of Florence. Baldassarre catches the phrase, "Come,
O blessed promise," and repeats it, as he savors the prospect of
revenge against Tito. Just as Savonarola and the Florentines are immersed in their passion for their city, so is Baldassarre immersed in
his private passion. History and fiction fuse together.

As the narrative unfolds and reveals the important events, the
characters, both those who are entirely fictional and those imagined
from history, often take on symbolic overtones which suggest a
movement to history. Briefly, as examples, the fictional Bardo, living on an historical street named for his family, represents the artistic scholarly Renaissance, gone blind and sterile, simply fondling
the relics from the past. Bernardo del Nero, a character with a dual
purpose, serves both as a fictional godfather to Romola and as a
representative of the best in the Medicean oligarchy and the best in
the same humanism in which Bardo represents the worst.
Savonarola is the puritanical, prophesying voice of a reformed
Christianity, which appears to be moving towards democracy but
moves instead towards dictatorship.

In a summarizing passage on Savonarola, George Eliot, through
the voice of the all-knowing narrator, tells us what to think about
this man, who of all the characters in all three novels comes closest
to being a "world-historical figure." The comment comes just
before Savonarola's execution:

> For power rose against him not because of his sins, but because of his
> greatness—not because he sought to deceive the world but because
> he sought to make it noble. And through that greatness of his he en-
> dured a double agony: not only the reviling and the torture, and the
> death-throe, but the agony of sinking from the vision of glorious
> achievement into that deep shadow where he could only say, "I
> count as nothing: darkness encompasses me: yet the light I saw was
> the true light." (Chapter LXXI)

Hope frustrated in the character of Savonarola is the turning
back of the historical moment; an almost "world-historical figure"
has almost forced a part of the world to turn "a corner of time"[16]
and become renewed, if not precisely new.

George Eliot's perspective on history, then, is complicated and
sophisticated, the whole novel being informed by her sense of history, which had been nurtured by her extensive knowledge of

philosophies of history, particularly those of Comte and Saint-Simon. She had absorbed at the source what Dickens learned through Carlyle.

As the Victorians returned to the past with Dickens, Thackeray, and George Eliot, they discovered it in different ways and through different perspectives. As we return to the same past in these three novels, we should keep in mind that our own perspectives will differ because we are different people reading the books more than a century after their publication dates. And we have our own views of history—less certain ones, I think, and perhaps held less certainly.

NOTES

1. Discussions of historical novels tend to fall into three categories. First, historical novels are indeed in a genre different from all other genres, as in the discussion listed under Note 2. Second, even though historical novels differ from other novels because of the history in them, the history is not nearly as important as the artistic elements. Third, historical novels are discussed as novels; the history is more or less ignored. My discussion reverses the usual emphasis of category two.

2. For stimulating and helpful discussions of historical novels, see Georg Lukács, *The Historical Novel*, trans. Hannah and Stanley Mitchell (London: Merlin Press, 1962); Avrom Fleishman, *The English Historical Novel* (Baltimore: The Johns Hopkins University Press, 1971); Andrew Sanders, *The Victorian Historical Novel 1840–1880* (London: The Macmillan Press, Ltd., 1978). For briefer treatment, see John Maynard, "Broad Canvas, Narrow Perspective," in *The Worlds of Victorian Fiction*, ed. Jerome Buckley (Cambridge, Mass.: Harvard University Press, 1975), pp. 237-265.

3. Lukács, pp. 46, 103.

4. In making the distinction between the "felt" and "recovered" pasts, I have been aided by two studies which make no such distinction. In these George Eliot becomes the author who evokes in a magical way the past. See Thomas F. Deegan, "George Eliot's Novels of the Historical Imagination," *Clio*, 1 (1972), 21-33, and Thomas Pinney, "The Authority of the Past in George Eliot's Novels," *Nineteenth-Century Fiction*, 21 (1966–67), 131–147; rpt. in *George Eliot: A Collection of Critical Essays*, ed. George R. Creeger (Englewood Cliffs, N.J.: Prentice-Hall, 1970), pp. 37-54.

5. Since all the novels cited are in print, often in a number of editions, for quotations I give the chapter number and, if necessary, the book number. I omit page numbers.

6. According to J. A. Froude, "Dickens carried a copy of it [*The French Revolution*] wherever he went." *Froude's Life of Carlyle*, ed. John Clubbe [an abridgement of J. A. Froude, *Thomas Carlyle: A History*

of the First Forty Years of His Life, 1795–1835; A History of His Life in London, 1834–1881, 4 vols., London, 1882, 1884] (Columbus, Ohio: Ohio State University Press, 1979), p. 358. For a discussion of Carlyle's influence on Dickens, see David D. Marcus, "The Carlylean Vision of *A Tale of Two Cities," Studies in the Novel,* 7 (1976), 56-67.

7.   For George Eliot's use of detail through her study of Florentine art and architecture, and the results of that study, see Ann Ronald, "George Eliot's Florentine Museum," *Papers on Language and Literature,* 13 (1977), 260-269. See also George Eliot's own comments in *The George Eliot Letters,* ed. Gordon S. Haight, 9 vols. (New Haven: Yale University Press, 1954–55, 1978), particularly IV, 301, and elsewhere in that volume.

8.   For Causabon as "a historian who ignores the evidence of history," see Barbara Hardy, *"Middlemarch:* Public and Private Worlds," *English,* 25 (1976), 5-26.

9.   For pertinent studies of *A Tale of Two Cities,* see Sylvère Monod, *Dickens the Novelist* (Norman, Okla.: University of Oklahoma Press, 1968), pp. 452-469; Sylvère Monod, "Dickens's Attitudes in *A Tale of Two Cities,"* in *Dickens Centennial Essays,* eds. Ada Nisbet and Blake Nevius (Berkeley: University of California Press, 1971), pp. 166-183; Gordon Spence, "Dickens as a Historical Novelist," *Dickensian,* 72 (1976), 21-29; and the essays in *Twentieth Century Interpretations of A Tale of Two Cities,* ed. Charles E. Beckwith (Englewood Cliffs, N.J.: Prentice-Hall, 1972), particularly helpful being G. Robert Stange, "Dickens and the Fiery Past: *A Tale of Two Cities* Reconsidered," pp. 64-75.

10.   For a compact, provocative study of Carlyle's philosophy of history, see Hugh Trevor-Roper, "Thomas Carlyle's historical philosophy," *The Times Literary Supplement,* 26 June 1981, 731-734.

11.   For the letter and a helpful note on Saint-Simonism, see *The Collected Letters of Thomas and Jane Welsh Carlyle,* eds. Charles Richard Sanders and Kenneth J. Fielding, 7 vols. (Durham: Duke University Press, 1970, 1977, 1980), V, 134-138.

12.   For perceptive studies of *Henry Esmond,* see chapters VI, VII, VIII, and IX of John Loofbourow, *Thackeray and the Form of Fiction* (New York: Gordian Press, 1976). Andrew Sanders, "Clio's Heroes and Thackeray's Heroes: *Henry Esmond* and *The Virginians," English,* 26 (1977), 189-211. The section on *Henry Esmond* in Lukács is reprinted as "*Henry Esmond* as an Historical Novel," in *Thackeray: A Collection of Critical Essays,* ed. Alexander Welch (Englewood Cliffs, N.J.: Prentice-Hall, 1968), pp. 121-146. For Thackeray as an historian, see Jane Millgate, "History *versus* Fiction: Thackeray's Response to Macaulay," *Costerus,* 2 (new series, 1974), 43-81.

13.   On modes of perception in *Henry Esmond,* see Mary Rosner, "Perspectives on *Henry Esmond," The Victorian Newsletter,* No. 56 (Fall 1979), 26-31. My colleague, John H. O'Neill, shared with me his unpublished essay on the same topic.

14.   The indispensable study of *Romola* is Felicia Bonaparte, *The Trip-*
tych and the Cross: The Central Myths of George Eliot's Poetic Im-
agination (New York: New York University Press, 1979). For stimulating discussions, see George Levine, "'Romola' as Fable," *Critical*
Essays on George Eliot, ed. Barbara Hardy (London: Routledge &
Kegan Paul, 1970), pp. 78-98; and Carole Robinson, "Romola: A
Reading of the Novel," *Victorian Studies*, 6 (1962), 29-42.

15.   On the "Proem," see Bonaparte, pp. 12-13.

16.   For the suggestive phrase, see Edgar Johnson, who adopts it from C.
S. Lewis's *Perelandra*, "Scott and the Corners of Time," in *Scott*
Bicentenary Essays, ed. Alan Bell (New York: Harper and Row,
1973), pp. 34-37.

Wilkie Collins's Cinderella: The History of Psychology and *The Woman in White*

Barbara Fass Leavy

The 1939 publication of Clyde K. Hyder's study of *The Woman in White* helped to illuminate the unconventional life of Wilkie Collins as well as to reveal an important source for his ingeniously plotted novel. The written account of a French case in which one Mme. de Douhault is incarcerated under a false name in the Salpetrière so that her brother might gain control of her inheritance so closely parallels the plot against Laura Fairlie in Collins's book as to leave no doubt about where Collins's idea originated. But Hyder's legacy to Collins criticism has not been a totally happy one. First, his claim that when "all is said, it is as a story that *The Woman in White* has most interest," since "Collins himself belongs among the great story-tellers rather than among the great novelists," seems to have blazed the trail followed by virtually all subsequent critics, who focus almost exclusively on the plot.[1] Second, the parallels between the plight of Mme. de Douhault and that of Laura Fairlie have turned interest away from the character who, after all, gave the novel its name. Even U. C. Knoepflmacher's brilliant study of the book reads as if there are only two heroines in it, Laura Fairlie and Marian Halcombe. Anne Catherick is virtually dismissed as a "deranged outcast,"[2] whose chief importance, apparently, is as a foil for her half-sister Laura. Knoepflmacher argues for the existence of a counterworld of Victorian fiction of which Collins was a member. Analyzing the contrast between Laura and Marian as parallel to that between Scott's Rowena and Rebecca, or

91

Thackeray's Amelia and Becky, Knoepflmacher has revealed about Collins what Philip Rahv revealed years ago about Hawthorne: the novelists never allowed themselves to validate those impulses or attitudes invested in their dark ladies, with the result that it is their relatively insipid blond heroines who win the day. In such an analysis *The Woman in White's* thematic importance is dependent upon this rich and allusive tradition, and the woman in white herself, Anne Catherick, is relegated to virtual insignificance.[3]

Third, Hyder's legacy has the unfortunate effect of deflecting attention away from British social history to France.[4] But, in fact, the serialization of *The Woman in White* in Dickens' *All the Year Round* from November 1859 to August 1860 coincided with the meetings of a special Parliamentary Select Committee "appointed to inquire into the Operations of the Acts of Parliament, and Regulations for the Care and Treatment of Lunatics and their Property."[5] The Committee began hearings in March 1859 and issued its final report in July 1860, just a month before the three-volume edition of *The Woman in White* appeared. It had been convened to investigate the adequacy of existing laws for the protection of both real and alleged lunatics, and many of the issues covered by testimony before it became significant elements in Collins's novel, which was appearing simultaneously. Close ties existed between members of the Select Committee and the professionals who testified before it, on the one side, and the literary world of England on the other. The connections between Collins and these doctors and legislators—both direct and via Dickens—explain why one of the major impediments to solving the legal and social problems concerning lunatics became an important thematic strain in *The Woman in White*. Collins was interested in the medical and legal problems of insanity; and his novel reveals a concerted attempt to create a psychological case history which goes far beyond the requirements of his narrative. In an effort to explain his own "lunatic," Anne Catherick, Wilkie Collins anticipated some of the major psychiatric theories prevalent today by embodying his insights in a mythical approach to one of Victorian England's favorite fairy tales, *Cinderella*.

I

The years 1845–1860 are particularly significant in the history of the British mental health movement. A century of agitation for reform had resulted in The Lunatics Act of 1845, which, according to the historian of the movement, "ended the first stage of reform"[6] of lunatic asylums which more closely resembled torture chambers than they did places to cure or help the mentally ill. Accounts of cures lead one to believe that released patients must have invoked every bit of sanity they possessed to escape conditions far worse than those which had led to their breakdowns in the first place. The evolving changes and heightened awareness which led to the 1845 Act mark "the culmination of a slow process of social revolution which transformed the 'Lunatick or mad Person' of 1744 into the 'person of unsound mind' of 1845."[7]

From the time that the Act was presented, however, there was agitation from parties who believed its provisions did not go far enough. And in 1853 some uncontroversial amendments further improved the methods according to which the ill were confined and the controls on many of the places into which they were committed. The old horrors associated with asylums, however, clung to the public imagination, and, as Collins ironically reveals in *Armadale* (1866), the modern and supposedly enlightened treatment of patients could be more insidious than the older, blatant abuses. In this novel, published six years after *The Woman in White* and after much of the public furor had died down, Collins suggests the persistent terror felt in thinking about lunatic asylums not so much in his description of an institution as in his description of the office of the doctor who ran and owned it:

> The doctor's private snuggery was at the back of the house, looking out on fields and trees, doomed but not yet destroyed by the builder. Horrible objects in brass and leather and glass, twisted and turned as if they were sentient things writhing in agonies of pain, filled up one end of the room. A great book-case with glass doors extended over the whole of the opposite wall, and exhibited on its shelves long rows of glass jars, in which shapeless dead creatures of a dull white color floated in yellow liquid. Above the fireplace hung a collection of photographic portraits of men and women, inclosed in two large frames hanging side by side with a space between them. The left-hand frame illustrated the effects of nervous suffering as seen in the face; the right-hand frame exhibited the ravages of insanity from the same point of view, while the space between was occupied by an elegantly illuminated scroll, bearing inscribed on it the time-honored motto, "Prevention is better than Cure."[8]

In 1858 the strength of the public outcry resulted in the appointment of the special Select Committee, which would deliberate for more than a year and hear testimony adding up to some 800 pages of transcription and summary. Some of the matters covered by the

1845 Act as well as some of what remained unresolved even after the Select Committee bear on much of the content of *The Woman in White*, written while the Committee was in the process of meeting and published in book form just one month after it issued its final report.

The 1845 Act appointed a new group of Lunacy Commissioners whose main powers lay in their responsibility to inspect both state hospitals and what were called "licensed houses," that is, private asylums of the kind to which Anne Catherick and later Laura Fairlie are confined. Those who soberly examined the situation concluded that some state institutions were making advances in improving the condition of patients through non-restraint (eliminating the use of mechanisms such as chains, or clothing such as straight-jackets) and through the establishment of conditions to match the prevailing theory that mental illness, like physical maladies, responded to good diet, fresh air, and exercise. The so-called private asylums, however, remained objects of suspicion: despite the new powers of the Lunacy Commissioners concerning the licensing of such houses, the profit motive behind such free enterprises made it difficult for public and political figures alike to shake the suspicion that proprietors of private asylums were liable to corruption. In 1858 the London *Times* articulated a position that was shared by the philanthropic Lord Shaftesbury, a prime mover in the 1845 Act: "It is not good to keep a man's interest and duty in perpetual antagonism . . . it never can come to good to place beings so helpless as lunatics under the care of persons whose interest lies rather in the continuance than in the relief of their disorder."[9] While Shaftesbury's testimony before the Select Committee in 1859 indicates that he did not think that people were being unjustifiably confined to asylums, he did worry about their being kept there unnecessarily and therefore thought that all asylums should be taken out of the hands of private owners and run by the government.

That the blatant physical abuse of patients was less an issue than their legal protection in the period from 1858–1860 is reflected in *The Woman in White* by the fact that it is the question of legal confinement that occupies Collins. In addition, that Hartright has no reason to suspect Anne of being an escaped lunatic suggests that she has not been mistreated in the asylum: she presents a clean, neat, and healthy appearance, however strange her behavior. Again, the Lunacy Commissioners were charged with the responsibility of inspecting all municipal asylums (those in the suburbs were inspected by local Magistrates), and their reports affected the issuance and renewal of licenses to private establishments. Also, it was the duty of the Lunacy Commission to inspect the legal procedures according to which a patient was confined to an asylum; part of the 1845 Act involved a revision of the kinds of petitions and medical certificates required before a private patient could be committed and detained. But the legal safeguards that were being devised—adequate or not—led to three perplexing medical problems, at least two of which, and perhaps all three, make themselves felt in *The Woman in White*. The first two concerned the difficulty in recognizing insanity when one was confronted by it.

The ability to diagnose insanity was related to the concern of the Select Committee about whether asylum proprietors were given notice before the Lunacy Commissioners arrived to inspect their premises. The obvious fear was that the owner would have a chance to clean up his establishment, and that he could devise some means to prevent the close questioning of a patient whose complaints might cause him some trouble or whose clarity of mind would arouse the suspicion that the proprietor was out of self-interest detaining someone whose release would reduce his income. Both the threat of illegal commitment and unjustifiable detainment were matters that plagued the public; again, it was the London *Times* that in 1858 voiced this general fear:

> The position of a lunatic appears to be one of the most terrible in which a human being can be placed. There is, however, a still worse condition, which is that of a person of sane mind who is treated by his fellow-creatures as though he were mad—of one who, being himself of sane mind, is incarcerated in an asylum, intended only for the insane,—who is, therefore, subjected to bodily restraint, and, still worse, to the moral and intellectual indignities consequent upon a supposed deprivation of reason. To be insane is bad enough—to be considered insane when a patient is not so in reality must, as far as present suffering is concerned, be incredibly worse.[10]

Public protest emphasized the assumption that the line between the insane and the allegedly insane was easy to draw.

John Thomas Perceval, the son of an assassinated former Prime Minister, whom Collins may have used as the basis for Percival in *The Woman in White*, is of special interest for his account in July 1859 to the Select Committee of his own confinement in an asylum. It is as a self-proclaimed champion of the mad and the allegedly mad that he sees himself:

I have said that I consider myself the attorney-general of all Her Majesty's madmen. I believe I am the only person, and, as far as I can see, my pamphlet is the only work that is published on the subject of maintaining the rights of lunatics. I consider that society or the Legislature, who shut up patients not only for their own benefit, which is generally looked upon to be the case, but for the benefit of society as well, in a very great measure—in a manner are compelled, in doing so, to violate the liberty of the subject, and to deprive him of the power of seeing his friends, and I think that they should most jealously respect all his other rights; he ought to enjoy them, and they ought not to interfere with them.[11]

In November of the same year, Wilkie Collins would begin serialization of a novel in which his own character, Percival, would represent the very dangers John Thomas Perceval was fighting. He would violate the liberty of, first, Anne Catherick, and then his own wife, Laura, committing each to a private lunatic asylum, not for either their own or the public good, but for his own. That Collins reversed the role of the real Perceval in portraying his own Percival is consistent with many similar, demonstrable reversals in his fiction in general and *The Woman in White* in particular.

Though public statements often inferred that the distinction between the insane and the allegedly insane was readily apparent, it was recognized at the time that insanity could present itself convincingly under the guise of sanity, and that it was not always possible to discern mental illness when it did exist. When asked by the Select Committee about whether it is "not the fact that, in lunatic patients, the symptoms of malady do not make themselves apparent, as they do in people in a sound state of mind," Shaftesbury provided a guarded response that reveals the scrupulosity with which he attempted to cooperate with the inquiry at hand, although it was the effectiveness of his Commissioners that was in part being called into question:

I do not know whether that is so. That is a mixed question, and I might have a private opinion upon it; but I may state that in respect to the testimony given by lunatics this is to be observed, and I think my colleagues will say the same, that the testimony of a lunatic, in respect of himself, is to be received with many grains of allowance; but the testimony of a lunatic, in respect of others, is oftentimes of the most trustworthy character.[12]

Perceval and Shaftesbury have been depicted as polite adversaries during the proceedings of the Select Committee; Perceval's main quarrel with Shaftesbury and the other Lunacy Commissioners was only that their safeguards both in terms of law and actual practice did not go far enough in guarding the rights of supposed lunatics.[13] On one point, however, they were in agreement: there would be no point in adding more physicians to the number of those who had to certify a patient in order to confine him. Shaftesbury and Perceval shared the prevalent belief of their time that the average intelligent person was as competent as any doctor (with the exception Shaftesbury made for experts such as John Conolly) in detecting mental illness. "The truth is," writes Perceval in the pamphlet written to expose the inadequacies of the 1845 Act, "that any person of sound common sense is in ordinary cases as good a judge of the sanity of a person of the same rank of life as any medical man whatsoever, and the friends and relations of a person of unsound mind are usually the best judges as to his insanity rendering him unfit to manage his property or to be at large." The qualification that Perceval adds to his claim is central to the plot of *The Woman in White*. For he continues that such relatives "are not blindly to be depended upon, because they may be influenced by corrupt motives, such as the desire to possess themselves of a ward's or kinsman's estate, or to get a person out of the way who interferes with their selfish gratifications."[14] It is clear that, once again, John Thomas Perceval is describing the two situations that Collins's Percival would set in motion: getting Anne Catherick out of the way in a private asylum because she "interferes with [his] selfish gratifications," and then doing the same with Laura Fairlie, out of "the desire to possess [himself] of a ward's or kinsman's estate."

In the argument that the average citizen is as competent as a physician to discern insanity, one finds a curious medical dilemma. On the one hand, it is admitted tht insanity can parade under the guise of sanity; a patient's claims on his own behalf are not to be completely trusted (although an insane person might be very astute where it came to another). But rather than leading to the conclusion that great expertise was necessary for some sound judgment to be made, this common belief led to the opposite conclusion: all that was needed was good common sense, possessed as well by the average person as by any doctor, provided that person were possessed not only of intelligence but also of good will. Such an individual is indeed portrayed as the hero and chief narrator of *The Woman in White*; and in the context of the perplexing legal and medical dilemma Collins's age had not yet worked its way out of, the scene in which Walter Hartright first meets Anne Catherick

assumes a significance far beyond the novel's acclaimed melodrama. When Hartright, after he attempts to help Anne, learns that
she had escaped from an asylum, he is overcome by the same difficulty that pressed upon the conscience of Collins's age:

> "She has escaped from my Asylum."
>
> I cannot say with truth that the terrible inference which those
> words suggested flashed upon me like a new revelation. Some of the
> strange questions put to me by the woman in white, after my ill-con-
> sidered promise to leave her free to act as she pleased, had suggested
> the conclusion, either that she was naturally flighty and unsettled, or
> that some recent shock of terror had disturbed the balance of her
> faculties. But the idea of absolute insanity which we all associate
> with the very name of an Asylum, had, I can honesty declare, never
> occurred to me, in connexion with her. I had seen nothing, in her
> language or her actions, to justify it at the time; and, even with the
> new light thrown on her by the words which the stranger had ad-
> dressed to the policeman, I could see nothing to justify it now.
>
> What had I done? Assisted the victim of the most horrible of all
> false imprisonments to escape; or cast loose on the wide world of
> London an unfortunate creature whose actions it was my duty, and
> every man's duty, mercifully to control? I turned sick at heart when
> the question occurred to me, and when I felt self-reproachfully that
> it was asked too late. (22)

Walter Hartright's bewilderment reflects the double dilemma
Victorian England faced with regard to its lunatics. On the one
hand, that Hartright could find no overt signs of lunacy in Anne is
not conclusive, since it was believed that the insane could feign
sanity or possess lucid intervals that did not cancel out the reality of
the disease. On the other side, Hartright's feeling that there was no
reason for the frightened young woman to be confined would carry
much weight at a time when it was also believed that such general
impressions were as valid as medical diagnoses, since there existed
no specific medical expertise to deal with what was nevertheless a
medical problem. Collins was able to use the conceptions of his
time, with their peculiarly conflicting logic, to advantage, heightening the mystery surrounding his woman in white by arousing genuine doubt about her madness. At the same time, he had emphasized the social theme of his novel, for his plot does not merely in-
volve the substitution of a sane woman for a deranged one in a lunatic asylum, but rather the substitution of an obviously unjustifiably
confined woman for another whose commitment is also questionable.

For Collins to be able in this fashion to employ the ideas of his time to heighten the ambiguity and hence the suspense of his story suggests a peculiarly sharp awareness of not only the legal but related medical issues surrounding insanity. To sustain his complex approach to his subject, he would have to construct for his own satisfaction at least a medical case history that might render Anne possibly mad but not necessarily so. Thus there may be more to his description of how he wrote *The Woman in White* than critics who invoke his account are aware of.[15] He tells how he first conceived of his "male devil," Count Fosco, but "let him wait, and [began] to think about the two women." He goes on:

> They must be both innocent and both interesting. Lady Glyde dawns on me as one of the innocent victims. I try to discover the other—and fail. I try what a walk will do for me—and fail. I devote the evening to a new effort—and fail. Experience now tells me to take no more trouble about it, and leave that other woman to come of her own accord. The next morning, before I have been awake in my bed for more than ten minutes, my perverse brains set to work without consulting me. Poor Anne Catherick comes into the room and says, "Try me." (596)

Although Collins clearly intended both his women to be interesting, modern readers find Laura not to their taste and poor Anne of little consequence. However, in the latter instance, her connection to what was happening in England concurrent with the writing and publishing of *The Woman in White* makes her a compellingly important figure.

II

In his study of private madhouses in England during the eighteenth and nineteenth centuries, *The Trade in Lunacy*, William H. Parry-Jones refers to the fears that "flared up, at intervals, throughout the nineteenth century" that for corrupt motives sane persons might be improperly confined to lunatic asylums.[16] It is his conclusion that "there is little well-documented evidence" of the practices attributed to private asylums and that much "of the hue and cry stemmed from the published recollections and accounts of alleged lunatics and ex-inmates of private madhouses."[17] Collins, of course, claimed that part of his conception for *The Woman in White* came from a letter he had received asking for his help in securing the release of an inmate from an asylum. Why Collins should have received such a plea is unclear, though it suggests that he was known to be interested in the problem.[18] An individual seeking such help would have done well to go to the Alleged Lunatics Friends Society. In fact, Perceval's intervention had secured the release from an asylum of one Charles Verity whose pamphlet, "A Voice From a Madhouse: By One Who Was Lately An Inmate of the Northampton Lunatic Asylum" was part of the public uproar in 1858.[19] Verity was, he claimed, first unjustifiably imprisoned for possession of stolen goods he had not known were stolen, and then, as a natural result of the stress caused by his unwarranted fate, he had exhibited symptoms that led to his confinement in a lunatic asylum.

Verity's pamphlet was but one of many appearing in 1858 when "one of those waves of suspicion and excitement which occasionally pass over the public mind in regard to the custody of the insane occurred. . . ."[20] It is with obvious satisfaction that the 1858 report of the Alleged Lunatics Friends Society is able to declare that

> there appears to be a growing opinion amongst society, that the system of confining persons in private asylums is wrong in principle and dangerous in practice, from the temptations which it affords to persons to make an unjust profit from the improper confinement of their fellow subjects, whilst they are unable also to afford such patients that proper care, attention, and medical and moral treatment which is requisite for their well-being and cure.[21]

At the same time the *Journal of Psychological Medicine and Mental Pathology* noted the number of insanity cases that were being heard by juries.[22] It was probably the notoriety created by these instances of alleged lunacy that did more than anything else, including the resultant Parliamentary Select Committee, to create the atmosphere in which *The Woman in White* appeared.

Most of the cases reported in the press involved persons whose ability to administer sizable estates was at issue. One of these jury trials, which occupied the attentions of the London *Times* for many days, is particularly noteworthy because of the arresting parallels between it and the dramatic beginning of Collins's novel, *Armadale*. The case invovled one Henry Meux, who, having married a much younger woman after a dissolute past, fathered an infant son before sinking into the last stages of a degenerative mental illness and general paralysis. Previously, he had changed his will; the wife who would earlier have received a generous bequest was now his sole beneficiary if no children survived. His family sued to prove that he was not of sound mind at the time of the new will. What was at issue was not whether Henry Meux was insane, but *when* he had become so and thus unable to make sound judgments about his estate. Despite days of testimony from those who knew him, and despite testimony from famous doctors appearing for both sides, the jury could not reach a verdict. This failure once again illuminated the problems attendant upon the diagnosis of mental illness at a time when England was suffering from the lack of sufficient theories to account for insanity. Nevertheless, the outlines of the case obviously impressed themselves on Collins; for it is unlikely to be a coincidence that in *Armadale* one finds a similar trio: the dissolute and now paralytic dying husband; the young wife; and her infant son, one of the book's two Alan Armadales. It is the document, a letter, if not a will, written by the dying man that sets in motion what is to follow in the novel.

But perhaps the most notorious case of the time, and the one that may have triggered the public agitation of 1858, involed one Mrs. Turner, whom a jury of her peers adjudged to be sane even though a reading of even the *Times* account makes one wonder what such a conclusion was based on. Apparently Mrs. Turner, when not married or cohabiting with her husband, was able to function well enough to handle her own affairs. But, again apparently, the pressures of wedded life were such that she exhibited symptoms of excessive jealousy and paranoia, leading her reluctant husband first to seek a separation, and then, because of her conviction that he was trying to poison her, to have her committed to an asylum. What made this case notorious was that Mrs. Turner seems to have fallen into the hands of one of those genuinely incompetent and cruel asylum owners, a Mr. Metcalfe, who ran an establishment called Acomb House. His mistreatment of her both in his asylum and after her escape from it were set out in detail for the public's use in confirming the suspicion of asylums it had been nurturing all along.[23]

It may have been the Turner case that caused an abrupt change in the attitude of the *Times*. In June 1858 it had reported favorably on private asylums when it noted that "most of these metropolitan asylums are agreeably situated in the suburbs, and have spacious gardens, lawns, and pleasure-grounds for the use of the patients."[24] But a month later, when reporting on the Turner case, it stated that "We cannot but entertain a fearful suspicion that the administration of Private Lunatic Asylums is carelessly conducted and that a sad tragedy which is never spoken of in the outer world occurs in these dismal abodes."[25] By August 1858 the *Times* concluded:

The fact would appear to be that under existing arrangements any
English man or woman may without much difficulty be incarcerated in a Private Lunatic Asylum when not deprived of reason.[26]

Walter Hartright's reference to the "most horrible of all false
imprisonments" echoes the newspaper's contention that the "position of a lunatic appears to be one of the most terrible in which a
human being can be placed," but that while to "be insane is bad
enough—to be considered insane when a patient is not so in reality
must, as far as present suffering is concerned, be incredibly
worse."[27]

Perhaps Collins's most lurid depiction of false commitment came
more than a decade after the composition of *The Woman in White*
with his publication of *The New Magdalen* (1873). It is a novel
whose initial interest proves greater than its final execution, a powerful beginning succeeded by a tedious and sentimentalized middle
and ending. Written when Collins's power as a novelist seems on
the wane, the book hearkens back to earlier plots and themes. Like
The Woman in White, *The New Magdalen* also deals with two
women whose identities are confused, although in a typical Collins
reversal, the self-made imposter proves the heroine, while the
woman she is falsely pretending to be is a kind of female villain.
When Mercy Merrick, a Victorian "fallen" woman, meets Grace
Roseberry, she has no thought of passing herself off as Grace to the
latter's relatives, who had in fact never met Grace. But the setting is
wartime, and when Grace appears to be killed by enemy fire, the
temptation to assume her identity and begin again proves irresisti-
ble to Mercy. She does not know that Grace was only wounded and
will later arrive at her relative's house to claim her rightful place in
the houshold which has come to love the imposter. Since the real
Grace lacks the papers to prove who she is, she finds protestations
of her identity futile. In turn, the family concludes she is not only a
nuisance but mad. Committing her to a lunatic asylum will rid
them of the inconvenience caused by her persistence. What Collins
focuses on during this part of the novel is not only the pangs of conscience suffered by Mercy Merrick, but the ease with which she
alone can save Grace from the asylum or allow her to be placed
there: "The terrible altenative that was offered to her had showed itself at last, without reserve or disguise. Restore the identity you have
stolen, or shut her up in a madhouse—it rests with you to choose! In
that form the situation formed itself in her mind."[28] And in that
form Collins turns back to an earlier period to confirm the *Times'*

contention of 1858 that "under existing arrangements" a Mercy Merrick might indeed possess such power.

The horror of the threat to Grace had already been illustrated by Collins through his portrait of the person summoned to carry her away. In this character Collins embodied all the fears that had swept through the public mind and had reached a climactic pitch more than a decade before he wrote *The New Magdalen*:

> He was not a gentleman; he was not a workman; he was not a servant. He was vilely dressed, in glossy black broadcloth. His frock coat hung on him instead of fitting him. His trousers were a pair of shapeless black bags. His gloves were too large for him. His high-polished boots creaked detestably whenever he moved. He had odiously watchful eyes—eyes that looked skilled in peeping through keyholes. His large ears, set forward like the ears of a monkey, pleaded guilty to meanly listening behind other people's doors. His manner was quietly confidential, when he spoke; impenetrably self-possessed, when he was silent. A lurking air of secret-services enveloped the fellow, like an atmosphere of his own, from head to foot. He looked all round the magnificent room, without betraying either surprise or admiration. He closely investigated every person in it with one glance of his cunningly watchful eyes. Making his bow to Lady Janet, he silently showered on her, as his introduction, the card that had summoned him. And then he stood at ease, self-revealed in his own sinister identity—a police officer in plain clothes.[29]

Such a description of the person who would spirit off to a lunatic asylum someone who did not warrant incarceration would satisfy the public imagination. A century of slow reform plus the 1845 Act and its 1853 amendments had not erased the images of neglect and cruelty associated with the treatment of the insane. In comparison to *The New Magdalen*, *The Woman in White* is positively restrained, more in accord with the Parliamentary inquiries of 1858 and 1859, intended to respond to public hysteria rather than to inflame it.

Collins, however, also addressed himself to the growing awareness that it was not possible to formulate purely legal solutions to the problems of real and alleged insanity. There was indeed a disparity between the Select Committee's theoretical conclusions and the effects of its actual recommendations to tighten the legal procedures necessary for committing the patient.[30] In theory, the Committee responded to the problem that the legal safeguards intended to protect the rights of the insane might in fact impede a patient's receiving prompt medical attention. What psychological theory existed at the time made a close connection between physical and mental illness; if in the former instance, prompt detection and treatment were necessary to save the patient, so would this be the case where it came to insanity. Thus Walter Hartright's fear that he had endangered not only the public but Anne herself in aiding her escape reflects less the public hysteria with regard to the issues than what might be called the concerns of the opposing side.

In 1853 the "asylum doctors" responded to the public opprobrium surrounding them by forming an organized group whose views were expressed in the *Asylum Journal* (subsequently the *Journal of Mental Science*, now *The British Journal of Psychiatry*).[31] It was not the policy of the journal to deny that there were defects in the law, but it voiced resentment that in what it called "The Newspaper Attack on Private Lunatic Asylums," the fault of the system should be "most unjustly attributed as faults to those acting under it."[32] In addition, it called into question the assumption that laymen could make sound decisions in matters concerning lunacy. Pointing to the famous jury trials of 1858, it argued that even a casual perusal of the accounts in newspapers indicated that the facts presented mitigated against the jury's conclusion that the person in question (for example, Mrs. Turner) was sane. A perhaps milder and more conciliatory version of this position was voiced about the same time by the *Journal of Psychological Medicine* as it attempted to strike some balance between the legal and medical problems that, unless reconciled, would create insuperable conflicts:

> It is necessary that this very natural feeling of the public should be respected; and it would be well if the press, while advocating a stricter attention to the civil rights of the insane, would also give some little thought to their social rights. . . . The person who has manifested the earlier symptoms of a disordered mind is often altogether debarred from receiving proper medical attention, unless he be first certified to be and registered as a lunatic—as being, in short, that which the medical man is anxious to prevent him becoming![33]

On April 2, 1859, in Dickens' *Household Words*, soon to give way to *All the Year Round*—that is, just four months before the serialization of *The Woman in White* began—there appeared an article entitled "The Cure of Sick Minds." Not only did the article take up certain theoretical questions concerning the origin and course of mental illness, but also, in contrast to what was going on in the newspapers, it took the stance of the medical community that at least as dangerous to the patient as a violation of his civil rights was the danger that a patient would not get needed help in time.[34]

Household Words was not so much concerned with the impediments created by legal safeguards as with the generalized ignorance and superstition that prevented families from seeking aid. It described how

> A young woman, liable to returns of insanity, and living fourteen miles away, left her home at four-o'clock one wet morning, and taking the railway as her guide, hurried to the asylum; she passed through several tunnels on her road, and arrived wet and exhausted. She said, "she dreaded being ill at home, for they treated her badly when mad. She knew the asylum was her best place, and she came as fast as she could to get help in time; she did not let her friends know of her intention, for she had asked them to bring her, and they were unwilling to do so."[35]

It is the contrast to Collins's plot that is so striking here, for the anecdote in *Household Words* is almost a mirror image of the journey taken by Anne Catherick. In one case, a woman perhaps unjustifiably committed to any asylum, and certainly committed because she is troublesome to her family, escapes from the institution to thwart the plot against her and her half-sister. Both girls are victims of the inadequacies of the legal safeguards which should prevent such conspiracies, and both Anne and Laura reflect the public's fear of a potentially lethal combination of greedy relatives and corrupt asylum keepers acting on the worst conceivable motives. In striking comparison, *Household Words* presents an equally dramatic if condensed escape of a young woman, this time from her home *to* the asylum, because ignorance would prevent the needed treament available to her when she is ill. These mirror-image plots, so to speak, embody Victorian England's attempt to decide in 1860 whether its most pressing concerns with regard to the insane were legal or medical.

Clearly the appearance of *The Woman in White* coincided with a very crucial period in the British mental health movement. A year before Collins began writing his novel, public concern about the legal safeguards involving commitment to lunatic asylums had reached a fever pitch. Private pamphlets, the accounts of ex-patients, the sensationalism surrounding some cases that were reported in the newspapers, the continuing agitation from agencies such as the Alleged Lunatics Friends Society—all these led to the convening of a Parliamentary Select Committee whose hearings ran virtually parallel to the serialization of *The Woman in White*. The Committee and those who testified before it were obviously sincere in their efforts to deal with the reform of existing conditions where necessary, but they were hampered by some unresolved problems concerning the commitment of the insane. On the one hand, it was recognized that the insane could often feign sanity, hiding the reality of their illness. Piling up more and more legal safeguards, therefore, did not solve all the problems concerning rightful confinement and detention of patients. On the other side, the belief that persons possessed of common sense and good intentions were as able as almost any physician to diagnose a case requiring commitment did not eliminate the possibility that those asked to make a judgment would act from self-interest. And, finally, although the thrust of public concern from 1858–1860 was over the civil rights of patients, there was another voice to be heard. It came from physicians, asylum proprietors, and even from popular journals such as *Household Words*. Believing that mental illness, like physical illness, required prompt attention if the disease was to be arrested, many feared that general public ignorance and prejudice would prevent the treatment of those sorely in need of early help. What is also clear is that the discussion was severely hampered by a lack of the theoretical knowledge about the nature and causes of insanity that might resolve some of the existing dilemmas.

That Wilkie Collins was ironically aware of the paucity of theory available is reflected in *The Woman in White* in a passage that, as far as narrative itself is concerned, seems to have no special importance. When Hartright first arrives at the Fairlie home, he is met by Marian Halcombe, who apologizes for the failure of her uncle to greet the man he has hired to teach his niece how to draw. "Mr. Fairlie is too great an invalid to be a companion for anybody," explains Marian. "I don't know what is the matter with him, and the doctors don't know what is the matter with him and he doesn't know himself what is the matter with him. We all say it's on the nerves, and we none of us know what we mean when we say it"(28).

Collins, of course, was less interested in presenting theories than in dramatizing human problems. In *The Woman in White* he fictionalizes the subtle problems that Victorian England was grappling with in its attempts at reform. Naturally the plots against Anne and Laura typified the legal concerns of the time. A combination of a private asylum proprietor, whose self-interest would make it difficult for him to be disinterested even if he were well-intentioned, and a family plotting the elimination from its midst of a troublesome member, were sufficient to lock away an individual who was either sane or at least not clearly insane. It is, of course, noteworthy that Collins does *not* intensify the sensationalism of his book by portraying any asylum keeper such as the notorious Mr. Metcalfe of Acomb House. Neither Shaftesbury nor Perceval believed that this gentleman was typical of those who ran asylums. If he were, so the thrust of Perceval's testimony went, then the social ills of the time would be speedily cured as a result of the blatancy of the abuse. No, the danger was a more subtle therefore more insidious one: so long as asylums were in private hands, then it lay in the interests of proprietors to hold on to their fee-paying patients. Such proprietors, even if they did not actually cooperate in such plots as Sir Percival Glyde's and Count Fosco's, were vulnerable to their machinations.

Actually it is the more paradoxical medical problem that seems to have intrigued Collins, for it shows up in the ambiguity of his central, most dramatic scene: the meeting of Walter Hartright and Anne Catherick on the night she escapes from the asylum. Here Walter's inability to judge the reality of Anne's alleged insanity illustrates one of the most perplexing problems facing England's legislators. That she did not appear insane to Hartright is at one and the same time inconclusive and significant. This ambiguity suggests that Collins's story is not quite the obverse of the anecdote told some months earlier in *Household Words*, where the thrust of the article concerned the medical, not the legal, problem facing Victorians, who, if they tightened the safeguards involving commitment of the insane, might tragically deprive these poor persons of the prompt care they needed. On the surface, the contrast between Collins's plot, which involves a dramatic escape from an asylum, and the anecdote, which tells of a flight to an asylum, seems to bring the legal and medical issues face to face. Rather, Collins seems to have recognized that the legal and medical were ultimately inseparable. There would be little need for him to construct a case history for Laura Fairlie. Her commitment was clearly unjustifiable. Of much more complexity, and therefore of more interest, would be the case of Anne Catherick. It was she on whom Collins's inquiries into the nature and development of mental illness would focus.

III

To reconstruct the history of lunacy in England during the time that Collins was writing and publishing *The Woman in White* does not of and by itself demonstrate any particular contact between the author and the events of his time, or between Collins and the men associated with these events. As it happens, however, there were very close connections between the Victorian world of letters and that involved in the treatment of the insane. In some instances the connections to Collins are direct. But since, in others, the links exist mainly by way of a mutual link to Dickens, it may be appropriate to quote Richard Renton's qualification as he tried to describe the uneasy association between Collins and John Forster: "My friend whom I introduce to you, is by virtue of that introduction, your friend also, but not as I am your friend, or you mine."[36] Nevertheless, because Collins and Dickens were so close, especially during the period in which *The Woman in White* was written, it is reasonable to think that the combination of Collins's interest in lunacy, and what will be shown to be Dickens' friendship with people involved in both the Lunacy Commission and the Select Committee, would result in Collins's particular awareness of what was going on.

"As the dear and close friend of Dickens, Collins must, in the nature of things, and as from personal knowledge I know he did, have 'rubbed shoulders' with Forster in such fashion as to qualify him for the title and position of 'friend of the house.'"[37] That the relationship between the two was uneasy is familiar to all Dickens scholars, but it is in Nuel Davis's *Life of Wilkie Collins* that an important though speculative connection is made between Collins's fiction and Forster's place on the Lunacy Commission. Davis writes that "Forster, who held a dignified and profitable sinecure as Commissioner of Lunacy, probably was the unwilling source of some of Wilkie's ghastly asylum details in the latter part of *Armadale*."[38] It is interesting that no consideration is made of the possibility that Forster, to whom indeed *Armadale* was dedicated, might have influenced *The Woman in White* as well. Again one finds an instance where the earlier and better book is thought of so exclusively in terms of its story that it draws little inquiry about Collins's sources for his conception of madness and asylums. But, in fact, the post held by Forster at the time Collins wrote *The Woman in White* is as close to the central concern of that book as his later post would be to *Armadale*. Before he was Commissioner of Lunacy, one of whose duties would be to inspect asylums and interview patients, Forster had been Secretary to the Lunacy Commissioner. Renton notes that this office, taken on in 1855, was not arduous, but that it "absorbed much valuable time."[39] Among the hours Forster would have spent as Secretary would have been those in which he inspected the certificates, submitted to the Lunacy Commission, which testified to the need for a patient's commitment to an asylum. These certificates formed part of the due process that stood in the way illegal confinement; if they were not in order, it was the Secretary's obligation to set in motion the procedures that would secure the patient's release. From Forster—whether directly or through Dickens—Collins would have learned not only about asylum condition but about legal procedures involving the commitment of patients. In 1859–1860, when *The Woman in White* was written, Forster was still Secretary to the Lunacy Commission and had not yet become a Commissioner himself.

Collins had another source of information concerning the workings of the Commission and the administration of asylums. When Forster assumed the secretaryship in 1855, he was replacing Dickens' friend, Brian Procter, better known in Victorian letters as Barry Cornwall. Not only is Procter an instance of the crossover between the British world of literature and the realm involving lunatics and those entrusted to look after them, but it is to him that Collins dedicated the first edition of *The Woman in White*. In brief, both that novel and *Armadale*, fictional accounts of abuses associated with asylums, were dedicated to literary figures, friends of Dickens who also held the post of Secretary to the Lunacy Commission.

When Procter resigned his secretaryship, an appeal for the job on behalf of Forster was made to the Chairman of the Commission, the Earl of Shaftesbury, who was to be an important witness at the Select Committee hearings. Shaftesbury was, as well, an acquaintance of Dickens, and therefore, according to Renton, of Forster. Renton indulges himself in the fancy that it was no coincidence that "that which Dickens hoped for, and strove, by a terrible picture of the truth, to induce men to do, *Lord Shaftesbury did.*"[40] Renton thus speculates that Shaftesbury may have been inspired by Dickens' writing. It is no more fanciful to suspect that Collins may have been impressed by Shaftesbury's outspoken opposition to private lunatic asylums, as well as by his testimony to the Select Committee concerning difficulties in taking the word of a lunatic concerning his own condition, although his reports on another might often be uncannily accurate. Again, Collins's portrait of Anne Catherick is ambiguous on this point. Her clear-eyed view of Laura's plight is no sure sign of her own sanity. But her confinement in an asylum probably would not have occurred had the proprietor not been inclined to cooperate with her unfeeling mother and the scheme of Sir Percival Glyde. On both these points, Shaftesbury had addressed the Select Committee: on the dangers of the profit motive behind private asylums, and the difficulty of believing a patient concerning his own state of sanity. And given the Dickens-Shaftesbury-Forster connections, it is conceivable that Collins was familiar with Shaftesbury's views. The latter was the first witness before the Select Committee, and thus his testimony was given shortly before *The Woman in White* began appearing.

That Anne Catherick need not have been committed to an asylum, and that Collins had reason to portray her as as much a victim of wrong in this regard as Laura Fairlie Glyde was later to be, is a point whose demonstration also benefits from the friendship of Dickens for a witness before the Select Committee. It has only been in recent years that the close relationship between Dickens and one of the renowned psychiatrists (as he would now be called) of his age has come to light.[41] Dr. John Conolly was one of those physicians who was generally excepted from the claim that any intelligent layman could do as well as a physician in diagnosing insanity. Both his long-term experience with lunatics as director of the Hanwell Asylum and his writing on the subject of lunacy had established his expertise. Conolly's chief claim to fame in the history of British psychiatry, however, has to do with his advocacy of non-restraint in the treatment of the insane, a point which is not in fact significant for a consideration of *The Woman in White*. Anne's mistreatment in the asylum is not an issue except in terms of her being there at all. But Conolly's book, *An Inquiry into the Indications of Insanity*, a work familiar to Dickens, is quite explicit about the confinement of such patients as Anne. The *Inquiry* has as one of its purposes the urging that physicians be trained in asylums as they are in hospitals, so that they may acquire the same understanding of lunacy as they do of physical ailments. After learning to *diagnose* mental disturbances, from which Conolly excludes various forms of eccentric behavior, the physician would have to make a judgment about whether confinement to an asylum was either necessary or advisable. For Conolly by no means believed that a positive diagnosis was always to be followed by the commitment of the patient, and there were certain cases of mental disturbance for which he believed confinement was unwarranted.

It is noteworthy that Conolly did not testify on these important matters to the Select Committee, which drew mainly on his experience as a hospital adminstrator and was interested in such matters as staff-patient ratios. If Collins were familiar with his theoretical ideas, he would probably be so through Dickens or because Collins too had read *Indications of Insanity*. While it is not possible to demonstrate that he had done so—although it would be surprising if he had not, given his interest in the subject—there is one section of Conolly's book that touches on the plight of Anne Catherick who, had she been Conolly's patient, would not have been confined to an asylum even if he had confirmed the belief of Mrs. Fairlie and the doctor who examined Anne that she suffered from some form of intellectual impairment. For the man whom *Household Words* had called "the highest living authority" on the subject of insanity[42] was quite explicit in his belief that among those patients improperly put into asylums, not necessarily because of malice but because of ignorance on the part of his own profession, were what his age called "idiots"—people not so much insane as mentally retarded or in other ways defective. In his statements on this subject, Conolly may have provided Collins with another source for Anne and her plight:

> Another class of patients for whom a lunatic asylum is a most improper place, consists of those who, in various periods of life, become affected with various degrees of weakness of intellect. The portion of the nervous system, through which intellectual power is manifest, is liable, like those portions on the integrity of which other functions depend, to impairment, either to direct impairment, or to sympathetic injury, in consequence of the disordered state of other organs: the impairment may be temporary, or it may be permanent; and may be compared to a partial paralysis. In this state there is a general imbecility of mind, accompanied with the irritable feelings of hasty and fickle moment which belong to states of weakness; but there is a little or no extravagance of action, still less is there any thing in the condition of the patient which would make his liberty dangerous, or, if he were properly attended to and watched, even inconvenient to others or to himself. Nothing can be more lamentable than to observe the unconcern with which [such] individuals [are abandoned by their families].[43]

Conolly's description of a "general imbecility of mind" which, however, may be temporary, shows up in *The Woman in White* when Mrs. Fairlie writes to her husband about the little girl who has recently become her charge:

> I was left to discover (which I did on the first day when we tried her at lessons) that the poor little thing's intellect is not developed as it ought to be at her age. Seeing this, I had her up to the house the next

day, and privately arranged with the doctor to come and watch her and question her, and tell me what he thought. His opinion is that she will grow out of it. But he says her careful bringing-up at school is a matter of great importance just now, because her unusual slowness in acquiring ideas implies an unusual tenacity in keeping them, when they are once received into her her mind. Now, my love, you must not imagine, in your off-hand way, that I have been attaching myself to an idiot. (49-50)

That Mrs. Fairlie denies that Anne Catherick is an idiot may reflect the growing awareness that *Household Words* expressed in its second essay on the subject—"Idiots Again"—that its age had misconceived and hence mistreated that form of mental impairment.[44] Mrs. Fairlie's admonition that her husband must not jump to conclusions attributes to him the kind of prejudice that Conolly was attempting to deal with. The doctor's influence on Dickens is documented; that he also influenced Collins's perceptions is likely.

When Conolly described the lamentable condition that occurred when persons like Anne Catherick were sent to asylums because they were inconvenient to have around, he probably was not thinking about those situations that worried Perceval, where a family might be influenced by corrupt motives of the sort that form the plot of Collins's novel. The pathetic Anne Catherick emerges in *The Woman in White* as a victim not only of Sir Percival Glyde's and Count Fosco's machinations, but of the public and professional ignorance against which Conolly's *Inquiry in the Indications of Insanity* was directed, a general ignorance without which the villains' plots could not have been so effortlessly carried out. In Conolly's additional belief, as quoted by Dickens, that "every lunatic asylum should be the property of the state, and be controlled by public officers," and in his concern for the wrongful confinement of patients as the result of medical ignorance, one finds common beliefs linking three of the witnesses before the Select Committee: Shaftesbury, Conolly, and Perceval, two of whom at least were known by Dickens.[45]

Possibly Collins became aware of Perceval and his writings through his and Dickens' friend, Richard Monckton Milnes, who was a member of the Select Committee. Milnes's personal guest book shows that Collins was a visiter to Milnes's home in 1860, when the Select Committee issued its final report and Collins published *The Woman in White*.[46] An analysis of the questions Milnes posed to witnesses before the Committee reveals that while he may not have been the most active of the Parliamentary interrogators, he was not a passive member of the Committee either. His questions showed a keen interest in the investigation. Furthermore, since the relationship between the Milnes and Perceval families involved what Milnes's biographer calls one of the most interesting chapters in the "romance" of British politics,[47] Milnes himself must have been more than usually cognizant of Perceval's appearance before the Select Committee. Fifty-one years earlier their fathers had had a series of curious exchanges, and now as the sons faced each other on opposite sides during the Select Committee, Milnes possessed the power, influence, and connections to effect some of the changes Perceval was fighting for.[48]

There seems to be no way to prove that Collins and Milnes talked of Perceval. But Perceval testified in July 1859; Collins began publishing shortly thereafter a book in which one of his chief villains bears the same, unlikely and inexplicable name, standing in direct contradiction to the values of John Thomas Perceval and, in fact, illustrating the very fears that Perceval expressed in his testimony and writing. But it need not have been Milnes himself who acquainted Collins with John Thomas Perceval; the Alleged Lunatic Friends Society, while not exactly renowned, did draw the same kind of correspondence that Collins himself claimed to receive from persons seeking release from asylums; and Collins may very well have been familiar with Perceval's pamphlet concerning the inadequacy of the 1845 Act. But the Milnes connection strengthens the probability that Collins was aware of Perceval and knew what he stood for—this aside from the possibility that he actually knew Perceval. Finally, given the cross-connections among Dickens, Forster, Procter, Shaftesbury, Conolly, Milnes, Perceval, and Collins, and the mutual interest they shared in lunacy, lunatic laws, private asylums, and a patient's right to both sound medical treatment and legal protection, it would be surprising if Collins did *not* know of Perceval, the Alleged Lunatics Friends Society, the work of the Select Committee, and the overall issues with which it was concerned.

And, of course, there is Dickens himself, whose fiction, unlike Collins's, contains little about lunatics and asylums, but whose writings in general mark him as one of those Victorians with a keen interest in the subjects. Of the two articles that appeared in *Household Words* about idiots, the second reveals an increased theoretical interest in distunguishing among kinds of idiots as well as in the causes of idiocy.[49] This was the kind of intellectual exploration that unites Dickens with those who were beginning to understand that well-intentioned humanitarian efforts on behalf of the insane had to be aided by a better understanding such as Conolly was trying to achieve in his *Inquiry into the Indications of Insanity*. Actually, Dickens' best-known writing on the subject of insanity was more in the mainstream of British concern with the conditions experienced by the insane in the asylums to which they were sent than with the more subtle issues that attracted Collins. In 1860 a privately printed booklet paired Dickens' well-known article, "A Curious Dance Round a Curious Tree" (*Household Words*, 1852), which recounts a visit to an asylum and pleads for improved conditions for patients, with an 1860 *Times* piece about a "Ball at St. Luke's Hospital."[50] The booklet, whose date once again reveals how important the 1858–1860 period was in the history of the British mental health movement, concludes with a brief account of the improvement that had taken place in eight years, but argues that more must be done and funds raised. Hence, Dickens' name justifiably figures among the Victorians concerned with the plight of the mentally ill, and given his close connections with many important figures discussed above, and his close friendship with Collins, whose *Woman in White* he was serially publishing, it is virtually impossible not to conclude that through Dickens as well as through his own friends and interests Collins stood very close to the events of 1858–1860.

IV

While the sad truth is that most insanity involves quite ordinary people unable to cope with the quite ordinary pressures of everyday life, most ages have their myths of mental illness according to which emotional problems are associated with persons seen as extraordinary. In the Victorian age, such myths led in two directions. In the first case, the lunatic is put into the role of the demonic and ghostly figures who fill the gothic novel, and in such a tradition Charlotte Brontë's Bertha satisfies the reader's imagination both with regard to its conceptions of insanity and its expectations concerning sensationalism in fiction. On the other side, however, the furor in England during the time that Collins was writing his novel made it possible to conceive of the mental patient as a victim of society, a kind of Cinderella, deprived of a life of privilege and thrust into an existence of privation, misery, and drudgery.

When Perceval devoted himself to the protection of lunatics, he distinguished among four categories. There were the criminal lunatics, who created and still create for society a plethora of moral and legal dilemmas. And there were the pauper lunatics, whose plight in Victorian England revealed the inadequacy of social consciousness and reform at that time. Perceval's other two categories, however, encouraged the popular notion that alleged lunatics were the fairy-tale-like victims of malicious families and an inadequately protective environment. One of these groups consisted generally of those confined in private establishments. From Perceval's point of view, they were those whose families exercised over them "despotic power" that was in turn delegated to the asylum owners. That they needed to be rescued from their plight was Perceval's clear message.[51] But nowhere was the abrupt transition from a life of presumed comfort to one of deprivation as sharply defined as in the case of the special category of the insane known as Chancery lunatics, most of whose situations were strikingly similar to those of Cinderella, a tale which Collins draws on in *Armadale* and in *The Woman in White*.

Chancery lunatics were wards of the Crown, people with sufficient wealth that committees were assigned to look after them and their property. The procedure involved in committing Chancery lunatics was unique. It once "involved a trial by jury of the case of an allegedly insane person whose relatives petitioned for a declaration of insanity to prevent him from dissipating a considerable fortune."[52] This had been replaced by an inquisition before the Masters in Lunacy (specially appointed Commissioners). But it was part of a continuing scandal over Chancery lunatics that their rate of release from asylums was even lower than the general rate of release from private institutions, which in turn was lower than the rate of release from public institutions.[53] Not only were the asylum keepers profiting from the illness of the Chancery lunatic, but so were the committee in charge (which drew salaries) and the family in whose financial interests it was to have the lunatic out of the way. That a Chancery lunatic was a veritable Cinderella can be seen in the anonymously written pamphlet intended to expose their sorry plight: the "wealthy lunatic wards of Chancery are placed, as it were, in living tombs, beyond which their voices cannot be heard, and within which their slightest comforts are dependent upon the needy and vulgar persons by whom each of them is surrounded by their Committees, and to whose care they are assigned."[54] He describes a patient of six hundred pounds income a year, reduced to "scouring the chamber pots, shaking the carpets, making the beds, sweeping the rooms, and carrying water. He was to be seen every day, when the weather was fine enough, seated on a stool in the garden, near the muck-heap, with tucked-up shirt-sleeves, and cloth in hand, washing out the chamber-pots in a tub of water."[55]

Cinderella, reduced from riches to rags, from a life of comfort to drudgery and victimization by her wicked stepmother can be paralleled by another Chancery patient whose

> clothes were scanty, threadbare, and very dirty. He was made a butt of, cuffed, and kicked about in a manner painful to one's feelings to witness. . . . He was too insane to have his liberty, but he was not too insane to do the keeper's work. It would have been quite impossible for him, *of course*, to have carried a tray up and down stairs, swept the passages, and cleaned boots and shoes in any other place than a madhouse! . . . Here was a man, probably a gentleman, accustomed to be treated with that delicacy which the feelings of a gentleman requires, reduced to become the menial of a menial, the humble and submissive slave of a madhouse keeper! kicked, cuffed, insulted, abused—exposed to every species of degradation and tyranny.[56]

The London *Times* of August 1858 voiced particular sympathy for the "most glaring cases . . . of cruelty and crime . . . among those poor but wealthy wretches who are subjected to the tender mercies of ablebodied attendants—'keepers' in out-of-the-way houses, under the precarious inspection—at the outside—bi-weekly visitation—of some well-meaning physician."[57] The system was such that what was clearly needed by the Chancery lunatic was the magical power of some benign fairy godmother.

The depiction of the Chancery lunatic as an implicit Cinderella coincided rather well with a perhaps common Victorian fantasy. During an age in which the middle class was gaining ground, and upward mobility became an increasing possibility, deprivation could be fantasized as the failure of great expectations. Such a view informs the plot of Collins's *Armadale*, in which the outcast of the two Alan Armadales about whom the story revolves is forced to take a name not his own and wander friendless about the world, the victim of a cruel stepfather and an indifferent mother (in Collins's major fiction, it is the real mother who plays the role of wicked stepmother). Armadale's first memory is of his stepfather beating him with a whip, and he responds thus to inquiries about where his mother stood in this cruel household:

> Yes, I remember her having shabby old clothes made up to fit me, and having fine new frocks bought for her two children by her second husband. I remember the servants laughing at me in my old things, and the horsewhip finding its way to my shoulders again for

losing my temper and tearing my shabby clothes. My next recollection gets on to a year or two later. I remember myself locked up in
a lumber-room, with a bit of bread and a mug of water, wondering
what it was that made my mother and my stepfather seem to hate
the very sight of me.[58]

But the private and public merging of fantasy and its reflection in
the Cinderella story lies still closer to Collins than the writings
about well-to-do lunatics. Michael Kotzin has shown how frequently *Cinderella* appears in Dickens, and Harry Stone has demonstrated both how it prevades the themes and plot of *Great Expectations*, as well as how it was employed by Dickens in his quarrel with
Cruikshank over the uses to which fairy tales might be put.[59] Stone
focuses on Dickens' conception of the fairy tale as an antidote to the
climate of an age in which the imagination was being stifled in
almost every activity of life, and in which an early nourishment on
fairy tales would allow the imagination to survive the light of common day. Because of this emphasis, Stone does not note the extent to
which his own depiction of Dickens' childhood reflects the story he
has already demonstrated to be so important in the novelist's fiction. Would Dickens' seeming banishment to a blacking warehouse
at a time when he expected his life to take a better path be very different from Midwinter's cruel exile from parental love and finally
the parental home, or the Chancery lunatic's plunge from comfort
to misery? As Stone portrays Dickens' plight, "Seen through the
somber dusk of his first year in London, his Chatham childhood
seemed serene and idyllic—appareled in that 'fairy light.' Seen
through the dark shadow of the blacking warehouse, it took on the
radiance of paradise itself."[60] But Stone does not comment on the
extent to which Dickens' own account turned his life into a
Cinderella story. "My father," Stone quotes from Dickens' writing,

> appeared to have utterly lost at this time the idea of educating me at
> all, and to have utterly put from him the notion that I had any claim
> upon him, in that regard, whatever. So I degenerated into cleaning
> his boots of a morning, and my own; and making myself useful in
> the work of the little house; and looking after my younger brothers
> and sisters (we were now six in all); and going on such poor errands
> as arose out of our poor way of living.[61]

If Dickens had been self-conscious about his self-portrayal as
Cinderella, or aware of how this identification worked its way into
Great Expectations, he had clearly altered his view from that time,

almost a decade earlier, when he wrote to Wills about Cruikshank's *Cinderella* that he meant "to protest most strongly against altera- tion—for any purpose—of the beautiful little stories which are so tenderly and humanly useful to us in these times when the world is too much with us early and late. . . . I shall want . . . the most simple and popular version of Cinderella you can get me."[62] That he went on to parody *Cinderella* in "Frauds on the Fairies" in order to satirize Cruikshank does not necessarily lessen his reverence for the power of fairy tales to redeem an imagination lost in the hazes of mundane reality.

There is no direct evidence of just where Collins stood in the quarrel between Cruikshank and Dickens over fairy tales, which is unfortunate, for such evidence might shed light on Collins's own frequent use of the Cinderella motif in his fiction. There is reason to believe that Collins was repelled by Cruikshank's stand on drinking alcoholic beverages, for it was the latter's temperance crusade that apparently caused Collins to decline to attend a testimonial dinner for the artist.[63] Therefore, he probably sided unequivocally with Dickens in the latter's aversion to Cruikshank's having turned *Cinderella* into a temperance tract. Ironically, however, Collins and Cruikshank seem from a contemporary perspective not only to have much in common with regard to the fairy tale, but to be closer to a modern view of its function than Dickens was—at least in theory if not in practice.

In lashing out against Cruikshank, Dickens insisted on the purity of the fairy tale, for reasons already discussed. And in Stone's valuable analysis, Dickens has the better argument, also for those reasons; Cruikshank, however, was much clearer than Dickens about the anthropological significance of the fact that fairy tales came not in pure versions which he or anyone could corrupt, but in multiple versions, some of them quite at odds with others. In one of his rebuttals to Dickens, he wrote, "I will just take the liberty of sug- gesting to those gentlemen who may feel inclined to criticise my editing of those Fairy Tales, that they had better make themselves somewhat acquainted with all the old editions of these stories before they find fault with my version."[64] It was not a Victorian practice to focus on the *function* of the folk and fairy tale as a reflection of conflicts within a society and the way that a given society found of resolving them. Clearly, however, Cruikshank intuited as much when he altered *Cinderella* for his own social purposes. Such a con- ception of the fairy tale would be quite threatening to Dickens' own view of a fairy world that was an antidote to rather than an expression of contemporary reality, and, again, it is difficult to know where Collins stood in theory between these two positions. To judge from his practice, however, particularly in *The Woman in White*, Collins could find in Cinderella an expression of private as well as social pathology. As a result, he was able to read into this story a psychological meaning that brought him astonishingly close not only to interpretations of *Cinderella* found today, but astonishingly close to modern psychology itself, for which *Cinderella* is a favorite object of study.

Collins's *The Woman in White* is a reworking of the popular *Cinderella* fairy tale. The Cinderella motif, of course, appears ubiquitously in the world's folktales, and five out of the six motifs that A. Aarne and Stith Thompson categorize in *The Types of the Folktale* as well as some of their major variations combine in the plot and the central episodes of *The Woman in White*.[65] The five motifs are: 1) The persecuted heroine; 2) Magic help; 3) Meeting the prince; 4) Proof of identity; 5) Marriage to prince. Two of the variations emphasize the two stepsisters and the stepdaughter at the grave of her own mother.

The first of Aarne's and Thompson's motifs, "the persecuted heroine," hardly needs elaboration; the whole story revolves about the plot to shut Laura up in an asylum so that Glyde and Fosco can acquire her wealth. The second motif, "magic help," involves the intervention on Cinderella's behalf of a fairy godmother or other supernatural agent whose best remembered gift to the fairy tale heroine is the beautiful gowns that allow her to go to the balls at which she encounters her prince. The counterpart to this theme in *The Woman in White* leads to the very title of the novel. Mrs. Fairlie, who has taken a fancy to Anne Catherick, writes to her husband that

> Although she is dressed very neatly, her clothes show a sad want of taste in colour and pattern. So I arranged, yesterday, that some of our darling Laura's old white frocks and white hats should be altered for Anne Catherick; explaining to her that little girls of her complexion looked neater and better in all white than in anything else. She hesitated and seemed puzzled for a minute; then flushed up, and appeared to understand. Her little hand clasped mine, suddenly. She kissed it, Philip; and said (oh, so earnestly!), "I will always wear white as long as I live. It will help me to remember you, ma'am, and to think that I am pleasing you still, when I go away and see you no more." This is only one specimen of the quaint things she says so prettily. Poor little soul! She shall have a stock of white frocks, made with good deep tucks, to let out for her as she grows. (50)

This is Mrs. Fairlie's practical Victorian version of the Cinderella ball gown.

The third of these motifs, "meeting the prince," has to do with the role played by Walter Hartright, who, if he is not exactly a royal suitor, is nevertheless the novel's hero. Anne first meets him in her flight from the asylum; and it is he who sets about resolving the question of Laura's true identity, just as the prince in *Cinderella* sets out to solve the mystery surrounding the identity of the beautiful woman with whom he has fallen in love.[66] And, of course, it is in Laura's eventual rescue and marriage to Hartright that the fifth motif, "marriage to prince," is fulfilled. It is the fourth motif, however, "proof of identity," that forms the crux of *The Woman in White* as Fosco conspires to have Laura confined to an asylum under the identity of the now dead Anne Catherick. In Collins's French source, proving her identity and right to her inheritance after securing release from the Salpetrière was precisely what Mme. de Douhault was unable to do. Once again, much of Collins's fiction hinges on this motif, including *Armadale* and *The New Magdalen*, which is derived from the episode in *Cinderella* in which the stepsisters try to pass themselves off as the woman the prince is seeking.

But it is in a little-known short story that Collins wrote early in his career that such a substitution merges most clearly with the fairy tale. What was malign in *Cinderella*, however, as the stepsisters hide Cinderella out of sight while the prince makes his house-to-house search for her, is tragically benign in Collins's "The Twin Sisters."

> Streatfield, the hero, falls in love with a girl he sees on a balcony as he drives by in his carriage. After considerable effort he learns her identity, gets an introduction, and eventually becomes her accepted suitor. At the pre-nupital banquet, however, he meets for the first time his fiancée's twin sister, Clara, and realizes it was she whom he saw on the balcony and with whom he fell in love at first sight.[67]

This kind of reversal of the fairy tale plot is not unusual in Collins's use of *Cinderella*. In *The New Magdalen*, again, the imposter is actually the deserving heroine, whereas the rightful claimant is the novel's antagonist.

Two of the popular variations to the basic Cinderella story categorized by Aarne and Thompson are central to *The Woman in White*. One of these has to do with the presence in the fairy tale of two stepsisters. In Collins's novel there are also three women, each of them half-sister to at least one of the others. Two, Laura and Marian, have the same mother, and two, Laura and Anne, the same father. No two have both the same mother and father. The complications shared by their mingled identities is nowhere so apparent as in the scene—also typified in the fairy tale classifications—where Anne visits the grave of Mrs. Fairlie and vows to protect the latter's real daughter, Laura. More will be said about this scene shortly; for the time being it is worth noting that the visits to the dead mother's grave by Cinderella are frequently cited in studies of the fairy tale in order to differentiate the passive heroine of Perrault's version of the story from the more active heroine of Grimm's fairy tales.[68] Collins had used elements from both Grimm and Perrault. Like the passive heroine of the latter, his Cinderella, Anne Catherick, is rescued by a fairy godmother in the person of Mrs. Fairlie, whose gift of a dress is given without any effort on Anne's part and in response only to her unhappiness. But like Grimm's more active Cinderella, who tends her mother's grave and seeks the help she needs, Anne also proves herself worthy of Mrs. Fairlie's love by actively trying to save Laura. Unlike Dickens, who sought in his quarrel with Cruikshank the simplest and purest version of *Cinderella* available, Collins gathered from the two most famous variants of the tale elements to weave into his novel.

V

But the renowned fairy tale did more than provide Collins in *The Woman in White*—as it had provided him in his other fiction—with the basic characters and actions he used for his plot.[69] From his insight into the potential meaning of *Cinderella*, Collins also was able to construct the case history which made the character whose invention had eluded and tormented him, Anne Catherick, a psychological study for his time. Collins's own theory of composition mandated that if he created a character who was or appeared mad, the nature and etiology of her illness had to be clarified—at least in his own mind. And it was Anne, not Laura, who caused Collins the difficulties he described when outlining his procedure in writing *The Woman in White*.

Cinderella has been as popular among contemporary psychologists as it was among Victorian novelists. A favorite fairy tale among young girls, the story has drawn questions about what, in particular, the tale means to them as children and adolescents, and about why the appeal lessens in adulthood. Cinderella complexes have from one perspective or another filled the pages of professional journals of psychology.[70] But a more encompassing theoretical account of *Cinderella* as it relates to the development of children can be found in two recent books which shed light on Collins's depiction of Anne and his treatment of this fairy tale in *The Woman in White*.

Bruno Bettelheim, in *The Uses of Enchantment*, argues that children intuit the deep psychological content in fairy tales, which thus aid them in working through the conflicts that beset them as they grow up. Taking a position unlike either Dickens' or Cruikshank's, Bettelheim nevertheless combines some important elements from each. He believes that children healthily nourished on fairy tales benefit from these stories because they move into adulthood better able to face the demands of maturity. Like Cruikshank, he sees these tales as instructive for those who search for that which gives life its moral significance. However, instead of being overtly didactic, fairy tales, for Bettelheim, contain complex structures whose meanings are apprehended unconsciously rather than consciously. Bettelheim's study of *Cinderella* focuses not unexpectedly on the theme of sibling rivalry, and on the relationship between the heroine and her antagonistic step-sisters. Such, of course, is not the case in *The Woman in White*, although the sibling relationships among Anne, Laura, and Marian prove to have great significance. What is, however, more important at present is the light shed by Bettelheim on the theme of the wicked stepmother and common fantasies which comprise what Bettelheim calls the "family romance," involving

> daydreams which the normal youngster partly recognizes as such, but nonetheless also partly believes. They center on the idea that one's parents are not really one's parents, but that one is the child of some exalted personage, and that, due to unfortunate circumstance, one has been reduced to living with these people, who *claim* to be one's parents. . . . These fantasies are helpful; they permit the child to feel really angry at the Martian pretender or the "false parent" without guilt.[71]

In short, Anne Catherick's pretense at the grave of Mrs. Fairlie that it is her real mother she is weeping over is played out in the normal lives of all children who express anger at parents through the pretense that the latter are really step-parents, thus protecting themselves against the guilt they would feel for the momentary hatred felt towards the real father or mother. But Bettelheim is describing an essentially normal process on the part of children who will learn to cope with such conflicts, especially if aided by exposure to fairy tales.

In *The Treatment of the Borderline Adolescent*, James F. Masterson presents an analysis of *Cinderella* (and *Snow White*) in which what Bettelheim calls the "family romance" is presented in a less benign context. The death of the "real" mother and her replacement by the punishing stepmother reflects the inability of the emotionally disturbed young person to see the mother—and consequently others—as whole human beings. As Masterson writes, "The image of the good mother is split and preserved by the dramatic device of relating that although she wanted (i.e., loved) the child very much, the good mother died shortly after birth. The blood mother loves the child. The same theme is noted in Cinderella," where again, "the image of the good mother is preserved through her death. The blood mother, not present, had loved Cinderella."[72] And in the case of *Cinderella*, unlike *Snow White*, "the envy and jealousy are further split off and conveyed not by the stepmother but by the sisters."[73]

The cast of characters in these unhappy dramas that Masterson sees repeatedly re-enacted in the lives of his patients is negatively completed by the passive father who fails to protect his child against the damages of his non-nurturing or aggressively angry wife. The result is a young child whose illness develops like a hidden abcess which erupts in adolescence, as deep depression explodes into self-destructive and rebellious patterns of behavior at odds with the accepted forms of action expected of a young person. Masterson might be describing Anne Catherick, whose anguish leads to the impulsive, rebellious behavior that initially leads to her being committed to an asylum. That the cast of characters found in common between the fairy tale and the families described in Masterson's case histories can also be found in *The Woman in White* reveals Collins's ability to turn *Cinderella* into a study of an aberrant Victorian adolescent.

Masterson points out that in neither *Snow White* nor *Cinderella* does the father have any role to play. In the former, only one line is devoted to the father: "after a year had passed the King married a second time." In *Cinderella*, Masterson ironically notes, the father "gets better treatment (four lines)" but still "plays literally no role in her life. 'Once upon a time there was a nobleman of France who took a second wife after the death of his first. He did it for the sake of his little daughter so that she would have a mother. Then he left for a journey that would take him a whole year. He believed that his daughter would be happy while he was away.'"[74] This depiction applies equally to the ostensible fathers of both Anne Catherick and her half-sister Laura Fairlie.

There are three passive fathers in *The Woman in White*. That they combine to form a single type is reinforced in two ways. First, Anne's ostensible father turns out not to be a blood relation, and Laura's father proves to be Anne's as well. This Mr. Fairlie is replaced after his death by his brother, also referred to as Mr. Fairlie, so that it is effectively difficult to distinguish the two from each other. It is the latter Mr. Fairlie who represents the "bad," that is neglectful, father of the fairy tales who fails to protect the daughter who should be able to count on his strength.

Even Anne Catherick's nominal father reflects the paternal figure in *Cinderella* who after marrying his second wife left on a year long journey. Mrs. Catherick's husband, who married her when she was pregnant by another man, emigrates to American on a more enduring journey because of the bad marriage he is forced to endure with Anne's mother. But Anne's real father, the acknowledged father of Laura, is hardly more of a presence in his family's life. Mr. Fairlie's death only literalizes the role he had played for Laura. This is made evident in the crucial letter that Mrs. Fairlie had written to her absent husband, the one in which she informs him that one of her pupils (Anne) in the school she runs has been taken under her wing both because of her sympathy for the poor creature and because of the close resemblance Anne bears to their daughter Laura. (Mrs. Fairlie does not know, and the reader does not yet know, that she is providing her husband with information about his own illegitimate child.) The letter has an important function in *The Woman in White*, since it gives Collins an opportunity to supply past information about his characters not otherwise easily made known. Therefore there is a narrative necessity in his supplying a motive for Mrs. Fairlie's having to correspond with her absent husband. Nevertheless, her reason proves consistent with the view of fathers and father-substitutes in the novel. As Marian explains to Hartright when she first mentions the existence of the letter, "I will pass the morning in looking over my mother's correspondence with Mr. Fairlie. He was fond of London, and was constantly away from his country home; and she was accustomed, at such times, to write and report to him how things went on at Limmeridge" (30).

The absent Victorian father, a common figure in the literature of the period, had gradually given way to the growing emphasis on the maternal role in child development. But that the family was experiencing the negative effects of his neglect was also a popular theme.[75] Laura can idealize her dead father nonetheless because, again, the evil effects of this neglect are embodied not in him, but in his brother, who becomes Laura's guardian after her father dies. Since referring to both brothers as "Mr. Fairlie" blurrs the distinction between them, Collins tends to fuse rather than separate the good and the bad fathers.

The reader first meets the guardian Mr. Fairlie—or more accurately does not meet him—when Hartright arrives at Limmeridge. Marian apologizes that she is the only one to greet him:

> "My sister is in her own room, nursing that essentially feminine malady, a slight headache; and her old governess, Mrs. Vesey, is charitably attending on her with restorative tea. My uncle, Mr. Fairlie, never joins us at any of our meals: he is an invalid, and keeps bachelor state in his own apartments." (26)

The dynamics of this passage are clear: there is a vulnerable, helpless heroine (Laura) ministered to by a "good" mother figure, while the passive substitute father secludes himself. Later, after Laura marries and both she and Marian leave the house, Marian comments, "As for Mr. Fairlie, I believe I am guilty of no injustice if I describe him as being unutterably relieved by having the house clear of us women. The idea of his missing his niece is simply preposterous—he used to let months pass, in the old times, without attempting to see her" (179). But it is not just a matter of women in general. Laura, his niece, is essentially his daughter in that he is her guardian, and he makes it clear to Walter Hartright in a private interview in his bachelor quarters that he cannot bear children:

> "There are no children, thank Heaven, in the house; but the servants (persons born without nerves) will encourage the children from the village. Such brats—oh, dear me, such brats! Shall I confess it, Mr. Hartright?—I sadly want a reform in the construction of children. Nature's only idea seems to be to make them machines for the production of incessant noise. Surely our delightful Raffaello's conception is infinitely preferable?" (36)

The pun here on the word "conception" is, of course, part of Collins's irony. Mr. Fairlie is referring to Raphael's portrait of the Madonna and Child hanging on his wall, a portrait in which a natural father for obvious reasons is missing. Mr. Fairlie has substituted art for life because he cannot confront the demands and responsibility incurred by human contact. Later in the book he himself narrates part of the story of Laura's misfortunes:

> It is the grand misfortune of my life that nobody will let me alone. Why—I ask everybody—why worry me? Nobody answers that question; and nobody lets me alone. Relatives, friends, and strangers all combine to annoy me. What have I done? I ask myself, I ask my servant, Louis, fifty times a day—what have I done? Neither of us can tell. Most extraordinary! (309)

Fairlie's bachelorhood is but the symbol of his attitude, although the family's lawyer, shocked when the guardian's passivity allows him to make a marriage settlement for his niece that exposes her to innumerable dangers, attributes to his single condition this gross mishandling of her affairs.

Masterson has argued that the disturbed adolescent has parents similarly suffering from the illness that afflicts the child. The father, in particular, "crippled by failure to solve his own developmental difficulties, is unable to respond to the mature demands of fatherhood which more often he sees as a threat to his dependent relationship with his wife rather than as an opportunity for satisfaction. Indeed, his own immaturity prevents him from sensing and enjoying that satisfaction."[76] Mr. Fairlie, of course, does not see his guardianship of Laura as a threat to any other relationship he has formed, but he does similarly see it as a threat to his self-imposed isolation. He has resolved the problems described by Masterson by not marrying and by retreating into his own quarters, losing himself in his art collections—one of the most grotesque caricatures of the aesthete to come to us from the Victorians. That his passivity can be traced to some emotional malfunctioning can be seen, again, in the explanation by Marian (quoted earlier) that his condition is attributed to his nerves, but that "we none of us know what we mean when we say [that]."

In his study of The Woman in White and the contrast between Collins's dark and fair ladies, Knoepflmacher implies that the process that informs Bettelheim's "family romance" was practised in Victorian England on a wide scale. Knoepflmacher writes of the

Victorian novelist that "one side . . . rejects the escapism or aggression that the other side indulges."[77] This is essentially what happens when the child splits the mother into disparate figures, in the
meantime protecting himself from the guilt wrought by his own ag-
gressive anger. In Masterson's analysis of *Cinderella*, based on the
French version in which the step-sisters are actually the instigators
of Cinderella's misery, the mother merely agrees "with the sisters
that they had best put Cinderella to work in the kitchen."[78] But the
step-sisters are also part of the splitting process that Masterson
describes and Bettelheim explains in a wider context. According to
Masterson, "the mother's negative attitudes towards the child are
introjected unconsciously *by* the child and become associated with
his own *fragmentary self-image*" (italics added).[79] It is possible that
just as the child may split the mother into two figures to keep intact
the fantasized image of an ideal parent, so is it possible that the
child can be similarly split, the bad side projected onto bad siblings.
Collins's adaptation of the step-sister motif from *Cinderella* involves him, however, not in a two- but a three-way split. The doubl-
ings and triplings that go on in his book (and in his writings in
general) are quite complex, as the moral climate of his time and not
only the family pathology he intuited in the *Cinderella* story con-
tribute to Anne's illness, Marian's seemingly enforced spinsterhood
and vicarious existence, and the insipid heroine, Laura.

Neither Anne Catherick nor Laura Fairlie are "good" or "bad"
sisters from a moral point of view; what they are, however, are sane
and possibly insane (at the least, disturbed) versions of the same person. Anne is what Laura could have become if she had been born to
Anne's mother; Laura is what Anne fantasizes she might have been
as Mrs. Fairlie's daughter. Indeed, her desperation to save Laura
from her demonic fiancé seems a desperate attempt to preserve that
fantasy. In a frantic letter sent to Laura warning about the impending marriage, Anne writes,

> Your mother's daughter has a tender place in my heart—for your
> mother was my first, my best, my only friend. (68)

The significance of that circumlocution, "your mother's daughter,"
becomes clear later when Anne's "friend" becomes the "mother" of
her fantasy; for had Anne had Laura's mother, then she would in effect be Laura. Crying on the dead woman's tombstone, which she
has been tending just as Cinderella in the Grimm version tends the
grave of her mother, Anne exclaims:

"Oh, if I could die, and be hidden and at rest with *you*!" Her lips murmured the words close on the gravestone; murmured them in tones of passionate endearment, to the dead remains beneath. "*You* know how I love your child, for your sake! Oh, Mrs. Fairlie! Mrs. Fairlie! tell me how to save her. Be my darling and my mother once more, and tell me what to do for the best!" (90)

It is possible to wonder why Collins created three half-sisters, since it is the doubling of Anne and Laura that is essential to his plot and theme; Marian could easily have been a cousin or even more distant relative and not lost any of her role in the sequence of events. Collins apparently has placed Laura between two half-sisters, one on each side, because each in her own way completes his heroine's character. Where it comes to Marian, Collins may have been indulging in his own wish-fulfillment or developing one side of a conflicted inclination, as Knoepflmacher would have it. Unable to endow his idealized Victorian heroine with the qualities of vibrancy, sensuality, and superior intelligence, he protects her from what his age might have viewed as negative female attributes by projecting them onto Marian, who herself describes the difference between her and Laura:

Except that we are both orphans, we are in every respect as unlike each other as possible. My father was a poor man, and Miss Fairlie's father was a rich man. I have got nothing, and she is an heiress. I am dark and ugly, and she is fair and pretty. Everybody thinks me crabbed and odd (with perfect justice); and everybody thinks her sweet-tempered and charming (with more justice still). In short, she is an angel; and I am——Try some of that marmalade, Mr. Hart-right, and finish the sentence, in the name of female propriety, for yourself. (27)

By facetiously casting herself in the role of devil, Marian portrays *herself* as the wicked half-sister, except that her so-called wicked-ness, a kind of Blakean energy not tolerated in women at that time, is turned upon herself, not her sister. Masochistically, she decides to sacrifice herself for the angelic sister, taking all that is negative upon herself to keep Laura free of it.

But if Laura, split away from the characteristics of Marian, is thereby less than a whole person, so is she incomplete without her other half-sister, Anne. When Hartright first meets Laura, the reader is treated to lengthy passages in praise of her beauty and charm. Then Hartright reports that "at the same time, [I was] most troubled by the sense of an incompleteness which it was impossible to discover. Something wanting, something wanting—and where it was, and what it was, I could not say" (42). He is subsequently haunted by the resemblance between Laura and the mysterious woman in white, whom he has come to believe is the girl once cared for by Laura's mother. But it is only on the happenstance of his next meeting with Anne that he comprehends what it is that Laura is missing:

> I had seen Anne Catherick's likeness in Miss Fairlie. I now saw Miss Fairlie's likeness in Anne Catherick—saw it all the more clearly because the points of dissimilarity between the two were presented to me as well as the points of resemblance. In the general outline of the countenance and general proportion of the features . . . the likeness appeared even more startling than I had ever felt it to be yet. But there the resemblance ended, and the dissimilarity, in details, began. The delicate beauty of Miss Fairlie's complexion, the transparent clearness of her eyes, the smooth purity of her skin, the tender bloom of colour on her lips, were all missing from the worn, weary face that was now turned towards mine. Although I hated myself even for thinking such a thing, still, while I looked at the woman before me, the idea would force itself into my mind that one sad change, in the future, was all that was wanting to make the likeness complete, which I now saw to be so imperfect in detail. If ever sorrow and suffering set their profaning marks on the youth and beauty of Miss Fairlie's face, then, and then only, Anne Catherick and she would be the twin-sisters of chance resemblance, the living reflexions of one another. (84)

The passage is, of course, a piece of foreshadowing. Later on, after her disastrous marriage has taken place, Laura actually meets her double, who reminds her:

> "You don't remember a fine spring day at Limmeridge . . . and your mother walking down the path that led to the school, with a little girl on each side of her? I have had nothing else to think of since; and *I* remember it. You were one of the little girls, and I was the other. Pretty, clever Miss Fairlie, and poor dazed Anne Catherick were nearer to each other, then, than they are now!" (252)

But, in fact, Anne is mistaken. The two are soon to be closer than either can imagine. In relating this incident to Marian, Laura reports how startled she had been while looking at Anne, "as if it had been the sight of my own face in the glass after a long illness" (252).

What Collins seems to be implying in his portrayals of the differences and similarities among Laura and her two half-sisters is a
kind of mass object splitting in the Victorian mentality which, in
order to protect its feminine ideal, had to keep her free of, on one
side, the sexuality and intellect of one sister, and, on the other side,
the maturity that comes from a confrontation with pain and suffering. But if Laura cannot become a complex and whole woman,
even when her experiences in the asylum have left their marks on
her beauty, Anne does not place upon her creator the same
restraints. And thus Collins in effect uses a technique that has in
modern times become more common. He tells much of his story
from the perspective of the villain's or underdog's point of view. For
example, a novel-length version of Cupid and Psyche has been written from the narrative point of view of one of the sisters who in-
stigates Psyche's fall. What would *Cinderella* look like from the
point of view of the step-sisters? If one can think of something
analogous going on in *The Woman in White*, it is possible to see
that from a psychological point of view it is not so significant than
under adverse circumstances Laura Fairlie could have been Anne
Catherick. Rather, the point that Collins seems to have wanted to
drive home is that under other circumstances his "poor Anne
Catherick" could have been Laura Fairlie. What Masterson says of
the young patients he has treated applies equally to Anne Catherick,
whose story also reveals "in a clinical metaphor the ancient
struggle of mankind against fate . . . condemned by birth and subsequent accidents of fate to be victims rather than masters of their
own fortune; they are emotionally attacked and impaled before
they have developed the resources and weapons with which to do
battle."[80] The circumstances that would have made Anne become
Laura seem to have hinged simply, or perhaps not so simply, on
having the good fortune to be born to another mother.

VI

In *Cinderella* there are two "good" mothers, and one "bad." The
first good mother is dead, but she is reincarnated in the "Good
Fairy . . . to banish Cinderella's feelings of abandonment by magi-
cally fulfilling her wishes."[81] In the story, it will be remembered,
she appears suddenly to provide Cinderella with the dress that will
allow her to go to the ball and meet her rescuer. In Collins's novel,
again, it is Mrs. Fairlie who similarly relieves Anne's feelings of
misery by similarly endowing a dress, even if one which can meet

the needs of prudent Victorian utilitarianism in its capacity for alteration as Anne grows.

Because Mrs. Fairlie dies before the book begins, although it is Anne's deep attachment to her that is at the heart of the story, it is necessary to provide in *The Woman in White* another if lesser "good" mother figure to help Anne when she escapes from the asylum and to provide the reader with information about Anne's blood mother. This figure is Mrs. Clements, whom Anne describes to Hartright:

> "Mrs. Clements is my friend. A good kind woman, but not like Mrs. Fairlie. Ah, no, nobody is like Mrs. Fairlie!"
>
> "Is Mrs. Clements an old friend of yours? Have you known her a long time?"
>
> "Yes; she was a neighbour of ours once, at home, in Hampshire; and liked me, and took care of me when I was a little girl. Years ago, when she went away from us, she wrote down in my prayerbook for me, where she was going to live in London, and she said, 'If you are ever in trouble, Anne, come to me. I have no husband alive to say me nay, and no children to look after; and I will take care of you.' Kind words, were they not? I suppose I remember them because they were kind. It's little enough I remember besides—little enough, little enough!" (87)

Collins adds special force to the good and bad mother theme in *The Woman in White* and in *Armadale*, by making the blood mother and not her successor the "bad" mother. However, Collins is perhaps closer to nature than is the fairy tale he is adapting, since it is the failure of the real mother to nurture her child which sets in motion the negative forces in his book. In the child, the

> need for affection and approval from his mother to build ego structure and grow are so absolute and his rage and frustration at the deprivation of these very supplies on the part of the mother so great that he fears these feelings may destroy her and himself. To deal with his fear and to preserve the feeling of receiving supplies, the infant splits the whole object of the mother into two parts, that is, a good and bad mother.[82]

The child clings to the image of the good mother as Anne clings to the memory of Mrs. Fairlie, and the anger at the bad mother is projected onto someone else or is in some other way acted out. Only once in *The Woman in White* does Anne reveal her anger and her capacity for object splitting; this scene occurs when Hartright questions her about her mother:

"Don't ask me about mother," she went on. "I'd rather talk of Mrs. Clements. Mrs. Clements is like you, she doesn't think that I ought to be back in the Asylum; and she is as glad as you are that I escaped from it. She cried over my misfortune, and said it must be kept secret from everybody." (87)

Anne knows that she and her mother do not have an appropriate relationship with each other: "I don't get on well with her. We are a trouble and a fear to each other" (87). But as she is directly confronted by Hartright with the reality of how her parents have abandoned her, her mother actually cooperating with her being sent to the asylum, her way of dealing with her anger is immediately to transfer her attention to one of her "good" mothers.

It is through this good mother, Mrs. Clements, that the reader first gets a detailed look at Mrs. Catherick. It is not, however, the first look, which had come through Mrs. Fairlie's letter to her husband:

Mrs. Catherick is a decent, well-behaved, respectable woman; middle aged, and with the remains of having been moderately, only moderately, nice-looking. There is something in her manner and in her appearance, however, which I can't make out. She is reserved about herself to the point of downright secrecy; and there is a look in her face—I can't describe it—which suggests to me that she has something on her mind. She is altogether what you would call a walking mystery. (49)

She is not, however, a mystery to Mrs. Clements, who nevertheless, unreliable reporter that she is, misinterprets Mrs. Catherick's erratic behavior towards her daughter. When asked how she had come to care for Anne, Mrs. Clements responds, "There was nobody else, sir, to take the helpless creature in hand. . . . The wicked mother seemed to hate it—as if the poor baby was in fault!—from the day it was born. My heart was heavy for the child; and I made the offer to bring it up as tenderly as if it was my own" (437). However, when asked if she had had constant care of Anne, she tells Hartright that she had not, but in an answer worth quoting at length, since it reveals better than any other passage in the book the extent of Collins's insight into the complex nature of the relationship Anne had had to her own mother:

"Not quite entirely, sir. Mrs. Catherick had her whims and fancies about it, at times; and used now and then to lay claim to the child, as if she wanted to spite me for bringing it up. But these fits of hers never lasted for long. Poor little Anne was always returned to me and was always glad to get back—though she led but a gloomy life in my house, having no playmates, like other children, to brighten her up. Our longest separation was when her mother took her to Limmeridge [where Anne forms the attachment to Mrs. Fairlie]. Just at that time, I lost my husband; and I felt it was as well, in that miserable affliction, that Anne should not be in the house. She was between ten and eleven years old, then; slow at her lessons, poor soul, and not so cheerful as other children—but as pretty a little girl to look at as you would wish to see. I waited at home till her mother brought her back; and then I made the offer to take her with me to London. . . ."

"And did Mrs. Catherick consent to your proposal?"

"No, sir. She came back from the north, harder and bitterer than ever. Folks did say that she had been obliged to ask Sir Percival's leave to go, to begin with; and that she only went to nurse her dying sister at Limmeridge because the poor woman was reported to have saved money—the truth being that she hardly left enough to bury her. These things may have soured Mrs. Catherick, likely enough—but, however that may be, she wouldn't hear of my taking the child away. She seemed to like distressing us both by parting us. (437-438)

Obviously, Mrs. Catherick's ambivalence toward her child, caring for it one moment and pushing it away another, had more to it than a desire to spite Mrs. Clements, although that is how that simple woman interprets it. What it actually was, Collins himself probably could not explain, although modern psychology could say a great deal about Mrs. Catherick's erratic desire to possess the child she was nevertheless unable to nurture.

Mrs. Catherick presents her own version of Mrs. Clements's story in a section of the novel in which, finally, Hartright has an opportunity to confront her, hoping to wrest out of her her daughter Anne's secret, which he believes to be the key to Laura's freedom. Mrs. Catherick proves with regard to her daughter to be one of the most chilling characters in the book—perhaps one of the most chilling in Victorian fiction.[83] In a confessional letter written to Hartright, she admits to more than the mere fact that she hardly mothered her child:

Pray understand that I do not profess to have been at all over-fond of my late daughter. She was a worry to me from first to last, with the additional disadvantage of being always weak in the head. You like candour, and I hope this satisfies. (494-495)

Believing her daughter to be insane, she also believes that her "worst responsibilities, so far as she was concerned, were all over

when she was secured in the Asylum" (499), especially as it was to
"A Private Establishment," and not to a "pauper Asylum" that she
helped to have Anne committed, thereby confirming all the fears
about such places and the families that sent their unwanted
members to them that swept England during the time Collins wrote
his novel.

Anne Catherick, daughter of a father who never made himself felt
in her life and a mother who in her inability to love her child reveals
her own mental pathology, is the Victorian version of the emotionally ill adolescent of modern psychology. The Victorians, who,
in general, hardly recognized adolescence as a separate category,
were only beginning to recognize childhood "insanity" as more
than a category of either idiocy or immorality. Deprived by her
mother of those emotional resources that would have allowed her to
grow into a healthy woman, Anne clings to the mother of her double as the good mother of her longings. As Hartright describes the
attachment to Mrs. Fairlie, the latter does emerge as the fairy godmother of the fairy tale:

> The old grateful sense of her benefactress's kindness was evidently
> the ruling idea still in the poor creature's mind—the narrow mind
> which had but too plainly opened to no other lasting impression
> since that first impression of her younger and happier days. (85)

This fixation is Anne's defense against her misery. Abandoned by
her real mother, she is obviously given to depression. Mrs. Clements
describes her as a gloomy child, and the death wish Anne articu-
lates more than once in the book expresses her melancholy. But her
opportunities to act out in order to guard against what Masterson
calls the "abandonment depression" are limited, since the gross
delinquency of the time would have been unthinkable for her. Yet,
both Mrs. Clements and her mother speak of Anne's stubborn
whims, one of which is her insistence on wearing white even when
her mother tries to prevent it in her attempt to break the bond between Anne and Mrs. Fairlie. It is this blatant disobedience in an
age in which childhood obedience had absolute value that leads to
the quarrel between Anne and her mother whose final result will be
Anne's commitment to a lunatic asylum. It is Anne's inability to
control her angry impulses, however, that sets in motion the events
that lead to her incarceration. When Sir Percival, Laura's future
evil husband, insults her by calling Anne an "idiot," she threatens
him with the secret that can ruin him, as her mother explains in her
account of the scene,

She had always had crazy notions of her own about her dignity; and that word, "idiot," upset her in a moment. Before I could interfere, she stepped up to him, in a fine passion. "Beg my pardon, directly," says she, "or I'll make it the worse for you. I'll let out your Secret! I can ruin your life, if I choose to open my lips." . . . He sat speechless, as white as the paper I am writing on, while I pushed her out of the room. (497)

Mrs. Catherick, nevertheless, has no hesitation in cooperating with Sir Percival's scheme to commit Anne to a lunatic asylum.

But what, specifically, could Collins have made of the behavior of his own creation, Anne Catherick, once he had overcome the obstacles her invention had posed? In the Victorian age, a growing awareness of mental disturbance on the part of children was reflected in the report published in the *Journal of Psychological Medicine* that there are some children who are strange even in their nurse's arms,[84] and Mrs. Clements does muse over what strikes her as Anne's strange behavior:

"Queer," she said to herself, "always queer, with her whims and her ways, ever since I can remember her. Harmless, though—as harmless, poor soul, as a little child." (82)

The *Journal* reports on this phenomenon as a kind of mental retardation, and Collins seems to have considered this possibility when he has Mrs. Fairlie call in a physician to diagnose Anne's apparent slowness in learning. But in the letter to her husband, Mrs. Fairlie explicitly rules out a judgment of "idiocy." Collins may have faced the same dilemma as Marian Halcombe who says of her uncle that he suffers from nerves, although no one quite knows what it means to say that. What he therefore depicts is a young woman who, made ill by the absence of mothering during her formative years, might have recovered or grown out of her malady had her fairy godmother not proven more helpless than her counterpart in fairy tales.

That—despite the absence of theoretical knowledge on which to draw—Collins was able to anticipate such insights of modern thought proves him to be a novelist skilled in psychological analysis as well as clever narrative in *The Woman in White*. It should no longer be necessary to appeal to the importance of plot in fiction in order to win this book a wide circle of appreciative readers.[85]

NOTES

1. Wilkie Collins and *The Woman in White*," *PMLA*, 54 (1939), 303.
    H. P. Sucksmith, in his introduction to the scholarly edition of *The
    Woman in White*, invokes Aristotle to argue that the novel is in no
    way denigrated because of Collins's emphasis on story (London: Ox-
    ford University Press, 1975), p. x. Citations will be to this edition. R.
    P. Ashley's biography of Collins argues that when judged "by the
    standards of melodrama and sensation—the only standards by
    which it is fair to judge it"—the novel is a "masterpiece": *Wilkie
    Collins* (New York: Roy Publishers, 1952), pp. 69-70. Also see
    Walter M. Kendrick, "The Sensationalism of *The Woman in
    White*," *Nineteenth-Century Fiction*, 32 (1977), 18-35.
2. "The Counterworld of Victorian Fiction and *The Woman in
    White*," in *The Worlds of Victorian Fiction*, ed. Jerome H. Buckley
    (Cambridge, Mass.: Harvard University Press, 1975), p. 363. Aside
    from Knoepflmacher's major excursion into the novel's meaning,
    there have only been occasional glimmers of a thematic approach.
    In *Victorian Conventions*, John Reed argues that in his famous novel
    as well as in *Armadale*, Collins was concerned "with abuses of law
    which permitted sane individuals to be confined" (Ohio Univeristy
    Press, 1975), p. 204. Reed's claim that Collins was not interested in
    current theories of insanity, however, is one of the points against
    which this essay will argue. D. B. MacEachen also stresses that Col-
    lins, who was trained in law even if he never practised it, "made his
    readers aware of existing legal injustices that might not have engag-
    ed their attention at all had he not incorporated these problems in
    [his] novels," and also claims that Collins, like Dickens and Reade
    "realized that the presentation of an emotionally stirring 'case
    history' was a far more potent means of reform, so far as the
    average, uncritical reader was concerned, than either satire or
    denunciation . . .": "Wilkie Collins and British Law," *Nineteenth-
    Century Fiction*, 5 (1950), 139, 133-134. But MacEachen does not
    discuss *The Woman in White*, and thus the question of whose case
    history is important in this novel remains open.
3. Probably the most explicit dismissal of Anne Catherick is made by
    Kenneth Robinson in *Wilkie Collins: A Biography*: "Anne Catherick,
    The Woman in White, suffers from an infirmity of mind, which,
    while appealing to our sympathies, nevertheless limits our interest in
    her and her fate, and she misses the tragic stature intended for her by
    the author" (London: The Bodley Head, 1951), p. 152. Peter Carac-
    ciolo comes close to an important point when he refers to Anne as
    "this harmless girl" who has been "put away by her mother and Sir
    Percival Glyde": "Wilkie Collins's "Divine Comedy: The Use of
    Dante in *The Woman in White*," *Nineteenth-Century Fiction*, 25
    (1971), 390. For the point that troubles the novel's chief narrator
    and hero, Walter Hartright, is the very point that critics tend to take
    for granted or dismiss as unimportant: whether, in fact, Anne's con-

finement to an asylum is any more justified than Laura's. But Caracciolo has other aims in his essay and does not pursue this theme.

4. Sucksmith, in his notes, acknowledges that abuses existed in England, but he refers the interested reader away from Collins's fiction to Charles Reade's, p. 606.

5. The charge appeared on the Committee's reports, three of which were issued. See Great Britain, Parliament, House of Commons, *Sessional Papers*: 1859 (Session 1), III: 75-470; 1859 (Session 2), VII: 501-752; 1860, XXII: 349-442.

6. Kathleen Jones, *A History of the Mental Health Services* (London: Routledge and Kegan Paul, 1972), p. 148.

7. *Ibid.*, p. 149.

8. *The Works of Wilkie Collins* (1890; rpt. St. Clair, Mich.: Scholarly Press, 1976), VIII, 426-427.

9. August 28, p. 8.

10. August 19, p. 6.

11. *Sessional Papers*, VII, 531.

12. *Sessional Papers*, III, 100.

13. Those, such as Kathleen Jones, who note the adversary positions of the Select Committee and the Alleged Lunatics Friends Society, which Perceval helped to form, neglect the points held in common by Perceval and Shaftesbury. See Jones, p. 159; William H. Parry-Jones, *The Trade in Lunacy: A Study of Private Madhouses in England in the Eighteenth and Nineteenth Centuries* (London: Routledge and Kegan Paul, 1972), p. 238; Richard Hunter and Ida Macalpine, "John Thomas Perceval (1803–1876) Patient and Reformer," *Medical History*, 6 (1962), 393–394.

14. *Letters to the Right Honourable Sir James Graham, Bart., and to other Noblemen and Gentlemen, Upon the Reform of the Law Affecting the Treatment of Persons Alleged to be of Unsound Mind* (London: Effingham Wilson, 1846), p. 35.

15. Sucksmith includes Collins's account, which first appeared in *The Globe*, November 26, 1877, in Appendix D of his edition.

16. P. 290.

17. *Ibid.*

18. While, to my knowledge, no one has challenged the veracity of Collins's claim to have received such a letter, neither has anyone proven its existence. Sucksmith includes Collins's reference to the letter, which appeared in *The World*, (December 26, 1877), in Appendix C, p. 591.

19. (Northampton: Privately Printed, 1858).

20. Daniel H. Tuke, *Chapters in the History of the Insane in the British Isles* (London: Kegan Paul, 1882), p. 190.

21. Read at the General Meeting of June 23, 1858, pp. 9-10. The Society issued only two reports, of which this is the second.

22. 11 (1858), xxx.

23. The actual inquisition concerning Mrs. Turner was not given the same attention as the Meux case, which was reported on daily from

June 9-18 (with the exception of the 13th). But the Turner case created an editorial uproar in the newspaper.

24. June 21, p. 12.
25. July 28, p. 9.
26. August 19, p. 6.
27. Already cited.
28. (New York: Harper and Bros., 1873), p. 197.
29. *Ibid.*, pp. 194-195.
30. See Kathleen Jones, p. 160. Jones entitles this chapter in her study, "The Triumph of Legalism."
31. *Ibid.*, p. 155.
32. *Journal of Mental Science*, 5 (1858-1859), 151.
33. 11 (1858-1859), xxxiv.
34. That the article in *Household Words* quoted from the *Journal of Mental Science* in the course of its discussion (p. 416) indicates that for the educated Victorian reader, there was no wide gap between popular and scholarly publications.
35. April 2, 1859, pp. 416-417.
36. *John Forster and his Friendships* (New York: Charles Scribner's Sons, 1913), p. 213.
37. *Ibid.*, pp. 212-213.
38. (Urbana: University of Illinois Press, 1956), p. 245.
39. Renton, p. 195. Renton also provides the information that it was Proctor whom Forster succeeded, p. 187.
40. *Ibid.*, p. 232.
41. Richard A. Hunter and Ida Macalpine, "Dickens and Conolly: An Embarrassed Editor's Disclaimer," *TLS*, August 11, 1961, pp. 534-535.
42. "The Treatment of the Insane," *Household Words*, June 5, 1852, p. 272. Quoted by Richard A. Hunter and Ida Macalpine in their introduction to John Conolly's 1830 book, *An Inquiry Concerning the Indications of Insanity: With Suggestions for the Better Protection and Care of the Insane* (London: Dawsons, 1964), p. 34.
43. *Indications of Insanity*, pp. 29-30.
44. April 8, 1854, pp. 197-200. Dickens and Wills wrote the first essay on "Idiots" in the June 4, 1853 issue; Harriet Martineau wrote "Idiots Again." Dickens' sustained interest, however, is in no way lessened because he delegated the subject to another writer.
45. Quoted by Hunter and Macalpine, *Indications of Insanity*, p. 34. Before Anne Lohrli's index to *Household Words*, there was a tendency to attribute to Dickens all that appeared in his magazine. "The Treatment of the Insane," in fact, was written by Henry Morley as was "The Cure of Sick Minds" in 1858. Again, this does not necessarily lessen the Dickens connection to these ideas. For a discussion of the authorship of articles on insanity appearing in *Household Words*, see Lohrli's biographical notes on Richard Oliver: *Household Words; a Weekly Journal 1850-1859* (Toronto: University of Toronto Press), pp. 388-389.

46. T. Wemyss Reid, *The Life, Letters, and Friendships of Richard Monckton Milnes, First Lord Houghton* (New York: Cassell Publishing Co., 1891), I, 463.
47. *Ibid.*, I, 17.
48. *Ibid.*, I, 10-17 for an extended account of the relationship between the elder Perceval and Milnes.
49. Already cited.
50. This booklet, "A Curious Dance," was privately printed by St. Luke's Hospital in 1860, and is in the New York Public Library Rare Books Room.
51. *Letters*, p. 29.
52. K. Jones, p. 156.
53. *An Address on the Laws of Lunacy: Especially as They Affect the Lunatic Wards of Chancery, for the Consideration of the Legislature* (London: Charles and Tiver, 1858). Anonymous author [Senex] protests against being a Ward of Chancery, p. 3.
54. *Ibid.*, p. 4.
55. *Ibid.*, p. 6.
56. *Ibid.*, pp. 5-6.
57. August 28, p. 8.
58. *Works*, VIII, 144.
59. Michael Kotzin, *Dickens and the Fairy Tale* (Bowling Green, Ohio: Bowling Green State University Popular Press, 1972), p. 51 and *passim*; Harry Stone, "Fire, Hand, and Gate: Dickens' *Great Expectations*," *Kenyon Review*, 24 (1962), 662-691 (the novel as an inverted *Cinderella*). In *Dickens and the Invisible World: Fairy Tales, Fantasy, and Novel-Making* (Bloomington: Indiana University Press, 1979), Stone devotes an important chapter to the significant quarrel between Dickens and Cruikshank. In *Victorian Conventions*, Reed also notes the importance of *Cinderella* in *Great Expectations*, but his argument that "Dickens means to convert the fable to Christian purpose" (p.30) rather puts the novelist in Cruikshank's camp. It is noteworthy that *Great Expectations* was the novel that followed *The Woman in White* as serial in *All the Year Round*. That both books should draw heavily on the Cinderella story suggests a possibly mutual awareness. For further connections between the two novels, see Martin Meisel, "Miss Havisham Brought to Book," *PMLA*, 81 (1966), 278-285.
60. *Dickens and the Invisible World*, p. 59.
61. *Ibid.*, p. 58.
62. Charles Dickens to W. H. Wills, July 27, 1853, Berg MS.
63. Robinson, *Wilkie Collins*, p. 189.
64. George Cruikshank, "To the Public," in *Cinderella* (London: David Bogue, 1854), p. 31.
65. Antti Aarne, *The Types of the Folktale: a Classification and Bibliography*. Translated and enlarged by Stith Thompson (Helsinki: Suomalainen Tiedeakatemia, 1961), pp. 175-177.
66. There are two biographical elements that should be considered in ex-

amining Collins's being influenced by *Cinderella*. First is Collins's own pride in his particularly small feet. Davis, for example, notes that Collins "had tiny hands which he took care to keep soft and white, and feet so small that they would slip about inside a woman's shoe," *Life of Wilkie Collins*, p. 53. Ashley relates that "Wilkie's feet were so small and delicately shaped that one night when he arrived at a friend's for dinner soaked to the skin, no shoes, not even the women's, could be found small enough to fit him," *Wilkie Collins*, p. 24. Then there is the often-quoted account by Millais that one night, when he was accompanied by Collins after a party, they heard a cry of a woman in distress. The iron gate of a nearby villa opened, "and from it came the figure of a young and very beautiful woman dressed in flowing white robes that shone in the moonlight." Collins is re-ported to have run after her, determined to find out who she was. There is an arresting parallel here between Collins and the prince de-termined to discover the identity of the beautiful woman (Cinderel-la) who flees the ball just before midnight so that he must make a house-to-house search with her lost slipper to find her. It is difficult to know where fact and fiction diverge in this supposed episode in Collins's life (see Sucksmith's notes, pp. 604–605).

67.   This is Robert P. Ashley's summary in "Wilkie Collins' First Short Story," *More Books: The Bulletin of the Boston Public Library*, 23 (1948), 105.

68.   See, for example, Phyllis Ralph, "Fairy-Tale Heroines in Nineteenth-Century English Fiction," *Folklore Forum*, 11 (1978), 124-139.

69.   In the context of the Cinderella influence on Collins, Fosco and his pet mice become a parody of the coachman who takes Cinderella to the ball.

70.   The interested reader can begin with Stanley Rosenman, "Cinder-ella: Family Pathology," *American Imago*, 35 (1978), 375-396 and follow the author's notes and bibliography.

71.   (New York: Alfred A. Knopf, 1976), p. 68.

72.   (New York: John Wiley and Sons, 1972), pp. 25, 28.

73.   *Ibid.*, p. 28.

74.   *Ibid.*

75.   See my essay, "Fathering and *The British Mother's Magazine*, 1854–1864," *Victorian Periodicals Review*, 13 (1980), 10-16. This essay is the result of the initial work I did on British psychology dur-ing the time that Collins wrote *The Woman in White*.

76.   Masterson, p. 75.

77.   "The Counterworld of Victorian Fiction," p. 352.

78.   Masterson, p. 28.

79.   *Ibid.*, p. 31.

80.   *Ibid.*, p. 17.

81.   *Ibid.*, p. 28.

82.   *Ibid.*, p. 24.

83.   It is also noteworthy that Collins, in focusing on the relationship of Mrs. Catherick to her daughter Anne as a source of the latter's ill-

ness, has written a Mother-Daughter novel in an age famous for its depictions of Fathers and Sons.

84. "On the Education of Children Predisposed to Insanity," 1 (1848), 493. In her book on *Mothers of England: Their Influence and Responsibility* (New York: D. Appleton & Co., 1844), Mrs. Ellis describes childhood melancholy as something mothers should watch carefully, and it is clear from her discussion that the reasons for this condition will not always be apparent. She also views what now would be termed depression in children as a terrible affliction (p. 90).

85. The scope of this essay has caused me to seek help from divergent sources. I would like to thank Drs. Eric T. Carlson, Helen E. Daniells, and Jacques Queen of The New York Hospital–Cornell Medical College for the aid I received from discussions with them. Dr. Carlson also made it easier for me to conduct research in England. Some of the material in the essay was presented on two occasions at the Research Seminars of the History of Psychiatry section of New York Hospital–Cornell Medical College. I also would like to thank Gloria and Fred Kaplan for their consistent interest in and support of this project.

Introduction to *The Novel on Blue Paper*

Penelope Fitzgerald, editor

The novel which William Morris began to write early in 1872 is unfinished and unpublished and also untitled. I have called it *The Novel on Blue Paper* because it was written on lined blue foolscap, and Morris preferred to call things what they were.

The only first-hand information we have about it is a letter which Morris wrote to Louie Baldwin[1] on the 12th of June, 1872.

> Dear Louie,
> Herewith I send by book-post my abortive novel: it is just a specimen of how not to do it, and there is no more to be said thereof: 'tis nothing but landscape and sentiment: which thing won't do. Since you wish to read it, I am sorry 'tis such a rough copy, which roughness sufficiently indicates my impatience at having to deal with prose. The separate parcel, paged 1 to 6, was a desperate dash at the middle of the story to try to give it life when I felt it failing: it begins with the letter of the elder brother to the younger on getting *his* letter telling how he was going to bid for the girl in marriage. I found it in the envelope in which I had sent it to Georgie to see if she could give me any hope: she gave me none, and I have never looked at it since. So there's an end of my novel-writing, I fancy, unless the world turns topsides under some day. Health and merry days to you, and believe me to be
>
> Your affectionate friend,
>
> William Morris.

The tone of gruff modesty, and in particular the catch phrase from Dickens,[2] is habitual to Morris and can be taken for what it is worth. In spite of the disapproval of Georgiana Burne-Jones, whose opinion he valued at the time above all others, he did not destroy his MS, but kept it; and after what was presumably further discouragement from Louie, he kept it still. He must have been aware, too, why he had been given no hope. Mackail[3] tells us that Morris "had all the instinct of a born man of letters for laying himself open in his books, and having no concealment from the widest circle of all," and (of the Prologues to *The Earthly Paradise*) that there is "an autobiography so delicate and so outspoken that it must needs be left to speak for itself." That, we have to conclude, was the trouble with the novel on blue paper; it did speak for itself, but much too plainly.

The background of the novel—the "landscape"—is the Upper Thames valley, the watermeadows, streams and villages round about Kelmscott[4] on the borders of Oxfordshire and Gloucestershire. Morris had gone down to inspect Kelmscott Manor House in May 1871, and in June he entered into a joint tenancy of the old house with Rossetti at £60 a year. The grey gables, flagged path, enclosed garden cram-full of flowers, lime and elm trees "populous with rooks," white-panelled parlour, are all recognisably described in this novel, although Morris when he wrote it had never spent a summer there. It was the house he loved "with a reasonable love, I think." Rossetti, not a countryman, had hoped that the place would be good for his nerves. But the seclusion, despite the constant presence of Jane Morris, and his intimacy with her, did his nerves little good. Morris had a business to run and was obliged to be in London a good deal. An inevitable tension arose among the three of them which has been so often and so painfully traced by biographers. To Morris it was "this failure of mine." Mackail, cautiously describing the subject of the novel as "the love of two brothers for the same woman," evidently saw no farther into it than the failure. Once, however, when I was trying to explain the situation, and its projection as myth, to a number of overseas students, one of them asked a question which I have never seen in any biography: "Why then did Morris not strike Rossetti?"

I hope to show that this question is very relevant to the novel on blue paper. Certainly Morris was not "above," or indifferent to, his loss. It is a mistake to refer his much later opinions, as reported by Shaw, or Wilfrid Scawen Blunt, or Luke Ionides, or as expressed in *News from Nowhere*, to his "restless heart" of 1868–73.[5] Which of us would like to be judged, at thirty-nine, by our frame of mind at the age of fifty-seven? Morris himself knew this well enough. "At the age of more than thirty years," he wrote in *Killian of the Closes* (1895) "men are more apt to desire what they have not than they that be younger or older."

And Morris's attitude toward his wife's infidelity may have been affected by the profoundly unsettling behaviour of his greatest friend, Edward Burne-Jones. Burne-Jones had been married since 1860 to Georgie, the charming, tiny and indomitable daughter of a Methodist minister. The Neds had started out in lodgings with £30 between them, and their happy and stable marriage, together with Burne-Jones's designs for the Firm, were part of the very earth out of which Morris's life and work took growth. But in 1867 the quiet Ned suddenly claimed, much more openly than Rossetti, the freedom to love unchecked. He had been totally captivated by a tempestuous member of the Greek community in London, Mary Zambaco.[6] Of this unpredictable young woman, he drew the loveliest by far of his pencil portraits; "I believed it to be all my future life," he told Rossetti. The affair came and went and came again, to the fury of Ionides, and the sympathetic interest of the Greek women. It lingered on, indeed, until 1873. Morris, stalwart, stood by his friend, but the effect of this new confounding of love and loyalty, on top of his own "failure," must have been hard to master; the effect of Mary herself can be guessed at, perhaps, from the strange intrusion of one of the characters, Eleanor, into the novel on blue paper.

Meanwhile, Georgie was left to manage her life and her two children as best she could. In his own loneliness and bewilderment Morris felt deeply for hers, and at this time he was apparently in love with her, or at least, he turned to her for affection; for gratification of the need to share thoughts and feelings; for the pleasure of believing himself understood.

Some of his drafts and manuscript poems of 1865–70[7] show this without disguise, though always with a chivalrous anxiety. He must not intrude; he thanks her because she "does not deem my service sin." A pencil note on one draft reads "we two are in the same box and need conceal nothing—don't cast me away—scold me but pardon me." He is "late made wise" to his own feelings, and can only trust that time will transform them into the friendship that will bring him peace. Meanwhile the dignity and sincerity with which she is bearing "the burden of thy grief and wrong" is enough, in itself, to check him.

> . . . nor joy nor grief nor fear
> Silence my love; but those grey eyes and clear
> Truer than truth pierce though my weal and woe . . .

Georgie in fact, was steadfast to her marriage, and strong enough to wait. "I know one thing," she wrote to her friend Rosalind Howard, "and that is that there is love enough between Edward and me to last out a long life if it is given us."

In the meantime, what was Morris's outward response to the assault on his emotions? Work, as always, was his "faithful daily companion." After returning from Iceland in September 1871 he illuminated the *Rubaiyhat* of Omar Khayyam, designed the Larkspur wallpaper, began his novel, and fiddled about in "a maze of rewriting and despondency" with his elaborate masque, *Love Is Enough*. But the moral of *Love Is Enough*, (as Shaw complained), is not that love is enough. Pharamond, coming back from his quest for an ideal woman to find that his kingdom has been usurped by a stronger man, accepts that frustration and loss are worthy—"though the world be a-waning"—to be called a victory in the name of love. But Morris knew, as Shaw knew, that this is nonsense. The victory, melancholy as it is, is for self-control. Renunciation is achieved through the will and strengthens the will, not the emotions. And this, with a far more positive hero than poor Pharamond, is, I believe, the real subject of the novel on blue paper.

Morris had been delicate as a child; but as soon as he grew into his full strength, he was subject to fits of violent rage, possibly epileptic in origin. To what extent these were hereditary, it is impossible to say. When Morris was eleven he was sent as a boarder to his school at Woodford, although it was only a few hundred yards away from his home. What seems strange in his later life is the attitude of his close friends, who seem to have watched as a kind of entertainment his frenzied outbursts, followed by the struggle to control himself and a rapid childlike repentance. At times he would beat himself about the head in self-punishment. "He has been known to drive his head against a wall," Mackail wrote, "so as to make a deep dent in the plaster, and bite almost through the woodwork of a windowframe." Yet with the exception of the day when he hurled a fifteenth century folio at one of his workmen, missing him, but breaking a door panel, there is no record of his making a physical attack on anyone. To return to the student's question, it is possible that Morris did not strike anybody, least of all the ailing Rossetti, because he waged almost to the end of his life a battle of self-control; though his acceptance of Jane Morris's infidelity, repeated in later years with Wilfred Scawen Blunt, also has to be taken as a fact an itself, subject to some other psychological explanation.

The recognition of restraint as an absolute duty may be referred back to the tutor who prepared Morris, when he was seventeen years old, for his entrance to Oxford. This tutor, the Rev. F. B. Guy, was one of the faithful remnant of the Oxford Movement, who had survived Newman's conversion, or desertion, to Rome. Morris believed at this time that he was going to enter the Church, and probably learned from Guy the Movement's insistence on sacrifice and self-correction, even in the smallest things. The Tractarians saw the religious impulse not as a vague emotion, but as a silent discipline growing from the exercise of the will. All that we ought to ask, Keble had said, is room to deny ourselves. And Morris, willingly enlisted in a struggle which he was never to win, persisted in it long after he had parted from orthodox Christianity. At the age of twenty-three he concluded that he must not expect enjoyment from life—"I have no right to it at all events—love and work, these two things only." In 1872, when love had betrayed or rejected him, he wrote: "O how I long to keep the world from narrowing on me, and to look at things bigly and kindly!"[8]

The most telling expression of Keble's doctrines in fiction was Charlotte M. Yonge's *Heir of Redclyffe* (1853). It was said to be the novel most in demand by the officers wounded in the Crimean War, and it was the first book greatly to influence Morris. Here he read the family story of a tragic inheritance. Guy, the Heir, has the ferocious temper of his Morville ancestors, and has to struggle as best he can with "the curse of sin and death." All his "animal spirits," all his great capacity for happiness is overshadowed by the temptation to anger, and he is driven to strange extremes, cutting up pencils, biting his lips till the blood runs down, and refusing, in obedience to a vow, even to watch a single game of billiards. "Resistance should be from within." He sees his whole life as "failing and resolving and failing again." Phillip, on the other hand, the high-minded young officer, provokes the Heir and leads him, from the best possible motives, into temptation. Here the novel sets out to show the evil that good can do, and when Guy dies to save him from fever, Philip is left to suffer for ever "the penitence of the saints."

The Heir of Redclyffe, as an exemplary text, asks for a kind of inner or even secret knowledge from its readers. From page to page we are reminded of Kenelm Digby's *Broadstone of Honour*, which held up the example of mediaeval chivalry to Young England. That is why Guy's nearest railway station is called Broadstone. Again, Guy and his sweetheart Amy are, in a sense, acting out the story of *Sintram*[10] (the book which Newman would only read when he was quite alone.) Sintram, tempted by the world, the flesh and the devil, and burdened by his father's crime, has to toil upward through the snows to reach Verena, his saintly mother. That is why the widowed Amy calls her child Verena. And *Sintram* itself makes mysterious reference to its frontispiece, a woodcut version of Dürer's engraving *The Knight, Death and the Devil*, over which Morris and Burne-Jones, as students, had "pored for hours."[11]

These potent images remained with Morris, even though in *The Earthly Paradise* he had unlocked half the world's tale-hoard. In the second of his late romances, for example, *The Well at the World's End* (1892–3), Sintram's evil dwarf reappears. In 1872, the time of his greatest emotional test and stress, he set to work on this novel which is a temptation story, although the hero must proceed simply on his own resolution, without prayer, without divine grace, without the saving hand of the loved woman. And most unexpectedly, Morris returned from his dream-world, the "nameless cities in a distant sea," to place the story in a solid English parsonage, or, to be more accurate, in Elm House, Walthamstow, the first home that he could remember.

Morris opens his tale with the sins of the father. One of those impulses which "sometimes touch dull or dulled natures"—a distinction which Morris was always careful to make—arouses the train of memory in Parson Risley. Eleanor's letters follow. The parson's sin is not that he was Eleanor's lover. This is shown clearly enough later in Mrs. Mason's reproach: "Mr Risley, if my husband likes to make love to every girl in the village he has a full right to it if I let him"—a remark which blends well with the "sweet-smelling abundant garden" and the fertile melon beds. Risley's guilt then, is not a matter of sexuality but a denial of it, firstly through cold cowardice in rejecting a woman "like the women in poetry, such people as I had never expected to meet," and secondly through his vile temper. These two aspects of his nature are his legacy to his sons.

The Parsonage, as has been said, recalls the house in Walthamstow where Morris was born, and in the two boys, John and Arthur, Morris represents the opposing sides, as he understood them, of his own character. In some ways the brothers are alike or even identical. Both are romantically imaginative and given to dreaming their lives into "tales going on," both are fond of fishing (not a trivial matter to Morris), both, of course, love Clara, both dislike their father and both resemble him. "As to the looks of the lads by the way it would rather have puzzled anyone who had seen them to say why the little doctor should have said that either was not like his father; some strange undercurrent of thought must have drawn it out of him, for they were obviously both very much like him." John, however, is manly, open, friendly, bird-and-weather-noticing; Arthur is a book-worm, and sickly. ("Love of ease, dreaminess, sloth, sloppy good-nature," Morris said, "are what I chiefly accuse myself of.")[12] Arthur is "versed in archaeological lore," while John is in touch with earth and water—"with a great sigh of enjoyment he seemed to gather the bliss of memory of many & many a summer noon into this one"—and yet, perversely, Arthur is to be the farmer and John the businessman. From the guilty father John inherits anger, Arthur cowardice. John's loss of temper alarms Arthur; "are you in a rage with me? Why do you know, your voice got something like father's in a rage." But just as Parson Risley fails to answer Eleanor's letter, so Arthur conceals John's.

John's struggle for self-control is marked by very small incidents. Resistance, as the Heir of Redclyffe recognizes, must be from within. At the beginning of the day's outing, when Clara greets Arthur tenderly, "they did not notice that J turned away to the horses head." At Ruddywell Court, when Arthur begins to do the talking and Clara is entranced, John "got rather silent." On the return to the farm, when Clara kisses Arthur, John is left "whistling in sturdy resolution to keep his heart up, and rating himself for a feeling of discomfort and wrong." When she is poised for a few moments between the two of them in the rocking boat, but at length sits down by Arthur, so that both of them are facing the golden sunset to which John's back is now turned, he pulls at the oars "sturdily," exerting his strength for them in silence. These small everyday victories of the will lead up to a disastrous failure, the furious and destructive letter, and the despairing attempt to redeem it by a postscript—"Tell Clara I wrote kindly to you."

Arthur, on the other hand, the "saint" of the novel, is shown indulging himself in the sweetness of his dreams and the horror of his nightmares; and even when he becomes the centre of consciousness, this self-indulgence is obvious. Clara's love for him is founded, in the Chaucerian mode, on pity. When he reads John's letter, he is afraid. He lies to Clara, who against her better judgement accepts the lie. Arthur is, in fact, almost without will-power, while John, in his blundering way understands keenly the importance of the will. "Nobody does anything," he tells Mrs. Mason, "except because he likes it: I mean to say even people who have given up most to please other people; but then theyre all the better people to be pleased by what's good rather than by what is bad." And he has "a feeling not very pleasant of not being listened to."

In 1872 Samuel Butler published *Erewhon*, Hardy, *Under the Greenwood Tree*, and George Eliot, *Middlemarch*. All of these seem very far removed from the unfinished tale-telling on blue paper. But when Morris told Louie Baldwin that he was impatient at having to deal with prose, he underrated the poetry of his story. This lies in the interrelationship of the three journeys—the passage of a summer's day, the first walk upstream to the paradise of the farm, and the crucial turning-point of John's adolescence. The June prologue of *The Earthly Paradise* opens, (also in the meadows of the Upper Thames):

> O June, O June, that we desired so,
> Wilt thou not make us happy on this day?
> Across the river thy soft breezes blow
> Sweet with the scent of beanfields far away,
> Above our heads rustle the aspens grey,
> Calm is the sky with harmless clouds beset,
> No thought of storm the morning vexes yet.

This is the exact poise of the novel, between past darkness, present happiness (John when he first goes to Leaser is "happier than he was last year") and the coming unknown discontent. And so John, at seventeen, stands on the confines of his own home, with

> the expectant longing for something sweet to come heightened by rather than chastened by the mingled fear of something as vague as the hope, that fills our hearts so full in us at whiles, killing all commonplace there, making us feel as if we were on the threshold of a new world, one step over which if we could only make it would put life within our grasp—what is it? Some reflex of the love and death going on throughout the world, suddenly touching those who are ignorant as yet of the one, and have not learned to believe in the other.

Mackail quotes this passage in part, but dismisses the novel as "certainly the most singular of his writings." Jane Morris's comment on the *Life*, however is interesting: "You see, Mackail is not an artist in feeling, and therefore cannot be sympathetic while writing the life of such a man."[13]

NOTES

1. Louisa Baldwin (1845–1925) was the youngest surviving child of the Methodist minister, George Macdonald, and the sister of Georgiana Burne-Jones. On her eleventh birthday she was taken as a treat to meet Rossetti, and became a pet of the whole circle. Although her marriage to the manufacturer Alfred Baldwin was a happy one, Louie's health failed and she became a chronic invalid.
2. *Little Dorrit*, Book 1, chap 10. The Circumlocution Office "was beforehand with all the public departments in the art of perceiving HOW NOT TO DO IT."

3.   J. W. Mackail, O.M. (1859–1945) married Margaret, the Burne-Jones's daughter, and was commissioned to write his classic *The Life of William Morris* (2 vols. [London: Longmans, 1899]) by Burne-Jones himself. Mackail's letters and unpublished notes show that he was obliged to exercise a great deal of tact and to omit some episodes altogether.

4.   Historically speaking, the village should be spelled Kelmscot and the house Kelmscott, but the villagers themselves seem to have given up the distinction.

5.   "Morris was a complete fatalist in his attitude towards the conduct of . . . all human beings where sex was concerned." (Bernard Shaw, *Morris As I Knew Him,* 1936). "Women did not seem to count with him." (Luke Ionides, *Memories,* 1925). "He was the only man I ever came in contact with who seemed absolutely independent of sex considerations." (W. S. Blunt, British Library MS. Additional 45350.) Blunt did not know him well until 1899.

6.   The head of the Greek community in Victorian London was Constantine Ionides, "the Thunderer," a wealthy stockbroker and a generous patron of the arts. Mary Zambaco was a granddaughter of the House of Ionides, a wealthy beauty with "glorious red hair and almost phosphorescent white skin," who had left her husband in Paris in 1866 and come to London. She was also a talented sculptress, with a temperament which Burne-Jones described as "like hurricanes and tempests and billows . . . only it didn't do in English suburban surroundings." In 1868 he made his first attempt to break with her; she threatened to throw herself into the Regent's Canal. In 1869 he painted her as Phyllis pleading with Demophöon, with the epigraph *Dic mihi quod feci? nisi non sapienter amavi* (tell me what I have done, except to love unwisely). Rossetti was in their confidence, writing in 1869 to Jane Morris that Mary had become more beautiful "with all her love and trouble . . . but rainy walks and constant journeys are I fear beginning to break up her health."

7.   British Library MS. Additional 45298. Some of these poems were included, in variant forms, by May Morris in the *Collected Works* volume XXIV and volume I of the supplementary volumes.

8.   Letter to Aglaia Coronio, 25 November 1972.

9.   Sir Kenelm Digby, *The Broadstone of Honour; or The True Sense and Practices of Chivalry,* 1846.

10.   H. de la Motte Fouqué, *The Seasons: Four Romances from the German* (English trans: 1843). *Sintram and his Companions* is the winter romance.

11.   Guy stands looking at the woodcut "as it were a dream," but Philip thinks it "hardly safe for so excitable a mind to dwell much on the world of fiction." *The Heir of Redclyffe,* chap. 5.

12.   Mackail, II, 158.

13.   Letter to W. S. Blunt, May 6, 1899. Fitzwilliam Museum Library.

Our story begins in a village not so very far from London,
yet in a country out of the track of the busiest
people, and at any rate for whatsoever reason,
with a remote and unchanging air about
it, that put it beyond dulness, and made the
common place people, who wore away their monotonous
and thoughtless lives there, seem, to the dreamy wanderer through them as if they must
deal with a different code of right and wrong,
different ways of hope and fear and pleasure and
pain. It was an old village of middling size
with no squire's house in it or near it, because
a very great lords house some 5 miles off swallowed
up almost all the land thereabout: the rectory
on the other hand was rich and the rector served
for squire in the village of Ormstead, which
nearly on the borders of a
rich grazing country and a strange open
waste, sometimes wooded & sometimes bare,
called Scolton Chase. Old as the village street
was it looked still older, for, in that country of
good building-stone, people kept on building
all decent houses with little mullioned windows
a good hundred years later than in most
parts of England, and the houses here were
mostly built of this brown stone with
stone slate roofs; a queen little old red-brick house
with stiff iron railings and two yards of garden
along its front had a brass plate on the door
and held the doctor; another red brick
house, as small and not lacking the railings
& garden, but new, and with a blue slate roof,
had a general shop below it, and rooms where

The Novel on Blue Paper

William Morris

Our story begins in a village not so very far from London, yet in a ~~place~~ country out of the tracks of the busiest people, and at any rate for whatsoever reason with a remote and unchanging air about it, that put it beyond dulness, and made the commonplace people, who ~~lived~~ wore away their monotonous and thoughtless lives there seem to the dreamy wanderer through the streets as if they must deal with a different code of right and wrong, different ways of hope and fear and pleasure and pain than him. It was an old village of middling size, with no squire's house in it or [very] near it, because a very great lords ~~estate~~ house some 5 miles off swallowed up all the land thereabout: the rectory on the other hand was rich and the rector served for squire in this village of Olmstead, [and to his house we must go; where we have said, for the rest, that this village of Olmstead] which stood [nearly] on the borders of rich grazing country and a strange open waste, sometimes wooded & sometimes bare,

---

A Note on the Text

This text exists only as British Library MS. Additional 45328—fifty-three sheets of lined blue foolscap with a Britannia watermark.

Morris's lineation and pagination have not been retained, although extra space has been added to indicate original page breaks. All of the words in square brackets were deleted by Morris; they have been retained where it is necessary to complete a sentence. The words which have been struck through also were deleted by Morris, but they only intrude on an otherwise complete sentence. This manuscript is printed in this manner to enable the narrative to proceed without unnecessary interruption and to make clear, at the same time, what Morris cancelled, even in those places where, in this unfinished work, he never got round to filling in the gaps the cancellation had created.   —Ed.

the curate lodged above : another, originally ~~the~~ made of
two of the ordinary houses knocked into one
had been taken possession of by a retired ~~ship~~
skipper, who ~~spent had long~~ spent his days
in building rockwork about the garden, fowl-
houses and stables like castles, in wood & plaster, and an arbour with a
tin dome to it. the other houses were all of
one type only bigger or smaller, differing in being and in some of
them having little gardens in front which most
lacked, the little white haired freckled children
building their mud-pies right up against the
brown stone walls of them: the village inn
was not among the biggest; it stood back a
little from the road, a big pollard elm in
front of the door with a circular bench round
its roots, and thrust out the sign halfway up its
bole ~~was the sign~~, from where one could still dimly
see the two white harts and the bugle of the
Scotton arms. ~~Near the end of~~ Near its end the long street
was cut across by a road ~~near its end~~, the
northern arm of ~~ro~~ it: led up through rising
ground to the Chase, the southern into the
heart of the ~~fair rising country~~ undulating hedged meadow
land; ~~broken here & there by~~ just down
this road lay the Rectory first, & then the
Church : the ~~first~~ Rectory a handsome old stone
house with a ~~bi, ~~ ~~walled~~ garden whose
long high wall ran alongside the road,
~~& it~~ and had a square turret-like pleasure arbour
at the corner of it, a common fashion there
abouts : the church and churchyard ended
the village on that side : and the ground sloped
quickly away from them into ~~deep rich m~~
~~&~~ fields, heavily hedged as aforesaid ;

called Scolton Chase. Old as the village street was it looked still
older, for, in that country of good buildingstone, people kept on
building all decent houses with little mullioned windows a good
hundred years later than in most parts of England,[1] and the houses
here were mostly built of this brown stone with [grey] stone slate
roofs; a queer little old red-brick house with stiff iron railings and
two yards of garden along its front had a brass plate on the door
and held the doctor; no a red another red brick house, as small and
not lacking the railings and garden, but new, and with a blue slate
roof, had a general shop below [it], and rooms where

the curate lodged above; another, originally made of two of the ordinary houses knocked into one had been taken possession of by a
retired [ship's] skipper, who spent had had long spent his days in
building rockwork about the garden, fowl-houses and statues like
castles in wood and plaster, and an arbour with a dome to it. The
other houses were all of one type, only differing in being bigger or
smaller, and in some of them having little gardens in front which
most lacked, the little white haired freckled children building their
mud-pies right up against the brown stone walls of them: the village
inn was not among the biggest; it stood back a little from the road, a
big pollard elm in front of the door with a circular bench round its
roots, and the sign thrust out from halfway up its bole [was the
sign], where one could still dimly see the two white harts and the
bugle of the Scolton arms. Near the end of Near its end the long
street was cut across by a road near its end the northern arm of wh:
led up through rising ground to the Chase, the southern into the
heart of the hedged grazing country undulating hedged meadow
land; broken here and there by just down this road lay the Rectory
first, & then the Church: the first Rectory a handsome old stone
house with a [big great walled] garden whose long high wall ran
alongside the road, with and had a square turret-like pleasure arbour at the corner of it, a common fashion thereabouts: the church
and churchyard ended the village on that side: and the ground
sloped quickly away from them into [deep rich] fields, heavily
hedged as aforesaid;

[and just about the village mostly grassgrown; but sprinkled about]
Looking from the crazy paling of the churchyard one might see the
rich countryside, not very far indeed for it soon swelled up into a
hedged slope again, a patchwork at some times of the year of
ploughed field & grass mead, but this June tide all green, the just

and just about the village mostly of grass grew, but sprinkled about. Looking from the crazy paling of the churchyard one might see the rich countryside, not very far winded for it soon swelled up into a hedged slope again a patchwork at some times of the year of ploughed field & grass mead, but this June tide all green, the just cleared hay fields and shewing bright among the beans and corn: between the first slope & the church had been a battle once: the whole countryside had been much fought over in the parliamentary wars; and in the time when Oxford was Charles' head quarters a regiment of royalist horse surprised a band of roundhead levies marching toward Reading, and beat them into rout after a fierce skirmish; many men fell in the village street itself, and in the parish register was record of eighteen troopers buried on the north side of the church. nearer to the river again the partizans of the luckless Richard the second had had one of their last scatterings, but the place of this was grown dim by this time; on the north side of the village history went back with a great leap, for on the borders of the chase were 3 barrows and the farmhouse they stood by had kept at any rate the popular idea of what they were in its name of Danesko Hall. The church itself was one of those architectural oddities of wh: there are so many in England: the chancel high walled, rich with carving, a very lantern of traceried windows, and with a low roof covered with cleared hay fil field, [and] shewing bright among the beans and corn: between the first slope and the church had been a battle once:[2] the whole countryside had been much fought over in the parliamentary wars; and in the time when Oxford was Charles' headquarters a regiment of royalist horse surprised a band of round head levies [there] marching towards Reading, and beat them into rout after a fierce skimish; many men fell in the village street itself, and in the parish register was record of eighteen troopers buried on the north side of the church. Nearer the river again the partizans of the luckless Richard the Second had had one of their last scatterings, but the place of this was grown dim by this time; on the ~~other~~ north side of the village history went back with a great leap, for on the borders of the Chase were 3 barrows and the [meadow] farmhouse they stood by had kept at any rate the popular idea of what they were in the name of Danesho Hall. The Church itself was one of those architectural oddities of wh: there are so many in England: the Chancel high walled, rich with carving, a very lantern of traceried windows, and with a low roof covered with

lead: the nave barnlike with low aisle walls and a high roof patched in all sorts of ways and ruinous enough; this latter again nearly swallowed up the low square tower, in wh: there was scarcely a stone awry, and the tangled carving of whose Norman door was sharp and clear still; inside there were remnants of painted skreen work struggling among ricketty deal pews, the rich farmers in ~~lack~~ default of squire's pews ~~eush~~ cushioned and red curtained; this in the nave, then the now bare magnificence of the chancel beyond, so startling, so little cared for; [the] rich chantry by the side of it whose alabaster images ~~were~~ had been scored all over with initials of Bumkin's sweethearts through generations of slumbrous sermons; and in the chancel itself [half] wasted and broken remains of ~~the parap~~ necessities of the old worship; half the altar stones built into the pavement, figures in stained glass without heads or turned upside down, painted tiles in the pavement, a brass or two, a half dozen of hatchments on the walls; and amidst it all blocking up a wind: bay, the tomb of a member of the rector's family; it was a family living, who some 50 years ago had been a professed dilettante and a travelled man, and had enlightened his native place with an Italian work of art in memory of his wife, and himself when he should come to die; this was a marvel for miles around; there was a death and his dart in it and the rector on his knees, and his wife of her own accord opening lead: the nave barn like with low aisle walls and a high roof patched in all sorts of ways and ruinous enough; this latter again nearly swallowed up the low square tower, in wh: there was scarcely a stone away, and the tangled carving of whose Norman door was sharp and clear still: inside there were remnants of painted screen work struggling among rickety deal pews, the rich farmers in default of squire's pew carpetted cushioned and red curtained; this in the nave, then the magnificence of the chancel beyond so startling, so little cared for; the rich chantry by the side of it whose alabaster images had been scored all over with initials of Bumkin's sweethearts through generations of slumbrous sermons; and in the chancel itself wasted or broken remains of the necessities of the old worship; the altar stone built into the pavement, figures in stained glass without heads or turned upside down, painted tiles in the pavement, a brass or two, a half dozen of hatchments on the walls; and amidst it all, blocking up a window but, the tomb of a member of the rector's family; it was a family living, who some 50 years ago had been a professed dilletante and a travelled man, and had enlightened his native place with an Italian work of art in memory of his wife, and himself when he should come to die: this was a marvel for miles around; there was a death and his dart in it and the rector on his knees, and his wife of her own accord opening

death's door in the towering marble rockwork ~~and an~~ amidst which
an angel held a scroll of fiat Voluntas tua and the date, simpering
meantime on a stained glass bishop in the opposite window ~~whose
head held~~ who for all return grinned queerly on him from his aureoled head held in his hand. The church was wretchedly kept enough
amidst all these signs of former wealth, and was rather a place for
an antiquary than for a seeker after the picturesque; and the village
again full of architectural and historical interest as it was, would
not have been called pretty or charming by people; and certainly I
should not have called it cheerful though there was nothing squalid
about it: the general absence of gardens toward the street, the
brown walls & brown road meeting, the brown-faced heavily-
walking [bent] men, the brown-faced anxious looking women, the
silence of the world as it were among the many noises of this
summer afternoon, the landscape beyond so rich and so limited, no
big hill no wide river to lead ones thoughts or hopes along: was it a
place to crush passion or to soothe it, or rather to nurse and foster it
with brooding, with a sense of isolation and imprisonment?
I have told of the inside of the church, I will now do as much for the
rectory: there was little modern or gay in; inside its high wall you
came into a court with a drive round it and a grass plot in the middle, the stable on one side & the kitchen garden on the other; roses
enough trained on the wall

right up to the topmost windows old fashioned these were but not
the mediaeval ones of the poorer houses; a stone porch led into a big
white panelled hall, with unclerical enough matters for decoration
[a good deal consisting of foxes in fact: a stuffed fox with a hen in
his] not only with the hunting-field but with reminiscences of
travelled members of the the family the principal one being a stuffed
tiger in the corner, carefully dusted, but bald and shining in many
places now, whose death was the handiwork of the late rector, once
an [Indian] sepoy captain, who laid aside his sword to be inducted
into the family living. To him also were to be referred one or two Indian cabinets and a carved ivory junk[3] in the [long] low-ceilinged
square drawing room, and a carpet growing threadbare in the
[long] low-ceilinged long dining room once a pleasant room enough,
but dealt with unluckily by him of the monument [who had dab-
bled] so that it is now drab and bare with horsehair chairs and stiff
legged sideboard with a sarcophagus cellaret underneath it, and
with 4 vulgar portraits on the walls. There stood the present rector
now leaning against the fireplace, though there was nothing in the

death's door in the towering marble rock-work,
amidst which an angel held a scroll of fiat Voluntas tua
and the date, simpering meantime on a
stained glass bishop in the opposite window
whose too adulatory grimed queerly on him
from his aureoled head held in his hand.
The church was wretchedly kept enough amidst
all these signs of former wealth, and was
rather a place for an antiquary than for a
seeker after the picturesque; and the
village again full of architectural & historical
interest as it was, would not have been
called pretty or charming by people; and
certainly I should not have called it cheery
though there was nothing squalid about it,
the absence of gardens toward the street, the
brown walls & brown road meeting, the
brown faced men, the brown faced
anxious looking women, the silence of the
world as it were among the many noises
of this summer afternoon, the landscape beyond
so rich and so limited, no big hill no
wide river to lead our thoughts or hopes
along: was it a place to crush passion
or to soothe it, or rather to nurse and foster
it, with brooding, with a sense of isolation
and imprisonment?
I have told of the inside of the church, I will
now do as much for the rectory: there was
little modern or gay in; inside its high wall
you came into a court with a drive round
it and a grass plot in the middle the stable
on one side & the kitchen garden on the
other: roses enough trained on the wall

grate but pink & white strips of paper, and a little hard-bitten apple-cheeked old man visibly a doctor stood opposite to him with his hat in his hand ready to go: Well said this latter, he'll do now is beginning to eat like a trump: the rector grunted acquiescence pleasure

anything you will, and the Dr. looked at him rather hard for a time & then said What a d How different he is to you in looks I mean: [he's a clever lad was] not much like his mother was either: the rector didnt answer and the Dr. said again after a pause: he's a clever lad your son; I hope he mayn't turn out too clever and give us the slip. Which do you mean said the other, [rather] in a tone as if he repented his rudeness in not answering before, yet didn't wish the talk to last. Why Arthur of course werent we talking of him: no John is all right; though he's clever enough too; but sharp and full of sense—o he'll do—will die a rich man, I should say—the rector smiled faintly but said nothing, and the little Dr. smiled too as the pleasantest way of showing that he knew he was to go and bustled out of the room, leaving the usual Dr.'s injunctions behind him. When the rector had shut the hall door upon him, he turned—sauntered slowly into the drawing room and thence down through an open glass door down a high flight of stone steps and out into the old fashioned flower garden with its terrace and mulberry tree,[4] and straight cut flower borders, and the great row of full foliaged elms that cut it off from the fields without; he stopped presently in the yellow light of the sinking sun amid the sweet scent of the June flowers, and stared hard at the beauty before him, muttering she was right that day it was a dull place to bury oneself in. [Something] a pang compounded of the memory of hopes and fears, pleasures and pains of many past years shot through him as he spoke: one of those sparks of feeling

which sometimes touch dull or dulled natures for a moment: if they could only catch at them and grasp in them the thread that would lead them out of the wretched maze; for the scent of summer evening had somehow mingled with thoughts that the talk about his sons had begun in him and for that moment he remembered what he might have been rather than what he was; old aspirations old enthusiasms the kindling of what he thought true love—and the slaking of it—it was too bitter to let him muse long; he turned back again into the house, feeling that less of a prison than the sweet summer garden that led into the fields that lead into other fields that led he didn't care where—: he flung himself down into a chair and took a

right up to the topmost windows old fashioned
there were but not the mediæval looking ones
of the poorhouses; a stone porch led into
a big white panelled hall, with unclerical
enough matters for decoration ~~a good deal~~
~~consisting of foxes in fact: a stuffed fox with~~
~~a tail his~~ mostly with the hunting field,
but with reminiscences of travelled members
of the family the principal one being a
stuffed tiger in the corner, carefully dusted,
but bald and shining in many places now.
whose death was the handiwork of the late rector,
once an ~~Indian~~ Sepoy captain, who laid aside his
sword to be inducted into the family living.
to him also were to be referred one or two
Indian cabinets and a carved ivory chest
in the ~~long~~ low-ceilinged square drawing
room, and a carpet growing threadbare in
the ~~long~~ low ceilinged long dining room
once a pleasant room enough, but dealt
with unluckily by him of the monument
~~who had dabbled~~ so that it is now drab and
bare with horsehair chairs a stiff legged
sideboard with a sarcophagus cellaret underneath
neath it, and with 4 vulgar portraits on
the walls. There stood the present rector now
leaning against the fireplace. though there was
nothing in the grate but pink & white strips of
paper, and a little hard-bitten applecheeked
old man visibly a doctor stood opposite to him
with his hat in his hand ready to go: Well said
this latter, he'll do now is beginning to cub like
a trump: the rector granted acquiescence pleasure

stupid book of travels in his hand and didn't read it—sooth to say he did not look like a man likely to have pleasant thoughts: he was a handsome man too; liker to a captain of dragoons than a parson one would have said; tall and well-knit, with black hair, black eyebrows over fierce looking grey eyes, a straight well made nose, a well fashioned mouth and large chin & jaw; all the features cast in a fine mould—yet all spoilt; his brow knit in an ugly half scowl, his eyes with little expression in them but suppressed rage, his nose [grown] swelled and reddened, his mouth and chin grown coarse & lumpy—an unlovely face. People in general are not very quick to read character in a faces but the simplest people had found out that

Parson Risley was of no use to them in spite of his good looks; it must be said though that he had always in any case when it was possible acted with a reckless cruelty which in rougher times would perhaps have developed and won for him the reputation of an Ezzelin;[5] and though he had tempered this from time to time by giving great gifts, yet this man of over just forty with what seemed an easy life to live, dealing with no very important matters, without ambition as it seemed, without serious opposition, or without fear of having his position lessened, without anything much to grasp at, had managed to make himself both feared and hated in the limited society in which he moved—Yes—even as the [solemn] beautiful church was a grave and a ruin: the comely wellconditioned village [a dull prison], the fair sweet scented country side a sort of dull enchanted valley to be escaped from so was this handsome house and handsome man its owner the scene and actor of a tragedy without meaning without ending, a curse without a name, a lurking misery that could not be met and grappled with because its very existence had slain sight & memory & hope—that of pain itself that quickens those whom God will not have die while they seem to live. Parson Risley had taken the living of Ormslade[6] as a young man; [he was newly] married then, [when he had been there a year] and his wife bore him two sons at Ormslade and died a year after the birth of the 2nd, little regretted by

him; she had been a pale thin querulous flaxen haired woman with blue eyes whom he never treated with even a show of respect; and for this as for everything else she didn't seem to care seriously; yet when she was sickening for her last illness (she died in childbirth of her 3rd child, who died with her) it is certain that she had in her mind a great longing to live till one of her sons grew up that she

might tell him a grievance of hers, and perhaps entrust a hatred to
him; a hatred to his father; nobody was with her when she died
except the hired nurses and the little village Dr. of this latter she
asked many questions as to when he thought children grew old
enough to understand matters of of love and the like; questions wh:
he parried as well as he could, and in his turn asked leading question to see if she would not tell him the story whatever it was; but
she didn't open herself to him, and died and left all unsaid; after all
it was no great thing that she had to tell; only how she had found 3
or [4] letters in an old [forgotten] pocketbook of her husband's hidden away among clothes. Here they all are in order that we may
make an end of the rector's history at once before we begin that of
his sons with whom our tale will chiefly have to do; they all dated
before his marriage; the first is in his own hand—

Hasted Hall.

My love, my darling

   I could not do it yesterday; though

I came up to London for nothing but to tell you; and yet I was going
to do it the last half hour we were together; though you were so happy and bright; didn't you notice how confused and stupid I was; but
then when you took me upstairs to see your newly furnished bed
room, and were so pretty over talking about all the things, and
showed me your dear clothes in the drawers and I saw your little
slippers lying about, and all the dear things that ~~you have to~~ touch
your body that I love so, then my heart failed me as I thought I
should never lie with you in the new pretty bed, and I came away
with the kisses that I feel now, and leaving that lie behind me—For
you know the kind of thing I ~~mean~~ have to say; don't curse me; live
and think of me, as I shall think of you—I am to be married next
Thursday—who knows we may meet again—my wife may die
before we are either of us very old—you know dear that life won't
be very pleasant to me; so don't be too angry; at all events be sure
that I don't love her; ugh! I haven't told you a word about it, and
now when all is over why should I; yet I must say this much, that I
should have been clean ruined if I had not; just a hint to my father a
month ago about what might have happened to me made him quite
mad and you don't know how I ran in debt—there you forgive don't
you, as you

have forgiven me so many things; ah my God if I were only back with you to give and be forgiven over and over again how can I do it how can I do it? to lie & pretend to love this ugly stupid woman, hard-hearted too she is—when I have had the cleverest and most beautiful woman in the world in my arms—why was I born among rich people loving all sorts of comfort for?—one thing more I shall go to my rectory as soon as I am married, my wife is rich; I can easily afford to send you ~~100~~ 250 a year so you will be richer now than you have been; I must try to think how you can write to me; for I must hear of you for indeed & indeed I shall always love you my precious my darling my own!—O if you could only kiss your poor James.

The 2nd letter was this in large well-formed woman's hand.

There is your letter back again; take it and the curse with it you pretend to dread; yet if I curse you I don't curse God; I bless him rather for showing me what you are while I could yet escape from you; yes even at the cost of all the pollution I have suffered from you, the loss of the house, a dull loveless enough one certainly I left for you—curse you & your money; the money for wh: you have sold me & yourself; I will have none of it Who cares whether I die or

not—~~ah~~ and for you—I know you now my eyes are opened all sorts of little things come back to me now and I see what they mean; I stifled all doubts in me all disgusts I hid to myself—I should soon have got to be as base as you. Ah why am I ~~spe~~ writing to him and telling him of my feeling as if we were still—lovers—but note this— May your life grow duller & duller in the dull place you are going to bury yourself in—may you have no escape in the whole world from dullness—I say I know you; may all your grossness and falseness increase on you till every thing hates you, till your face that I kissed and hung over changes as your base soul works on it curse my curse upon you—ah why are words so weak?—I will not die—do you hear? I will live and curse you—

The 3rd with the date of the next post in the same hand:

O no no no I didn't mean it: and you have forgiven me! indeed I will live and wait and hope and try to keep young and—and handsome for you—O what a letter I could write—If you only knew how full my heart is of love for you; yes I shall be happy with my love whatever happens—I could tell you many things only shame and horror of my last miserable words keeps returning; what did I do that night I sent the letter off—last night it was: let me tell you that for I know you will be pleased to hear about me, that you are forgiving me as you read this: I wandered about the street after post time till it got dark, went right down into town; it was such a fine bright evening, and I felt so strange not at all like I expected to feel, I can't tell you how, but not mad at all; so it got dark and still I walked about all through the city at first & then I turned westward & got into the Strand, and people spoke to me as if I was—well I shall never be that never; I will live [pure] and be good till I can be with you again my darling—and then I began to love you so again and I cried and put my veil down, and I stopped at the turning off to Waterloo bridge and went half way down the street toward the bridge[7]—and then there were so many people about; and I turned back and went straight to the Olympic; and I took a ticket for the stalls quite sensibly, and went in and sat in one of the stalls close by the door ~~an~~ just where we sat last week my darling, and Robson was acting in Medea[8] still though it was half over; wasn't it strange of me; and shall I tell you how I felt when the people laughed?—Well I thought quite distinctly now I needn't trouble to kill myself after all because I must have died and this is hell—you have forgiven me dear, havent you? that's why I tell you all this—well, Medea

came to an end and then there was a farce, and people laughed more & more till at last we all got up, and I got my bonnet and walked straight home and it was raining and when I came to Waterloo Bridge, for I went that way home, there were few people about: but I walked straight home and ran sometimes. I don't know why but I had a feeling on me of being too late; well I got home and I daresay you can guess, poor child who must be so unhappy yourself as to how I felt when I had let ~~in~~ myself in—anything one calls home is the worst place to be in when one is unhappy isn't it dear. Yet I must have gone to sleep soon for it was broad daylight when I looked round again; broad daylight outside I mean for the red curtains in the little back room that you don't like; were drawn and made the front room dark and dismall—and I found myself wet, very stiff and tired; and footsore; and I crept upstairs to our— to my bedroom: then I began to take off my clothes—dear I cant tell you any more what I did, but it was all very dreadful: but dont grieve too too much for I am better now; because the sun rose after a bit, long & long before Martha was astir, and then I crept downstairs in those slippers dear and got the pen & ink and began to write this: and I felt quite happy at once

but tired & ill—your letter was very kind I know—so kind my darling that I know you have forgiven me—and you mustnt think me
lightheaded ~~with~~ for writing all this am quite sensible: and to show
you that I will talk about money matters—Of course I would take
your money dear if only to be obliged to you and to live by you still:
but it would be so very awkward for you to send it; and you must remember my telling you of Mr Dixon my godfather and how in spite
of all he wanted me to come & live with him I shall do so soon
now—he is one of the best old men who knows & cares [so little]
about the ways of society that I think he looks upon marriage as
quite as shocking as anything else—think of me dear among the
books and papers in his museum of a house on Stoke Newington
Common though I dont suppose you were ever near there—O darling darling think of me, and be as happy with your wife as you can
be—get children and love them—who knows what may happen as
you said in your letter—O my dear it almost the bitterest of all that
I didnt keep your dear dear letter; yet even if you dont write to me
again I shall know you have forgiven me—Yet your kisses, those
kisses you spoke are on my lips still—Goodbye goodbye. Your
Eleanor—

These three letters put in one envelope

and addressed in Mrs Risley's formal weak hand were found under
her pillow when she died—her husband took them glanced at them,
and made a motion toward the fire but didn't throw them in; one
may hope from this that at least a little pain shot across him as he
put them away in his bureau, but I think there was something of
fear too, and it must be said that he never answered no 3—that no 2
had not astonished him exactly but made him both uneasy and resentful; that he rather looked at himself as an injured man on that
score thenceforward—
About 6 weeks after Mrs Risley's death on a bright day in the middle of a wet February when the floods were out all about the river,
the parson came in from a solitary ride through the sopping country
and ~~was told~~ as he put his foot to the ground his servant said to him
there's a lady in the drawing waiting to see you sir— —[Who he
said. I dont know sir but she wouldnt] She would wait and said she
had particular business and he gave a card as he spoke on which the
rector read Miss Ullathorne—with an unconcerned look for the
name was utterly unknown to him; yet as he crossed the hall, the
conventional smile that he had drawn over his face, faded away,

and as with a strange feeling half of fear half of pleasure he opened
the drawing room door expecting to see he couldn't tell why the
writer of those two letters—he opened the door, and

went in and in spite of expectation turned pale and trembled when
he saw a tall woman standing with her back toward him looking
out of the window, for he knew it was she without seeing her face;
she turned round suddenly and faced him with a half startled half
joyous cry and held out both her hands to him: she was a beautiful
woman, black haired and dark eyed with full lips and gloriously
proportioned figure; but grown thin with her a face worn and haggard though flushed now as she came towards him with all her frame
trembling and her lips half-open, and her beautiful eyes eager &
flashing: she stopped after the first step and hastily took off her
gloves and came forward and stretched out more timidly it seemed
now one hand to him. I know not what change came over her face
as their hands met; for he took hers, as if he were afraid of it and let
it drop at once; and said in a short dry way; sit down Eleanor I am
glad to see you: but she stood still looking at him and hadn't spoken
a word yet and the change went on in her face all the while. What
can I do for you? he said after a while again in voice that tried to be
softer. She heaved a great sigh and seemed as if she would speak but
said nothing: and presently, he himself had sat down, moved her
hand as if to touch him but let it fall again: Did you come

from London today? how are you getting on now Eleanor?" he
spoke hurriedly almost as if in fear this time. She made no answer;
again he said You are looking ill: you must be tired; do sit down; let
me get you a glass of wine." She turned from him and slowly walked to the other end of the room, and stooped down over the glass
case that held the ivory junk with its painted and gilded puppets: it
was growing dusk now: he called out with growing trouble in his
voice Eleanor, is it really you? She turned and answered nothing: I
will do anything I can for you he said You have heard that my wife
is dead—not a word: he rose up from his chair in terror for he really
began to think she was ghost: all the dreadful threatenings of the
disbelieved or disregarded creed of which he was the priest flashed
across his brain mingled with naif or gross ghost stories read long
ago in queer little penny garlands with woodcuts; he put his hand
before his face for a moment as if he thought she would be gone
when he removed it but she was there facing him at the other end of
the room in the gathering dusk—My God Eleanor speak to me he

said or are you really a ghost? She understood his base fear, and a
smile passed over her face and she came towards him, he could see
through the twilight how deadly pale she was—when she came

close to him she spoke at last, but as it were deadly pain to her, yet
even then her voice was sweet and pure & he felt it so and shud-
dered as he heard it—No she said I am alive George—don't you
wish I were dead? A sound like no came from his lips, and he moved
from her a little; she spoke again slowly and as if it were with great
effort; George, she said, when I went to the other end of the room I
thought the door was there: I meant to go at once—but it is right in
these matters to leave nothing untried so I will speak—yes I will call
you by the old name: dear George my darling & my love do you
know why I came here: again he gasped out no—O my love she said
listen yet for the old days are not yet dead in my heart, and all may
go well with us yet: I came here because I heard you were free; I
came to be loved George to be called by the old pet names, to feel
your arms round me and your lips on my face—who knows; to be
married to you if you would; if you would not to have hope given me
pleasure—ah who knows what pleasure—George what will you give
me: a little will be enough—He stood listening in the gloom with knitted brows, and spoke at last—glad that he couldn't see much of her
face—Why will you talk like this: he said: I did what lots of young
men do: I never said I would marry you then even? did I?

and how can I marry you now: you talk about the old times do you
suppose 3 years haven't changed me more then they have changed
you: I wish you had written and asked me to meet you somewhere,
instead of coming here. "I cursed you once she said: He broke in turning fiercely on her. Yes you needn't remind me of it: look here
Eleanor the first words of that letter made an end of the whole thing:
even when we were getting on best together I was afraid of you I
wondered whether you wouldn't cut my throat some—no listen:
when I wrote that letter about my marriage to you I was thoroughly
trembling with fear, and when your letter came next morning and I
saw you had sent mine back I didn't open it for a couple hours — —
Now you who are so deuced clever tell me whether one loves people
one is thoroughly afraid of? You said in your letter you had found me
out, well I believe you had just for that moment—found out I believe
that I can't bear such furious women—My God I think its for me to
curse you now: you have made me a bad man: you and your beauty
that I was luckless enough to stumble over and I used to think how

clever you were too; and how you were like the women in poetry, such people as I had never expected to meet—you have made me an unhappy man—Eleanor I hate you and I wish you were dead—

He flung himself down into a chair as he spoke and wept aloud; she stood there quite silent till his weeping had sunk to sobs; then she said in a clear low voice I dont curse you now; I don't say farewell to you: I have nothing to wish for hope for think of: I am glad I cant see your face. He heard the room door open and shut, and then the outer door; then he slowly rose, and went out into the hall where the servant was lighting the lamp and a flood of disgust and horror as one damned on earth swept over him as the light flashed at last over the passing things: the man stared at him as well he might as he went to the outer door and opened it: the night had fallen now, but the thin crescent moon was ~~there~~ was high & bright the boughs were tossing about in the wild wind, a great ~~rack~~ mass of rain clouds was far down to lee- ward, and light ragged clouds were drifting across the remote watery grey sky; he ran out bareheaded into the moonlight, but turned back when he had got his hand on the wicket latch and walked slowly into the house. If there is such a thing as punishment the [next few] hours of that night were a heavy one to him, and he came down the next morning haggard and aged; and in the course of the day sent for his curate, and told him that he was worn out with the terrible loss of his wife's death &

seeing to the future of his motherless children and that he should go away for a little rest and would write from the continent and so he set out on his travels, and took care not to look at a newspaper, an English one, for he went to Paris, for weeks: he never heard what became of her, nor need we:[9] she was young & might live to love again, if she could tide over a few months till the shame of having loved something that didnt exist had worn off her; if she could once more get to see any order or hope in the world. As for the rector, he came back in two months looking little changed enough; yet there was a whisper that all wasn't right about him; ~~nor~~ and people said his temper wasn't bettered by his wife's death; and his presence seemed to cast a blight upon any company he happened upon though he was a pleasant man enough as word goes especially if no one contradicted him: and so the days wore away: at one time the village people began to talk about his marrying again: the ~~daughter~~ sister of the only man with whom he could be said to be really in- timate, a small squire some 7 miles off, named Ralph Godby who

had been a college friend of his; he was a burly handsome good-
natured country gentleman who found deuce knows how some
pleasure in the society of this [haughty] moody irritable overbearing
man

who for the rest would have quarrelled with him for ever ~~if~~ but for
the proverbial necessity of ~~there being~~ its taking two to ~~perform~~ do
that deed; he used to go and stay with him for two or three days at a
time, and these visits got very frequent about 2 years after the death
of Mrs Risley & in fact the rector would have made love to Miss
Godby, ~~of~~ a handsome healthy round armed woman of 23 if she had
let him; but she as kindhearted as her brother, [and] with the grain
more of insight which a woman of otherwise the same capacity as a
man always has could not abide the sour morose parson who generally had a bad word for everybody & delighted in scattering to the
winds any little bit of kindly romance the simple hearted woman
might get up about people and things about her; so she carefully put
on her worst dress when he came there covered up her arms & neck
at dinner like a quakeresss; though to do her justice she was not generally sorry to let people admire them; never would ride when he
was there—got tired of her archery; and laid aside her sketching;
and in short showed her wholesome hatred of him in the simplest
and most straightforward ways so the parson got more & more overbearing and quarrelsome with these friends of his, till at last his
visits got sparser and sparser, and the gossips of the

countryside said which was not true that he had made an offer and
been refused. Meantime his children were growing up and had
everybody's good word, yet but little notice from their father; now
& then when they got to be boys instead of children they went to
stay with Mr Godby where Miss Edith spoilt them terribly, and
where they picked up materials for many a future dream in the
library and on the lake in the park; and then they spent a day ~~with~~
at one or two of the farmers houses in the parish of one of which
more anon; but this was all the change they had except their school
where they went rather late and which no further than Hamington
a country town ten miles from Ormslade.

Their father would often go up to London and spend a month at a
time there, and would go abroad for two or three weeks, not
heeding whether it were their holidays or not and indeed thinking
next to nothing of them; they for their parts were not all glad when
he came home; both because their having the run of the whole

house and the constant society of the footman gardiner & cook was very delightful, and also because their father, whom they always feared was particularly morose and ill tempered when he came back from these absences, as they grew up they often enough heard their father spoken of in a misterious halfhushed way, and themselves with a condescending pity which though it troubled

them, didn't puzzle them for long, for they soon divined what sort of a man their father was, and with no little shame shared perforce the general dislike of him, or hatred rather call it. So passing over a good many years let us come back to the day we began with when John the elder was fifteen and Arthur the younger 14 years old. Passing up the wide carved staircase we come at the top of the house to a large low-ceilinged room with 3 windows at one end over looking the kitchen garden, though that was pretty much hidden now by the thickleaved boughs of the great limes that brushed against the open windows and from which delicious scent and sound came that evening; the room was white panelled like the greater part of the house, with 3 or four of the queerest and most oldworld pictures ~~stuck~~ hung on its walls, an old sampler and ~~another worsted~~—~~worked~~ picture worked in brown worsted of Abraham and Isaac among them; and besides these, pictures from illustrated ~~pictures~~ papers pasted up here & there, a stuffed polecat with a partridge in its mouth arranged on the mantelpiece without the expense of a glass case, which had however been granted to the remains of a great big-bellied [deformed] crooked looking roach, such a recent trophy that he had not turned brown yet, and to crown all the lads library in hanging shelves at one end of the room and a single barrelled gun and a goodish collection of tools and fishing rods by no means neatly disposed

about the room. On a little deal table in the middle of the room was a huge bunch of summer flowers stuffed into a great brown jug, and then there were the two white hung beds, in one of which lay the sick lad Arthur just turning the corner of a low fever; ~~and~~ by whom John sat reading to him out of a new green coated book, Lanes Arabian Nights[10] to whit; in that queer sort of way boys read sometimes when they cannot read quite quick enough for their eyes or their eagerness over the story; he stopped to laugh sometimes too as well he might for it was the tale of Maroof[11] he was reading, but came to an end at last when the sick lad fell back on his pillows and said; thanks old chap; what a jolly story, what asses they were to leave it

out of the old book lets have a look it will you. He turned over the
book the other leaning over him to look at the pictures till his hand
fell and he said. Well it was kind of father to get it me wasnt it? Yes
said John shortly turning away and fidgetting about among an open
draw of fishing tackle——I think he's a generous man and all that
sort of thing said Arthur, I'm bound to say with his money: John
said nothing: ~~Has~~ After a pause Arthur said has he said anything
more about your going to Oxford: since that day? Youre such a
close fellow I know you wouldn't have

told me if there had been a row especially while I was ill." "O there
was no row, said John, he did speak to me yesterday week, and so I
said the same thing over again, that I had heard him grumble at being a clergyman that I didn't want to any more than him. I was going to say I thought it wrong if a fellow didn't very much wish to be
but I knew he would laugh at me & so I held my tongue." "Well
what did he say." said the other: I dont think he cared a bit: he said
well that he wasn't rich enough to keep me idle and that if I wasnt
going to take the living after him I must turn to at something next
year, and mustn't be too particular either; I said was quite ready
whenever he wished it—~~I sh~~ and there was an end of the talk; I
should think he would ask you sooner or later old fellow. Well I
wasn't said Arthur emphatically, just think I should have to be his
curate; I know what I should like to be—a farmer, but not about
here: I declare [the] last holidays I felt quite queer when we came into the George at Hamington, and there were some farmers we didnt
know for fear they should begin to talk about father: and I say I
havn't told you this before but when I was dreaming last week
when I about at my worst I kept dreaming[12] about him—don't you
say a word about it though? I said John that's a likely joke! Well
look here

I dreamed he asked me to come out a ride; here, you know, and just
as I got up on the poney he groaned dreadfully; then we rode away
beastly fast, but though we rode out of our gate I didnt know the
place a bit, but presently I felt dreadfully afraid and turned round
to look at him, and his face was all aflame; I mean as if it were
made of glass with fire behind ~~he~~ it, and when I looked at him he
screamed quite loud; so I tried to get away from him & whipped the
poney and somehow I did get ahead of him and I went so fast and
knew he was behind me all the time, though I didn't hear any noise
behind me and I didnt feel as if I were gallopping but was going on

just I were a puppet pushed along a slide and so I went till I was in a dark lane with trees on either side and it seemed like twilight, and there was an opening ahead and the sky showed, as if there were an open heath there, and I wanted most dreadfully to get there, and then there was a noise like when one swings round a flat piece of wood [round] with a hole in it, dont you remember; but presently I did get out on to this open place and it was so still, and yet things seemed to be going round and round; and I was on foot again and quite alone—and so I walked on and on till I got to where there was a canal on each side of a paved road and the water in the canal was quite black and seemed as if it were boiling though there was no steam coming from it,

and then all at once I saw a man sitting in the middle of the road with his hands before his face and got more horribly afraid at that but couldn't help going on till I stood over him, & then I saw by the clothes that it was father; and I touched him and he didnt move— and then I touched him again, and felt him tremble, and then just as I was going away he jumped up and just think he was a skeleton, all but his face which was his sure enough and all like a glass mask with fire behind it, and he opened his mouth, and made the most horrible noise that kept growing louder & louder and I couldnt run away and—I say Arthur, dont go on with that said John—you'll make yourself ill again. I wish the deuce we hadn't got on this talk, tell me another time—shant I read you another story? No thank you said Arthur, I am tired: besides its getting dusk and you had better go and look after your worms." I say old chap, said John with rather an effort: if you wish it a bit I won't go to morrow; I'll stay and read to you: no he said you go Mrs Hadow will sit with me, and tell me stories about the farmers here about and the great people of Scolton Manor: besides I want you go and tell me how Clara is, and what shes doing: very well then said John; good bye for the present. And out he went and not too slowly either; for he certainly looked forward to his tomorrows fishing as well he

might that beautiful June weather having been a good deal shut up with the sick lad. As to the looks of the lad by the way it would rather have puzzled anyone who had seen them to say why the little doctor should have said that either of them was not like his father; some strange undercurrent of thought must have drawn it out of him, for they were obviously both very much like him; and were handsome and well grown; the sick boy as he lay white-cheeked in

his bed, had certainly a great delicacy of feature that had no counterpart in his fathers coarsened face: while John was light haired,
burnt brown and freckled with the June tide, with less serious and
merrier eyes than his brothers' even had the latter been well; a bigger mouth & fuller lips and more massive jaw and chin, and was in
the lower part of his face very like his father; just as Arthur was in
his black hair and forehead and nose though his eyes big like his
father's and of the same colour, had a far away & dreamy look instead of a fierce & restless one—So John ran quickly down stairs and
out into the garden, where the sun was already set and a cloudless
golden sky was burning through the elms at the bottom of the
garden.

John ran into the tool house and took up a garden fork prepara-
tory to going off to the melon ground where the worm populated
old dung heaps were: for some strange reason that moment and the
half hour were one of the unforgotten times of his life, and in after
days he could never smell

the [earthy] mixt scent of a tool house, with ~~mixed with the smell of~~
its bast mats and earthy roots and herbs in a hot summer evening
without that evening with every word spoken and gesture made
coming up clear into his memory: it struck on him as he came out of
the tool house again into the glow of the evening, and all his boyish
visions of the great red finned basking chub, and the shadowy flitting bleak and the great water lily leaves spreading over the perch
holes vanished and left him with that vague feeling of disappointment in life past, yet hope of life to come; the expectant longing for
something sweet to come heightened by rather than chastened by
the mingled fear of something as vague as the hope, that for fills our
hearts so full in us at whiles, killing all commonplace there, making
us feel as if we were on the threshold of a new world, one step over
which if we could only make it would put life within our grasp—
what is it? Some reflex of the love and death going on throughout
the world, suddenly touching those who are ignorant as yet of the
one, and ~~do not~~ have not learned [dis] believe in the other? he
passed slowly over the grass growing dewy now still moving me-
chanically towards the melon ground, and ~~had~~ entered a walk that
led to the walled kitchen garden, and covered over with thick
clipped yew trees was very nearly dark now and so just as he was
reaching out his hand to the latch of the door it opened suddenly,
and he started back with a queer

sound of terror one would not have expected to come from the strong healthy looking youth; it was his father, who stopped a moment startled too it seemed and looked at him & then walked on again swiftly; John passed on into the kitchen-garden with his heart still beating violently and a sense of shame upon him; it was much too dark for him to see his father's face in that moment; but he had fancied a look of disgust & almost hatred in it: anyhow it was a relief to come into the [broad] light ~~of~~ that yet was over the sweet smelling abundant garden, and strip the first white currant bough of its fruit; more of a relief still to hear a heavy tread close before him, mingled with the squeak of a pair of stiff corduroy breeches, and presently he ~~came~~ met with a smiling face the ~~gardeners cowb~~ the under gardener and cowboy[13] so called for he was near 60 years old at least; Going after brandlings Master John said he, I've got you a lot well scoured because I guessed youd be too busy with Master Arthur and Mrs Hadow told me youd be going fishing about as now; therewith he put the bait box in his hand & they both walked back together; the breeches performing with great regularity till the boy said; Shall you be going to Fairmead Farm on the way, Master John? perhaps Jack said he conscious that he was blushing in the dusk; give my duty to my old missus if you do, and little Miss; Im told she asked you why I didnt come up and see her hayhome time and that.

She's a kind woman is Mrs. Oldham:[14] lord, that was a pleasant house to be at: sometimes I wish to God I hadn't married: not but what Master's a good master too he added hastily: and then after a pause a little awkward perhaps—Its a year since I saw Miss Clara. So you told me yesterday Jack said the lad. Who do you think ill marry her sir—Bless us Jack what a queer question to ask me? Well it ill break her mothers heart if anything ill comes of her; and there a drowsy lot hereabout drink and sleep and dodder about I cant think anybody about heres good enough for her. Ha I know you came from Wiltshire Jack and despise us butter makers eh; well, Clara shall go a journey to your chalky Paradise and bring away a moonraker.[15] I dont know what you mean Master John said the boy with a grin, but Miss Clara's father was as learned as a parson and almost as sour begging your pardon sir; How did he get on with father Jack? Well said the boy; it aint exactly the sort of thing to talk about to you; but I think if Mr O hadn't died of cholera, one or other of em must have busted they couldnt live together in a 20 mile ring—I'm a going down toward the cowhouse Mr. John—they did hate each other so: I daresay youve heard tell that Mr. O. wasnt right about his religion, not exactly a dissenter you know, but thought there was no bible nor miracles, nor nothing; and so he didn't come to church and you know I daresay somehow

that put the parson's back up: ~~you~~ though no offence Mr. John but folk say the parson would be best pleased if the church were to walk off to London, so that nobody mightnt come to it: well there was a many things went atwixt and atween; mongst others a row about your going there you & Master Arthur when you was little; and the nurse sent away for taking you there; and she believed to be a little drunk Mr. John; and that was about the time I came to your honoured father; and Ill tell you no lies but I must say I think it was because I was under a cloud up at Fairmead that parson took me in; for that damned thief Jenkins[16] a porridge-faced Welshman he said I took the oats, a man with a wife & family to say that: that was just before I was married sir, and I often wish I'd got his head under my spade I do; well I should (not) tell you ~~you~~ only you must remember that, that your father was as soured as might be because Mr — had given you and Mr Arthur half a crown apiece that day. Yes I remember Jack said the lad though I was only about 9 then; it was a big tip for a farmer to give such a little chap—ah he was always a liberal man was Mr — well you know I was with your father then sir and he came down the peach walk of a hot day of June swearing more than I thought to hear a parson swear; and if I don't lie he said as he passed

by me: Ill find something for him to do with his halfcrowns. and then you know youre rather young to know about things like that; but Kitty Churchill at the post office she fathered her child at Mr. — and my wife's sister who was still at Fairmead she said there was a fine row there; anyhow next day down comes Mrs — to the rectory, and she goes and gives your father a bit of her mind; for Ill tell you right out Mr John, it was in everybodys mouth that the parson set Miss Kitty on to that business; well you know the housemaid she told my wife that she listened at the door, and Mrs — she was proud & stiff and talked beautiful and your father roared and made a noise—and this she heard her say Mr. Risley if my husband likes to make love to every girl in the village he has a full right to it if I let him; and let me tell you says she that if ~~you~~ he was to what he would be hanged for, he would be a better man than you who havn't the spirit to do either right or wrong—she's a good woman she is; and if I had a taken the oats I'd work on anything short of a treadmill to pay her back—but I ask your pardon Mr John I haven't got anything to say against your father—beside you'll have heard this often enough before; well some of it perhaps Jack but not quite in the same way

I say I must get back home, its getting quite dark; its going to be fine tomorrow isn't it? Why you wont burst yourself eating all you catch Mr John; the water's as low as low: Never mind Jack he said I'll give you everything I catch above 2 lbs; just take the fork home will you; and he went off whistling from the garden into the field from which they had come, just as the low moon was yellowing, through the windless summer night, in which the nightingales were beginning to sing now: one may easily imagine that his nervous sentimental mood had vanished before the gardener's talk.

Yet so it was that it didnt pain him much to hear his father spoken of so at any rate that thought wasnt the uppermost in his mind as he startled the blackbirds out of their roosts in the thick leaves; nay whatever there was of sordid about the story had slipped off him and left a pleasant feeling of life active and full of incident and change going on about him, with I know not what of sweeter, of sweetest lurking behind it all; and the little pleasures lying ready to his hand they also were so keenly felt so full of their own beauty; how happy he was as he strode out into the light that the just lit up house threw over the dewy lawn; strong & happy and full of life what should touch him or harm him? He ran straight up-stairs to his brothers room when he got

and found him alone with the candles just lighted and looking so particularly happy that he said. Hilloa Arthur whats happened old fellow? How pleased you look? Why I was just going to say the same thing to you he said—but I say fathers just been up and he said as I was getting on all right and he was out of anxiety about me he was going up to town and he thought he shouldnt be back till the holidays were over; and that he would come & see us at Hampton & tip us and then he left 5£ for the two of us. and so he's gone—then presently he said I wonder what people would say if they heard us two talking about father—for, after all you know he isn't unkind to us.'

I don't care quoth John, but I know were right when all's said; once for all I will have no more to do with him than I can help: he don't care a bit for us Mrs — is a great deal more like our mother

than he is our father; I am a precious deal more pleased to see Mrs
Hadow and little Stoneman (the doctor) Meantime when I come
home; when I we sit with him he has nothing to say to us except
'don't do that:' and hang it all I think were old enough to be talked
to now; and do you know old chap when I hear him preaching in
church with that beastly put on voice, I feel not ashamed of myself,
for I dont feel as if I belonged to him at all, but in such a rage—blast
his sermons—" I say John

said Arthur raising himself a little Whats the matter now; are you in
a rage with me? Why do you know, your voice got something like
father's in a rage—"O I didn't mean anything he said: only sometimes I feel a little cooped up here: we see nobody & go nowhere like
other boys do: I intend next summer to ask him to let you & I go
somewhere to the Continent or somewhere. I dont think he'd say
no—How queer said Arthur that was just what I was thinking of
when you came in, & how jolly it would be—but I say I shall be on
my legs again in a week; couldnt you knock up going to some place
or other with Clara tomorrow for of course you'll go & see her?
Well queer again said John for I was thinking of that;—therewith he
began to busy himself with the fishing-tackle, and presently the two
were deep in talk about bait and lines fish and chances had and
lost, and in this that & the other water: for all the country side was
good for boys fishing a lasy little stream that ran into the river
threading big pounds here & there, especially in one place where a
great old house had stood long ago pulled down except its flowery
iron gates. At last the housekeeper came in & drove John out for the
sick boys behoof who indeed soon fell asleep, and John went down
to supper with his father; who looked

particularly glum John thought at first and was if possible even
shorter in his words than usual; yet as the lad looked hard furtively
at him from time to time he began to see think that his father must
have been weeping lately and surprised a strange feeling in his own
heart at the discovery about which he could only tell that it was
painful & yet something like a pleasure; but if he could have known
it he would have found surprise & pity there tempering what was
really hatred, yet mixed with a kind of rage & the cruelty of young
and happy people against suffering they cannot understand: his
father seemed to feel his eyes upon him for presently he said impatiently, Jack just put out one of those candles I can't stand the light
I've got a cold I think: fancy having a cold in the middle of

summer." So the evening passed: father & son read at first, but presently the rector got up & walked out of the room and John could hear him pacing the drawing-room up & down, and with a vague fear that something ~~wa~~ bad was brewing let his eyes wander from his book, and his mind stray into many strange ways of thought, and was so deep in them that he started when his father came into the room again though he only sat down and took up his book again; however he had something to say and said it presently though it was nothing very terrible. Jack yes

father. Lets see how old are you? ~~17~~¹⁷ last February father: well you see next year you might have gone to Oxford; but as you won't why you're quite old enough now to turn to business: so look here I have got two openings ~~with~~ for you; you can take which you please of them; one is to go my brothers sollicitor, Mr Jackson & be articled to him; and he will shove you and you will be a partner if you work one of these days; the other is a place in a Russian merchant's house Woollaston & Co. Mr. — ~~promised~~ talked to me about it the other day, and its a good enough opening for a young fellow like you; Now that all Ive got to offer you, there isnt a third course for you except to loaf about on a small allowance (which in any case I shall give you). but even that I won't say no to as far as giving you house room goes—but I dont think you would like it and I am sure I shouldn't—so I give you till I see you again some 2 months hence to consider—Thanks father said John its very kind of you; and he spoke as if he really thought it so; for there was something either about his father's tone or else it came from thoughts in his own heart that rather softened him; and he began to build up a romance for his father in his own mind, ~~for though he was no his fa that his~~ partly a history of what he imagined might have been

and partly of what he imagined might be: he playing a large part in this latter for sentiment and greatheartedness. His father said nothing for a while and they both seemed to be at their books again: but after a while he looked up & said—Jack, don't you be too close friend with that woman at Leaser Farm & her brat: they will serve you a turn my boy one of these days; Don't you hear me, eh?" For John sat now with his dream gone and with something like a scowl ~~on~~ mingling with the flush on his face. both sat silent a while till the rector said. Well, a nod's as good as a wink to a blind horse: and I know that whatever I do or say, you will be always there when Im gone. How many pretty stories of me did you hear last time you saw

[the] widow Mason? O father said Jack you dont suppose they talk to me about things about you; and he got very confused at the emphasis he had laid on the me—Risley laughed grimly, and said: They'd have given people something to talk about I daresay if they had been as unhappy as Ive been: ~~boys~~ children and happy people oughtnt to be so ready with their hard words and thoughts about those who are down, and don't know where to turn to for something pleasant to think of. Why whats the matter with me tonight he said as if you ~~don't~~ cared whether I live or die—or anybody he said with a groan as he got up and strode out of the room; leaving John with an

wretched feeling of having been unjust upon him, and a strange interest growing up in him and mingling with the real disgust he had of his father—the rector didnt come back again and after he had sat a while trying in vain to arrange the confused whirl of thought that swept through his head, stole up to his room in a guilty manner; hoping principally it must be confessed that he should not think of his father the next day, and spoil thereby pleasure of more than one kind he was looking forward to. Next ~~morning~~ day just as the fresh June morning was getting hot John was striding fishing rod in hand basket on shoulder down the road past the church which ran between the Battle Meads[18] as they were called in memory of the old fight; till he had got past the church he felt as if somebody would call him back at the last moment, and he had walked so fast that he was flushed hot enough now; he slacked his pace presently and wiped his streaming face laughing the while as the thought aforesaid came to him. No shadow of last nights fears and doubts was on his face now and he looked and was as happy a fellow as might be found within the narrow seas; both the lads and he especially would have been called very childish at most times by superficial observers, from the agonies with which they caught little pleasures, their shyness, and when they were talking

to strangers this clumsiness of expression and the care with which they avoided any words or talk that expressed strong feeling of any kind;[19] and certainly John was more excited with his days fishing than one would have expected a big fellow of 17 to be—he soon gained the top of the first slope, and from the brow of it could see the line of alders that indicated the windings of the stream, through a narrow valley soon bounded again by another cultivated slope; he stopped presently at and old stone bridge and began fitting his rod together there and disposing of his tackle on the parapet; by the side of the bridge was a stile that led down to the footpath which followed the river for some way through the fat green meadows; the stream itself was a sluggish one, ~~overhung~~ with steepish clay banks, & much overhung with alders, and maple; not very inviting certainly but ~~he~~ it had the attraction for our brothers that running water always has for boys and John stayed with looks of real affection over the lichen grown parapet: [presently] as he stood thus came a sound of wheels, and presently ~~he~~ turning round he saw Dr Stoneman's gig & old white mare coming pounding along—the Doctor pulled up suddenly when he saw him, and said—Well hows the sick one this morning—getting on allright said he; he woke at 7 this

morning & said he had slept all night: he said he wants to get up tomorrow: Well he had better wait till I come: I shall be with him at ½ past 12—hows your father this morning he didn't look very well? eh grinning you dog (there was not a ghost of a smile on John's face). You think I want to make another patient nolens volens—I think he's all right doctor—hes going to London today to stay away some time—~~When~~ Oh said the Dr, staring hard at John as if he expected something more to come, in default of which he sang out well goodbye you wont catch anything today, Ill bet—and he was just shaking the reins, when John said Stop a bit Dr. When do you think Arthur will be about again so as to be able to walk I mean: oh about 10 days said Dr. — Lord John how bright and pleased you look to day he said suddenly. has anything happened? No sir—I am going into business after Xmas though—Eh said the Dr. where— who'll take the living? ~~wh~~ Why mr. Stoneman you don't suppose either Arthur or I want to be dangling about waiting for fathers shoes: besides we've both of us made up our minds we wont be parsons—Im going with a Russian Merchants[20] Mr Stoneman said John rather proudly for in fact it hadnt taken him long to make up his mind—There said the little Doctor I'm a prophet John; I was telling your father yesterday you would make your

fortune in no time—well good bye again—I wish I were going with you: I say: does Miss Clara treat you still as little boys and kiss you eh? The wheels drowned his cackling laughter as he spoke, so John had his scarlet blush all to himself: to say the truth he would have blushed nearly as much ~~as~~ if the Dr. had mentioned Claras name:

nay he would have blushed at the mention of almost any lady between the ages of 12 and sixty if she were anything short of being
his aunt; for he was of that age—however he was not so ill pleased
by the Drs joke as he ~~said~~ went down the footpath and throwing his
line into the water began to fish assiduously, enough, & as luck
would have it falsified both the cowboys & the Drs prophecy by taking a fair number of fish—so the day wore, and cloudless still began
gather ~~ed~~ that purple haze about the horizon which makes the summer noon so threatening; John seemed to get more restless and
passed quickly now from pool to pool; and at last when it was nearly ½ past twelve deliberately put up his rod and walked down the
river bank for some furlong or so till he met the meadow-path
again; just here the ~~stream~~ whole landscape got freer and more
cheerful, the southern slope was a good deal drawn back from the
stream now and left wide flat meads on that side with a fringe of
hedgerow elms at the hills foot; the stream itself grew

shallow and ran over gravel or pushed its way through beds of blue
flowered mouse ear and horesmint[21] and was bordered by willows
instead of the harsh dark alders that hung over its black pools
higher up, the meadows were full of great sleekskinned cows who
grazed quietly or sat under the big trees scattered here and there
about them; John went along rather fast as though he had to get to
some place by a known time but singing and happy, he met a little
brown faced girl with a basket and a solemn stumped tailed mon-
grel of a dog; the girl bobbed to the parson's son and the indis-
criminating dog growled at him; then as he passed a muddy shallow
of the stream in which the heifers were standing swinging their tales
in a sort of cadence, he met a white-haired lad who pulled his forelock to him [and he grew happier still if it might be he felt so home
~~like~~ in the well remembered place] he stopped when the lad had
passed; with that puzzled sense of its all happened before till with a
great sigh of enjoyment he seemed to gather the bliss of memory of
many & many a summer noon into this one and wondering
deliciously why he was so happy he walked on again as swiftly as
before for presently as he ~~turned the corner followed~~ came to a tree-
less & shallow bight of the stream [he saw under a nook of the hills
that ~~was fair as fair~~ again gravelly and wooded drew nearer to the
stream now the clustering roofs of an ~~farm~~ old farmstead among
lime and elm trees: a retired and far away spot it was indeed, yet as
distinctly with an air of cheerfulness & happiness about it as there

was of gloom and want of hope about Ormslade village; he turned towards the stead with quickened steps, smiling in anticipation as he saw coming towards him one of the farm men

who stopped as if expecting greeting and talk as he came near; of him so the natural questions of fish & sport being disposed of John asked with little anxiety indeed after the mistress & her daughter—All well sir said the man as they always are I think and always deserve to be: I heard the mistress talking of writing to you sir about Master Arthur: if you make haste youll find them in the garden Sir—I hope Mr Arthur is better Sir—Yes hes getting all right, Will, I'll get on—good bye—so he went] that ran on now straight towards a grey old bridge some 50 yards ahead, and the wide expanse of the beautiful meadow was broken by a line of thick quickset hedge that guarded a rod a little raised above the fields in a way that told of winter floods; but now without looking as if by instinct his feet turned[22] from the river on to a footpath that cut off the corner to a big homestead lying at the foot of the foot of the slopes, that grassclad, and rich with elm trees again drew nearer to the river; the grey roofs showed among plenteous lime trees populous with rooks, and a row of huge walnut trees walked as it were up the hill [just] from beside the farm yard gate; the honeyed scent of the limes floated across the mead to him as he walked on eagerly through the blazing sun, and the pleasant sounds of the farm came with it, & brought him and a feeling of rest and coolness to come: the farm men were just slowly going off to their work again, as he came up to the gate; he stopped amongst

them and spoke a few words to tall young fellow there, a fishing shooting companion of a good many years, and then watched them walking slow off between the walnut trees to the upland fields, lingering again over his happiness before he went into the yard: indeed it was place on that bright day to exhilerate and older and more worn heart than his—or the heart of a stranger either; for though there was nothing marked or impressive about the landscape here any more than at Ormslade, village; yet just as an atmosphere of dullness & hopelessness hung about that, so about this was one of quietness and rest the rest not of death but of happy life: almost all the farm buildings were old but quite trim & in good order the one or two where the stone was whiter were built much like the others; a paved footway led up to the house, and gave one the idea of the farmer & his family come home from church to the Sunday dinner the house itself was old not late than Charles the 1st time in fact, for there was 1639 carved with the initials [W] L S. above the lintel of the door way, and in appearance it was older still with its three little gabled [finished] roofs running into the larger main roof, [and] the gables themselves being finished with a stone ball threaded on an iron spike; the gable-end of the said main roof was windowless & covered all over with a great pear tree, and at the corner of the wall furthest from where John stood was an old yew tree nearly blocking up the narrow space between the house &

farmyard wall: as John was just pushing the gate, a peacock suddenly swept up from inside the yew tree and perching on the coping sent forth his harsh cry that rang with no unpleasant sound somehow from out that dark corner of the sunny place; John stopped a while moment again to look at him, but presently he swept down into the field outside, & John heard light footsteps coming along the wall side, he swung the gate open quickly and passing in and glancing coming down along the way that led to the front of the house was a tall girl clad in a light dress, bare headed, & holding a letter in her hand, she gave a little start & a pleased cry when she saw his smiling face coming towards and running towards him, shifted her letter into her left hand, caught his right hand in hers and kissed his cheek quite frankly, and without noticing apparently that it was scarlet with blushing; for in fact and any youth was think of what Stoneman had said to him, and all the way up from the river, and was wondering whether she would kiss him or not, and whether he manage to ask her too if she didn't; for he hadnt seen her since the Xmas holidays owing to Arthur's illness & he thought that he was really growing up to very manly. Im so glad to see you after all this long time; why I wonder when you will have done growing John: he laughed frankly too, and said O I have've done now, I'm a man & am going into business soon: and youre a woman, and havent grown a bit this last year I think though youre a year younger than me—but where were you

going without your bonnet in this hot sun? Why she said, I wrote a letter to Arthur this morning and I had just come out to find the boy & send him off with it, and she held the letter out: it was fat and puffy; what have you got inside, he said. Why our big aloe has blossomed this year and I was sending him some blossoms because you know they say they only blossom once in a hundred years, and I thought he should have something to remember his being ill this year—Dr Stoneman saw mother yesterday and so I know he's better—Im so glad. he gave her back held the letter out to her again to take: but she said no wont you take it home to him poor lad: as he did so putting his hand back she touched his it with hers: and he thought what a difference the summer made, for he wasn't anything like a happy the last time he saw her which was no not long after Xmas on a cold rainy day the beginning of February & they turned now and went side by side toward the door of the house that led into the farm yard, she with her eyes cast down & her brow a little eas knitted as though she were thinking of something hard to grasp; he looking at her all over with his eyes wandering from one part of her to another, and wishing if it might be that he could see her all at once—and indeed it was a good wish, for if he were to live to see the aloe blossom again he would not see so good a sight: she had really stopped growing some months: and was slim & thin, though without a suspicion of ill health about her: she was a little above the middle hieght of women

in writing to John Arthur is to tell him that he has heard her telling the kid about him and what a fine chap he was—talk about getting old at the picnic[23]

well-built and with a certain massiveness about the figure in spite of her present thinness: her hands were [beautifully made and] long-nailed & delicate in make, but not very small, and they were browned with the sun too, with even a little freckle[24] here & there on them: her face like her figure had something strong & massive amidst its delicacy, somewhat sunburnt too like her hands, beautifully clear of skin but without much red in her cheeks: dark brown abundant silky hair; a firm clear cut somewhat square jaw and round well developed chin; lips a little over thin a little too much firmly closed together for her youth & happiness, a straight nose with wide nostrils and perfectly made but somewhat short; rather high cheek bones that gave again too much of a plaintive look to the her cheeks, a wide forehead and beautiful shaped head above it; and to light all this up large grey eyes[25] set wide apart fringed with dark lashes; so capable of all shades expression that they were liable from their expressiveness to be missread, so sympathetic to the soul that shows through them that in times of strong emotion, before the lips had begun to tremble the whole change would have come over the eyes: amidst apparent acquiescence they would be cold with disdain, amidst apparent coldness they would be tender, O how tender, with love; amid apparent patience they would burn with passion; amid apparent cheerfulness they would be dull & glassy with anguish. No lie or pretence could ever come near them. They were [as it were] the index of the love and greatness of heart that wielded the strong will in her, which in its turn wrought

on those firm lips of hers & that serious brow which gave her the air of one who never made a mistake, an ~~expression~~ air look which without the sanctification of the eyes ~~would~~ might perhaps have given an expression of sourness & narrowness to her face. I have told of what she was like here; and it is true that even at this time all this was in her face; yet certainly undeveloped much of it; boundless simple love rather her face showed now, and the frankest pleasure in whatever was delightful—and yet how serious it was sometimes; and as John walked beside her now, he felt rough & rude & awkward & common and began to shuffle, and to tremble when her dress touched him: by the way one must say something about the said dress though there was little to be told about

She was dressed in a white cotton gown fresh and pleasant looking in the hot sunshine, and though it was all very plain there was nothing clownish about her rather a very visible taste in the make of her clothes; [rather everything and] all was [trim and] dainty, from her collar of coarse old lace to her trim sandalled shoes; on the second finger of her dear right hand she had a flimsy old fashioned ring of two or three coloured golds & turquoise, and a little brooch at her throat of the same manufacture; these were all her ornaments; and even these perhaps would have seemed excessive for a work-aday to the canons of taste that ruled the system she had been brought up in, which at all events implied ~~that~~ if they did not declare that all ornament was display: She led him into the cool clean house with its sanded passages, past the kitchen wherein a sound of washing up was going on; past the parlours right and left, and the foot of the queer heavily balustraded staircase:[26] the house was small enough, as I said before it had been but a farmhouse panelled all over with rather rude panelling, left unpolished in these stairs & passages, and polished dark in the parlours: however more of these hereafter; they went out of the front door into a little ~~garden~~ grass-plot with a border of delicious summer flowers all round it growing as such things [only] do in those old gardens and railed off with a little green railing from a large orchard scattered over rather sparsely with old and decaying

trees, and bound by the high road and a great untidy hedge, all dusty now. In the orchard was wandering an old grey purblind horse,
that was sauntering out the end of his days in utter peace, since the
good widow could not make up her mind to finish it with a bullet;
half a dozen geese pecked away gravely almost between his legs,
and a peahen with two chicks wandered about restlessly. nearer to
the house the long white stony drive that swept about the old tree,
will bring us again to the gate in the green fence from which a
flagged path led up to the green-painted front door with its gleam-
ing brass knocker: (aloe on other side) a little way from the sunniest
side of the flagged path was a big mulberry tree, under which sat
the widow on a wicker chair, dealing with many yards of calicoe,
and making the deuce knows; she turned to them as she heard the
sound of their footsteps and got up from her chair to greet them: she
was a woman of not more than 36;[27] much taller than her daughter,
of looser make and most certainly beautiful, but little like her
daughter; her hair had was abundant dark and crisped, her she had
great soft brown eyes, and a large mouth with full lips; she was thin
now, and her face look worn but not un unhappy; but the principal
expression on it was one of kindness; that expression of yearning
softness that expects its full reward of affection

and indicates an exacting and rather restless heart / a pleasant look
of welcome lighted up her face now as she took John's hand and
fairly wrung it. O John she said I am so glad to see you; Ive been
thinking of you so much these days past, & how lonely you dear
boys must have been all this time since you came home—Im so glad
to see you. There was a visible tone of sympathetic pity in her voice
that rather embarassed J. who felt as strong and happy as a lad need
do; he reddened and said—O thank you Mrs. Mason were getting
on all right now; but I can tell you we were frightened about Arthur
the poor chap didn't sleep for days & days and its upset all ones fun
this last holidays of mine—I say I've brought you some fish perch.
and therewith he unslung his basket and poured his catch out on the
grass—poor things! said Mrs. M. I hope you wont care about fishing
when youre a few years older John—Well he said fish never look
very much alive—do they Clara. She had been standing a little
behind him with a thoughtful look on her face but stepped forward
when the fish fell on the grass and she said now—The're very pretty
I like to see them: and they certainly don't look very much alive
now: well mother suppose you say thankyou for the fish and ask
John to have something

to eat, and he can tell us all about Arthur while he's having his dinner: O Im ashamed of myself, me a farmer and all—but you know we've just done our dinner; and I'm afraid I'm like other people and when I feel hungry I feel as if everybody else must be so too, and the same if Im glad or sorry or dull—John made a mighty effort and he said with a great blush—No Im sure you are not a bit like other people Mrs. M. so kind as you are—Ah my dear she said sometimes I think kindness of people like me may bring on dreadful things; I mean to say when ones kind because one wants other people to be kind to one. He stammered at his own boldness as he answered: Why if you make it like that nobody does anything except because he likes it; I mean to say even people who have given up most to please other people: but then the're all the better people to be pleased by whats bad good rather than by what is bad: they had all three talked themselves into the oak parlour by now; John perhaps with a feeling not very pleasant of not being listened to, which made him very silent now it was a beautiful old, deliciously cool in that hot afternoon the lowest sweeping boughs of the limes brushing the window at one end, a bay tree pruned away from the little side window which looked into the farmyard: the furniture was none of it modern, and

there was a big old sideboard of earlier date than the house: on a little spindle legged table by the window was half covered up with Clara's work, innocent looking portions of a dress she was making for herself, and the other half was cleared for that letter of hers; and the pen was still in the inkstand: on another table a rough piece of carpentry was bowl of goldfish, and there stood a big table with bulgy legs in the middle of the room: an old chintz covered sofa, and square armchairs and half a dozen queer bandylegged chairs of Queen Anne's time completed the furniture of the room: the dark panelled walls were decorated with 6 old engravings of W. 4 3rd's London and Westminster framed in old black frames, and with (these latter hanging on each side of the mantel-piece) two tolerably good engravings from Italian pictures; which the taste of the late farmer had introduced: again the room like the outside of the house looked full of quiet happy life; and apart from the neatness and cleaness of everything and the signs of the occupations of the two beautiful women scattered about it no doubt helped the impression that which clung to the whole house, that though old, [and] handsome in decoration and picturesque in outline it had never been built for anything different from what it was: everything was what

old English green ware punch bowl potpourri

was thought fit for a rich farmer of that passed day, and everything
added had grown on to the place as naturally as

the growth of the big limes & walnuts the old dead landreve had
planted for the first tennant: John sat down dazed with the hot sun,
and familiar with the room as he was it had a strange look of interest that day, and again he felt that [queer] feeling of something
going to happen and his heart beat in an excited way: Clara had left
them at the door, but presently he heard footsteps & the musical
jingling of glasses, and he noted her foot setting the door left ajar
fully open, and there she stood with a tray for his benefit heavy
enough: he jumped up, feeling awkward still, and hurried to take it
from her; she shewed no coquetry in letting him take it for it was
heavy enough as aforesaid; but gravely helped him to get it into
order on the table, and he fell to without any pressing and with
good will enough, as might well be for everything was of the
freshest, from his own schoolboy appetite to the crisp lettuces: the
elder lady sat busy over her work meantime and asking him little
matters of parish gossip, [a great grey cat jumped] and he ought to
have been getting at his ease long enough ago, (the bees never
ceased their music, the fowls cackled in the farm yard: there came
now and again the distant sound of wheels from the road and it
seemed that even if these had been silent there would have been a
musical murmur about that marks the high tide of a bright summer
day) but he felt restless and uneasy, and wondered why Clara didnt
talk, for she was ~~walking~~ wandering up & down the room restlessly,
now taking up her work and picking the threads out of the unfinished

seams, now sitting down in the windowseat and reaching a hand to
the clematis that hung over it, now dipping the tip of her fingers into the gold-fish glass and then coming up to her mother as if she
were going to speak; a great grey cat jumped through the open window and came purring & rubbing up against her, but got a very
careless acknowledgement from her: so John eyed her, till he began
to answer Mrs. rather at random, for he thought in himself was she
too waiting for something to happen as he felt he was or might be.
They were all three silent now, John had done his eating & had
drawn his chair & was absently enough playing with the cat, at last
Clara sat down, and pulling a clematis flower to pieces with her fingers laid before her on the table, broke the silence by saying What
was it you said just now John about your going into business will

you have to go up to London. Dear me child how you made me start
said her mother: what is it Master John; I thought we shouldnt lose
you; you always seemed so fond of the country here. Well Mrs. said
he I have no choice as to going somewhere unless I take the living
after my father; and you wouldn't have me waiting for his
shoes—though I—though you don't like him Mrs. Mason—besides I
shall like it: why should you think me different from other young
men who want to see the world and get on? Well said she; I have
always thought you & Master Arthur very different

from other lads—there I must make you blush by saying much
better: and we're such childish ignorant people here, that Im half
afraid you will forget us: how hard it is when things change & people without any fault on either side forget each other! Do you I wish
you & Arthur were older, just as I have wished of late that Clara
were my sister instead of my daughter: and then there wouldnt be
so much chance of a different set of hopes & wishes separating
us—Well he said: I dont want to boast but I don't think I shall
change much: and as for going away I know I shall often enough
long to be back but somehow I think it isn't so bad for people to be
apart a bit; so that they may have something else to think of than
themselves and each other: and sometimes lately—he stopped himself and reddened as his custom was when he got to talking or indeed thinking much about his feelings—What John, said she—O nothing he said I cant express myself properly—and that was true; yet
there was something more than a vague thought in his head: a feeling he was half ashamed half afraid of; had fallen on him at whiles
lately; of discontent and hopelessness—of emptiness in the summer
country about him—Well she said I see what it is John you want
some good excuse for explaining your being so glad of getting away
from us to new people—and I dont see who is to blame you—well I
should be more disappointed if Arthur were going instead—I dont
mean to be unkind

she said hurriedly—only I think he is the softest-hearted of you two.
But when are going John broke in Clara: Not till after Christmas he
said; its to be in a Russian merchants house and now you know as
much about it as I do, except that Mrs. M you don't know how I
shall miss you all. There I didn't mean anything: she said only Ill
tell you the truth I was so vexed to hear that you were going that I
was ill tempered and fell on the nearest and that was you: so youll
forgive me; and come & see us often these holidays, with Arthur

when he can go about again. Can you come often now? Yes said he
fathers gone away for some months—but that reminds me—Arthur
will soon be about again; and we want you to take us to Ruddywell
Court and ~~the~~ let us ~~have~~ give Clara and you a pull on the river and
have a picnic on that little eyot in the river—please come: Clara
looked up grown ~~joyously~~ suddenly and said O when shall we go
Mother: I do so want to see the beautiful old house again and that
room with red bed in it dont you know: that Arthur & I liked so
much and you didn't John—I daresay I shall like it this time he
said—When shall we go Mrs. Mason: Arthur ~~and~~ will be about &
quite able to go in 10 days time—[Its very true] O I shall be as
pleased to go as any of you she said brightening up Ill let you know
in a couple of days, Mr. John when I can manage it there's not
much to do this time of the year

The afternoon was getting on by this time & for the last ten minutes
there had been the sound of cows lowing by the farmyard, and in
this pause Mrs. seemed to catch the sound, & said—there now the
cows will be milked in a few minutes Im sure youre not too much of
a man to drink a syllabub[28] Master John and without waiting for an
answer she hurried out of the room to get the necessary foundation
for that pastoral delicacy. So the young folk were left alone—and
~~still Clara seemed restless not very happy: but John seemed to be
quite unconscious now of anything but enjoyment~~ eyed each other
rather shyly at first; till John said: fathers given Arthur such a good
new Arabian Nights, not like the old one you know, a new translation would you like to have a Vol: O I should she said I do so love
tales—but heres and idea John bring a volume the day we go to
Ruddywell & let someone read aloud in the eyot; I don't like
swallowing my stories so greedily as you boys do; when I get
something I like, I like time & place to go with it: Well I know he
said I sometimes wonder if I shall have read all the good books
before I die: how dull it will be but Im not such a book worm as
Arthur: I remember when we were all little reading about this room
one snowy day about Xmas; and he and I read ours wallowing
about on the floor; while you sat solemnly in the inlaid chair at the
table, with your

sugarplums handy: but I got tired first; and then you, and then we
both bullied Arthur for reading in the twilight by firelight don't you
remember?—Yes she said. So well I think I can see myself looking

[margin note: talk at A. says peoples lives & theirs would make dull stories]

up & watching the great snow flakes growing less & less visible as the light faded, surely she said after a pause we three have been the happiest children that ever lived. What a sweet voice youve got Clara he said suddenly: I mean when you talk—she blushed and laughed merrily, and it was indeed sweet to hear: then she said: Thats the first time youve ever said anything of that kind to me John so I dont wonder at your blushing at it. He was blushing with a vengeance but he laughed too and said: this is the first time I ever saw you blush Clara I do believe: so youre no better than I am— then they were both silent a while till she said gravely now: its strange we should both have remembered that we—so distinctly isnt it? and be talking about it like old people: I wonder if perhaps in years to come we shall remember this afternoon: the sunniest day in the year at all so cool & dim in here: and hark John the cows just let into the farm yard & mother here with the green dragon bowl com-ing: looking so fresh and handsome. Whats that Clara said Mrs. col-ouring up too: about people suddenly remembering little scraps of time gone by mother—ah child I hope youll never wish you could forget everything but today—No no I should

never wish that she said whatever had happened to me: I should wish to keep it all[29]—but please mother don't look as if you were going to cry; and she went up to her & began fondling her; John standing by half pleased half embarassed: and with a strange feeling that had gathered over him amid Clara's talk as if he had got a pain or some great pleasure, which yet set him longing so much for something still greater that it was a pain— Im an old fool quoth Mrs. M. not to remember that nobodys griefs are interesting to anybody but themselves—come along I'm going to milk her myself under the big walnut tree; come and get in the hay first Clara: She had indeed put a clean big cooking apron over her silk dress wh: was somewhat showier than one would have expected a farmers to wear even as rich as she was—Out they went all three Clara talking merrily about the milking & the cows & her poney and pet lamb that was grown an unwieldy great wether now; and John rather looking as if it were all a play got up for his special pleasure; and so to the big barn with its cool dusky depths, where with her dress tucked up she jumped lightly over the quarter-board: John following in amid huge admiration of her ankles; there she was for thrusting her hand into a truss of sweet hay but he cried out against it, yet she was obstinate and the two hands went in together with laughter enough, so out they

both passed again blinking at the white hot sun; but as they stood together just outside the barn ~~looking at~~ looking to see the cows that
stood huddled together by the byre door, lo a tramp & a jingling and
there was come the team from field X a sunburnt redlipped freckle
faced boy swinging about on (X two iron grey leaders, a dapple grey
wheeler, and behind a red roan and another dapple grey and a brown
horse) the first one: Clara went up to the second irongrey while the lad
stopped his charge grinning & pleased, and made much of him, and
cried out laughing to John to feed him with his wisp of hay—why
shouldnt mine go in the syllabub he said: why said she I meant you to
drink off mine; but since you wont well mix them half & half: she took
his wisp and he stood blushing (again) there and gave him back the
two halves & then took the ~~horses~~ black forelock of the horse in her
right hand while she held the clean hay away with the left: it was a
pretty sight thought Mrs. M; and she wished Arthur there to see it—so
away went the team to their stable, and then Mrs.M. turned with no
little affection to her cows, and singling out a great strawberry coloured Durham, coaxed it easily enough from the rest the 4 went off to
the walnut tree in procession first the goodwife with the china bowl
then the cow lowing & slobbering; then Clara holding a great trail of
sweet clematis & John with the pail & milking stool—so the syllabub
and further milking went on, Clara twisting the clematis in the cows
horns who repaid

that attention by eating as much of it as she could get at) and singing the while a snatch of a sweet old tune, a Xmas carol no
less—while John did the looking on—then came the cowboy for the
cow, and the syllabub was drunk with laughter enough as they sat
about on the flowering grass, and a little west wind got up to cool
the fiery afternoon, and Clara began to sing again in a pause of the
merry talk, and at first with a dreamy serious face till her mother
joined in and the two raised their voices while John listening grew
serious to melancholy as he looked at Clara's sweet eyes and wide
brow drawn into a little frown by her eagerness, yet felt more
melancholy still when the song was done. they sat nearly silent after
this for some while, with the crickets chirupping about them and
the afternoon was wearing fast; till to bring them back to earth
again there was a heavy footstep behind them and the farm bailif
came up, a commonplace businesslike looking man who shook
John's hand and asked with overdone appearance of interest about
the health of the rector; then tried a compliment to the ladies and a
warning against sitting in the grass as they got up and turned

toward the house again, then came tea; and after that ~~Clara~~ the bailif went away a while and they all sat under the mulberry tree again, quiet, & rather sad perhaps, till again the bailif with books that needed Mrs.Ms attention; and then J who had not spoken for a long while said. Well

I must go Mrs.M. I ought to have gone long ago you wont forget our day will you—She smiled pleasantly on him as he turned away, and Clara said Ill go with him a little way mother unless you want me to help you write out at once: no it will do when you come back dear said she—so Clara's bonnet was on in a minute and the two went round the house by the same path by which Clara had first come to him that day & then the two went slowly & soberly in the golden evening down to the river; she talking to him, asking questions about Arthurs illness then of what books they were reading; and then shyly & hesitatingly she asked about the Latin & Greek books they learned at school; he answered and talked well enough now, but at every turn he said that Arthur could answer her better and so they went slowly enough along the border of the stream, till he bethought him of taking home some of the water flowers to stuff the jug on the bedroom table with and had soon gathered a great bundle which he thrust into his empty fishing basket she standing by all the while and going on with her talk: this was just at the end of that more cheerful part of the river, & the evening was so far spent that the sun was setting in a cloudless orange sky; so when he had shut his basket: I must go back again now John—Yes dont tire yourself he said with a mighty effort

She walked though a little with him silent, till at last she said now I must go—dont forget the letter to Arthur—O no he said—John she said Im afraid I havn't been quite myself to day—O youve been cleverer & brighter than ever he said; and—Well she said I didn't feel so—you don't know how startled I was by your saying you were going to London; and though I know you must, and I always knew you would have to: but I don't like it—But you mustnt think that we shan't see each other often after a time again he said—something is sure to happen that will bring us together—I hope so, she said give my love to Arthur—good bye and she took his hand, and seemed as if she was going to kiss but did not, and turning [quickly] with a kind frank smile went swiftly on her way back again. He stopped a moment looking after her, with something that was certainly pain; then strode on quickly, thinking how long the day had been since the morning; but the pain softened soon, and he was soon dreaming of her feet brushing through the dewy grass and the night wind rustling her dress, and her great lovely eyes turning slowly to look at the yellowing moon as it ~~rose over~~ should shine through the willow boughs. The sun was down before he had got to the bridge and by then he was walking between the Battle Meads it was already something more than twilight. his father's house seemed dull and uninteresting as he stood before the doors of it; duller still

as he let himself into the dark hall, for the house was not lighted up yet; the servants mostly loitering about the back door that lovely evening: he went into the dining room and rang rather impatiently, and yet managed to swallow his feeling of dissappointment & weariness before the light came, and went whistling up stairs to his brothers room with his hand on Clara's letter in his pocket the while: there was no light in his brothers room when he got there; Mrs. was sitting there with him; hilloa old fellow he said, pulling his water-flowers out of the the fishing basket how are you getting on, very well said Arthur rather faintly: he's been up Mr.J. said Mrs. — and I think he's tired himself a bit. I Well I wont stop here long with him Mrs. — he must make up his mind to sleep. Don't go yet a bit John said the sick lad; I shall freshen up bit presently before I go to sleep: How the good folks up at Leaser Farm Mr.John said the housekeeper: Arthur turned round to the wall as John answered: ~~First~~ as well as well Mrs. the whole place is like the kingdom of heaven; it would be better to be a horse or a cow there than a man in most other places. Well she said I hope all will go on well: but Mrs.Mason has always spoilt that girl dreadfully; would ask her advise about things, when the child shouldn't have known that there were such things in the world: Yes master John I don't say but she's a fine girl & will marry well too; but if you'd seen her mother ready to go

down on her knees to her, when she ought to have had the rod across her back, you'd have been almost inclined to call the old lady a fool. Well well shes not so very old said John laughing and is nearly as pretty as her daughter. Ah said she laughing in her turn you'll be like all the men Master John; and I don't say there not a pretty pair widow Mason and her daughter: besides I like them both very much: but the widow isnt one of the wise ones: Miss Clara maybe. Well Ill take myself off and come up with Master Arthur's supper presently; and then you must take yourself off Mr.J. [then] J fell to stuffing a 2nd [blue] white jug with the mouseear, but as soon as the door was fairly shut Arthur raised himself up on his

pillows and how was Clara old fellow: Id never seen her look so
well: you remember saying in February what boys we looked beside
her; she's much more of a woman now, and I felt such a hobblede-
hoy & such a lout beside her: I don't think you would though you
always had the grace of the family—Nonsense said the other visibly pleased though; You dont suppose Clara notices things like
that—I say did she send any message to me—love & hoped you were
better, and a letter, here it is—he stepped up to the bed side with it,
Arthur took it eagerly, then lay back on the pillow with flushed
cheeks still holding it in his hand, then slowly put it under his pillow
not noticing how John was looking at him with a certain surprise at
first as

though he had expected him to open & read it: and then turned
away suddenly; for once more the commonplace of his life was broken into by he knew not what pain, what wild hope—but presently
Arthur began talking quite cheerfully about the farm & his fishing
& what Dr Stoneman had said about him; and then John speaking
rather constrainedly at first and happily enough afterwards told his
brother of the affair of the pleasure party; and then fell to talking of
his own prospects and the London sojourn that was to be: so that
they were both of them cheerful enough when the housekeeper
came up with the supper: so at last John said good night & went his
way and the housekeeper was following taking the candle and leaving only the ~~rushlight~~ the ghostly sickroom looking rushlight in the
room when Arthur called out O, Mrs. please leave the candle by me
I may want to read: hereon a short argument followed the dame
pleading fire & fever; the lad ~~sle~~ weariness & sleeplessness; and as he
was obstinate he had his way, and the departed having set the can-
dlestick in a bason on a chair by the bedside with a book or two: she
was scarcely gone before Arthur's hand stole under the pillow and
forth came the precious letter that he opened with beating heart:
though it was pretty much what he expected, it was little like we
should have from what we have seen of Clara; it was partly childish
partly stiff; it began Dear Mr.Arthur & ended your sincere friend &
well-wisher Clara Mason: it was long enough and began and indeed
went on nearly to the end with talk

about ~~the~~ her mother & the cows and her poney and the weather &
the garden, not forgetting the seldom flowering aloe: then it began
stiffly enough with not a few long words to talk of his illness and the
regrets for it: but at last came this: perhaps Mr.Arthur you will
think it strange for a girl of my age; and I am aware that I cannot

put it into proper language but I cannot help telling you about it
how I felt this morning as I lay awake quite early: I was thinking
about you and your brother and wishing that I could see you and
hoping so that you were better; then I began to wonder how 3 lives
would run on together, and then all of a sudden, I felt so strange, as
if I understood all about it why we alive and liked each other so,
and it felt so sweet and delightful that I never felt so happy in all my
life and yet I was longing for something, but the longing didn't seem
any pain to me: I cant tell you now what I thought of in that
minute—though if you had been by I think I could have then; but it
had slipped away very fast and left me wondering what it was that
had made me so happy: and so I thought & thought on till I grew
quite tired and got up and dressed and it was quite early only 5
oclock then; and I went out and walked a long way down the river,
and I got so tired that I had to sleep in the afternoon—But I must
ask you pardon for writing such a long letter and fatiguing you so
with nonsense, when you are just recovering from so severe an illness. It will give me the greatest pleasure to meet you again quite
yourself: meantime believe

me as aforesaid—Between weakness & transport the lad wept the
sweetest tears over his letter, and kissed over & over and put it at
last on his bosom and so with a happy face turned round to sleep,
and dropped off pretty and passed the ~~lig~~ night with faint vague
dreams of pleasant things, waking the gardens, going to hear music
& the like; and woke in the earliest dawn, to hear the birds begin-
ing their and a cow lowing a long way off: he felt about for his letter
& began in the happiest way to dream awake of the fields and
stream by Clara's home all grey & cold with the mist now; then he
[set himself in the midst of the scene and] thought of himself
wandering about in these meadows sick with the longing that he felt
amid his happiness, and then the farmyard gate swinging open and
Clara running to meet him her shoes all shining wet with the dew,
and putting her arms round him and kissing him less timidly than
she did [perhaps] really, and with something in her eyes that he had
not seen there yet; and then the two turning together and going into
the little garden in front there, and spending the day as if there were
no one else in the world; and still he kept beginning over & over
again the sort of things she would say to him; the way in which she
would kiss him, for still every sweetest way seemed not quite sweet
enough, till wearied out at last he fell asleep again just as the eastern
sky was beginning to redden, and his waking dream

turned into a sleeping one without changing much at first except
that it was suffused with a vague excitement and luxury and ~~horror even~~ fear withal that ~~he~~ had ~~not felt~~ been absent before; and he was
walking with Clara through ~~other~~ meadows not at all like the
Leaser meads which yet they both agreed to think were none other
it seemed; they were thickly studded with apple-trees in bloom, and
it was moonlight, yet the birds were singing in full chorus; and
Clara herself was clad in light fluttering raiment like he had seen on
angels in old pictures instead of her usual dress, and she spoke to
him in verse in the rhythm of some fragment of old poetry that he
had forgotten awake, and so they passed on till as it happens in
dreams the landscape changed and there were big blue mountains
~~and~~ all about the mead and a rushing stream through it, and suddenly his heart seemed to stop beating for fear and she stopped him
& faced him, with fear in her eyes too, and as he tried to speak &
could not, she had turned into his brother and they were both quite
children again and he thought that they had lost themselves & were
to die, and the rush of the stream seemed to get louder & louder, and
the wind to rise & howl about the hollows of the mountainside, and
presently a horse came gallopping past, and then a herd of cows
rushed up and then a great flock of sheep ~~the~~ seemed to fill up all
the valley their endless backs all moving like a sea, and the sounds

of the bell whethers filling up all the air, and then with a sense of
something dreadful going to happen he woke panting & gasping
with an unuttered cry, and the horror of the dream was so strong on
him that at first he seemed to wake into a world of white flame; but
as he ~~woke up~~ came fully to himself he saw the broad sun flooding
the room, and smiled to himself with returning comfort as he heard
the sound of a scythe being whetted outside for the mowing of the
rough piece of grass called the drying ground; then came the sound
of the musical church clock and he counted 7, and the full memory
of his happiness came on him as he felt the letter by ~~the~~ his side, and
lay listening to the sweep of the scythe in the swathe, the rattle of
the gardeners barrow, and all the little noises that go to make up the
music of a June morning: he soon grew drowsy again & fell into a
dreamless sleep, from which he was only woke by John & Mrs.
coming with his breakfast. the sick lad mended fast enough now
and wrote to Clara little notes every day telling her how he was,
there was little else in them though every night he pleased himself
by imagining tender little sentences he would write the next day,
but his heart always failed him when the paper lay before him; ~~shall~~

nor could he even get further in his signature than your affectionate friend, though he tried hard; they were a great pleasure to him however and the days passed happily for both the lads, and John went 3 times to Leaser farm, and came back the third time with the pleasure party day

duly settled for the day after tomorrow; this brought the time to the end of June; there had been broken stormy weather for near a week and all the farm people went to bed the night before with fears about the weather, Mrs.Mason being at least as eager as the others; the day dawned with a heavy mist, and would have looked unpromising enough to an unweatherwise person, but John was none such, and announced joyfully to his brother that they were going to have a wonderful day; as indeed it turned out for the mist was clearing even from the low ground about Leaser Farm as the brothers drove their phaeton into the orchard befo and stopped before the little green railings; where the two women stood ready dressed beside the in the door not to lose time. My youre not so well as I expected to see you Mr.Arthur said Mrs.M. as they all stood together beside the carriage and indeed, Arthur was pale and trembling as he after Clara's and stood leaning with one hand on the carriage after Clara's kiss, and rather timid welcome, and the two brothers looked for the moment different enough for John's face was flushed through its sunburn amidst his ruddy brown hair, and yet his brows were knitted anxiously while Arthur was smiling with the look of a sick person that has suddenly got a great pleasure. O its nothing he said, I shall be all right when we are going through the air again. Mrs.M. turned into the house for a glass

of wine while Clara looked rather grave, said she are you quite sure you can go Arthur: o dear he said Dr. said it would do me good didn't he Jack; he made a half step forward as he spoke, and touched her sleeve with his hand, and then let it slip onto hers; she held it quite simply & kindly and her eyes were fixed on him with a tender and anxious look that made the poor lad forget everything else, and they did not notice that J turned away to the horses head, but when in a moment Mrs.M. came out of the house with the Arthur drew his hand away rather hastily and flushing so that Mrs.Mason cried Why what ails you? You two haven't been quarrelling in this minute have you: Arthur laughed tho rather awkwardly; Clara flushed too, but still looked steadily at him, and with that John was come back to the carriage door in high spirits;

~~and~~ a ~~hamper~~ big handled basket with a white cloth was handed by
the redcheeked blackhaired maid into the ~~front~~ drivers seat, John
nodded to her & shook hands with her and jumped up into his place
without ceremony leaving the three to to help themselves up into
the inside where Arthur was set despite his politeness leaning back
in the roomy back seat with Mrs.Mason discreetly sitting by him,
and Clara opposite her mother; so off they went, John turning
round to talk in extra merry ways; and ~~Mrs.~~ answered at first by
Mrs.Mason only but soon as they drove through the now bright

sun and the fragrant shadow of the high hedge & lanes, all
awkwardness wore off the other two as well, as they all seemed as
happy as might be. the two women were clad as for merry making
and both gracefully enough; the mother in black silk with an Indian
shawl over her, a ~~n~~ sort of an heirloom of ~~the~~ her mothers; the
daughter also in a dress whose material came out of the chest on the
landing at home; it was an ~~Ita~~ India muslin soft and fine with a little sprig worked over it in floss silk; over this she had nothing but a
~~scarf of~~ delicately assorted shaded scarf: at her throat was a broach
made of a faint miniature of some long dead ancestor of her fathers,
a red-coated crested-helmed militia man, set in a coppery gold
frame; and a thin chain of the same material was over her neck.
these were her own private treasure, but her mother had lent her for
the occasion an old fashioned bracelet of thin chains of genoese
gold: clasped with a clasp of the same fashion as the ring on her
[dear brown] finger described before; and she wore it on her left
wrist, so much whiter than her [beautiful] hands from which she
had pulled the glove now; rather still as though she were committing an impropriety.—When she first got in she had a bunch of
beautiful cabbage roses in her hand which she held in her hand for
some time looking at Arthur all the while, yet with a strange faraway look in her lowlying eyes as though she did not see him, but ~~in-
a while~~ that melted away in a while into mere tender kindness as
she reached out to him, and put it into his hands saying I meant
them for you they are the last we shall have: so they drove on merrily enough by roads running along the side of the hills till after going
down a steep descent they came over to a little village scattered
about a goose green and then turning round a corner came upon the
ancient garden wall

over topped with fig trees & mulberry of Ruddywell Court: they
stopped before the great Queen Anne iron gate presently; and

Arthur and the two ladies got down there and walked slowly up the beautiful old yew hedged garden toward the front of the house; while John drove off to stable his horse at the Sun wh: lay nearer to the river: ~~at~~ the house was too much like other fine Elizabethan houses to need any particular description, so one need only say that it was ~~only~~ among the completest though not the largest existing of its kind: being received by the housekeeper they sat down in the cool deserted looking hall and waited for John who came back presently, and they were soon all four wondering each in his or her own way at the show things: Arthur and Clara both got very eager over the pictures, though to most people there would have been nothing very interesting about them as they were some few bad copies of well known Italian masters or endless ancestral portraits some not genuine, some dull works of fourth rate painters of such things and [some two or] three naif queer productions of the Holbein & Janet[30] school: these latter all of them boastfully calling themselves works of the first master were hung in the room with the red beds Clara spoke of the other day ~~more of wh~~ to which they came presently: the place was all full of old furniture tapestry & armour some of it really remarkable—they enjoyed themselves hugely among all these magnificences; the housekeeper was a friend of Mrs.Mason's

So they were not trotted through at the usual rate but sat about in special corners, and handled everything at their pleasure: Arthurs eyes sparkled with pleasure, and he did the talking for almost the whole company for was really somewhat versed in archaeological lore; and could tell scraps of stories from old chronicles & the like: John had got rather silent now, ~~and~~ but made little jokes from time to time which rather jarred on both his brother & Clara: she for her part ~~stuck~~ kept close by Arthur, listening with real pleasure to his talk; taking care that he should have the best seat when they halted; following him to the window when he went there to enjoy the deep green garden: so at last they came to the room with red beds which was was called Queen Elizabeth's room and was hung with tapestry[31] of earlier date than the present house: in which knights and ladies were walking & playing amid ~~the~~ a faded grey garden populous with pheasants and rabbits: a great red hung bed in the darkest corner and a smaller one of the same material & colour beside it: a suit of bright steel armour was in the other corner, and on the wall were the three pictures in question two handsome bearded men in slouched hats, and a wonderfully ugly big-nosed lady in a rich dress holding a pink in her fingers. the one deeply recessed window look-

ed over the corner of an orchard on to wide flat meads, and a
flashing river beyond; the sun had gone from that side of the house
now and the room was deliciously cool and full of that feeling of
rest that a shadowed room

has on a hot day: so when they had looked at the pictures & tapestry
& embroidered coverlets Arthur sat down somewhat wearily, &
Mrs. said. 'Dont you think you had better rest a bit here Master
Arthur before dinner: you wont last out till the end of the day if you
are not careful of yourself." Arthur demurred and Mrs.Mason was
just going to speak again when Clara said do stay & rest Arthur and
Ill stop with you Im rather tired too. The burly housekeeper smiled
for he had seen that Mrs. was going to offer to stay behind ~~and~~ but
she wasn't over sorry to be rid of Arthurs to her stupendous lore, so
that she might have her say: and didnt want to lose her chance of
talking to her friend—so she said: Yes you two young ones and
solemn ones stay if anybody must; for I know you are on the lookout
for ghosts & romantic matter, and one could see a ghost at noontide
I am sure I should come to this room to look for it: so they passed on
J. talking merrily to the housekeeper: and left the two there: Arthur
sitting a big chair near the corner and Clara near him her dainty
fresh skirts brushing against the old hard armour: almost without
looking he was conscious that she had laid her left hand on the
breastplate, and even though he half saw it he began to dream
about it as his way was, ~~making~~ about everything; to make it something different from what it was; all the morning as he talked he
imagined her thoughts about him, and had changed her clinging
kindness into heaven knows what dream of singlehearted passion,
and now as she stood silent there, and he sat trembling

and afraid to break the sweetness of being at one with her, he imagined her in like case: and now she turned her head a little and their
eyes met; hers so tender and compassionate for she saw a worn anxious look in his face: Are you very tired dear she said in a sweet low
voice: it thrilled all through him with inexpressible sweetness for
she had not yet ~~called him dear~~ used so soft a word to him; his face
lighted up as he shook his head and reaching out his hand touched
the sleeve of her left arm and then as before let his hand fall down
on to her palm, that yielded passively to him while a look like surprise came into her face which he noted despite his dreaming and
began to talk hurriedly, without losing her hand though. Wouldn't
you like to know all about the old fellow that wore it Clara? ~~when~~

how he went to & fro, and the people were he was fond of—Yes she said though I suppose people were dull & stupid then like they are now when they fall in love and are happy and unhappy: and write poetry too—Ive never seen any old books of that time Arthur—There are some old chronicles at home, he said, I don't know why Ive never lent them to you; you see when we three have been together lately we have been busy talking about things going on; besides I wasn't sure that you could read them easily without someone to help let me come over and read pieces to you this summer out in the garden. Yes do she said. You know, he went on, one has fits of not caring for fishing & shooting a bit and then I get through an enormous

lot of reading; and then again one day one goes out and down to the river and looks at the eddies, and then suddenly one thinks of all that again; and then another day when one had ones rod in ones hand one looks up & down the field or sees the road slowly winding along and I cant help thinking of tales going on amongst it all and long so for more & more books—don't you know—Well she said one day goes so much like another with me, and she gave a little unconscious sigh, and women have so much less of stirring things to look forward to than men; and yet I won't say that I don't make tales to myself too. She blushed scarlet as she spoke and Arthur felt the hand he was nursing tighten on his a little: his heart leaped at it, and again what tales he told himself; he was silent as he watched the colour fading out of her face again: at last he said with a great effort. Clara you get more & more beautiful every day—there I never said a word about that before, and if youre not angry I'm so glad I said it now: If he expected to see the blush come into her face again he was disappointed; she only looked at him with such serious eyes as she answered: Why should I be angry Arthur; I'm pleased because I think you know about such things, and people about here dont much I fancy: and though I don't think I should set my heart on it much I can't help being pleased at being—being ~~good~~ well-looking. Youre a great deal more than that he said

I hope ~~youll~~ we—you will be happy, for somehow beautiful people so often seem to be unhappy: Oh she said with a real merry laugh—don't say such unlucky things or it will fall back on yourself, for she did colour again a little here, ~~while Arth~~ Ive heard mother say that you were like to turn out the handsomest men she had ever seen and that you were far the handsomest of the two there are you angry she

said laughing again for his face was scarlet: besides she said gravely
& rather primly, people are always happy when they do what is
right. He laughed out at this and said Ill luck for me Miss Clara who
don't do a 20th part of what I ought—and never shall—come I
know you don't belive that?—I don't know she said, turning toward
the armour again; she had gently drawn her hand away for a minute or two; tell us Arthur could a man like this have walked about in
our house—No he said don't you remember the date; this fellow is
as old almost as the chancel of our church theres a brass just like
him in the floor. he rose as he spoke, and took the halberd out of the
mailed hand, and lowered the blade of it for her to see the engraved
ornament on it, she drew to it with a pleased smile as he began to
talk about it and tell her what the figures meant, her face was so
near to his that he felt her breath upon it and he was as happy as
might be: and as he moved

to put it back in its place [again] the look of surprise came into face
unnoted by him as he led her to the window seat on which he knelt
while she leaned forward by him; then they talked about the day
and how delightful it would be upon the river, till suddenly the
voices & footsteps of the returning party were heard & Arthur
loosed her hand and turned with start to meet them; if he had
looked at her face he would have seen something like trouble in it
now;—and would certainly not have put it down to the right
cause—as for her she greeted them with Mrs Arthurs quite rested
now mother—Yes whoever else is tired quoth the housekeeper grinning.—O were not tired said Mrs.Mason simply not seeing the cun-
ning old lady's grin—or noticing her emphasis—though if we must
say the truth she would not have been greatly distressed if she had
seen lovemaking going on between the two after her first qualm of
fear at the parson's violence of indignation at his brutality; of doubt
as to whether John would not have made the better lover. Well they
walked slowly back through the corridors & cool dark rooms happily enough all of them; the young ones full of eager life [and] made
miraculous by vague dreams for the future; dreams that were
shared more or less by Mrs.Mason amid the regrets of her widow-
hood

for she whose nature sweet & kindly feelings hardly included passion as her dreamy & vague mind hardly included reason, found her
failing interest in contemplating the future of her daughters heart,
whom she loved tenderly scarcely remembering it maybe that she

was her daughter. So they passed out of the house, and turning along the front of it went by the housekeepers invitation through the gardens toward the little inn that standing where the Ormslade river[x] combined in itself the character of inn lockhouse & ferry house: the Ormslade river crossing the road became a sort of garden canal to Ruddywell Court, and turned what would have been very beautiful and quaint old gardens into a positive paradise, and the young folk grew nearly wearied by their pleasure amid the redundance of the old garden through which they loitered sitting down for long spells here & there: at last they came to where they had to cross a bridge, built in naively pedantic imitation of the glories of Palladio,[32] and taking leave of the complaisant housekeeper passed out into the highway a few hundred yds from the ferryhouse. a rod or two further on the backstream from above the lock crossed the road and ran into the Ormslade river, and there the two together slipped into the broad stream which there is all the less necessity for any naming as the people thereabout never called it anything else than the River and indeed they might be excused if they forgot that there was any other river in

world, so beautiful this stream was, such a look of history and romance and promise of great things to come it bore upon its eddies, and already high up in that remote countryside had that look of nobility, which never belongs as I fancy to any river that does not personally meet the ~~strea~~ sea. There were no longer hedges on either side the way now nothing but wide clear ditches full of yellow flowered segs & water flowers, and the road was a little raised above the broad meadows that spread out long distance on this left bank of the stream, rows of willows here and there marking the course of some brook or big ditch, countless kine & horses wandering about, and the lapwing wheeling about with his peevish cry: on the right bank ~~after~~ low hills hill rose up just a rod on the other side of the tow-path, though just opposite the ferry they fell off into wide slopes of grass meadows through which the road wound, and afterwards upstream fell away from the river while down stream they rose steeper and here & there showed broken escarpments of sandy bank pitted with sand martins nests—so they came down to where the inn a little low stone slateroofed house with the sign of the Rose hanging ~~at~~ from it, stood ~~on~~ at the brink of the wide pool below the lock; [then] on a sloppy willowy piece of land even in this June almost as much water as earth, a casting net hung spread out and

[x] as people called it though old folks and the maps had the Blackwater ran into the big navigable sea-going stream.

dripping still on to the dry dusty road by the door, and a mangy old grey

~~and~~ with a very small brown child babbling about him and hanging on to his tail, and inside through the cool dusk of the house one could dimly see shining pots hanging up—a very unlikely place it looked to get ones dinner at; it looked at the very end of the world; for the road ~~seemed to~~ that ended in the shallow on this side, rose from the water on the other all grass grown & little used and was now indeed ~~little but~~ hardly more than a bridle way, and seemed to lead nowhere at all—So here Mrs M. made Arthur go into the house for a Rest while John went to get the boat ready and see about the necessaries for the feast: Arthur looked over his shoulder to see if Clara were coming [and] but she said quietly I must go & look at the lock therell be plenty of time, and walked off briskly as she spoke, [drawn by the attraction of the great stream] and presently her feet were bruising scent from the great horse mint as she picked her way between the willow stems; then she scrambled up a little bank into the blazing sun and so to the lock head where she stood leaning on the sluice tops and watched the water gurgling ~~into~~ under the shut sluices, and the shadowy faint green bleak flitting about at the top of the water; [somehow] the look of the black depths made the day seem hotter & more luxurious, as the scent of the marshland hay and clover, and the hum of bees and tinkle of sheep bells ~~from~~ was carried to her across the wide meadows then as she looked up in a while the sound ~~tinkling~~ of church bells, fell sweet upon the light wind

from a little steeple she could just see at the foot of the furthest spur of the higher ground, bringing that inevitable melancholy with it that deepened upon her till with a sigh she was just turning to go, when she felt a hand upon her shoulder, and said, Arthur? No its me quoth his brother. how grave you look Clara; you look as if you could see through me. her eyes changed kindly as he spoke, and she said I think the bells made me melancholy—John let us come to the boat: he turned slowly saying what were you thinking of though? Well she said people can't expect to be answered when they ask such questions as that, but for once I think I can tell you; I was thinking that it would be very dreadful to live here if one got to be unhappy: How strange he said, I suppose the bells set me thinking too, for as I came along I was thinking and wondering what I should do to pass the days if I were living here an old man with all ones friends dead—or at Leaser Farm he said, stammering & reddening; She didnt answer & he was silent as they walked on; he took her firm fine hand to help her down the bank and his face grew graver & graver, till she said suddenly [raising her eyes and] you bring the book? Yes he said—Im so glad I have been looking forward to hearing those stories; and it will be so delightful to remember them with the beautiful place & this happy day—They got to the boat with this where Mrs. & Arthur were already seated: Clara was rather eager to row but John rather grave still and awkwardly enough

edging in some compliment to her skill with the oar, objected on the score of haste in getting into the shade being advisable so Clara sat down beside the two others in the stern smiling but a little vexed: at any rate this pleased one person Arthur to wit who ~~leaned back~~ sat with the rudder strings in his hands ~~& his~~ her cheek nearly touching his shoulder supremely happy; and presently ~~seeing that John~~ she laughed merrily & said John I was getting ill tempered; but you must have been picking up grand manners somewhere, to beat about the bush like that, when you know I can't row a bit. All right he said laughing himself You shall row going back—You & your mother together if you like—we can start in good time—Worse & worse said Mrs. —unless, you really mean a compliment by thinking us such fine ladies that our arms would ache at the first stroke of the oar: if you saw Clara and I washing our own smart laced things you would think better of them Mr.John—The two lads blushed & felt happy & shamefaced at this but said nothing, John laying vigorously on the oars, and Arthur pumping himself in the pride of his oarcraft, though the great big green-painted old tub was not particularly suitable for that display: betwixt this small pleasantry and others they got to the eyot wh: ~~stood~~ was just a long bank high and dry above the weedy shallow that John pushed

the boat through with some difficulty—; but in the middle of said bank some one had planted a ring of willows, and this dry time the turf under them was soft & pleasant enough so there they spread their feast out, Arthur lying down and John trying to help and looking awkward & because both the women would not let him, pretending to be afraid of his breaking things: so there was plenty of laughter over their dinner, ~~and~~ Mrs.M codling Arthur hugely which he was still weak enough from his illness to like rather, and Clara watching his somewhat startling appetite with amusement mingled with pleasure too—the business of eating over they fell to the book, Arthur reading at first, to whom Clara drew near, and sat watching his eager face with ~~the~~ a little frown on it; ~~but w~~ with kind & serious eyes; but turned in the pauses of the tale to talk about it to John, who spoke well and without any shyness now; then John took the book & read, not so well as Arthur because he couldn't help thinking of what was coming further on in the tale, and Clara having arranged the cloths Arthur lay on about a tree-trunk sat by him, and still watched his face, and he sat conscious of it and not liking to turn to her lest she should look away, and when the sun was fairly falling and before it began to get colder they got into the boat and the two women took the oars, and they dropped slowly down stream amid a good deal of merriment

from the lads; and they stopped here & there to gather wild flowers on the bank, and wandered about from side to side of the stream, doing all those little untellable things that go to make a happy day with happy people; and they were all very happy together till at last Mrs.Mason cried out that it was already over late for Arthur to be out and they must turn at once; so she who was sitting aft moved to give her place up to John and he went forward and met Clara in the middle of the boat, and it was a little difficult for them to pass one another, ~~so there she~~ and as they stood thus with her hand on his shoulder ~~they stood with~~ she stopped and said John look at the sunset now, Mother and ~~John~~ Arthur turn round and look; for a sudden change had gone over the sky by the drift of light clouds & the whole was full of strange golden ~~& green~~ light, and in the west ~~it was~~ the clear sky passed from orange to pale yellow & green, and the long strips & light flecks were deep crimson, unmeasurable colours: they looked silently, while the stream gurgled past them and the water hen cried among the weeds and the big eyed heifers stared at them from the bank but Arthur turned soon to look at her: there she stood with her hand still on John's shoulder, and he holding the other hand: ~~her head~~ she had half bared her arms beautiful but slim as a young girl's are, her head was bare and little locks of hair were floating about her face in the light wind, her lips were a little parted ~~with the~~ amid pleasure and thought—and her eyes fixed full on the sky, as if she would never

think of anything of earth again—but even as he gazed in ecstasy with a strange pang at her exceeding beauty that seemed too great for her to notice him; ~~She~~ a happy smile crossed her face, her kind

eyes fell to his, and she stepped aft lightly and came & sat down by
him, laying her hand on his in the fulness of her heart. The John sat
down & threw the oars into the rullocks, with a heavy splash the ~y~
~were~ boats head swung round, and presently the two were facing
that western glory to which J.'s back was turned and he pulled back
sturdily toward the lock: it had not wholly faded by then they got
into the carriage there though the clouds were dusky purple now instead of crimson & the stars were beginning to show and the high
moon to colour.— So on they drove, through the odorous June night
steeped too completely in happiness to remember that their pleasure
day was nearly at an end. Arthur was rather worn out amid his
delight, and Mrs.M. had made him lie as much along as he could on
the back seat the carriage after much opposition on his part: he had
Clara's ~sat~ roses in his hand for he had made them put them in
water at the little inn and they were quite fresh now: she sat opposite to him quite hanging over him, not saying much but listening to
him when he spoke almost (he thought) as if there were no-one else
in the world; and indeed she thought how happy she was to have
such dear friends & so fond of her as he—and his brother were—

Yes and as he talked to her now telling her how he had thought of
her in his illness, & of his dreams she had come into, that fever had
sometimes turned into horrors, the tears gathered in her eyes with
pity and affection, and though with a thrill of fear she felt despite
herself glad that he seemed fonder of her than John did—But here
was Leaser Farm at last and the little green railing and the lights
flitting about the windows for it was fully night now; and now
Clara's lovely eyes were blinking at the candles in the oak parlour
hot and stuffy now while the two lads drove on still through the
cool night., Arthur's heart beating still with the boldness ~with~
~which~ that had filled him at parting to pass his lips from the cheek
she had ~offered~ him to her averted lips, and his lips trembling still
with the sweetness of very unbrotherlike kiss; John whistling in sturdy resolution to keep his heart up, and rating himself for a feeling of
discomfort and wrong that sooth to say was not new to that hour of
parting but had been hanging about him all day long. As to Clara
she found her mother perhaps a trifle cross and disagreable after the
days pleasuring; but herself at least might have passed for gay, and
at last when she had put her candle out and was lying alone in her
dear little room looking at the faintly moving trees and stars be-

tween them that showed through her little half opened white curtained window, all wordly troubles had past

away from her, and wrapped in the happiness ~~of~~ her own beautiful
& simple soul made for her she thought of her love for those that
loved her till night weariness had their way with her & she fell
asleep in the fragrant peaceful place, and dreamed of herself grown
very old but happy still, with no one lost of those that loved her.
Arthur lay abed ~~to his breakfast~~ the next morning happy enough,
and John sat with ~~with~~ him at his breakfast; with the feeling that
life had got very commonplace & stupid, fit enough in any case for
the day after a merrymaking, and longing sorely for something
startling to happen but doing his best to carry on something of talk
with his brother and going every now & then to the open window &
leaning out of it in a restless manner; at last came the short sharp
double ring at the bell that indicated the postman, and J started,
though it may easily be believed that the lads correspondence was
so small that neither of them need expect a letter because of that;
nevertheless on this occasion a letter was brought up presently &
given to John, who said Well by Jove heres a letter from father, and
tore it open ~~with~~ eagerly and with some apprehension too wh: latter
Arthur rather more than shared: what is it old fellow? he said before
J could have half read it through: Why said J after he had hastily
skimmed through to the end its a case of Goodbye—and he threw
him the letter, which ran thus:

My dear J. You remember my telling you last time I saw you that
you must make your choice of a business, well you must choose at
once; for I have just got a letter from Godby telling me that the
place in the Russian house is just vacant; if you take my advice you
will take it; Godby's friend will push you; and by then you are
twenty-one you might put your Mother's money into the affair and
become a junior partner; i.e. always if you work hard these 4 years
& learn the business: if you determine to go it must be at once: Godby has asked you to go and stay with him for a couple of days before
you go up; that will be about as much as they will allow you: but he
will put you up to things in London: for he is a good natured fellow
and likes young people better than I do: write to him at once:
Mr—~~will~~ has instructions to get a lodging for you & to pay you.
Godby will tell you all about that: you are old enough to see about

all you want with the housekeeper; tell her to give you money to get
up to London—There—work hard & try to make money: ~~and don't~~
~~g~~ you will find the making of it more amusing than anything else,
besides all the amusement you can buy with it: dont get into a mess:
I did when I was young and that has tainted my position ever since;
if you think this queer for a parson to write I can't help it—I am not

[33]You say I shall not be surprised perhaps: surprised! why
when I was down there with you the whole air seemed full of this; it
lurked in dark corners in the ~~twigh~~ twilight, and the dark throbbed
with it as I lay alone on my bed, till I felt as it it would burst out into
a cry; and as I went up in the train the noise of the wheels & engine
seemed to be telling the world of it; and when the murkiness of London drew near, there it seemed to be lying in wait for us: (in my
dark room) (I expected to see it), as I hurried up the stairs, and as I
lay awake in the night I told myself the story over & over again till I
could lie still no more & yet was too weak to get up—look I am writing nonsense to you—but how could I be astonished. and now I will
talk sense & give you advice; and believe me for whatever reason, I
am inspired tonight, and if you follow my advice all will be well
with you; if otherwise, if you let any half-heartedness decieve you
~~there is nothing~~ it will be better for you to grow miserable & die,
than ~~than to live~~ & to be contented and live: again you think ~~ma~~ me
mad, ~~but~~ forgive it—but read on—if you are sure, as you say you
are, that Clara loves you and that you love her heed nothing heed
nobody but live ~~with~~ your life through with her, crushing everything. that comes in your way—everything—unless perhaps there
were somebody who loved her better than yourself: yet as you will
not be able to imagine that if

you really love her, the first word stands; everything & everybody—
I do not understand why you should hesitate—as to father; why, if
he had loved us as passionately as one reads of sometimes, I would
say disregard him—so there is no need to say that he loves us little
enough, that his whole life is mingled with some blind hatred—be
sorry for him, as I am—love him as I cannot,—and thrust him aside
from out your path—what else is there? Clara's mother? make her
yield man, make her yield! she is weak & sentimental a long face or
two a little crying & the thing is done: and she will have no grief, only a little discomfort: let her bear it! there is not much need to pity
her. Well, I won't do you the injustice to think you really care what

the world will say; nor think that you are really so stupid as to think that she with those eyes, that body that her soul has made, can care; and so you have nothing left; for you shall have at the very worst 2 thirds of any money I can make; and if you are poor, how sweet your ambition to get on will be when it is for her—bah, why need I preach to you about that. Oh you are happy—what need of me to call on God to bless you: for be sure that his blessings are showered down on the strong lucky people who come near enough to the fire to thrust their hands [into the fire] and snatch the gold

out of it: they cannot heed if they would, the wailing or the silent misery of those who are old or blind, or weak with the horrible fever of longing that can never be satisfied—O how beautiful you must think the world!—Stop though! are you sure that she loves you as you love her? Nay do not be indignant—find out without blinding yourself ~~what~~ how the matter goes; and if you find she does not then—~~and~~ why then still strive with all your might to get her, to be with her, if not for many years, yet for a year; if not for a year for a ~~mnth~~ month; if not for a month for a week—for a day, an hour a ~~mint~~ minute—do anything, stoop to any humiliation, tell any lie, commit any treachery—but do not die as—as some people must, with your love barren & unsatisfied, when you can make it otherwise: do not hesitate on the score of her happiness; if you feel real love you must know that you really think the whole world exists only to minister to your passion—O think of the happiness if you can feel this, and be satisfied—yes even without any return it is happiness; it is worth passing through all the pain that clings about it[34]— and if you do not feel this, you are not in love: and the ~~feeling~~ desire you have will pass away into something else—into friendship, or into disgust or hatred?—how should I know or care which? what does it

matter; all is either love or not love; there is nothing between; everything else; friendship, kindness, goodness, is a shadow & a lie! Yes you must test your love in this way, and even then you may fall into the misery a third ~~possibbil~~ possibility will bring you to: Oh my God it is all a matter of chance; for my words are only words to you unless you are really in love: who can judge false love without having felt the true? but try your best, try your best for all our sakes, and then God help you and all unhappy people!

your brother J.Risley.

P.S. This is a wild letter, but it is all I can write just now: do not be frightened of me when I meet you next; and tell Clara I wrote kindly to you, and was very glad that you were going to be married: you see I am so anxious that the only two people I love in the world or ever shall love, should be quite happy; quite without a cloud on their love; tell dear (scratched out) Clara that I advised you to carry the matter through if you were in torment (scratched out) in spite of everything. P.P.S. I must come & see you soon. Good bye J.R.

Arthur's face grew pale enough as he read his letter and when he had done it he walked up & down the room many times; but without saying a word; without indeed forming one in his heart; at last he walked out of the house & straight to Leaser Farm: there he found Clara & her

mother sitting together, and after the first greeting sat down with no attempt to make talk, and answered at random to Mrs.M's anxious questions about his health: Clara [could not bear to see him suffering thus] sat silent for a little time, and presently said to him quite abruptly: Come out and look with me Arthur I want to show you something: he rose without a word, and though Mrs.M: would have followed them, Clara's bluntness and a tone of real resolute sternness in her voice stopped her, and she sat there alone in great agitation: so when the two had gone a step or two got among the low hanging lime boughs Clara turned round on him and said: What has gone wrong Arthur? he caught hold of her hand and began nursing it to his breast, and the colour had come back to his cheeks again as he answered, "Nothing nothing; I wrote to John & have an answer—it was so kind—" She turned deadly pale: "What's the matter? is he ill?" she said—"No no dear: he said he was so very very glad and said I should be so happy, and advised us to carry the matter through, in spite of everything." She was still pale: "Arthur," she said, are you telling me the whole truth?"—"I mean she said, are you breaking some dreadful thing to me—don't torment me? it isnt kind to do those sort of things—you know I love you." "O my darling," he cried, drawing her to him, "and how I love you! there is not a word more of his letter to tell you, than that, and that he seemed tremendously

excited about it: and if I looked pale and anxious just now, it was because I had quite made up my mind to tell my father all about it and that we must be married at once; and it was a little apprehension & a greal deal of excitement that's it. O my own my sweet, and my cowardice and nervousness has made you suffer—dear I wish you could hurt me in return for it: but I know you are too kind and cannot." ~~her cheek touched his~~ he trembled all over with pleasure as he spoke, for her cheek touched his, and while he stood dreaming in his old way, ~~he heard her~~ he felt her sigh, and then her lips had stolen round to his, and there was no pang in his heart but of long-ing still unsatisfied as they kissed together there. I am so glad he was pleased she said as they walked back to the house, and now you're going to tell mother all about it—"Yes," he said dreamily. You know she said, "I haven't told her about it, "but I am sure she knows that something has happened: I must make her happy Arthur she has always been so kind to me; and I know you are fond of her. "Yes very much" said Arthur and they went hand ~~and~~ in hand into the room: where indeed there was little need to say much, for Mrs.M: met them halfway as soon as Arthur had opened his mouth; and perhaps the two lovers were a little ashamed of her raptures, Arthur at all events—Arthur went away in the evening scarcely feel-ing the ground he trod on, and kissing over & over again some little love tokens she had given him, a glove, and a little silk handkerchief she used to wear round her neck; yet ever and anon came a thought that

was like the shadow of a crime on him, this that he was glad she had not asked to see J.'s letter: and for her she said to herself aloud when she was alone: "I wish I had asked to see John's letter: and then again presently; No I ~~must can~~ cannot now, after that unlucky speech about its being the whole truth, he would think I half sus-pected something wrong: & it would look ugly & not as if I were his love.

THE CONCLUSION

By now Morris has got into trouble with his time scheme. Parson Risley and Eleanor see *Medea* at the Olympic in 1856 and he mar-ries shortly afterwards. John is born presumably in 1857, and origi-nally Morris tells us he is fifteen, bringing us to 1872, the exact time of writing, when the book opens. But on p.41 John has become "17 last February," so we are in 1874. Some years must elapse before Arthur and Clara marry, and more before "the kid" can be told about his uncle (p.54). If John is in his thirties the date will be

around 1890, so that his experiences will be truly news from nowhere. This is proof, if any more is needed, of how impetuously
Morris dashed into his tale. Mackail (*Life*, I, 287) considered that
the novel was about one-third of the way through, and that it was
"evidently going to take a tragic turn."   —Ed.

NOTES

1. Philip Webb, Morris's faithful friend and architect, wrote of the
    Kelmscott district: "It is known fact that in outlying places, when
    stone mason's work is the chief part of the building, and there are
    many quarries giving the same formation of stone, the prevailing
    traditions of building lasted longer in one place than another. This
    makes it often difficult in such places to be sure of the dates from the
    style of masonry," and of Kelmscott Manor itself, "the work was
    really later than it looked to be." J. W. Mackail, *The Life of William
    Morris* (2 vols. [London: Longmans, 1899]), I, 231-232. In *News
    from Nowhere*, Morris calls this part of Oxfordshire "the stone-
    country, in which every house must be built, walls and roof, of grey
    stone or be a blot upon the landscape."
2. See note 18, on "Battle Meads."
3. Ormslade Rectory seems to be a recollection of Elm House,
    Walthamstowe where Morris was born and lived till 1840, when he
    was six years old. The carved ivory junk in the drawing-room there
    was one of his earliest memories.
4. "Elm House . . . was a plain roomy building of the early years of
    this century, the garden front facing south on to a large lawn sur-
    rounded by shrubberies and kitchen gardens, with a great mulberry
    tree leaning along the grass." Mackail, I, 4. By the time Mackail
    wrote it had been pulled down and the site had been built over.
5. Ezzelino da Romano, (1194-1259) the ferocious governor of Verona
    and Padua.
6. Olmstead becomes Ormslade at this point.
7. Presumably Eleanor was thinking of throwing herself off the bridge.
8. The Olympic Theatre, Maypole Alley, Drury Lane, was a favourite
    haunt of Rossetti's; he used to take Burne-Jones and Morris there
    when they came to London as young men in 1856-7. The chief at-
    traction was the incomparable comic actor, almost a dwarf, "Rob-
    son of the Olympic" (Frederick Robson, 1821-1864). He appeared
    in *Medea, or The Best of Mothers, With A Brute Of A Husband* in Ju-
    ly 1856. This was a burlesque of the Euripides *Medea*, (which was
    playing nearby at the Lyceum), and was very successful. Dickens
    praised Robson's "frantic song and dagger dance," which was a
    frenzy of comic rage and jealousy.
9. Eleanor's role is Dickensian, and one would think that as a wronged
    woman (Rosa Dartle, Helena Landless) she must be intended for a

dramatic reappearance. But Morris calmly dismisses her from the story.

10.   Edward William Lane's translation of sixty-two of the *Arabian Nights Entertainments* was published originally in monthly parts, from 1839–41. A three-volume popular edition "for family reading" was published by John Murray in 1847, and a one volume edition in 1853. Lane included more stories than any earlier translator and Morris "revelled" in the book as a boy. The *Nights* were a favourite in many Victorian homes (it was one of the few books Christina Rossetti enjoyed as a child), but Georgie's family never possessed a copy until Morris gave them one in 1856. "It entranced . . . all of us, so that even the youngest sister would sit by the fireside on her little stool, reading it as long as ever she was allowed, whilst the outside world passed away and her sisters were looked at with dim eyes and addressed as 'O daughters of my father." G. B. [Georgiana Burne-Jones]. *Memorials of Edward Burne-Jones* (2 vols. [London: Macmillan, 1904]), I, 142. This was Louie, to whom Morris sent the MS. of the present novel.

11.   Lane, III, 671-732. Maroof, a poor cobbler, was bullied and nearly ruined by his wife, Fatima the Dung (Lane translates the Shrew), but ended up as a wealthy man and the husband of a Princess.

12.   Morris was supposed to have the gift of dreamless sleep, whereas Rossetti, Jane Morris and Burne-Jones were always recounting their latest dream. However, in *Frank's Sealed Letter* (1856), which, Mackail tells us, has "many details which were directly taken from his own life" the hero recalls "how I tried to wake, to find myself with my heart beating wildly, and the black night round me, lying on my bed; as often, when a child, I used to wake from a dream of lions, and robbers, and ugly deaths, and the devil, to find myself in the dear room, though it was dark, my heart bounding with the fear of pursuit and joy of escape." At the end of *News from Nowhere*, when the vision fades, Morris sees "as it were a black cloud rolling along to meet me, like a nightmare of my childish days."

13.   Jack, the under-gardener, seems to be drawn from Philip Comely, the cottager who looked after Kelmscott Manor, and who embarrassed Morris by constantly touching his hat as though by "a trick of machinery." There may also be a reminiscence of *The Heir of Redclyffe*, Chap.VII, where Guy helps with the haymaking, and "[Laura] watched the old cowman come up, touching his hat, and looking less cross than usual; she saw Guy's ready greeting, and perceived that they were comparing the forks and rakes, the pooks and cocks of their counties." As to the brandlings, the worms Morris himself preferred for bait, "they are striped & don't smell nice—that is their sign" he told his wife. (16 Aug. 1877)

14.   Oldham was the married name of Morris's favourite sister, Emma. The Rev. Joseph Oldham was a High Chuch clergyman and as the "Mr. O" of Morris's story "wasn't right about his religion" and appears to have been rather dissipated. Morris must have had second thoughts about using the name and changes it later to Mason.

15. A moonraker is a native of Wiltshire, and proud of the story that some of his ancestors dragged a pond to try to catch the reflection of the moon, or alternately that this was the excuse they made to the excise man who caught them hiding barrels of smuggled brandy in the pond.

16. Jenkins is also the name of the thieving groom in *The Heir of Redclyffe*.

17. From this point Morris changes John's age to 17, Mrs. Oldham's name to Mason, and Fairmead to Leaser Farm.

18. The name Battle Meads suggests that Ormslade Village is Radcot, about two miles downstream from Kelmscott. There was a skirmish here (thought of in Radcot, however, as a battle) during the Parliamentary wars. The stone bridge at Radcot, partly fourteenth century, is the oldest on the Thames. John lingers on this bridge to talk to Dr. Stoneman and then walks two miles downstream by the river path to Kelmscott.

19. Morris was well aware of the effects of his own shyness. In the letter to his mother (Nov. 11, 1855) explaining why he intends to become an architect instead of entering the church, he reproves himself for "speaking indeed far off from my heart because of my awkwardness." He was then twenty-one.

20. In sending his hero to Russia, Morris may have had in mind the experiences of his friend Crom (Cormell Price, 1835–1910). In the spring of 1860, having thrown up his medical studies and, as he put it, "burned his baggage," Crom applied for a post he had seen advertised in the *Times* as tutor to the family of Count Orloff-Davidoff, and went out with them to St. Petersburg. Before long he began to have serious differences over the education of the Count's not-very-intelligent son, Sergey; Crom wanted to develop the boy's imagination, the family demanded a kind of forcing system. In 1863 Crom resigned his post without much regret on either side (though the Count presented him with a silver cigar-cutter). Looking back on his years in Russia, he saw them as a "period of purgatory" and added "God grant that they may have eradicated many of my weaknesses." (Information from unpublished letters and diaries in the possession of the Price family.)

21. Morris wrote to his daughter Jenny from Kelmscott (Aug. 24, 1888) "The fishing is pretty much as it was; the river higher and the weeds uncut, though not very visible at first glance because the water is high. Altogether a very pleasant river to travel on, the bank being still very beautiful with flowers . . . the purple blossom of the horse-mint and mouse-ear and here and there a bit of meadowsweet belated . . ." Mouse-ear, however, has white flowers, and since Morris writes of it (p. 47) as "blue-flowered" he perhaps means the water forget-me-not, *myosotis scorpioides*.

22. Cf. *News from Nowhere* 1890 ". . . almost without my will my feet moved along the road they knew. The raised way led us into a little field bounded by a the backwater of a river on one side; on the right hand we could see a cluster of small houses and barns; new and old,

and before us a grey stone barn . . . over which a few grey gables showed." May Morris noted that the High House "in an ingle of the river" at Upmeads, to which the hero returns in *The Well at the World's End* (1896), was also Kelmscott Manor. In 1872, of course, Morris (although he knew the Upper Thames valley well) had never spent a summer at Kelmscott. He and Rossetti signed the lease in June 1871 and in July Morris went to Iceland. But just as he had dreamed of Kelmscott before he ever laid eyes on the place, so he recognized it as an image of self-renewal and peace years before he ever found it there.

23.   This working note is written, partly in pencil, on the back of p. 51. in Morris's MS.

24.   From the 1870s onward Morris shows his appreciation of open-air, sun-browned, unladylike beauty, as opposed to the ivory-pale women of his earlier poetry and prose. Rossetti had been angry when Frederic Stephens pointed out that Elizabeth Siddal had freckles; Morris seems to have been a pioneer in this matter as in so many others.

25.   The grey eyes are unmistakeably not Jane Morris's, "grey-lit in shadowing hair," but Georgie Burne-Jones's. Her granddaughter Angela Thirkell described them as "eyes of light and frankness and depth of feeling," and the artist W. Graham Robertson wrote of their "direct gaze" which "would always cost me a little subconscious heartburning, not for fear of criticism or censure, but lest those eyes in their grave wisdom, their crystal purity, should rest upon anything unworthy . . . ." After a moment "the impression of awe" passed, and she was simply "making an awkward boy feel quite comfortable and happy." (W. Graham Robertson, *Time Was*, [London, 1931]). William de Morgan declared that neither Georgie nor any of her sisters ever began a sentence without knowing exactly how it would end.

26.   Leaser Farm consists of the earlier part of the Kelmscott Manor buildings (*c.* 1570–1670). There is a ground-floor plan of the house, and a photograph of the "queer heavily balustraded staircase" in *Kelmscott: An Illustrated Guide* (1969) written for the London Society of Antiquaries by A. R. Dufty, F.S.A.

27.   Mrs. Mason's character, or at least her function in the book, seems to have changed since she boldly defied Parson Risley (p. 36). Morris now presents her as kindly, but somewhat nervous and sentimental. Her appearance suggests his mother-in-law Anne Burden (née Maizey) from whom Jane Morris inherited her dark good looks. Anne Burden died in 1871. But it was Morris's own mother who embarrassed him at times with her enthusiasm. When Burne-Jones first came to the family home at Walthamstow, Mrs. Morris "welcomed [him] kindly, and seeing his affection for her son would willingly have told him many stories of his childhood; but at this Morris chafed so much that the anecdotes had to be deferred." (*Memorials*, I, 87). There is a hint that Mrs. Mason who "isn't one of the wise ones" (p. 58) may be the innocent cause of some disaster. Her "restless

heart" recalls Morris's own judgement on himself in the November Prologue of *The Earthly Paradise*, "these outstretched feverish hands, this restless heart."

To his own mother Morris was always loving and dutiful. "My old and callous heart was touched," he wrote when she died in 1894, "by the absence of what had been so kind to me and fond of me. She was eighty-nine, and had been ill for nearly four years."

28. A drink or dessert made by curdling milk or cream with wine or other acid. For a real syllabub, the cow should be milked straight into half a pint of sherry, so that the warm milk forms a curd.

29. Cf. Morris to Jane Morris 3 Oct 1870: "For me I don't think people really want to die because of mental pain, that is if they are imaginative people; they want to live to see the play played our fairly—they have hopes that they are not conscious of—"

30. Hans Holbein (1497–1593). Francois Clouet, Jeannette or Janet (d. 1572). Morris was faithful throughout his life to Fra Angelico, Van Eyck, and Holbein as the three greatest painters of past ages.

31. Although Ruddywell Court seems to stand some way up the little river Leach, (which falls into the Thames near Kelmscott), Morris is perhaps remembering his Essex childhood. "Well I remember as a boy my first acquaintance with a room hung with faded greenery at Queen Elizabeth's Lodge by Chingford Hatch in Epping Forest (I wonder what has become of it now?), and the impression of romance that it made upon me." (*The Lesser Arts of Life*, 1882). The Lodge is a fine old timbered building, which is now a natural history museum for Epping Forest.

32. Antonio Palladio (1518–1580), the classicizing Italian architect.

33. Morris begins renumbering the pages here from 1 to 7. There is no indication as to how much time has passed since the visit to Ruddywell.

34. At this point the novel approaches the same point as *Hapless Love* (1869), the Prologue to the *Volsunga Soga*, and the close of *Love Is Enough*, where Pharamond, having lost both his kingdom and his quest, is told that those who "toil and suffer with no answer from the land of love" have not spent their lives in vain. But John's letter seems to give something of the reality behind Morris's variant expressions of it.

Review of Brontë Studies, 1975–1980

Kathleen Blake

There are more studies of the Brontës than ever, and that is saying a lot. I offer a broad sampling of a half-decade's work, growing more personal in my selection of publications postdating available bibliographies. I follow the emphasis in the reading I have done and devote more attention to Charlotte than to Emily Brontë and much the least attention to Anne Brontë. Again following the reading, I stress *Jane Eyre*, *Villette*, and *Wuthering Heights*. While Charlotte Brontë's juvenilia and first novel *The Professor* figure significantly in biographically oriented studies and those committed to comment on the whole canon, few critics present them as works of independent merit, and so I save space for other things by passing over them here. Still generally regarded as a flawed work, *Shirley* has been gaining a measure of critical recognition, as will be seen, and some fine work on Emily Brontë's poetry bears covering. The reputation of *Villette* has been growing dramatically, and many now honor Charlotte Brontë's last completed novel as her greatest.

The field is rich and diverse, but areas of common interest appear, creating a sense of collective discovery and advance. I have not organized this review chronologically. Rather, beginning with Bibliography, Editions, and Biography, I move to Criticism, organized under the following headings: Mother-Child-Family Romance; The Erotic; Anger and Protest; Guilt and Deathwish; Relation to Literary History and Achievement of Authorship; Narrative Techniques and Authorial Control. Throughout one finds biographical, psychoanalytical, literary-historical, feminist, and, to a lesser extent, Marxist, Bloomian, and deconstructionist approaches. I sometimes note earlier work which has initiated main lines of thought in the 1975–1980 period. Most significant has been the impact of feminist literary criticism since Kate Millett's 1969 *Sexual Politics*.

BIBLIOGRAPHY

Anne Passel's *Charlotte and Emily Brontë, An Annotated Bibliography* (New York and London: Garland, 1979) aims at comprehensive coverage through 1977, and while devoted to the more famous sisters, it contains sections on Anne, Branwell, and the Rev. Patrick Brontë. With a total of 1379 entries, its thoroughness, organization, annotations, and indexes make it useful, and it also lists other bibliographies, such as that of G. Anthony Yablon and John R. Turner, *A Brontë Bibliography* (London: Ian Hodgkins; Westport, Conn.: Meckler Books, 1978), a good source for hard-to-find early works.

EDITIONS

The important Clarendon Edition of the Novels of the Brontës under the general editorship of Ian Jack has given us the 1847 *Wuthering Heights*, ed. Hilda Marsdan and Ian Jack and *Shirley*, ed. Herbert Rosengarten and Margaret Smith (Oxford: Clarenden, 1976, 1979). Also welcome are *Two Tales by Charlotte Brontë*, "*The Secret*" & "*Lily Hart*," ed. William Holtz (Columbia and London: University of Missouri Press, 1978) and *The Poems of Anne Brontë*, ed. Edward Chitham (Totowa, New Jersey: Rowman and Littlefield, 1979). *Two Tales* is an attractive volume offering a facsimile of the texts in the author's famous tiny handwriting and then the edited version, indicating crossed-out words and so on. One finds a general introduction but not many notes. The *Poems of Anne Brontë* includes fifty-nine poems along with elaborate notes, appendices, and bibliographies, and an introduction making claims for the value of this poetry. Chitham prefers the non-Gondal to the Emily-Brontë-oriented Gondal pieces as more characteristically Anne's—personal, pious, moral, didactic, yet overall "a poetry of search, not statement" (p. 30). In style, the works are simple and forthright, conventional but not trite, linked to the tradition of the evangelical hymn. Of interest biographically are Chitham's correction of the usual view of Anne as gentle to the point of weakness and his tracing in such a poem as "Spirit of Pride" of a likely rift between Anne and Emily. Chitham credits Anne's longest poem, "Self-Communion," with "Rossetti-like depth and intensity" (p. 39). He believes that these poems have dissatisfied readers because they expect high Romanticism from any Brontë. While Anne's novels are tinged by Romanticism, the poems express a different consciousness. Chitham's edition may promote the critical regard that has been lacking. But between 1975 and 1980 the poetry has gone mostly unnoticed and even the novels have failed to generate much independent consideration.

Two reprints should also be noted—Thomas James Wise and J. A. Symington, *The Brontës, Their Lives, Friendships, and Correspondences*, part of the Shakespeare Head Brontë (1933; rpt. Oxford: Blackwell, 1980), 4 vols. in 2; and *Poems by the Brontë Sisters*, rpt. of the 1846 *Poems by Currer, Ellis, and Acton Bell*, introd. M. R. D. Seaward (Wakefield, England: E. P. Publishing; Totowa, New Jersey: Rowman and Littlefield, 1978).

BIOGRAPHY

Older books newly available are the first full-length study of Emily Brontë, A. Mary F. Robinson's *The Life of Emily Brontë* (1883; rpt. Philadelphia: West, 1978) and Winifred Gérin's *Anne Brontë, A Biography* (1959, rpt. London: Lane, 1976). John Cannon's *The Road to Haworth, The Story of Brontë's Irish Ancestry* (London: Weidenfeld and Nicolson, 1980) represents a traditional delving into background. We learn about the Irish Bruntys, about Patrick Brontë's literary ambitions and his father Hugh's renown as a barely literate storyteller. Cannon shows the corelation between certain family stories and the plot of *Wuthering Heights*. Not scholarly (no notes), Cannon's book is readable and rather beguiling.

But just because a biographical approach is so traditional in Brontë studies, it is challenged by Tom Winnifrith in *The Brontës* (London and Basingstoke: Macmillan, 1977). The opening chapter systematically seeks out the gaps between the lives and works. It notes the hypotheses and conjectures in biographical study and the areas of factual uncertainty and impossibility of verification. Winnifrith is an iconoclast. For instance, he questions the reliability of the heroic myth of Emily Brontë, founded on sparse evidence such as "a few courageous escapades involving dogs" (p. 21). He proposes to free criticism of overemphasis on biography so as to allow fuller insight into the books. Thus in considering *The Tenant of Wildfell Hall*, if one ceases to stress an identity between Huntingdon and Branwell, one may begin to see Helen as a factor in Huntingdon's fall, whereas Anne was *not* a factor in Branwell's fall. Righteousness becomes Helen's limitation. She herself is the product of a girl's education, ignorant of sin and ineffectual in contending against it, so that her attempts to reform her husband do as much harm as good. This is an interesting interpretation. However, Winnifrith's hopes for relative "de-biographicalization" of Brontë studies have not been realized.

Two guides for the general reader or student incorporate the usual biographical introductions and interpretations. These are F. B. Pinion's *A Brontë Companion, Literary Assessment, Background, and Reference* (London and Basingstoke: Macmillan; New York: Barnes & Noble, 1975), and Margaret Howard Blom's *Charlotte Brontë* (Boston: Twayne, 1977). (Both of these offer more sustained discussion and more scholarly and critical relevance than John Halperin's and Janet Kunert's *Plots and Characters in the Fiction of Jane Austen, the Brontës, and George Eliot* [Hamden, Conn.: Archon; Folkestone, England: Dawson, 1976].) The fairly standard views of Blom and Pinion define points of departure for the major biographical studies which have given us new ways of looking at the Brontës, in particular Charlotte Brontë. Margot Peters' *Unquiet Soul, A Biography of Charlotte Brontë* (Garden City, New York: Doubleday, 1975), Helene Moglen's *Charlotte Brontë, The Self Conceived* (New York: Norton, 1976), and Robert Keefe's *Charlotte Brontë's World of Death* (Austin and London: University of Texas Press, 1979) are richer in new perspectives than new facts. Feminism provides the perspective for Peters, psychoanalysis for Keefe; Moglen unites the two viewpoints. Peters's biography is careful, thorough and very substantial, while the speculative boldness of Moglen and Keefe augments both their interest and openness to challenge (by those of the Winnifrith persuasion, for instance).

Whereas Pinion cites Robert Southey's letter to Charlotte Brontë discouraging her literary ambitions but omits the parts of the letter which mark the message as one directed specifically at female literary ambitions, the author's sex in relation to her personal and artistic development is of paramount concern in Peters's biography. Thus the Southey letter gets full treatment. Peters transforms our view of Charlotte Brontë without transforming her into a doctrinaire feminist. But according to an expanded understanding of feminism, her life and art eloquently protest and triumph over the limitations faced by women in the period. Particularly fresh and effective is Peters's presentation of Charlotte Brontë's relations with women friends. Her friends since schooldays, Ellen Nussey and Mary Taylor, define two poles of possibility for women's lives and help to place Charlotte between them. Ellen Nussey was the gentle and dutiful, quite conventional and self-abnegating Victorian home-daughter and spinster. Mary Taylor was the independent, overtly feminist New Zealand emigrant and entrepreneur, also unmarried. The appearance of Mary Taylor's letters in *Mary Taylor: Friend of Charlotte Brontë*, ed. Joan Stevens (New Zealand: Auckland University Press, 1972) aided Peters greatly. Peters also treats Charlotte Brontë's relations with friends of later life, Mrs. Gaskell and Harriet Martineau. She shows Brontë and Gaskell reading and discussing Harriet Taylor Mill's "Enfranchisement of Women." She characterizes Brontë and Martineau as the "great feminine rebels of their day" (p. 313). According to Peters, the discussions with Gaskell reveal Charlotte Brontë's uneasiness about Mill's undervaluation of love in women's lives, and she broke with Martineau over the same thing (when Martineau attacked *Villette* for overvaluing love). In this way Peters shows the importance of the issue of love for Charlotte Brontë and certain conflicts it posed for her feminism, while she does not stress the degree of ambivalence felt over the erotic issue, as some later commentators do. However, there is a fine new interpretation of Charlotte Brontë's marriage, sensitive to the mixed motives leading to it, the tempered satisfactions which it yielded, and the limitations it imposed on the writer.

It is interesting to notice elements in Peters's biography which have grown to dominate and somewhat sensationalize the treatments of Moglen and Keefe. First is her observation that the death of the Brontës' mother created an indelible insecurity in the children. Second is her question, "was [Brontë's] death to be in a sense voluntary?" (p. 405). Like those after her, she makes use of Philip Rhodes's "A Medical Appraisal of the Brontës," *Brontë Society Transactions*, 16 (1972), 101-109, to suggest that the author may have died not of tuberculosis or a cold but of *hyperemesis gravidarum*, a psychologically induced overreaction to pregnancy which can render morning sickness a fatal disease. For the most part, however, Peters presents a picture of frustrating yet productive struggle between living as a dutiful woman and breaking convention as a woman of genius, while Moglen and Keefe darken the picture to stress neurosis and self-destruction.

Both Moglen and Keefe mix biography and literary criticism, and (as Moglen says about herself) each takes for granted other more exhaustive studies and risks partiality for the sake of emphasis. Typifying Moglen's approach is language found in the section on the elder sister's death: "Again, one imagines" (p. 22). Similarly, Keefe subtitles his opening biographical chapter "A Meditation on Charlotte Brontë," and the word "probably" is indispensable to his style.

Important for Moglen's purposes and reflected in her title, *The Self Conceived*, is the idea that Charlotte Brontë could not give birth to the child she had conceived but died of "the last of her neurotic illnesses; the last of her masochistic denials" (p. 241). In large part, she could not become a mother because of the dark tangle of her feelings about her own mother. For the Freudian Moglen, the infrequency of any reference to this mother signals repression and vouches for her psychological importance. Moglen outlines the consequences of losing a mother at five years old: feelings of abandonment, betrayal, responsibility, guilt, insecurity, and self-doubt. The trauma is recapitulated and deepened by the death of a motherly sister and results in a "lifelong fear of childbearing" (p. 21).

Thus far Moglen's thesis bears a strong resemblance to Keefe's, as he recognized upon reading her book after developing his own study independently. Both make much of Charlotte Brontë's account to Mary Taylor of a dream so painful that she did not wish to think about it. It concerned the return of her two dead sisters (one the mother surrogate Maria), beloved and loving in life but returning much changed, forgetful of all they had cared for, and critical of the very rooms. This appears in the light of a survivor's dream. Keefe is even more thorough and fascinating than Moglen in his analysis of the element of resentment for abandonment; this creates a reaction of guilt, self-blame, and leads to punitive discipline of a seemingly unworthy self.

Moglen also treats what she calls masochism. But she derives only part of it from the mother trauma. Even more comes from Charlotte Brontë's situation as a woman. For this part of the analysis Charlotte's relation to Branwell and Byronism becomes crucial. She put herself second to Branwell as a sister to a brother, a daughter less valuable in her father's patriarchal eyes than his only son. In addition, both she and Branwell embraced Byronism in their joint Angrian fantasy. They embodied the Byronic hero in Zamorna and both identified with him. However, a girl could never feel fully adequate to be the arch-masculine Zamorna. In fact, Moglen well shows that the Byronic model necessarily subordinates the female to the dominant male. Moglen very interestingly analyzes the juvenilia to reveal a developing criticism of Zamorna and the women who submit to him. She concludes that Brontë reached a critical understanding of female masochism in love though she did not truly overcome it herself. In fact, the impossibility of reciprocation from M. Heger "provided an appropriate outlet of Brontë's masochistic tendencies" (p. 67). Moglen presents a woman much more deeply smitten by feminist ambivalence over love than Peters and draws attention to her fictional portrayal of dominance and submission in the relations between the sexes, which others have also taken up.

Moglen claims that Branwell's demise was essential to Charlotte's autonomy and authorship, for he was the Zamorna she could not herself be, the brother to whom she deferred, the demand on her womanly sympathy and self-sacrifice finally too outrageous to meet. Always provocative, this analysis gets complicated and sometimes murky. A certain amount of confusion testifies to the breadth and intertwining of Moglen's concerns. Keefe manages to be consistently clearer by narrowing his concern to the trauma of mother-loss. He does not go beyond the realm of personal neurosis to examine cultural forces which could help traumatize a woman into conflict, self-doubt, and even self-destruction. However, Moglen overstates her case by concluding that Brontë "could not bring to birth the self she had conceived" (p. 241). After all, a child is not actually oneself, nor did Charlotte Brontë have a strong maternal self-image to which she failed to give birth. And, despite everything, she did conceive and bring forth herself as a writer.

CRITICISM

Mother-Child-Family Romance

Of course, mothers are important in both Keefe's and Moglen's readings of Charlotte Brontë's novels. Both perceive Jane Eyre's orphan state as a representation of the author's own sense of maternal abandonment. Both present Jane as Cinderella facing not only male antagonists but also evil stepmothers and stepsisters (Reeds, Ingrams, etc.). Moglen goes beyond Keefe in treating the good mothers and sisters in *Jane Eyre*. For instance, she points out the aid of supernatural mother figures, while Keefe has surprisingly little to say about this. While passing over such important mothers, he sometimes strains to give importance to others, such as Rochester's mother, whose jewels Jane refuses to take as his gift. Surely her re-

jection has more to do with him than his mother. Moglen makes
Bertha Mason into a mother figure without citing much explicit evidence. But her basic insight is convincing and valuable—a good
family (the Rivers) replaces the bad ones, and this helps Jane to
achieve autonomy and a better balance of power with the domi-
neering Rochester, though Moglen does not perceive true sexual
equality at the end, for Jane assumes the mother role in the marriage.

Attention to a heroine's search for a mother owes a good deal to
Adrienne Rich's "Jane Eyre: The Temptations of a Motherless
Woman," Ms., 2 (Oct. 1973), and her Of Woman Born, Motherhood
As Experience and Institution (New York: Norton, 1976). Thus Barbara Hill Rigney in Madness and Sexual Politics in the Feminist
Novel, Studies in Brontë, Woolf, Lessing, and Atwood (Madison:
University of Wisconsin Press, 1978) treats the importance of Jane's
relation to mother nature as a metaphoric moon mother, a Jungian
symbol to women of "belonging only to themselves" (p. 35). A thorough presentation of this family romance side of the "Cinderjane"
story it that of Maurianne Adams in "Jane Eyre: Woman's Estate,"
in The Authority of Experience, Essays in Feminist Criticism, ed.
Arlyn Diamond and Lee R. Edwards (Amherst: University of Mas-
sachusetts Press, 1977), pp. 137-159, and also "Family Disintegration and Creative Regeneration: the Case of Charlotte Brontë and
Jane Eyre," in The Victorian Family, Structures and Stresses, ed.
Anthony S. Wohl (London: Croom Helm, 1978), pp. 148-179. Adams
finds the Marsh End episode, in which Jane finds her family of
sisters, so important that the novel might have ended here. In an
essay on "Women's Writing: 'Jane Eyre,' 'Shirley,' 'Villette,' 'Aurora
Leigh'", in 1848: The Sociology of Literature (Essex: University of
Essex, 1978), pp. 185-206, the Marxist-Feminist Literature Collective applauds Brontë's recognition of the role of kinship as well as
economics in defining Jane's position on the bourgeois marriage
market.

Moglen does not make much of the obvious mother in Shirley,
Mrs. Pryor, while Keefe criticizes this novel for regressively fanti-
sizing the recovery of mother love. As Keefe acutely obeserves, this
recovery depends on Caroline Helstone's willingness to die; also
her mother comes to love her in response to her inadequacy, not
her adequacy. In that self-sacrifice and self-depreciation bring
back maternal love in the novel, Keefe discerns morbidity and
guilt in the author's own mother complex. Not surprisingly, he is
on the look-out for mothers who threaten the heroine's psychologi-

cal security in *Villette*: Mrs. Bretton, Miss Marchmont (threatening in that Lucy loses them), her enemies Madame Beck and Malevola, also stepmother Reason and the hag Human Justice. Even Cleopatra in the painting, because she is recumbant, appears to the somewhat obsessed Keefe "like a mother who has fallen inexplicably ill" (p. 171).

As interest in the mother motif has grown, so has interest in the child motif. Jane Eyre's strange child-dream attracts more and more criticism. For Moglen, it is prophetic for the author when her heroine lets the burdensome child fall. Brontë is herself the child fallen away from its mother and the mother who lets it fall. William R. Siebenschuh devotes an article to "the Image of the Child and the Plot of *Jane Eyre*," *Studies in the Novel*, 8 (1976), 304-317. He concludes that Jane must escape from the fears of her childhood (herself the child in the dream) to achieve maturity (herself a mother figure). In contrast, Rigney cites the child-dream in evidence of Jane's rejection of maternity. As part of their massive work *The Madwoman in the Attic, The Woman Writer and the Nineteenth-Century Literary Imagination* (New Haven and London: Yale University Press, 1979), Sandra M. Gilbert and Susan Gubar suggest that Jane is the child in a dream expressive of her own hostile wishes for the fall of Thornfield.

A major study of Emily Brontë also takes up the mother-child configuration in the family romance. This is Margaret Homans's *Women Writers and Poetic Identity, Dorothy Wordsworth, Emily Brontë, and Emily Dickinson* (Princeton: Princeton University Press, 1980), a work preceded by her "Repression and Sublimation of Nature in *Wuthering Heights*," *PMLA*, 93 (1978), 9-19. In a sophisticated and rather exhausting argument with debts to feminism, psychoanalysis, and Derrida (e.g., "Deconstruction ought to help displace phallogocentrism," p. 35), Homans presents two main aspects of Emily Brontë's poetic identity as a woman writing without the help of a female poetic tradition. One is her embodiment of her own imaginative powers in male figures, a problematical practice for a woman author. The other is a certain "matrophobia" or what may be termed a mother-nature complex. Motherhood provides no model for the creative artist, according to Homans, and so "the first project for any poet who is also a daughter must be to keep herself from becoming a mother" (p. 17), and she must likewise avoid indentifying with the nature-as-mother found in poetic convention, for to identify with nature would prohibit its (her) being "other" enough to write about. Homans sometimes strains to muster evi-

dence of conceptual linkage between motherhood, nature and poetic identity. For instance, a cited school devoir shows Emily
Brontë's mixed feeling about mothers, but contains nothing about
nature or writing. A poem addressing nature as a "mother" with
"kindly breast" does not prepare us to accept the analysis of "distrust for nature on the part of the feminine poet" (p. 149) except insofar as distrust for maternal nature has been previously discovered
in Dorothy Wordsworth and Emily Brontë is said to resemble Dorothy Wordsworth. Presenting Catherine's horror of her image in the
mirror as horror of her impending motherhood and of the maternity of nature, Homans concedes that "this reading may be extravagant"(p. 157). Homans's extravagances are mostly stimulating for
they are the results of intricate-minded speculation. However, she
can be oddly simple-minded, too. She declares *Wuthering Heights*
relatively free of the mother-nature complex because it is a novel
and as such freer than poetry of the Romantic mother-nature tradition. She overestimates the freedom of this or any novel from literary heritage. Indeed, most critics have associated *Wuthering
Heights* with Romanticism.

The Erotic

Turning from the family to the sexual romance, we encounter
various views of Charlotte Brontë on love between the sexes. She is
seen as celebrator and/or critic. *Jane Eyre*'s Bertha Mason and *Villette*'s Nun frequently supply focal points of discussion in this area.
  Ellen Moers' *Literary Women* (Garden City, New York: Doubleday, 1976) links the feminism of *Jane Eyre* with an affirmation of
sexuality. A work of similar stature in feminist literary criticism,
Elaine Showalter's *A Literature of Their Own, British Women Novelist from Brontë to Lessing* (Princeton, New Jersey: Princeton University Press, 1977) also links sexuality and the rights of women, or
to be more exact, sexual repression and female oppression. Thus a
constrictive Victorian sexual code for women produces Bertha Mason, figure of bestial and terrifying return of repressed. Showalter
has followed up her interest in Bertha Mason with an article on
"Victorian Women and Insanity," *Victorian Studies*, 23 (1980),
157-181, which indicates that strong female sexuality was indeed
considered dangerously akin to madness in the period.
  Showalter's sympathetic discussion of *Jane Eyre*'s madwomen is
one of number of precursors of Gilbert's and Gubar's study titled after Bertha Mason, *The Madwomen in the Attic*. Among these pre-

cursors are Jean Rhys's novel about the first Mrs. Rochester, *Wide Sargasso Sea* of 1966, and Gilbert's own "Plain Jane's Progress," *Signs*, 2 (1977), 779-804. There is also Nancy Pell's "Resistance, Rebellion, and Marriage: The Economics of *Jane Eyre*," *Nineteenth-Century Fiction*, 31 (1977), 397-420. This places Bertha at the center of the novel, a woman victimized and maddened by the patriarchal Victorian marriage market and devaluation of female sexuality. Her appearance in the book coincides with the famous passage about Jane's feminist longings. She becomes emblematic of the extremes of oppression and revolt between which Jane must find a middle way. Broadly analogous interpretations are found in the works of Moglen, Adams, Rigney, the Marxist-Feminist Literature Collective, also in Carol A. Senf's "*Jane Eyre*: The Prison-House of Victorian Marriage," *Journal of Women's Studies in Literature*, 1 (1979), 353-359. Cited here as well as elsewhere is an influential early essay by Robert Heilmen on Brontë's charging of stock Gothic figures (such as the Madwoman and the Nun) with new psychological significance—see his "Charlotte Brontë's 'New' Gothic" in *From Jane Austen to Joseph Conrad*, ed. R. C. Rathburn and Martin Steinmann (Minneapolis: University of Minnesota Press, 1958).

Gilbert and Gubar make the culminating statement on the "'gothic' lunatic who functions as the more sedate heroine's double" (p. 314). Again, the central confrontation is not with Rochester, but with Mrs. Rochester. Gilbert and Gubar place less emphasis than some on Bertha Mason's sexuality, more on her rage. The "ridge of lighted heath" of Jane's feminist anger escapes repression and returns with a vengeance in Bertha's incendiary impulses and the ultimate Thornfield fire. (Even saintly Helen Burns "burns" in her "fever," according to the very insistent argument, p. 346.) Still, besides anger, sexuality remains important for Gilbert and Gubar. The opening sentence of their book poses the question, "Is a pen a metaphorical penis?" They put up no fight against the Freudian metaphor of pen as sexual organ; rather, they explore various women writers' questioning (direct, indirect, or failed) of the particular sex of the sexual organ. Throughout, they connect repression of sexuality with repression of anger with inhibition of female literary creativity.

Placing a feminist value on sexuality, Gilbert and Gubar perceive substantial sexual fulfillment in *Jane Eyre* and *Villette*. They see substantial equality in love between Jane and Rochester, Lucy and M. Paul. For them, the Nun of *Villette* is entirely negative, a figure of constriction, self-abnegation, desexualization. They recognize

that Lucy's ambivalence about love and men generates the Nun
(and also the witchlike Malevola, whom they well observe to be
linked with the Nun). However, they do not recognize the feminist
force of this ambivalence as much as some critics do. As they see it,
Lucy must free herself of the Nun. They belong with Moers and the
other critics who find in Brontë a feminist affirmation of eros.

In contrast are those who stress her erotic ambivalence, some
even perceiving in the chaste Nun a positive value. As I have indicated, Moglen observes a dynamics of dominance and submission
in Brontë's treatment of sexual relations, which persists to the end of
Jane Eyre and undercuts any certainty of equality in marriage.
Shirley also shows Brontë's critique of these psychosexual dynamics
and lacks any very favorable resolution, according to both Moglen
and Keefe. Pell is one of a number of critics who reinterpret Richard Chase's well-known formulation "The Brontës or Myth Domes-
ticated," in *Forms of Modern Fiction*, ed. William Van O'Connor
(Minneapolis: University of Minnesota Press, 1948) (the essay originally appeared in 1947). That is, Chase chides Brontë for an "insane suffragettism" intent on castrating the hero because his masculinity threatens the heroine. But feminists often revise this to suggest
that such suffragettism is not insane, given cultural patterns of
masculine dominance and female submission which make painless
and peaceable readjustment of sexual power unlikely.

In the view of Jean Kennard in *Victims of Convention* (Hamden,
Conn.: Archon, 1978), Charlotte Brontë fails to find a way of recon-
ciling the conflict experienced by her heroines between indepen-
dence and passion. She feels that the "two-suitor convention" of the
love-story novel plus an habitual conception of masculinity in
terms of domination of the female cause Brontë to compromise the
autonomy of Jane Eyre and Shirley Keeldar. Though the author
manages to avoid a final marriage in *Villette*, "To Lucy, love is still
bondage" (p. 106). Adams considers *Jane Eyre* "at its heart anti-romantic and anti-marriage," despite a marriage ending which she
finds unsatisfactory ("Family Disintegration," p. 173). Rather like
Kennard and Adams in favoring a non-marriage ending on feminist
grounds is Carolyn Platt in "How Feminist Is Villette?" *Women &
Literature*, 3 (1975), 16-27. And Nina Auerbach and Judith Plotz
salute the Nun as a positive persona for Lucy Snowe in *Communi-
ties of Women, An Idea in Fiction* (Cambridge, Mass., and London:
Harvard University Press, 1978), pp. 97-113, and "Potatoes in A
Cellar: Charlotte Brontë's *Villette* and the Feminized Imagination,"
Journal of Women's Studies in Literature, 1 (1979), 74-87, respec-

tively. For Auerbach, the Nun initiates Lucy into a world of female power, such as that found in convents and girls' academies. She stresses the ambiguity of attitude toward Paul at the end. His absence leaves Lucy in possession of her own school. Plotz argues Lucy's achievement of the austere autonomy of the nay-sayer. She says "no" to every inadequate option offered to her sex, so that Plotz entitles one section "Embrace of Negation: Lucy as Nun." A sharp contrast between Auerbach and Plotz and Robert Bledsoe, "Snow Beneath Snow, A Reconsideration of the Virgin of *Villette*," in *Gender and Literary Voice*, ed. Janet Todd (*Women & Literature* new series) (New York and London: Holmes & Meier, 1980), pp. 214-222, sums up the contrast between those who see Brontë as critical of eros and those who insist on her erotic affirmation. Bledsoe argues that Lucy Snowe's virginal incapacity for marriage marks the author's sense of her morbidity. But Leroy W. Smith examines a conflict between autonomy and love in several Brontë heroines, and his findings lead him to entitle his essay "Charlotte Brontë's Flight from Eros," *Women & Literature*, 4 (1976), 30-44.

   Turning to Emily Brontë, we find that criticism of the love theme is much less rich. However, there is a fine piece by T. E. Apter called "Romanticism and Romantic Love in *Wuthering Heights*" in the collection of essays *The Art of Emily Brontë*, ed. Anne Smith (London: Vision; Totowa, New Jersey: Barnes & Noble, 1976), pp. 205-222. Apter believes that Emily Brontë values without sentimentalizing the romatic love of Catherine and Heathcliff, but that she also places it in a critical perspective through the commentary of Nelly Dean and through the second generation's alternative style of love. He argues that the young Catherine and Hareton achieve romantic intensity without making it depend on suffering and impossibility of consummation except in death. This essay has a good deal more to offer than Colin Wilson's "A Personal Response to *Wuthering Heights*," pp. 223-237 in the same volume. Wilson dislikes the sadism in the novel. Had Emily Brontë found her own Heathcliff, he casually speculates, she might not have written such a warped love story. Or better yet, she should have mated with George Henry Lewes!

Anger And Protest

   In keeping with their main theme, Gilbert and Gubar make out "Eyre" a pun for "ire." All of the feminist critics attend to anger and protest in Charlotte Brontë's works. Hence their attention to

Bertha Mason, figure of female passion made mad and murderous by confinement. Two nineteenth-century critical statements supply touchstones for feminist readings stressing anger and protest. One is Elizabeth Rigby's attack on Brontë in *The Quarterly Review*, 84 (1848), 153-185, for asserting the rights of man in unfeminine fashion. The other is Matthew Arnold's remark in a letter of 1853 about the "hunger, rebellion, and rage" in *Villette (Letters to A. H. Clough)*.

The Marxist-Feminist Literature Collective sees social protest closely allied to Brontë's feminist protest. They appreciate Terry Eagleton's *Myths of Power, A Marxist Study of the Brontës* (London and Basingstoke: Macmillan; New York: Barnes & Noble, 1975) though they criticize the author for separating social and sexual issues. One would expect the novel most explicitly concerned with social problems to impress a Marxist critic more than it does. But Eagleton is no more enthusiastic about *Shirley* than most others. (Treatment of the woman question raises the novel in the estimation of feminists but has not made it a favorite.) Eagleton feels that focus on proletariat versus ruling-class conflict deflects Brontë from the more acute analysis seen in *Jane Eyre*. There she portrays the heroine as a petty bourgeoise in conflict with a higher class and at the same time desirous of joining it. While he finds much to interest him, Eagleton takes a rather sour view of the fairy-tale ending that allows Jane to accommodate bourgeois and genteel values. He is most enthusiastic about the novel seemingly least concerned with social protest, *Wuthering Heights*. Compared to Charlotte, Emily Brontë is "more penetrative, radical, and honest" (p. 98) because she does not soften stark class antagonisms by means of fantasy endings. Eagleton carries forward Arnold Kettle's work on *Wuthering Heights* in the first volume of *An Introduction to the English Novel* of 1951. Catherine's and Heathcliff's love represents freedom and rebellion against society (this society or any society?—a Marxist critic should be clearer here). Catherine betrays this love by choosing Edgar and gentility, which leaves two options open to Heathcliff. He can run wild, to achieve only the freedom of the despised outsider, or he can exploit the exploiters, using his freedom to foster unfreedom. Heathcliff chooses the latter, and Eagleton sees in this an even more bitter irony than Kettle does. For Kettle, Heathcliff's revenge for oppression leads him to subvert his own humanity, but he recovers it in his final change and death. For Eagleton, the bourgeois tactics used by Heathcliff in his anti-social maneuverings actually help advance social forces he hates. The second generation inherits both houses but abandons the Heights for the Grange. Thus

Eagleton would have us see the new industrial bourgeoisie (Heathcliff) undermining the old yeoman class (Heights) and infiltrating, transforming, and strengthening established agrarian capitalism (Grange). Emily Brontë pleases Eagleton by showing that such vengeance on society as Heathcliff's misfires because it fails to align itself with a new revolutionary class. Those interested by this substantial Marxist study might also look at Ronald Frankenberg's "Styles of Marxism, Styles of Criticism: *Wuthering Heights*, a Case Study," in *The Sociology of Literature, Applied Studies* ed. Diana Laurenson (Keele, England: University of Keele, 1978), pp. 109-144.

Guilt And Deathwish

I have already covered deathwish hypotheses in biographical studies of Charlotte Brontë by Peters, Moglen, and Keefe. Keefe writes compellingly about both guilt and an impulse towards death even in the righteous survivor, Jane Eyre. No one else makes us attend so closely to *Jane Eyre*'s opening section on *Bewick's Birds* with its images of death, crime, and punishment. No one so well observes Jane's attraction towards death along with her fear of it in the Red Room, her guilt over her own deathwish along with her indignation at unjust treatment. Keefe's thesis is the steady attrition of self-justification and instinct for survival traceable in Brontë's works. Whether or not one wishes to explain Brontë's attitudes by reference to her loss of her mother, it is worth paying attention to the attitudes themselves, as represented in the fiction.

Patsy Stoneman mounts another argument in "The Brontës and Death: Altenatives to Revolution," in *1848: The Sociology of Literature*, pp. 79-96. She suggests the subversive implications of death in the works of Charlotte and Emilly Brontë. Death presents an alternative worth considering to women denied viable options by society. Inside/outside imagery in *Jane Eyre* and *Wuthering Heights* implies social constraints versus transcendence. Emily Brontë favors transcendence through death for Catherine Earnshaw. However, Stoneman perceives an irony in this escape from society. Catherine may be seen to pass into the dubious "outside" of the social outsider, the fallen woman, not so much transcendent as victimized by death. This interpretation relies on the scanty evidence that the dead Catherine is termed a "waif" and "a woman," instead of being called more respectfully by her name. The upshot is Stoneman's greater admiration for Charlotte Brontë's portrayal of heroines who may compromise but still survive. She has a point in observing the limitations of sickness and death as forms of rebellion, especially for women in an age which considered female invalidism and morbidity so socially acceptable. An arresting idea is that Emily Brontë herself refused to pine and die in the proper feminine fashion. By implication, this makes her death more of a protest. But it is easier to imagine Emily Brontë a rebel than to prove her one.

Relation To Literary History And Achievement Of Authorship

As already suggested vis-à-vis Bertha Mason and the Nun, relations with the Gothic generate considerable comment. The Gothic is a subspecies of the Romantic, always deemed important for the Brontës. Thus Anne Brontë suffers with readers because she does not meet an expected Romantic standard, according to Chitham. Typifying work on Brontë Romanticism is Richard Dunn's comparison of Charlotte to Wordsworth, Coleridge, Shelley, and Hawthorne, "The Natural Heart: *Jane Eyre's* Romanticism," *Wordsworth Circle*, 10 (1979), 197-204.

However, Lawrence Jay Dessner observes a conflict between realism and romance in *The Homely Web of Truth, A Study of Charlotte Brontë's Novels* (The Hague: Mouton, 1975), and feminist critics are especially insightful in analyzing the ambivalence of both Charlotte and Emily towards the Romantic. Moglen explores the charm and dangers that Byronism held for Charlotte Brontë. Gilbert and Gubar and Homans show how the male literary heritage in general and Romanticism in particular influenced but also threatened the Brontës as women authors. Whereas Harold Bloom postulates any writer's "anxiety of influence," Gilbert and Gubar swerve from this notion to propose an even more acute female "anxiety of authorship." A pen/penis image denies women means of expression. Gilbert and Gubar and also Homans write compellingly of "The Masculine Tradition" (Homans's chapter title) which casts in doubt a woman's literary ambitions. Homans stresses Emily Brontë's difficult relations with Milton as well as with the Romantics. Likewise, Gilbert's and Gubar's chapter on "Milton's Bogey: Patriarchal Poetry and Women Readers" shows the difficulty of female identification with the very male voice of Milton. Women are left with Eve as a model, but as here audaciously proposed, Eve has Satanic affiliations in the poem, and these supply a specific female route to Romantic Satanism, thus Byronism, thus Jane Eyre-Rochesterism. Thus the indomitable Eve of *Shirley*

and the rebel angel Vashti of *Villette*. But for a woman, the Eve-
Satan heritage remains equivocal, in just the way that the Byronic
heritage does (here Gilbert and Gubar and Moglen explore common ground). That is, besides a woman's fantasy identification
with the hero are "feelings of female powerlessness [which] mani-
fested themselves in her conviction that the closest she could really
get to being Satan was to be his—creature, his tool" (p. 207), and
even his victim, like Eve and Satan's consort Sin. If this raises
problems for women readers, it is all the more troublesome for
women writers.

The Marxist-Feminist Literature Collective also suggest the div-
isiveness of the Romantic legacy for Charlotte Brontë, insofar as
Romanticism celebrates the irrational, yet irrationality has attach-
ed to women as a stereotype and stigma, inhibiting accomplish-
ment. And another study shows that Emily Brontë could be as
anti-Romantic as she was Romantic. According to Nina Auerbach's very striking essay "This Changeful Life: Emily Brontë's
Anti-Romance," in *Shakespeare's Sisters, Feminist Essays On Women Poets*, ed. Gilbert and Gubar (Bloomington and London: Indiana University Press, 1979), pp. 49-64, the Romantic elements of
Wuthering Heights are almost entirely missing from the poetry.
Auerbach presents an amazing contradiction—between the Romantic fixation in the novel on childhood, the past, memory, and a
single love and lost unity to be recovered only in death, and Gondal's anti-Romantic devaluation of all of these in favor of mutabil-
ity and multiplicity of experience in love and everything else.
Auerbach reminds us that Emily Brontë spent more of her creative
life in the world of the poems than of the novel. Though *Wuthering Heights* is hardly conventional, this critic makes the poems
seem more original, almost anomalous in a Victorian age much influenced by Romanticism. We may note a difference of opinion between Auerbach and Homans, who finds Emily Brontë freer of an
inhibiting Romantic, masculine literary tradition in the novel than
in the poetry.

Certainly, Auerbach, Homans, and Gilbert and Gubar credit
both Brontës with achievement of strong female authorship.
Homans and Gilbert and Gubar take special interest in works
which can be seen as dramatizing the finding of female voice. Thus
for Gilbert and Gubar *Villette* concerns an overcoming of the anxiety of female narratorship. Originally evasive as a narrator, Lucy
Snowe comes to realize that the painful history of her "buried life"
can make a story worth telling. The "buried life" reference weakens

this argument somewhat, for the phrase is Matthew Arnold's who doubted the power of psychic pain to provide action and edification enough to sustain a work of literature, as he said about his own *Empedocles*. Thus Lucy does not seem to overcome specifically feminine doubts. Still, increase in narrative assertion may outweigh any other form of progress shown in *Villette*, and Gilbert and Gubar give us a more subtle and original Bildungsroman than earlier interpreters. Ultimately, they do not, like Moglen, question whether Brontë could bring forth the self she had conceived, or like Kennard, depict her as the victim of literary conventions. Indeed, Showalter shows that she set a standard for later women writers to live up to.

Narrative Techniques and Authorial Control

Critics continue to explore the narrative complexity of *Wuthering Heights*. In her introduction to *The Art of Emily Brontë*, Anne Smith finds "the choice of Nelly Dean as a narrator . . . a master-stroke" and, throwing discretion to the winds, calls Nelly "the most fully-drawn, complete human being in the novel—or possibly in any novel" (p. 18). She takes a next step beyond those critics who have questioned Nelly's reliability to the point of making her out a villain and suggests that Nelly's superstitutions also partially ally her with the supernatural vision of Catherine and Heathcliff, though she reduces the supernatural to folklore.

Charlotte Brontë's narrative techniques also increasingly interest critics. Many observe the importance of alter egos as structural devices, as we have been in discussions of Bertha Mason and the Nun. *Shirley* is still viewed as lacking in narrative cohesion, but *Villette* has grown greatly in critical estimation for the odd effectiveness of its narration. Some continue to identify author and narrator—Blom and Cynthia A. Linder view Lucy Snowe's Christian faith and fatalism as Brontë's own. (See Linder, *Romantic Imagery in the Novels of Charlotte Brontë* [London and Basingstoke: Macmillan; New York: Barnes & Noble, 1978].) But others explore labyrinthine unreliability in this narrator and separate her from a creator who leaves her open to judgment. Janice Carlisle in "The Face in the Mirror: *Villette* and the Conventions of Autobiography," *ELH*, 46 (1979), 262-289, analyzes the narrator's evasions and secretiveness, her lapses and distortions of memory, her displacement of the reader's attention from herself to other characters who turn out to function as doubles. By such narrative concealments does

Lucy actually reveal her repressive self. Carlisle, like Gilbert and Gubar, finds the most persuasive signs of psychological growth within the developing narration itself, which shows the heroine's increasing capacity to tell her story straight.

While both Emily and Charlotte Brontë are found technically fascinating as writers, Emily currently receives more credit for being a "conscious artist," in Anne Smith's words (p. 28). Thus Gilbert and Gubar recognize Lucy Snowe's achievement of narratorship and her creator's achievement as a woman writer, but they tend to depict the latter as to a significant extent unintentional and uncontrolled. Charlotte Brontë, is "essentially a trance-writer" who produces "dreaming sentences," "obsessive and involuntary," expressing "secret, ungovernable rage," enacting and evading her impulses in work which subverts its ostensible morality, "not always conscious of the extent of her own duplicity" (pp. 311-317). Throughout *The Madwoman in the Attic* run notions of covers and veils in women's writing. In Freudian fashion, what counts most is what is most covert and even inadvertent. Similarly, the Marxist-Feminist Literature Collective puts Derrida and especially Pierre Macherey in the service of feminism. *Villette* is "haunted by the unacknowledged phantom—the Machereyan 'not-said' of feminism itself." Seemingly the author as well as the narrator is haunted and "can only be silent" on certain themes. Meanings "inscribed in the margin" carry more interest and authority than those in the text itself (pp. 197-198). Just so, in "*Villette*'s Buried Letter," *Essays in Criticism*, 28 (1978), 228-244, Mary Jacobus refers to "the novel's unconscious." "What the novel cannot say is eloquently inscribed in its subtext" (pp. 228, 233). (Note: Jacobus belongs to the Collective.)

To treat the Brontës as creating half unaware is neither unusual nor unprecedented. Eagleton presents Charlotte Brontë as an author in the grip of her fantasies of upward class mobility. Keefe believes that personal tragedy and need pushed her towards wish-fulfillment in *Shirley*. An important article published in 1971, Carol Ohmann's "Emily Brontë in the Hands of Male Criticis," *College English*, 32, 906-913, shows how often in the past the art of Emily Brontë has been regarded as "involuntary" and how often this view has correlated with sexism. A critic did not have to acknowledge a woman writer's craft and control. It is strange to see some feminist critics now led by Freudian and deconstructionist methods to appreciate the more involuntary aspects of female authorship. By comparison, Linder's book on Charlotte Brontë seems plodding and old-fashioned—it shows that melodramatic features (e.g., the Madwoman, the Nun) are thematically integral and that nature imagery provides objective corelatives for states of mind. But the book is notable for its simple insistence on the author's deliberateness and control. It cites her various statements of intention and shows how she fulfilled them.

* * *

Briefly reviewing this review of Brontë studies, 1975–1980, I must express again my sense of a rich diversity of work. At the same time I find commonalities of concern, summed up in my headings, and a collective advance in understanding and appreciation. In terms of the attention paid to her, Charlotte has overtaken Emily Brontë, and it is possible that Anne is poised for a comeback. Interest in biography has not waned, and psychoanalytical discussion has burgeoned. The two famous Brontës loom larger than ever in literary history, while their relation to that history has undergone significant revaluation. Above all, feminist scholarship lends fresh excitement to the enterprise of Brontë studies. By way of finale, I will list the works which stand out, for me, as most important: Passel's bibliography, volumes in the Clarenden Press edition of the Brontë novels, Chitham's edition of Anne Brontë's poems, Peters's biography of Charlotte Brontë and biographical-critical studies of Charlotte Brontë by Moglen and Keefe, and criticism by Adams, Apter, Auerbach, Carlisle, Eagleton, Gilbert and Gubar, Jacobus, Kennard, Homans, the Marxist-Feminist Literature Collective, Moers, Pell, Showalter, L. Smith, and Winnifrith.

Recent Dickens Studies, 1980

Sylvia Manning

There were not many books on Dickens this year: not a good year for a reviewer to earn her mite in complimentary copies from obliging publishers. Lots of chapters in books, sometimes two chapters, but as to entire books, only two "completed" *Droods* and a fine volume on Dickens' illustrators. And so this reviewer indulges herself by opening with a book from 1979, Susan R. Horton's *Interpreting Interpreting*, justifiable because it was omitted from the Volume 9 counterpart of this essay, and indulges herself by closing with a book from 1981, Mark Lambert's *Dickens and the Suspended Quotation*, justifiable only on its merit. In between, the organization is based on such categories as seemed to fall naturally from the material at hand. Many things are omitted, some because the reviewer found them worthy of omission, others, no doubt, because the reviewer's bibliographic method was not wholly systematic, and a few because this review was prepared during the period when most libraries in southern California sent their 1980 journals to the bindery. Unfortunately, since all are omitted equally, the reader will not be able to distinguish one type from the others. Finally, a fourth category of omissions is constituted by the essays in Volume 8 of this *Annual*, omitted for obvious reasons of propriety. These essays are listed herewith without commentary: Fred Kaplan, "The Art of Biography. An Interview with Edgar Johnson"; Robert Newsom, "'To Scatter Dust': Fancy and Authenticity in *Our Mutual Friend*"; Colin N. Manlove, "Neither Here Nor There: Un-

easiness in *Great Expectations*"; Richard D. Altick, "*Bleak House*:
The Reach of Chapter One"; Sarah A. Solberg, "'Text Dropped into
the Woodcuts': Dickens' Christmas Books"; John Kucich, "The
Purity of Violence: *A Tale of Two Cities*"; Janet Larson, "The Arts
in These Latter Days: Carlylean Prophecy in *Little Dorrit*"; Fred
Kaplan, "Recent Dickens Studies: 1977–1978."

READERS READING

To risk a bit more candor. *Interpreting Interpreting* is included in
this review not merely because there were few books on Dickens this
year and because the *Annual* review for 1979 missed it, but because
I very much wanted to read it, and just at the time that I was supposed to be at work on 1980. The book beckoned not only with its
clever title but with the sub-title, *Interpreting Dickens's Dombey*,
promising an extended work applied to Dickens and dealing directly with all the new insights, new problems, and new shibboleths of
the newest criticism. The promise was sustained at its very outset:
Stanley Fish in the first sentence—the first line—along with E. D.
Hirsch, Maimonides, and Augustine. (Hirsch was made short work
of, Maimonides and Augustine were soon dropped, but Fish persisted to the very end.) And the promise got a good way towards fulfillment in the early chapters. Horton offers an impressive review of
the problems that an honest regard for differences in interpretation
creates. Her attack on the critical assumption that all elements of a
text "signify" thematically is good, though perhaps a bit unfair to
the perspicacity of some thematic critics, many of whom do
recognize certain elements as mainly or wholly technical or personal. Less satisfying is her elaborate demonstration that differences in
interpretation arise from critics' seeing different units of a work as
its basis or looking at different levels of the work. This explanation
comes with a three-page chart (printed horizontally) of the "interpretive ladder" that places the levels in a hierarchy, which may be
supposed to be the equivalent of the graph in other analytic disciplines but which, unlike a good graph, does not really make
anything clear that the ordinary text did not. And what both the ordinary text and the ladder tell us is that the observer shapes what he
or she sees—not exactly a startling revelation.

Horton's alternatives to the fallacies of others are not always
soundly argued. She never makes the case, for instance, for her
claim that interpretation should explain why the elements of a text

are there, rather than what we make of them however they got there. Her minute exploration of those why's, though fascinating, may be more an evasion of hermeneutical conundrums than their solution. The exploration is in large part a pursuit of facts, with which this book is much concerned. Facts appear in the title of chapter 1, and by chapter 5 we are told that "facts" of the author's life at the time of composition "are facts of the text just as surely as is the structure or langauge of the book itself. Only by reference to the conditions under which it was composed can the interpreter have any hope of distinguishing formal necessity from personal necessity; thematic element from technical exigency." From these "facts" Horton moves to a structure for *Dombey and Son* built upon the words "borne down" as opposed to "borne away" and the concept of motion to-and-fro as opposed to a resting place. She says that the phrases "borne down" and "borne away" and their synonyms pervade this book and also Dickens' letters of this time just as the ideas they convey pervade the plot of the novel, but she demonstrates neither their pervasiness in *Dombey* and the contemporary letters nor their relative absence from the rest of his writings. And then she generalizes from the pressures upon Dickens during this period to the pressures upon Victorian society in a world of rapid change.

Knowing facts, of course, is very different from divining intentions, and the book recurs to the impossibility of the latter, sneering at the "privileged information" of benighted critics who have spoken of Dickensian intention. But when Horton says that "Description in a Dickens novel exists always first and foremost for its own sake," surely intention is posited, if not spoken. The conclusion to this book is also anti-climactic: *Dombey and Son* is inexhaustible. *Interpreting Interpreting* scarcely answers its own questions, but it does a very good job of raising them. Its interpretation of *Dombey*, though not authoritative, is better than interesting.

Others in 1980 dealt with readers and variety of perception less ambitiously, sometimes more successfully. Malcolm Andrews, in "A Note on Serialization," one of a number of essays on Dickens in Ian Gregor's collection *Reading the Victorian Novel: Detail into Form* (London: Vision Press; New York: Barnes and Noble), remarks that serial publication encouraged a leisurely reading of detail that gave the part its intensity, in contrast to the rush for plot that book-form creates. He points out that the context of parts published in periodicals (*Hard Times*, for example, in *Household*

Words), affected perception of those stories, and that reading aloud, as the parts often were read, gives a fuller experience of the text. Others have attempted to recreate or approximate the original conditions of reading, offering experiments to Andrews' theory. Michael Lund ("Teaching Long Victorian Novels in Parts," *Victorian Notes* 58), presents the commentary of two students who read *David Copperfield* in "installments" (every other week, commentary intended to demonstrate significant differences in the reading experience when we read serially. The approach might be interesting, but in this instance it does not yield much. Perhaps bolder than Lund, Keith Carabine himself read *David Copperfield* for the first time in installments, with a day between each ("Reading *David Copperfield*," Gregor volume). The experiment does not seem to have achieved more than Lund's, and the essay moves on to another of those triumphs of modern sensibility over the placid Victorianism of the mid-career Dickens that have become familiar in criticism of *Copperfield*. But this reviewer, unreasonably irritated by the phrase "a first read" followed by a "dramatic 'wait,'" may well be unfair to Carabine.

Richard D. Altick approaches the matter of the original readers' responses to serialized novels by taking, like Susan Horton, *Dombey and Son* as his example. The purpose of "Varieties of Readers' Response: The Case of *Dombey and Son*" (*Yearbook of English Studies* 10), he says, is "to outline the directions and scope of such an inquiry and to indicate the methodology and types of evidence involved." He does so in a highly informative essay that has the historical richness Horton calls for but lacks. An essay that does not seem to intend to raise the issue of a reader's treatment of the text but does so with an excellent crux is Graham Mott's "Was There a Stain upon Little Dorrit?" in *The Dickensian*. He moves from the poles of Leavis's argument that the stain is on Clennam and Cockshut's assumption that it is on Little Dorrit to the tension in Dickens' own view of the matter, which he compares fruitfully to Dickens' ambivalence concerning the Meagles family. The result is an interesting meditation on meaning and intention perhaps pursued not as far as it might be and too readily resolved into the components of Dickens' notions.

In the *TLS* of April 18, in "*Little Dorrit*: The Prison and the Critics," Philip Collins inquires how "a new literary interpretation becomes diffused into the general consciousness" by using the prison imagery in *Little Dorrit* as an instance. Like Gibbon on the impercipience of the Pagans to early Christian miracles, Collins wonders about the critics before Edmund Wilson, who hardly noticed the images, but unlike Gibbon, he concludes that the imagery really is there and he offers some explanation for its late appearance in commentary.

THE DICKENS ILLUSTRATIONS

The major work on Dickens for 1980 is Jane R. Cohen's *Charles Dickens and his Original Illustrators* (Ohio State). A full and principally narrative account of each of the illustrators and their relations with Dickens, it would be valuable for its bibliography alone. Its strengh is in its historical, primarily biographical, emphasis, steering clear of most of the fog that has threatened much criticism of the illustrations and their relation to the texts. Yet the book is analytical where it needs to be, and only in the last chapter does the method weaken—and then we are past Dickens, concerned with the decline of the illustrated novel after 1870.

The shadow of Cohen's book dwarfs the year's minor writings on the illustrations. Cohen supersedes John Turpin's otherwise interesting account in *The Dickensian* of "Maclise as a Dickens Illustrator," and makes Sarah Solberg's various notes seem scattershot. In "A Note on Phiz's Dark Plates" (*The Dickensian*), Solberg suggests an economic motive, having to do with the novel's first appearance in the unillustrated *All the Year Round*, for Browne's failure to use dark plates in the illustrations for *A Tale of Two Cities*. In "Bull's-eye's 'Eyes' in *Oliver Twist*" (*Notes and Queries*) she complains about the "misleading" inclusion of Bull's-eye in the *Oliver Twist* illustration "The Last Chance" because the text says that the dog was hiding and because the unwary reader might take Sykes's "The eyes again" as referring to the dog's staring instead of to a vision of Nancy. For Solberg, this kind of error cautions against criticism that insists upon the importance of the illustrations in reading the texts, an issue that she takes up at greater length in "Dickens and Illustration: A Matter of Perspective" (*Journal of Narrative Technique*). Her argument here is based upon comparisons of sales figures for the Cheap Edition and illustrated editions, upon comparisons of sales figures for *A Tale of Two Cities* in its simultaneous publications in illustrated monthly parts and unillustrated in *All the Year Round*, and upon Dickens' references to Browne and his use of Forster as a go-between in discussions of the illustrations for *Dombey and Son*. The caveat of this essay is important, but the essay is over-written and occasionally smug in our academic way (for example, as it triumphs over Q. D. Leavis). On the other side, Stephen Lutman's "Reading Illustrations: Pictures in *David Copperfield*" (Gregor volume) looks at the interaction of text and illustration without claims that strain credulity and with a series of interesting points. He remarks, for instance, on David's interest in pictures on walls and their frequency in the novel, on how the illustrations, unlike the text, readily avoid David's narrative viewpoint, on how they can summarize and point forward across the linear development of the text, can "help to mediate comic and tragic aspects of the narrative," can point up parallels and contrasts of characters that the novel does not make explicit.

BIOGRAPHY

Avid readers of Dickens will be interested in Diana Orton's *Made of Gold: A Biography of Angela Burdett Coutts* (Hamilton) not for what it tells of Dickens, who appears throughout but whose portrait is familiar, but as a highly readable, ample account of Miss Coutts. There is new information in David Parker and Michael Slater's "The Gladys Storey Papers" (*The Dickensian* for Spring, with a further note in the Autumn issue), which concerns papers relating to *Dickens and Daughter* now deposited in the Dickens House. Also in the Spring *Dickensian*, Margaret Diane Stetz prints the text of a letter donated to Boston University's Mugar Memorial Library in 1974, too late for inclusion in volume III of the Pilgrim *Letters*, in which Dickens prepared a plea for public support of the sanatorium founded by Thomas Southwood Smith in 1840 ("Charles Dickens and 'The Sanatorium': An Unpublished Letter and Manuscript"). In contrast, Robert Woodall's "Charles Dickens, 'Faithful Stenographer'" in *Blackwood's* December issue does not tell us anything more about Dickens' career as a reporter and is only briefly interested in its relation to the politicians we find in the novels.

INFLUENCE ON DICKENS AND OF DICKENS

Source studies this year are not numerous but of great range. At one extreme, Anne Lohrli establishes in "Dickens and Meadows Taylor" (*Notes and Queries*) the evidence that Dickens had read Colonel Taylor's *The Confessions of a Thug* (1839), a book that may have more significant bearing on *Edwin Drood* than the note develops. At the other, Donald Stone's chapter on Dickens in *The Romantic Impulse in Victorian Fiction* (Harvard), "Death and Circuses: Charles Dickens and the Byroads of Romanticism," analyzes several of the novels in a manner gratifyingly compatible with what they are like when read. His theme of Romantic influence allows a discussion of novels from *The Old Curiosity Shop* to *Drood* that not only traces a strain of influence but often illuminates individual novels. The problem with the method is that after a while the terms "Byronic" and "Wordsworthian" begin, through sheer repetition, to lose meaning, and one is made more than a little uneasy by the simplification inherent in such adjectives when they refer not to the figures as people but to some conception of them. Stone writes of "Byronic willfulness" and "Wordsworthian quiescence" almost as though he—and we—had forgotten that Byron was also sometimes quiescent and Wordsworth willful, as though the qualities were to the poets as wetness is to rain. Still, the essay is well worth reading.

In "Charles Dickens and Rockingham Castle" (*Northamptonshire Past and Present*), Philip Collins discusses with his usual lucidity the relationship between Chesney Wold (*Bleak House*) and Rockingham Castle, countering the sort of foolish equation found in Michael and Mollie Hardwick's *Dickens England*. In "A 'Discipline of Feeling': Macready's *Lear* and *The Old Curiosity Shop*" (*The Dickensian*), Paul Schlicke looks at Macready's acting text of *Lear*, rather than the Shakespearean text, for its influence on *The Old Curiosity Shop*. He attends to the elevating pathos in both; to the oppositions between melodrama and the "integration of tragedy"; to our resistance to Nell's death as in part a function of our discomfort with the topic itself, and not just Dickens' handling of it. His essay goes beyond the parallels of plot to the tensions in the work: the nature of the conflict and the attendant emotions.

Studies of Dickens' influence on others perhaps hold less interest for Dickensians than othersians. Laurel Boone's "Tiresias and the Man from Somewhere" (*South Atlantic Quarterly*), for instance, draws parallels between *Our Mutual Friend* and *The Wasteland*, finding them in all possible, plausible, and less plausible *minutiae* and looking in particular at images of dust, at the Thames, and at the figure of Harmon in relation to the figure of Tiresias. The result may do something for our apprehension of *The Wasteland*; it does not illuminate *Our Mutual Friend*. Charlotte Walker Mendez, in "Scriveners Forlorn: Dickens's Nemo and Melville's Bartleby" (*Dickens Studies Newsletter*), argues for Nemo as one of the sources of Bartleby and then moves to parallels in theme and imagery that are less exciting than she claims. Even more modest is John S. Martin's note "Copperfield and Caulfield: Dickens in the Rye" (*Notes on Modern American Literature*), which points to David's "caul" in the name "Caulfield": it is a note on *Catcher in the Rye*, not on Dickens and not meant to be. Similarly, Arnold Johnston's chapter on *The Pyramid* in his *Of Earth and Darkness: The Novels of William Golding* traces parallels between *The Pyramid* and *Great Expectations* with emphasis upon *The Pyramid*, though the effect enriches the meaning of both works. More broadly, Jerome Meckier in "Why the Man Who Liked Dickens Read Dickens Instead of Conrad: Waugh's *A Handul of Dust*" (*Novel*) writes about Waugh on Dickens and Conrad, whom he sees as humanists asserting the continuance of Christian feeling and morality without the Christian forms. The most limited form of these studies is a silly note by J. W. Wheale in the *James Joyce Quarterly* called "More Metempsychosis? The Influence of Charles Dickens on James Joyce," which surveys parallels noted earlier between Joyce and Dickens (or sources for Joyce in Dickens—the issue is a bit muddied), adds a few more, and concludes gratified that Dickens is not the source for Joyce's greatness.

Sue Lonoff looks at once at influence on Dickens and the influence of Dickens in "Charles Dickens and Wilkie Collins" (*Nineteenth-Century Fiction*), reviewing what Dickens did for Collins and talking about what Collins did for Dickens, both generally and in detail with regard to certain novels, especially *Edwin Drood*. The essay is a valuable fact-filled summary that overshadows William Baker's note "Wilkie Collins, Dickens and *No Name*" (*Dickens Studies Newsletter*), which asserts that most Collins/Dickens studies look only to Collins's influence on Dickens and then looks at letters and at the manuscript of *No Name* to demonstrate Dickens' influence on that novel.

THEMATIC STUDIES

Thematic studies of Dickens in 1980 fall rather neatly into three groups: studies based in psychoanalytic theory, studies about death in the novels, and studies of the shorter fiction. Dianne F. Sadoff, in one of the two *PMLA* essays on Dickens for this year, "Storytelling and the Figure of the Father in *Little Dorrit*," argues that in this novel Dickens "demonstrates . . . that the purpose of narrative, including the narrative about purpose or vocation, is to seek the figure of the father, to write the paternal metaphor, and to acquire paternal authority." I do not see how this thesis is demonstrated about narrative, but it is convincingly argued about the particular narrative at hand, and perhaps the generalized statement should be regarded as the kind of grand theoretical statement that suits a good essay to *PMLA* editorial policy. The essay is fully decked in Miller, Lacan, Freud, Barthes, Ricoeur, *et al.*, and loaded with things ironic, but a powerful rendering of the novel and its motives emerges from the baggage. Sadoff is especially convincing in her remarks about the novel's ending.

Michael G. Miller constructs upon a Freudian basis a series of Oedipal parallels that join Murdstone and Heep and thus bridge what are often taken as two parts of *David Copperfield* ("Murdstone, Heep, and the Structure of *David Copperfield*" [*Dickens Studies Newsletter*]). When Micawber defeats Heep, he argues, the good father expels the bad—and then considerately betakes himself to Australia. Derek Brewer devotes a chapter of *Symbolic Stories* (Rowan and Littlefield) to *Great Expectations*. He uses fairy-tale typology and psychoanalytic concepts such as splitting, condensation, and oedipal conflict to analyze the novel as a version of the family drama of adolescence. Though the essay is interesting, its insights are hardly new, and its method is such that it offers nonetheless only one footnote, to A. D. Hutter. Gordon D. Hirsch, the most programmatically psychoanalytic of this group of writers, has two essays this year: "A Psychoanalytic Rereading of *David Copperfield*" (*Victorian Newsletter*) and "Psychological Patterns in the Double Plot of *Our Mutual Friend*" (*Hartford Studies in Literature*). In the former his aim is to "chart a course between the Scylla of moralism [the theme of the disciplined heart] and the Charybdis of Oedipal reductivism" in an analysis of *David Copperfield*. With theory taken from Erikson, George S. Klein, Kohut, and Mahler, he shows the novel re-enacting over and over the loss, the "narcissistic blows," of separation as well as the failure to individuate in child-parent relationships. His David ends up with a tenuous victory in the struggle for fidelity to life. The essay on *Our Mutual Friend* argues that the "unity and coherence" of the novel is to be found through an examination of the way the two main plots "explore similar patterns of 'filial' response to paternal and social authority." The essay proceeds to this examination in a thorough and workmanlike fashion that is not inspiring but that does yield notes of interest. The theory here is a much simpler Freudianism that tends toward the reductive.

John Kucich, in Dickens' second *PMLA* article for the year ("Death Worship among the Victorians: *The Old Curiosity Shop*"), says that his purpose is "to examine, first, the nature of the negative transcendence that can be represented by death and, second, the way a writer can legitimate desires for death by merging them with a positive cultural ideal." The notion here of negative transcendence could use sharper definition, but that problem is lesser than the slipperiness of the logic. Death legitimized society for the Victorians because society recognized death as its originating event. They affirmed it as "transcendent violence, as the final rupturing and negating of restrictive, inauthentic human limits." Thus to affirm death is to affirm life—but a more conservative affirmation is desired, because Quilp affirms death and we do not want to be like Quilp. And so "the most important means of presenting experiences of release through death in some acceptable conservative form is the role given over to art as a vehicle for social organization." What happens to this sentence as a role becomes a means is analogous to what happens to the argument as a whole. And it is hard to say whether the problem is logical or lexical, or rather, whether the logic requires the lexicon or the lexicon governs the logic. It is interesting, however, that when Kucich replies to an attack on his essay in the October issue (F. S. Schwarzbach: letters to the editor), he is quite convincing. This essay should be read not against Schwarzbach's reply but against Stone and Schlicke above, both of whom deal with the Victorians and ourselves in response to Nell's death more readably and more persuasively.

The issue of Victorian response to the death scenes is raised again by W. L. G. James in "The Portrayal of Death and 'Substance of Life': Aspects of the Modern Reader's Response to 'Victorianism'" (Gregor volume), but the essay fails to answer its own questions. It does remind us of the context that might more explicitly inform Kucich's essay (though the mortality rate in 1820 was half that of 1720, forty percent of the population still died by the age of six); it does not tell us what we might conclude therefrom.

Attention to the short fiction has been modest. In "Dickens and Christmas: His Framed-Tale Themes" (*Nineteenth-Century Fiction*), Ruth F. Glancy combines an interest in the framed Christmas tales (either written and framed or only framed by Dickens) as vehicles for autobiographical storytelling, with some interest in the theme of memory that the form provoked. The essay provides a good summary of the history and themes of these tales. Gordon Spence presents "Mugby Junction" as a re-doing of themes from

"The Haunted Man" but "in a low key, omitting the Gothic and supernatural elements, dispensing with the doctrinal insistence on the importance of memory and dissolving the autobiographical connection" ("The Haunted Man and Barbox Brothers," *The Dickensian*). Not much remains, but the essay is nonetheless more convincing than John Daniel Stahl's "The Source and Significance of the Revenant in Dickens's 'The Signal Man'" (*Dickens Studies Newsletter*), which argues that the narrator is a revenant, the signal-man's double, and that the tale is a warning of a doom no technology can forestall.

STUDIES OF CHARACTERS

These are mostly, this year, studies of characters as characters or persons, as opposed to studies of how Dickens creates or deploys characters. In "Alienation and Integration in *Barnaby Rudge*" (*Dickens Studies Newsletter*), Joan B. Frieberg shows the characters of the novel to be alienated from society rather than integrated with it and the good, or saved characters to achieve community while the bad ones fail to do so. The thesis works, but it is a bit trite for this stage in Dickens studies. Russell M. Goldfarb, in "John Jarndyce of *Bleak House*" (*Studies in the Novel*), enjoys greater originality. He argues that Jarndyce is neither all good, as he is usually portrayed by the critics, nor all bad, but merely wanting "to live out his life with the least possible disturbance to his well being." For Dickens, however, this is probably the same as all bad, and one suspects it is for Goldfarb too, since he goes on to an inventory of Jarndyce's faults, concluding that if "enough good people were as rich as Jarndyce and did as little, then surely, the novel suggests, evil would indeed triumph. But the world contains people such as Esther. . . ." He concludes that in the end Esther deserves to marry Woodcourt and no longer live in service to prick the "conscience" of a rich old man. One wonders how no one else, in over 125 years, has grasped this point. Or is it that in this essay Jarndyce is standing outside the realm of novels? A surer embedding is achieved by Paul Eggert in "The Real Esther Summerson" (*Dickens Studies Newsletter*) as he attempts to steer between the extremes of sheer irritation at Esther and a vision of her conducting a conscious and a successful quest for identity. Yet his interpretation of Dickens as sharply critical of her debility is at odds with her roles both as narrator and as moral standard. And he makes some very odd points. He sees her reaction to Guppy's proposal as "almost hysterical," alerting us "to an underlying hardness or inflexibility of disposition in her." How superbly male a point of view that is! I, in contrast, find her reaction perfectly appropriate to the repulsive self-assertion of a Guppy. Eggert also finds the adjective "happy" "not consistent with the described events" when Esther and Ada, reunited in chapter 36, fall weeping to the floor. I cannot tell why. All told, however, the essay is interesting in its hypothesis and fairly convincing in its outline.

Anne Humpherys's "*Dombey and Son*: Carker the Manager" (*Nineteenth-Century Fiction*) is a finely argued essay dealing with the contradictions in Carker by seeing him "as a character reflecting a contradictory set of characteristics which had adhered to the Gothic hero-villain," with the "various elements of his personality not fully integrated." She traces these elements carefully. Mark Kinkead-Weekes analyzes character in terms of structure, following in "The Voicing of Fictions" (Gregor volume) the changing voices of *David Copperfield* to trace its development of meaning. He traces Davy, Daisy, Doady, and David, arguing against spatial readings. The essay is evocative.

ASPECTS OF TECHNIQUE AND FORM

In an amusing note called "'His Truncheon's Length': A Recurrent Allusion to *Hamlet* in Dickens's Novels" (*Dickens Studies Newsletter*), Lionel Morton brings into focus the recurrent allusion to the Ghost of Hamlet in Dickens' writing and suggests its relationship to Dickens' concern for return to life, especially of fathers. Neil Grill, in a purple style ("elemental" used twice in four sentences, with different referents), traces "home" imagery in *David Copperfield* to conclude that the house is "a symbol of the basic need for warmth and protection in a world of impermanence and flux" ("Home and Homelessness in *David Copperfield*" [*Dickensian*]). We really ought to heed Philip Collins's call, issued some years ago, for a moratorium on image studies. Even worse is Don Richard Cox on "The Birds of *Bleak House*" (*Dickens Studies Newsletter*), relentlessly chasing the bird imagery in a plenitude of reference with a minimum of enlightenment, unaware equally of the way in which his hunt empties the sign of meaning and of a long prior essay on the same subject.

Much more effective is Robert W. Duncan's analysis of "Types of Subjective Narration in the Novels of Dickens" (*English Language Notes*). The essay proceeds by dividing subjective narration into four kinds and concludes that it is used "when the dramatic or thematic situation is penetrated by the impulse of the narrator, abandoning the formal structure and participating as a sympathetic spirit of a choral leader." Its contention that Dickens achieves in this way "nuances beyond the reach of quoted speech and indirect statement" is supported by a fine regard for detail.

For Michael Hollington the grotesque is a term "for that cardinal simultaneity of magic and comic effect so distinctive of Dickens' mature art." He seeks its sources in pantomine and medieval gothic and is concerned with "innocent" as well as demonic grotesque. In addition to Hollington's brief treatment of gothic in relation to grotesque, two books on Gothic in 1980 give some attention to Dickens. Judith Wilt's *Ghosts of the Gothic: Austen, Eliot and Lawrence* (Princeton) is a nervy book, exhilarating if you are willing to go along with its wonderfully sweeping hypotheses. She treats Dickens only briefly, focussing upon his "exploration of the Gothic potentiality of character." Her remarks on the double are arresting: "Increasingly, it is this shadow, this brother, the double, that fascinates Dickens: Magwitch/Compeyson, Bradley Headstone/Rogue Riderhood, Carker/old Dombey, the pure deadly evil spirit clutching and feeding its passion upon the human corruptible soul until the only nobility left in the victim is the will to destroy the incubus, at the price even of its own life." This passage is also a good example of the style of the book. David Punter, in *The Literature of Terror: A History of Gothic Fictions from 1765 to the Present Day* (Longman) is more conservative and less interesting. The chapter on Dickens, Collins, and Sheridan LeFanu suffers from its range. We learn that Dickens learned from the Gothic tradition that fear is the best way to hold attention, and learned some techniques for heightening it. Dickens is said to be a poor instance of Victorian sensationalism because he formed his "complexly original novels" from a number of genres, and indeed though Dickens can be seen in terms of this history, it does not do much to illuminate his work.

Conceptions of comic form offer an alternate way of organizing or understanding Dickens in 1980. Roger B. Henkle's *Comedy and Culture: England 1820–1900* (Princeton) often either is opaque or fails to demonstrate its theses. It appears to have in mind an audience that needs more explanation and plot summary than Dickensians are likely to enjoy, and it suffers from a tendency to let its illustrations and secondary arguments run it off track. It makes assertions such as that "Dickens's personal experience uniquely shaped his imagination to deal with such a scene" (I doubt it matters what sort of scene such was), talks about Dickens' "artistic objective," works in the middle class and the City without much illumination. The two chapters on Dickens are not without insight, particularly in the matter of the change Henkle asserts in Dickens' comedy; one must take the good with the bad.

We can find an instance of how willful interpretation is by a conjunction of an example in Henkle with an example in a three-page treatment of Dickens in Ann Jefferson's *The Nouveau Roman and the Poetics of Fiction* (Cambridge). The latter book is about Butor, Robbe-Grillet, and Sarraute, but in the process of arguing that the nouveau roman's "curious self-obsession" is "simply a more explicit and exaggerated form of a necessary reflexivity endemic to the genre as a whole," Jefferson uses Micawber's letter in chapter 27, with its comic reversal immediately subsequent, to show how "speech within speech . . . becomes also speech about speech," how the limitations of content turn us to langauge and how the languages of David Copperfield and Micawber react upon each other (to the disparagement of Copperfield's). Henkle treats the same passage quite solemnly, seeing Micawber's behavior as evidence of stress in the disintegrating world of the City.

Robert M. Polhemus's chapter on Dickens in *Comic Faith: The Great Tradition from Austen to Joyce* (Chicago) is a great deal more rewarding. It is mostly a fine essay on *Martin Chuzzlewit* that treats the clash in the novel between its moralism and its comedy, a clash rooted and expressed in language, so as to explain brilliantly the ultimate failure of the novel (though he never calls it failure). The latter part of the chapter is weaker, both structurally and in its argument. A system of sub-headings with numbered subsections appears to mark a refusal to seam the essay, and the sections on food, time, and space barely cohere. But the work on satire and the liberation of comic language is superb. An often similar understanding of *Martin Chuzzlewit* and the power of its language governs Patrick J. McCarthy's "The Language of *Martin Chuzzlewit*" (*Studies in English Literature*), which argues that the linguistic effects of the book, which have "tended to validate whatever is energetic, extreme, and unique" are subordinated to the "tranquil, calm, and happy" conclusion, so that the "clear, formal implications are that the wild exhilarations of disorder have been safely contained." The argument is demonstrated with care and should be pondered alongside Polhemus's. A less satisfying treatment of language than either of these is Roderick F. McGillis's "Plum Pies and Factories: Cross Connections in *Hard Times*" (*Dickens Studies Newsletter*). The thesis that this novel "is about language as much as anything else" is not demonstrated—perhaps that is just as well—in part because the self-indulgent style of the essay (one paragraph begins with "This reminds me of . . . .") allows McGillis to review a variety of loosely connected matters, some more interesting than others. The principal concern is the importance of nursery-rhymes and fairy-tales in the language of *Hard Times.*

Peter Brooks's "Repetition, Repression, and Return: *Great Expectations* and the Study of Plot" (*New Literary History*) is, as the title indicates and the opening sentence announces, primarily a discourse on plot, but its instance, *Great Expectations*, is discussed extensively. Grounded in a philosophical Freudianism (very different from the clinical Freudianism represented by Hirsch) that finds life, in essence, a detour on the road to death, the essay ultimately discovers in the novel a critique of reading: "human interpretation in ignorance of the true vectors of the text." A good deal of its critical reflexivity, however, is made convincing by the coherence of ingenious argument, and the essay must be forgiven its occasional turgidity and various jargons for the frequently startling power of its rendition of, as it promises, the plot.

William C. Spengemann's segment on *David Copperfield* in *The Forms of Autobiography: Episodes in the History of a Literary Genre* (Yale) analyzes the novel in the context of a work that seeks "a theory, or rather a description, of autobiography that will recognize both its perduring relation to the self-biographical mode and its apparently increasing tendency to assume fictive forms in the modern era." Following this description, *David Copperfield* "is autobiographical only to the extent that it expresses through the deployment of conventional narrative *personae* and through the allegorical tenor of its language Dickens' over-riding concern with the realization of his self, the achievement of true being"—only, that is, in the first fourteen chapters. Spengemann's further concern is less to demonstrate this thesis than to analyze the fourteen autobiographical chapters. The method leads through the not surprising assertion that "To redeem this past but ever-present time, Dickens had to square not only its disgraceful appearances with his present success but its private vision with his publicly avowed belief in moral justice," to a quite astonishing rendition of Mr. Dick and Aunt Betsey as sharers of David's role in representing Dickens' "several past and present selves." The argument is intriguing, and one is disappointed that the interests of this book lead Spengemann away from more discussion of Dickens.

The most provocative work on Dickensian form in 1980 is to be found in Peter Garrett's two chapters in *The Victorian Multiplot Novel: Studies in Dialogical Form* (Yale). Dialogical form is form with dual logic, especially when the opposing logics are of single and multiple focus. The chapters on Dickens are designed to demonstrate, in the earlier and later novels, that the effect of dialogical form is to give us "not the realization of a secure and comprehensive vision but a continual, shifting, unstable, and unpredictable confrontation between single and plural, individual and social, particular and general persepectives," and they do so with varying success. Sometimes the insights are valuable independently of the thesis, but for the most part the thesis is more interesting than its applications to Dickens. When Garrett tries to make Doyce's modesty and sense of himself not as inventor but as discoverer of existing laws into a part of the theme of denial of responsibility (hence, suspect), the thesis is playing havoc with the novel. When he makes the alternative conclusions to *Great Expectations* significant, he is making meaning of an editorial habit. Yet although I am not convinced that the world of *Little Dorrit* (along with *Bleak House* and *Our Mutual Friend* the focus of the second chapter) is as surely lacking in "transcendent truth" as Garrett states (not quite demonstrates), his approach to this novel, as to the others, develops lines of tension that other readings tend to suppress, and the effect is liberating. The first Dickens chapter does fine work with the association in the early novels of spatial, elevated perspective with power and fear, its conflict with individual perspective and its temporality. The method leads Garrett to examine closely passages that are not those everyone else uses. All told, the work is sometimes cavalier in its handling of the text, but too often enlightening to miss.

DICKENS AND . . .

Essays about Dickens and something were highly various in 1980, both in subject and in quality. They include Dickens and Italy, Dickens and the angels, Dickens and the new woman, Dickens and the hearth, Dickens and Jews, Dickens and social reform, Dickens and industrialism, Dickens and the Arctic. Dickens and Italy is the subject of a chapter devoted to Dickens in Kenneth Churchill's *Italy and English Literature 1764–1930* (Macmillan [London] and Barnes and Noble [New York]). Churchill argues that *Pictures From Italy* is a plea to the English to abandon their insularity and treat their European neighbors "as fellow human beings." He sees Italy in *Little Dorrit* not as mere background but "a country whose rich environment would be used . . . to bring out the qualities and states of mind of a character exposed to contact with it." As such, it changed the possibilities of fictional use of Italy. J. M. Cameron's "Dickens and the Angels" (*University of Toronto Quarterly*) treats not so much of angels as of Dickens' religious attitudes generally, with humor and a degree of impatience for a writer "frightened of any suggestion of reality (over and above, that is, the expression of a rather vague moral attitude) in religion." Gail Cunningham writes with similarly refreshing style in *The New Woman and Victorian Novel*, and although any book that declares its interest in those minor writers who, "content for the most part to parade their arguments unencumbered with the literary trappings of imaginative power or psychological plausibility, give stark and forceful expression to the new feminist ideas" must charm us by its wit alone, the work on Dickens is limited to an account of his conventional portraits of fallen women in Lady Dedlock and Edith Dombey and brief mention of Miss Wisk and other feminists. In "Dickens's Hearthless Hero: The Failure of Home and Family in *Great Expectations*"(*Illinois Quarterly*), Irwin Weiser summarizes a great deal of plot to point out that in *Great Expectations* at least, Dickens "can no longer accept the values of the home and family as a reward for his characters." He does not explain how Dickens can do so in *Our Mutual Friend*. The essay seems written for a non-specialist reader.

Anne Aresty Naman begins with the problematic and ultimately unworkable thesis in *The Jew in the Victorian Novel: Some Relationships Between Prejudice and Art* (AMS Press) and proceeds to a lengthy but unilluminating discussion of, among others, Dickens. A simplistic and tedious methodology does not surprise us with insightful readings. We learn, for instance, that Fagin is a more sucessful stereotype than Riah because Fagin is evil and Riah suffers as do most of Dickens' good characters, and that Dickens used stereotypes, not only the racial one of Jews, to fulfill moral intentions.

Carol Snef, in "*Bleak House:* The Need for Social Reform" (*Dickens Studies Newsletter*), extends the image of vampirism from Vholes through Krook, Chancery, to all parents battening on or neglecting children, all parasites, all whose allegiance to the past obscures their perception of present needs, all locked in the past—until the concept is no longer very useful. The conclusion, though it is eccentric, might have come from any reading of the novel, and hardly seems to arise from this one: at the end of the story, the reader suspects that it is only a matter of time until the second Bleak House is infected.

There is more substance, though equal wrongheadedness, in Catherine Gallagher's "*Hard Times* and *North and South*: The Family and Society in Two Industrial Novels" (*Arizona Quarterly*). Against the limitations of *Hard Times*, which is organized on the "metaphoric principle of social paternalism," this essay champions *North and South*, in which "the family is metonymically, not metaphorically, associated with society." Gallagher argues that Dickens' themes are selected and developed on the basis of the metaphoric organization—an organization she inferred from the themes. Despite an obvious immersion in ecomomic history, the writer seems to believe that Mrs. Gaskell's solution to the class antagonism offered in *North and South*, that is, an inter-class marriage, would have been viable. Though the solution is seen to emerge from the metonymic method, it appears to be praised for its social applicability. Despite the theory and its odd partisanship, however, the essay offers some analysis of both novels that brings them usefully into contrast.

After Gallagher and Snef, it is particularly satisfying to read Philip Collins. In "Dickens and Industrialism" (*Studies in English Literature*), he reviews what Dickens knew and wrote of Industrialism, his various and inconsistent judgments, and his failure to speak of child-labor, looking at Dickens' primarily "modernist" attitude with Collins's usual fullness and grace. This solidly grounded essay is more valuable that the combination of ideology and literary theory that emerges from one like Gallagher's.

Another historical approach is Sheila Smith's in her extensive work on Dickens, especially *Hard Times*, in *The Other Nation: The Poor in English Novels of the 1840s and 1850s* (Clarendon). The purpose of this book is to see how the poor appear in early Victorian novels, "how the appearance accords with verifiable reality and what this reality can tell us of the imagination which created that fiction." The purpose is carried out more didactically than this statement implies. The novels are judged by the degree to which they measure up to Smith's high standard of confrontation, directness, and realism. There is no theoretical defense—none appears wanted—of the assumption that what a novel should do is render the poor imaginatively and without condescension. (I do not mean to imply in contrast that a novel should render the poor unimaginatively and condescendingly, merely that verisimilitude in a certain political vein is not a generally accepted mode of construing novelistic merit.) Withal, Smith writes with a fine and often undeniable irony. She calls Dickens' descriptions of St. Giles in *Sketches by Boz* and elsewhere "social horrors at a safe distance," arguing that Dickens "reduces people to wild objects producing a frisson of delight in the beholders." His treament of Stephen Blackpool, for instance, "stifles our sense of the man but increases our admiration for the director of the pathos." *Hard Times* comes in for altogether rough treatment. It is attacked for offering us fancy instead of imagination. Its governing symbols, Coketown and the Horseriding, are declared inadequate. Dickens' repeated use of "the three facts of smoke, flame, and sounding machinery" in descriptions of industrial centers (in *The Old Curiosity Shop, Bleak House*, and *Hard Times*) shows his "simple, crude reaction to the industrial towns." Dickens cannot win: he is criticized for comparing Coketown to "the painted face of a savage" on the grounds that for him "savage" is replete with nasty connotations (Smith assumes that the simile is to the populace, not merely the structures), but his "exceptional, protective treatment of Stephen implies condescension rather than understanding." The latter is a good point: Smith argues that when Dickens takes a character seriously he is free to laugh at him. I am not sure the distinction is an entirely reliable index of Dickens' attitudes (surely he is as solemn about Agnes as he is about Stephen, and surely he takes Agnes quite seriously), but it certainly helps to define what is wrong with the portrayal of Stephen. Dickens comes of poorly in this study, but so does everyone else. The novelist who is most successful in this book's terms is Gaskell, though in the end Smith gives Dickens credit for a firmer historical and political context than hers and for the power of his "image of human dispair."

In diametric contrast to Smith, Carol L. Bernstein in "Nineteenth-Century Urban Sketches: Thresholds of Fiction" (*Prose Studies 1800–1900*) dissolves city into text and description into referenceless rhetoric. She employs the current rhetorical mode to distinguish Dickens' descriptions of the city from the ostensibly more realistic urban sketches of writers like Sala. A more traditional historical inquiry than either of these is David Roberts's "Dickens and Arctic" (*Horizon*), which sets *The Frozen Deep* in the context of Dickens' response two years earlier to the reports from Canada concerning the end of Sir John Franklin's arctic ex-

pedition. The popular play touched on the popular issue, affirm-
ing, against recent evidence to the contrary, that in extremes of
service to one's country, character gains strength for nobility and
self-sacrifice.

EDWIN DROOD

Work on *Drood* this year includes two articles and two completions. Edgar Rosenberg, "Dating *Edwin Drood*" *(The Dickensian)*
places the *Book of Memoranda* entry on the novel as autumn or
winter 1860, as opposed to Forster's bogus letter offering July
1869, thus demonstrating that Dickens had been thinking about
Edwin and Rosebud a long time. At the other extreme of practicality and factualness, Robert F. Fleissner in "Drood the Obscure:
The Evidence of the Names" *(Armchair Detective)* performs an
elaborate exercise in puns and association to demonstrate that
Drood is innocent (rood) Jasper evil (asp), Neville good (n/evil):
other analyses do not lead anywhere in particular.

The two completions share a number of features. Both depend
upon Jasper's being schizophrenic and include the killing of Neville; they envision the same marriages for Rosa and Helena, and
they make use of the Sapsea tomb. On the other hand, in addition
to differences in the solution of the plot, the two books present
themselves differently. Charles Forsyte's (pseudonym) *The Decod-
ing of Edwin Drood* (Scribner's and Gollancz) offers the completion in the first half of the book and an explanation in the second.
The first part is the better of the two. It is highly dramatic and
picks up a great many threads from the Dickens portion. The justi-
fication ranges from convincing to comic (when it finds crypto-
grams in Mrs. Crisparkle's cupboards or in the packing-boxes of
the Twinkleton girls). *The Mystery of Edwin Drood*, concluded by
Leon Garfield, introduced by Edward Blishen, and illustrated by
Antony Maitland (Andre Deutsch) is an attempt at a seamless joining of Dickens and Garfield that comes off very well but not perfectly. Dickens' style is more difficult than his plotting. The Dickens portion of this novel cuts rapidly back and forth from scene to
scene; Garfield becomes almost continuous and so loses this device
of mystification. Garfield also drops Dickens' frequent present
tense, to some detriment. But if you enjoy this sort of thing, the
novel will occupy a pleasant evening.

ADAPTATIONS

In "Two Film Versions of *Oliver Twist:* Moral Vision in Film and Literature" (*Dickens Studies Newsletter*), Barry Tharaud attacks both the David Lean 1947 and the 1933 Monogram Pictures films of the novel as lacking the novel's moral vision; he summarizes the films and makes grand statements about the moral-didactic value of the novel.

Nineteen eighty was notable not for work about adaptations but for an adaptation, David Edgar and the Royal Shakespeare Company's *The Life and Adventures of Nicholas Nickleby*, produced at the Aldwych and then on tour in 1981 at the Plymouth Theater in New York. *Dickens Studies Newsletter* offers a pair of reviews, Margaret Ganz unhappy with anything other than a recital of the novel, Richard Dunn quibbling but having enjoyed himself. Andrew Sanders's review in *The Dickensian* is glowing. This reviewer lines up with Sanders. By December, 1981, the Royal Shakespeare Company had surely brought us closer than the academy has or perhaps can to what Dickens must have meant to an audience, whether of readers, at Dickens' readings, or in contemporary adaptations (the price of admission excepted).

STYLISTICS, AND 1981

Mark Lambert's *Dickens and the Suspended Quotation* (Yale) is properly the province of next year's *Annual*. This reviewer can offer no excuse for reviewing it here except perhaps that the book deserves as much notice as it can get. Its opening sentences are: "Whales there are in Dickens, and a multitude of sprats. This is a book about plankton." The liveliness of style, the wit, the irony, do not diminish. At the end of the first chapter, Lambert promises his reader "a small but permanent shift in the way you perceive good nineteenth-century novels." The question at hand is simply whether, when, and why Dickens interrupts a character's speech with a phrase such as "said Mrs. Craddock, the landlady, peeping in." The answers are luminous, set in historical context, presented with enviable force and clarity. *Dickens and the Suspended Quotation* outruns the best of 1980, and compensates for the worst. If you must choose only one book on Dickens, or one book on nineteenth-century novels, choose this one.

IN CLOSING

One hopes that Dickens critics will continue to avoid using language so as to offend the inimitable ghost. Some in 1980 did not, and if the ghost is beyond such trivia, still we should be spared not only "a first read" but "transmit out" and "personalized," life and art "to transpose each other," "intensive" for "intense," "positive" and "negative" used, as our students use them, as all-purpose adjectives meaning "good" and "bad" and even, with all respect to the lexical freedom of current criticism, "expectative" and "futilization." One hopes too that critics will heed warnings such as Horton's relative to both what Dickens "must" have intended and what the text "must" show. We are surely now all skeptical when told that in Esther Summerson Dickens "had committed himself to a psychological study deeper, probably, than he had anticipated" or that the "world of the Victorian novel is a rational one." At one point in her other wise fine essay, Humpherys cites Alan Horsman's note that Dickens had originally intended Edith Dombey to become Carker's mistress but had changed his plan when Lord Jeffrey protested, and argues that despite this "late change in Dickens' plan, given their two personalities Edith's rejection of Carker is as inevitable as her elopement." Now Humpherys's explanation of the logic of rejection is very good, but is not "inevitable" a bit strong? What would the critic have written had Lord Jeffrey not interfered?

Taking the volumes as wholes, 1980 seems to have been a rather good year for the *The Dickensian* but mixed for *Dickens Studies Newsletter*. One can only be infinetely grateful, however, for the work of the latter's bibliographers, Alan M. Cohn and K. K. Collins.

Lewis Carroll: A Sesquicentennial Guide to Research

Edward Guiliano

Lewis Carroll was omitted from the editions of *Victorian Fiction: A Guide to Research* (1964 and 1978) and *Victorian Poetry: A Guide to Research* (1956 and 1968). Perhaps the editors could not make up their minds whether Carroll was a novelist or a poet. More likely, though, the editors decided that he was too minor a figure, one without a significant foothold in the college classroom or elsewhere in the mills of academe, to merit inclusion. But, curiouser and curiouser, interest in Carroll's life and art has mushroomed in recent years. His books continue to sell briskly and broadly; readers are turning with regularity not only to the *Alice* books but to his lesser-known works; his works are being taught and studied in courses in Victorian literature, children's literature, linguistics, and philosophy; and scholars and critics in English speaking as well as many non-English speaking countries are turning increasingly to Carroll and his art. These, I recognize, are strong assertions, but the listings for the past decade or so in the annual *MLA International Bibliography* or in the annual Victorian bibliography published in *Victorian Studies* provide some support for them; indeed, judging by quantitative standards, it appears that in terms of academic interest Carroll has begun to eclipse some of the most venerable Victorian authors. Putting aside the question of merit, if one asks now which Victorian writers will continue to be (not necessarily should be) read and studied a hundred or two hundred years from now, Lewis Carroll is a much safer candidate than anyone would have been willing to propose as recently as twenty-five years ago.

Since their publication, *Alice's Adventures in Wonderland* (1865) and *Through the Looking-Glass* (1871) have held a firm place in the popular culture. They have been quoted and misquoted, staged and filmed, commercialized and otherways bastardized. There have been floods of editions and translations of the *Alice* books, and, over the years, a broad range of other primary and secondary Carroll publications has also appeared. I propose to sort selectively through these works, emphasizing valuable recent ones, in this first prose guide to publications on Lewis Carroll.

BIBLIOGRAPHY, REFERENCE, AND COLLECTIONS

For more than a half century, the *Lewis Carroll Handbook* has been the standard bibliographical reference. This descriptive bibliography dealing almost exclusively with primary works was compiled first in 1931 by Sidney Herbert Williams and Falconer Madan and was based in part upon Williams's *A Bibliography of the Writings of Lewis Carroll* (1924). The *Handbook* was revised and brought up to date by Roger Lancelyn Green in 1962 and again by Denis Crutch in 1979. With each edition some material was dropped while much was added, so one can sometimes find useful information by checking an early edition. The *Handbook*'s listings of works published in Carroll's lifetime and the many subsequent editions cited are of unquestionable value; however, its checklist of materials about Carroll is severely limited, and virtually all of the materials catalogued are British or American publications.

The best source of information on secondary publications or on material published in languages other than English is Edward Guiliano's *Lewis Carroll: An Annotated International Bibliography, 1960–77* (1980). The data is arranged in four sections: Section A, Primary Works; Section B, Reference and Bibliographical Works and Exhibitions; Section C, Biography and Criticism; and Section D, Miscellaneous—Including Dramatic and Pictorial Adaptations and Discussions of Translations. Annotations are descriptive and not evaluative. Since reprints of books first published prior to 1960 are included and since reviews of books are cited with each book, the bibliography is reasonably comprehensive.

For information on translations of Carroll's works, consult Warren Weaver's *Alice in Many Tongues* (1964), supplemented by *Lew-*

is Carroll: An Annotated International Bibliography for more recent information.

Catalogs are, of course, an outstanding source of information on primary publications. For Carroll studies none is more valuable than the Brooks catalog of the auction sale following Dodgson's death in 1898. This catalog has recently been reprinted in facsimile along with three subsequent 1898 booksellers' catalogs offering books from Dodgson's library (Blackwell, Parker, and The Art and Antiques Agency) as *Lewis Carroll's Library* (1981), edited and with an introduction by Jeffrey Stern.

Other useful catalogs are Morris L. Parrish's scarce (limited to 66 copies) *A List of the Writings of Lewis Carroll* (1928) and its supplementary list (1933); the exhibition catalog of *The Lewis Carroll Centenary in London* (1932); the *Catalogue of an Exhibition at Columbia University to Commemorate the One Hundredth Anniversary of the Birth of Lewis Carroll* (1932); *The Harcourt Amory Collection of Lewis Carroll in the Harvard College Library* (1932); *Alice One Hundred: Being a Catalogue in Celebration of the 100th Birthday of "Alice Adventures in Wonderland"* (1966); and *Lewis Carroll and Alice, 1832–1982*, the catalog, with long discursive entries by Morton N. Cohen, of the sesquicentennial Carroll exhibition held in 1982 at the Pierpont Morgan Library.

Warren Weaver's census of extant copies of the 1865 *Alice* (*PBSA*, 1971) is an important bibliographical work. Weaver examined each of the nineteen surviving copies of this rare book and relates their individual histories and distinguishing characteristics. Speculation is always current that a few more 1865 *Alices* exist, and Selwyn Goodacre is currently preparing an up-dating of the Weaver census to appear in a Carroll issue of *ELN* (1982).

The Lewis Carroll societies in England and America have done much to improve the state of Carroll bibliography in recent years. Both societies publish newsletters which keep members abreast of the most recent publications (including ephemera). The Lewis Carroll Society of North America supports the publication of a continuing listing of "minor Carrolliana" that has appeared in the popular culture, *Lewis Carroll in the Popular Culture*, edited by Byron W. Sewell (1976–). The Lewis Carroll Society (England) also supports similar bibliographical works. *Jabberwocky: The Journal of the Lewis Carroll Society* regularly publishes bibliographical studies (and textual studies); for example, an extensive listing of *Alice* parodies, the collection owned by Lall Montgomery, appeared in 1972.

In 1890 Lewis Carroll wrote to the dedicatee of *Sylvie and Bruno,* his child-friend Isa Bowman, that "I really didn't dare to sent it [a presentation copy of *Sylvie and Bruno*] across the Atlantic—the whales are so inconsiderate." Contrariwise, in the years since Dodgson's death, most of the choice editions of his works, his letters and other manuscripts, his photographs, and much memorabilia have traveled safely across the Atlantic from England to America. Today the major repositories of Carroll material—thanks to the tenaciousness and subsequent munificence of a group of American collectors—are in the United States. The following libraries have preeminent and comprehensive Carroll holdings with strengths in all the major categories of the Carroll bibliography: The Houghton Library, Harvard University, which includes the Harcourt Amory Collection; the Humanities Research Center, the University of Texas at Austin, which includes the Gernsheim Collection (photographs) and the Warren Weaver Collection (noted for translations, etc.); The New York Public Library, notably the Henry W. and Albert A. Berg Collection; New York University Library, principally the Alfred C. Berol Collection but also the Fales Collection; The Pierpont Morgan Library, which includes the Arthur A. Houghton, Jr. Collection; Princeton University Library, principally the Morris L. Parrish Collection (which includes several of Dodgson's photograph albums); and The Philip H. & A. S. W. Rosenbach Foundation.

There are numerous other collections with choice but either less comprehensive or less important holdings. In England, perhaps only the British Library (British Museum) can be considered a major Carroll repository, and that essentially on the basis of assorted letters, books, information on printing history, and three stellar items; the manuscript of *Alice's Adventures Under Ground*, the surviving manuscript of Dodgson's journal (diary), and an 1865 *Alice*.

EDITIONS AND TEXTS

There is still not a complete edition of Carroll's works, or even definitive editions of his most popular works. Carroll, writing on a wide variety of subjects, published a great deal. Among his sixteen books are, of course, several works on mathematics and logic as well as a wealth of minor poetry and fiction. He published pamphlets covering such diverse topics as parliamentary procedure, election methods, mathematics, and several satires on Oxford politics and personalities. He was also one of the great Victorian letter writers. Up until recently, when his achievements as a photographer and as a logician became recognized, Carroll was widely known only for the *Alices* and *The Hunting of the Snark*—and this explains in part the absence of a thorough collected edition of his works. It would be desirable to have an edition of Carroll's works edited using modern scholarly standards, and it would be a relatively straightforward task because very few manuscripts of Carroll's works exist, the textual changes in published volumes are not extensive, and much of the preliminary bibliographical and textual spadework has already been completed.

There have been several collected editions of Carroll's works. In 1936 *The Complete Works of Lewis Carroll* appeared and was reprinted in slightly revised form in 1939. Despite its title, this Modern Library/Random House/Nonsense Press edition is by no means complete. It does not contain even all of the works signed "Lewis Carroll." It contains no material published for the first time, and no effort was made to establish a thoroughly reliable text. It is, however, a full and useful book, widely available, and has become a standard edition for many of Carroll's works. In recent years it has been reprinted several times in both hardcover and in paperback (Vintage). The second collected edition, *The Works of Lewis Carroll*, edited by Roger Lancelyn Green, appeared in 1965 (Hamlyn). It contains a wide, but far from complete sampling of Carroll's work including letters, essays, puzzles, and his Russian journal. It is not as widely used as the Modern Library edition. And like the Modern Library volume, its text was not established in accordance with modern scholarly standards. Forthcoming is *The Complete Illustrated Works of Lewis Carroll* (Outlet, 1982) which should be a useful compendium having as merits generally reliable texts of the *Alices*, *Alice's Adventures Under Ground*, *Rhyme? and Reason?*, *A Tangled Tale*, the *Sylvie and Bruno* books, and *Three Sunsets and Other Poems*, all with their original illustrations.

By virtue of its popularity and influence, Martin Gardner's *Annotated Alice* (1960), essentially a heavily footnoted edition of the two *Alices* in which Gardner identifies allusions, jokes, logical paradoxes, and puns, and provides additional background information and interpretation, has become the standard edition of *Alice's Adventures in Wonderland* and *Through the Looking-Glass*. Unfortunately, the texts used are not completely reliable and the positioning of the illustrations does not follow precisely the editions published in Carroll's lifetime. According to its publisher, more than one-half million hardcover copies of the *Annotated Alice* have been sold in America, and there are three British editions (including a Penguin

DICKENSSTUDIES ANNUAL

paperback), an American paperback edition, and translations into several languages. Gardner followed his *Annotated Alice* with the *Annotated Snark* (1962), which also has gone through several editions including a Penguin paperback edition, and recently was thoroughly revised and reissued in a volume on the Snark containing two other works on the poem (a bibliography and an essay on Holiday drawings). The new edition is published by William Kaufman (1981).

The Norton Critical Edition of *Alice in Wonderland*, edited by Donald Gray (1971), is a reasonably authoritative edition and also contains reliable texts of *Through the Looking-Glass* and *The Hunting of the Snark*. Gray, who used the 1897 text and includes corrections of printer's errors, makes a few judicious changes, but he does not consider Carroll's 1887 corrections. The placement of Tenniel's illustrations is, however, not always in harmony with editions published in Carroll's lifetime.

Selwyn Goodacre has provided textual notes and set up the apparatus for authoritative editions of the two *Alice* books (*The Library*, 1973). Nevertheless, there is little prospect for a definitive edition of the *Alices*. Goodacre, however, prepared an "experimental" text for the Sesquicentennial *Alice* illustrated by Barry Moser and introduced and annotated by James R. Kincaid (Pennyroyal, 1982). The text in this deluxe, limited edition is probably as close as we can hope for a definitive edition of *Alice in Wonderland*. The University of California Press is scheduled to bring out a trade edition of the Pennyroyal *Alice* late in 1982.

The most reliable text of *Through the Looking-Glass* appears in the Centenary edition illustrated by Ralph Steadman (1972). The text for this edition, also prepared by Selwyn Goodacre, is another amalgamation of Carroll's changes for a popular edition, and does not contain textual notes. Goodacre is currently revising his text for a forthcoming Pennyroyal *Through the Looking-Glass*.

It must be noted that the edition of the *Alices* edited by Roger Lancelyn Green that appears in the generally authoritative Oxford English Novels series (1971) contains serious textual flaws, and has been dealt with accordingly by Goodacre in a review (*Notes and Queries*, 1971). The Oxford edition does contain useful explanatory notes which echo and sometimes refine Martin Gardner's and contains as well a sober and wise introduction by Green. Macmillan's recent attempt (1981) at producing a definitive *Alice in Wonderland* has merit but also falls short of the mark.

In the absence of a reliable collected edition, and with no definitive editions of single titles, the many facsimile reprints of the first editions of Carroll's work in print are valuable and welcome. The series of reprints produced by Dover in paperback is handsome, reliable, inexpensive and widely available. The series (all currently in print) includes: *Alice's Adventures Under Ground* (1965), *Euclid and His Modern Rivals* (1973), *The Humorous Verse of Lewis Carroll (1960)*, *The Nursery "Alice"* (1966), *Pillow Problems and A Tangled Tale* (1958), and *The Unknown Lewis Carroll (Diversions and Digressions)* (1961). Dover has also reprinted three translations of *Alice in Wonderland*: the first French, *Aventures d'Alice au pays des merveilles* (1972); the first German, *Alice's Abenteuer im Wunderland* (1974), and Nabokov's (Sirin's) Russian version, *Anya v stranye chudes* (1976). Other facsimile reprints of *Under Ground* include University Microfilms' (1964), McGraw-Hill/Peter Smith's (1965), one which appears in Donald Rackin's *Alice's Adventures in Wonderland: A Critical Handbook* (1969), and the deluxe edition by Genesis Press (1979). These reprints are especially significant since *Under Ground* contains Carroll's own drawings, and these reprints have introduced Carroll's highly imaginative artwork to the general public. Other notable reprints include Garland Press's reprint of *Rhyme? and Reason?* (1976) and also *Sylvie and Bruno* (1976), and Mayflower Books' attractive *The Hunting of the Snark* (1981); *The Hunting of the Snark* has also been reprinted in facsimile in the trade edition of the *Snark* containing Martin Gardner's *Annotated Snark* (1981).

In the eighty-four years since Carroll's death there have been important publications of new primary material. The *Lewis Carroll Picture Book* (1899) contains a wide assortment of previously unpublished writings and drawings. *Tour in 1867* (1928; reprinted by Dover as *The Russian Journal* [1977]) is Dodgson's notebook of his trip to Russia with H. P. Liddon. A two-volume edition of his journals edited by Roger Lancelyn Green appeared in 1953 as *The Diaries of Lewis Carroll*. This invaluable work contains only about sixty to seventy percent of the extant diaries (several volumes also disappeared mysteriously since 1898). Genesis Press has announced plans to publish a facsimile edition of the complete manuscript diaries. Two of Dodgson's juvenile magazines have been published: *Useful and Instructive Poetry* (1954) and *The Rectory Magazine* (1976)—both reproduced in facsimile. Dodgson's poem "The Ligniad" is reproduced in facsimile and ably introduced by Roger Lancelyn Green in *Lewis Carroll Observed* (ed. Edward Guiliano, 1976), a volume that also contains previously unpublished photographs and drawings by Dodgson.

The equal of the diaries in importance to students of Carroll's life and art is the two-volume edition of *The Letters of Lewis Carroll* (1979), edited by Morton N. Cohen with the assistance of Roger Lancelyn Green. Cohen's editing is superb and the new information in this edition has already begun to promote a reassessment and better understanding of the man. If this edition, like the diaries, is flawed, it is only because it is a selected edition—in this case heavily biased in favor of Dodgson's letters to his child-friends. The edition contains 1305 letters, only about one-third of the correspondence Cohen assiduously traced in what has become twenty years of devoted study to Lewis Carroll. Even if Cohen has only traced a small percentage of the perhaps 75,000 letters Carroll wrote (the famed letter register of 98,000 letters included letters received as well as sent), the welcome news is that Cohen is in the process of following up his major edition with thematically related volumes which will contain many of the additional letters he traced. Although these will be large volumes treating Carroll and his publisher, Carroll and his illustrators, etc., one small follow-up volume has appeared: *Lewis Carroll and the Kitchins: Containing Twenty-five Letters Not Previously Published and Nineteen of His Photographs* (1980).

Another long-term editing project that has appeared recently is William W. Bartley, III's reconstruction of Carroll's "lost" volume of *Symbolic Logic* (1977). This advanced volume, *Symbolic Logic, Part II*, was published in combination with a newly edited Part I, and for the first time permits a just determination of Dodgson's position in the history of logic. I will return to this later.

Unquestionably, the most celebrated of the new publications is the long-lost episode of *Through the Looking-Glass* entitled *The Wasp in a Wig: A "Suppressed" Episode of Through the Looking-Glass and what Alice found there* (1977). This episode of an elderly wasp in a yellow wig, whose existence was announced on the front pages of the world's newspapers, is expertly introduced and annotated by Martin Gardner. Another publication of "sensational" Carroll material believed to be lost forever is *Lewis Carroll's Photographs of Nude Children* (1978), containing four photographic studies of nude children. (This work, introduced by Morton N. Cohen, appeared in a trade edition as *Lewis Carroll, Photographer of Children: Four Nude Studies*, 1979).

ILLUSTRATED EDITIONS, TRANSLATIONS,
STAGE AND SCREEN ADAPTATIONS
AND DISCUSSIONS THEREOF

Carroll's imaginative works of literature were originally intended for children, and in children's literature the wedding of text and illustrations is particularly crucial. Carroll's partnership with John Tenniel is certainly the sort of marriage that is said to be made in heaven. It is through Tenniel's portrayals that we remember the strange and fanciful creatures of Wonderland and Looking-Glass land. Also, Tenniel's illustrations complement and enrich Carroll's text so fundamentally that subsequent illustrators must think thrice before attempting a new interpretation of either *Alice* book. It is surprising that once *Alice*'s copyright expired in 1907 a flood of newly illustrated editions followed, and that today, a time when Carroll's popularity is so great, new illustrated editions gush forth as never before. Clearly the worlds Carroll created have fascinated artists as well as readers.

In the first half of this century just a few artists met the challenge of Tenniel—in my opinion, only Arthur Rackham (1907), Peter Newell (1901), Charles Robinson (1907), Willy Pogany (1929), and Mervyn Peake (1946). It seems that *Alice* has now become the challenge by which book illustrators are known and judged. Recently several artists have been worthy of the task.

The most renowned of these artists to render *Alice* in pictures are the Surrealists Max Ernst and Salvador Dali. In 1969 Dali produced a limited edition portfolio of twelve woodcuts and one lithograph. The following year Ernst illustrated the Mad Hatter's tea party in a lithograph where words are compressed into a mathematical pattern (1970). This was not Ernst's first attempt at illustrating Carroll's works. In 1966 he provided a long series of surrealistic images to accompany the first French translation of Carroll's work on logic, *Logique sans peine*. Worthy of more attention, however, is Ernst's 1968 illustrations for Carroll's perhaps most surrealistic work, *The Hunting of the Snark*. Ernst's *Snark*, published in Germany, appeared as a portfolio in a limited edition.

It is not surprising that Dali and Ernst were attracted to Carroll's work. From their start the Surrealists recognized a similarity between their work and ideas and Carroll's. The Surrealists had an obvious affinity with Carroll in their mutual use of the dream. Like Carroll, the Surrealists explored reality by questioning their quotidian existence, and challenged conventional ideas of language, logic, time and space. Carroll and the Surrealists both admired the child's worldview and the child's capacity to see things new. Both believed in a form of automatic writing as a mode of creation, and this led to their most fundamental similarity, the belief that thoughts, ideas and feelings do not have to be totally conscious or rational in order to be communicated. In "Lewis Carroll the Surrealist" (in *Lewis Carroll: A Celebration*, ed. Edward Guiliano, 1982), Jeffrey Stern explores in depth the affinities between Carroll and the Surrealists.

One contemporary artist, Ralph Steadman, has produced visual interpretations of all three of Carroll's major works: *Alice's Adventures in Wonderland* (1967), *Through the Looking-Glass* (1972) and *The Hunting of the Snark* (1975). Steadman's award-winning drawings are among the handful of interpretations that have clearly met Tenniel's challenge. They are particularly significant since the drawings represent an adult vision designed to appeal to adults. (They naturally can also appeal to children as children's editions have previously appealed to adults.) Steadman's effort is a radical attempt at reinterpreting Wonderland and Looking-Glass land and is rife with comparisons between Carroll's characters and present-day equivalents—comparisons that are surely lost on a child. His vision is astute and provoking and reflects an important characteristic of Carroll's current appeal, that the *Alices* and Carroll's other imaginative works are no longer merely children's works but adult works. Modern adult readers recognize the subtle humor, social satire and philosophical depth in Carroll's work; Steadman has captured this awareness in his drawings.

The most recent artist to take up successfully the test of Tenniel is Barry Moser in his Pennyroyal sesquicentennial *Alice* (1982). This is a distinguished edition and perhaps the most lavishly illustrated edition of *Alice*, containing seventy-five masterfully executed wood-engravings. Moser boldly chose to reveal Wonderland through the eyes of the reader's surrogate, Alice. Thus we rarely see Alice but see all that surrounds her. And often what we see is a bit sinister, bizarre, and threatening. By capturing this element in some of his renditions of Wonderland creatures, Moser has captured an element many readers find in *Alice* that is not evident or at least not so compellingly so in most previous illustrated editions.

Determining an order of merit when evaluating the dozens of illustrated editions that have appeared is a difficult and, in part, a subjective process. Illustrations speak differently to different viewers. The following are my additional selections of artistically merito-

rious or otherwise interesting, exciting and/or significant recent illustrated editions of Carroll's work: Adrienne Segur's *Alice* (1963),
Moritz Kennel's *Alice* (1971), Nicole Claveloux's *Alice* (1974),
Byron Sewell's *Alice* [Aborigine] (1975), Helen Oxenbury's *Snark*
(1970), Byron Sewell's *Snark* (1974), John Minnion's *Snark* and his
version of "Jabberwocky" from *Through the Looking-Glass* (1976),
and Leonard Lubin's version of "The Pig Tale" from *Sylvie and
Bruno* (1975).

It is appropriate to note here helpful background and critical discussions of various artists' attempts to illustrate Carroll's works.
Michael Hearn has discussed and evaluated Arthur Rackham's rendering of *Alice in Wonderland* ("Arthur Rackham's Adventures in
Wonderland" in *Lewis Carroll Observed*, ed. Edward Guiliano,
1976). In "Five Degrees of Frost" (*JJLCS*, 1976), Brian Sibley has
written perceptively on A. B. Frost's various illustrations of works
by Carroll, and in "Peaks and Chasms" (*The Mervyn Peake Society
Newsletter*, 1976), he has written on Mervyn Peake's illustrations to
the *Snark*. A valuable anthology of distinguished renditions of the
Alice books, *The Illustrators of Alice* (1972, rev. ed. 1979), was
compiled by Graham Ovenden and John Davis and contains a useful introduction and checklist by Davis.

The Tenniel-Dodgson relationship and the success of Tenniel's illustrations are the subject of an essay by Brian Robb ("Tenniel's Illustrations to the 'Alice' Books," *Listener*, 1965). In "Punch and
Alice: Through Tenniel's Looking-Glass" (in *Lewis Carroll: A Celebration*, ed. Edward Guiliano, 1982), Michael Hancher reveals the
previous incarnations some of Carroll's characters in the *Alice*
books had in Tenniel's *Punch* work and traces how some of the imagery Tenniel developed elsewhere is seen in the *Alice* illustrations.
In "The Appliances of Art: The Carroll-Tenniel Collaboration in
Through the Looking-Glass (*Lewis Carroll: A Celebration*, 1982),
Janis Lull focuses on the illustrations to the second *Alice* book. Richard Kelly focuses on the relationship of the text and the illustrations
in the first Alice book in "'If you don't know what a Gryphon is':
Text and Illustration in *Alice's Adventures in Wonderland*" (in
Lewis Carroll: A Celebration, 1982). In his discussion Kelly consid-
ers Carroll's thirty-seven illustrations to *Alice's Adventures Under
Ground* as well as Tenniel's renderings. Carroll's own illustrations
are also discussed at length by Donald Rackin in "Laughing and
Grief: What's So Funny About *Alice in Wonderland*?" (*Lewis Carroll Observed*, 1976).

Carroll's own illustrations appear in the previously noted facsimile reprints of *Alice's Adventures Under Ground* and in his juvenile magazines. *The Letters of Lewis Carroll* also contain a sampling of Carroll drawings, some not previously published. A collection of Carroll drawings, "Lewis Carroll as Artist: Fifteen Unpublished Sketches to the *Sylvie and Bruno* Books" appears in *Lewis Carroll Observed* (1976). These preliminary drawings were sent as suggestions to Harry Furniss, the professional illustrator of the *Sylvie and Bruno* books. They are important not only as evidence of Carroll's impressive imagination, but because they reveal a great deal about his working relationships with illustrators and suggest that the ideas for what turned out to be the cleverest and most memorable illustrations of his works were initiated by Carroll. In his introduction to these sketches, Edward Guiliano writes that

> Carroll's best drawings, like his best literary efforts, tapped deep springs of imagination that seem inconsistent with the outward appearance and manners of the Reverend Charles Lutwidge Dodgson. We do not expect expressions of violence and nastiness from here, but they are there in the *Alice* books and in illustrations, although not in his photographs. His photographic achievements derive from a different artistic impulse: a quest for purity and beauty. This drive, rather at odds with the impulse toward the grotesque evidenced in his drawings and writings, is more in harmony with the personality of Dodgson and with Victorian standards.

Although it is hard to prove, *Alice in Wonderland* has probably been both illustrated and translated more than any other so-called children's book. For the great illustrator and the great translator alike, *Alice* and the works by Carroll that followed present a supreme test, a game only grandmasters can play successfully. With its poetry, nonsense, parody, satire, nineteenth-century British cultural values and multiple appeals, *Alice* confronts the translator with seemingly insurmountable obstacles. Nevertheless, there has not been a shortage of players for this game.

Carroll of course was a devoted gamesman, and he personally refereed the translating of *Alice* into German and French. Since these first two translations appeared in 1869, there has been a tide of translations into other languages. The list has now grown to at least fifty-five, with eighteen new languages added since 1960. (It is even more startling that from 1959 to 1977, not counting reprints, there were twenty-four Japanese translations of *Alice* published, twenty-three Italian, and twenty-one Spanish.)

Through the Looking-Glass has not had quite the same appeal; still, there has been no scarcity of illustrated editions or translations of *Alice*'s sequel. The quantity of translations of the *Alice* books demonstrates that Carroll's following is international and that his art is part of the cultural heritage of non-English-speaking nations. Recently, more than just the *Alice* books are being translated. Prior to 1977 there were a few translations of *The Hunting of the Snark* and a few assorted selections from Carroll's other works. Now, his books on logic, his letters to child-friends, *The Nursery "Alice"* and *A Tangled Tale* have appeared in several languages. The most remarkable of the new translations are the first appearances of the *Sylvie and Bruno* books in French (1972), Spanish (1973) Japanese (1976), and German (1979). These books, long dismissed and ignored by British and American critics and readers, have been championed by the Europeans, particularly and French, who discovered merits in these books and created the impetus for others to turn to them.

It seems unlikely that any translation of the *Alice* books or *The Hunting of the Snark* will ever be so true as to rival the original in language and conception as do, to cite the classic example, Richard Wilbur's translations of Molière's plays. Yet several of the translations of Carroll's works stand apart as outstanding literary achievements. Henri Parisot, for instance, revised his translations of the *Alice* books for thirty years, and his work is by far the best among the many French translations. The same is true for his translation of *The Hunting of the Snark*. Christian Enzensberger's translation of *Alice in Wonderland* and *Through the Looking-Glass* (1963) has displaced all other German renditions. Klaus Richart's German translation of *The Hunting of the Snark* (1968) is also widely praised. Also most notable are Nina Demurova's Russian translations of the *Alice* books (1967) which have been held up as exemplars of the art of literary translation.

The game of translating Carroll's difficult works has even spawned its own critical tradition in which the problems and merits of translations are debated keenly like moves in a championship chess match. Christian Enzensberger's translation of the *Alice* books, for example, has been the subject of a doctoral dissertation by Susan Mango (Diss. American Univ., 1974). Shortly after Enzensberger's translations appeared, the failure of Antonie Zimmerman's first German translations were analyzed by Franz Lösel (*Hermathena*, 1964). Lösel has also analyzed the Remané German translation of Alice (*Beiträge zur Kinder- und Jungendliteratur*, 1968). Peter Rickard has thoroughly evaluated the leading French translations of the *Alice* books (*CLS*, 1975), and J. Dierickx has likewise analyzed the prominent French translations of *The Hunting of the* Snark (*Revue des Langues Vivantes*, 1974). Simon Karlinsky has evaluated the early Russian translations of *Alice* and finds Nabokov's by far the best (*TriQ*, 1970)—although Karlinsky did not consider the now standard Demurova translation. Demurova has written of the translation problems she faced in an extensive article (*The Art of Translation*, 1970 [title and text in Russian]). M. V. Panov has debated the comparative merits of various Russian translations of "Jabberwocky" (*Development of Modern Russian*, 1972 [title and text in Russian]). But among the critical articles on translating Carroll and the reviews of new translations that have appeared in recent years, the most unexpected, and another indication of the broad interest that exists in Carroll's art, is Lyndon Harries's discussion of the problems involved in translating *Alice in Wonderland* into Swahili ("Translating Classical Literature into Swahili," *Swahili: Journal of the Institute of Swahili Research*, 1970).

   If we consider illustration and translation as forms of adaptation, then it is appropriate at this point to mention two other forms: theatrical and cinematic renditions. The histories of stage and screen adaptations of the *Alices* are as long and rich as the histories of illustrated and translated editions. *Alice in Wonderland* appeared on stage for the first time in 1886 and on film first in 1903, and scores of adaptations followed. There is not a current listing of the stage versions of *Alice*. A list of film adaptations of Carroll's work exists, compiled by David Schaefer (*Lewis Carroll Observed*, 1976). David and Maxine Schaefer further discuss film adaptations in "The Movie Adventures of Lewis Carroll's Alice" (*American Classic Screen*, 1981). The most famous adaptation of the *Alice* books is, of course, the Walt Disney animated film (1951). This has been the subject of numerous discussions, notably from the Carroll perspective by Brian Sibley in "A Californian Yankee at the Court of Queen Alice" (*JJLCS*, 1974). The text of a successful stage version of *Alice in Wonderland* (1970) by André Gregory, it should be noted, has appeared as a book with one hundred photographs from the production (*Alice in Wonderland: The Forming of a Company and the Making of a Play*, 1973).

PHOTOGRAPHY

   Had Lewis Carroll never written the *Alice* books, we now know he would have earned himself a respected place in history as a photographer (and to lesser degrees as a logician and letter writer). For more than a decade there has been a great upsurge of interest in photo-history, and with the appearance of each new book on Victorian photography or photo-history in general, and with each new retrospective exhibition held at a major museum or gallery around the world, Lewis Carroll has become more widely known as one of the most outstanding nineteenth-century photographers, and certainly the most outstanding nineteenth-century photographer of children. He was one of the few early photographers who elevated picture-taking from a rather mechanical process to an art form.

The skill and beauty in Carroll's photographs have always been known by people deeply interested in Carroll's (here I should write Dodgson's) life and work; however, it was not until the late 1940s that his place in the history of photography became fixed through a thorough investigation by a photo-historian. At that time, Helmut Gernsheim literally stumbled upon a scrapbook of Dodgson's photographs while doing research on the photography of Julia Margaret Cameron. Not knowing anything about a photographer named Lewis Carroll, Gernsheim quickly recognized that the photographs were the product of "a genius at work," and began the first earnest study of Carroll's life with a camera. The result was Gernsheim's *Lewis Carroll: Photographer* (1949; reprinted in a slightly revised edition in 1969), the classic photo-history in which Carroll's genius is proclaimed.

Gernsheim's work was such a stunning landmark study, unequalled by anything before or since on Carroll's art, that rather than stimulate more work on the don's photography, it left little ground for other critics and historians. Only recently, thanks primarily to the work of Morton N. Cohen, have there been any significant advances in knowledge of Lewis Carroll as photographer; only recently have significant numbers of previously unpublished Carroll photographs appeared in print; and only recently has a proper catalogue raisonné of his photographs been undertaken (by Colin Ford, Director of the National Photography Museum, England).

The most notable collections of previously unpublished Carroll photographs that have appeared in recent years are: *Lewis Carroll at Christ Church* (1974), "Lewis Carroll as Photographer: A Series of Photographs of Young Girls" (*Lewis Carroll Observed*, 1976), *The Letters of Lewis Carroll* (1978), *Lewis Carroll, Photographer of Children: Four Nude Studies* (1978; rpt. 1979), which contains an introduction by Morton N. Cohen, and *Lewis Carroll and the Kitchins: Containing Twenty-five Letters Not previously Published and Nineteen of His Photographs* (1980).

The Christ Church photographs are a series of twenty-eight portraits of Oxford dignitaries. The collection is introduced admirably by Morton N. Cohen who argues rightly in his introduction that the album of photographic portraits proves that Carroll

> . . . was a distinguished photographer even before he decided to specialize in photographing children. This album is, in fact, much more than a gallery of Oxford dignitaries of the Victorian high noon: it is an exhibit of Dodgson's subtle artistic achievement. Here is Dodgson, the courageous craftsman, using the ordinary in an imaginative way, performing the miracle of creating a thing of beauty. And here too is proof that Dodgson's aesthetic instinct is as reliable when capturing the images of his world as it later proves to be in creating fanciful flights to Wonderland.

Since photographic portraiture was a widely practiced art, something that cannot be said for children's photography, this collection has added importance because it provides a sufficient sampling of Carroll's portraits to enable a valid comparison with other Victorian photographers. The Christ Church portraits fare well in all such comparisons; they are significant achievements and clearly demonstrate Carroll's skills and talents.

The Kitchin photographs and the suite of photographs of young girls are more representative of the majority of Carroll's photographs, hauntingly beautiful and artistically adventurous portraits of children—girls in diverse poses and costumes. Morton N. Cohen introduces the Kitchin photographs and Edward Guiliano the photographs of young girls, an introduction in which Guiliano offers several theories on the attraction photography held for Carroll. Guiliano writes on this same subject and on the sweep of Carroll's career as a photographer, his photographic achievements, and the state of our knowledge of Carroll the photographer in a sesquicentennial assessment, "Lewis Carroll's Adventures in Cameraland" (*A.B. Bookman*, 1982).

The appearance of the four nude photographs, long believed destroyed, was an event in Carroll studies that might have led to numerous insights into Carroll's life and art. It did answer some questions, and Morton N. Cohen sheds new light on Carroll's career in the introduction. But the questions about Carroll's sexuality and the reasons why he suddenly abandoned his cherished hobby after twenty-five years that many believed would be settled conclusively if surviving nude photographs were located have not been (see Guiliano's, "Lewis Carroll's Adventures in Cameraland"). (There is now a consensus, however, that it was the pressure of time more than anything else that moved Carroll to give up photography.) The nude studies were a surprise. They are unlike Carroll's other photographs, and, in fact, it is not strictly accurate to term them photographs. All four have been colored professionally: one is a watercolor based on a Carroll photograph and the other three are painted in oil. The figures are Carroll's but the backgrounds are not. All are nature paintings; two are elaborate seascapes and one is set on the bank of a pond or river. These four surviving nude studies are too small and too unusual a sample from which to draw definitive conclusions about Carroll's art.

The Letters of Lewis Carroll, it should be noted, contains a wealth of Carroll photographs, only some of which were published previously, and is perhaps the best collection of Carroll photographs alongside Gernsheim's book containing sixty-three images. A volume of previously published Carroll photographs that merits attention is a handsome deluxe album of fifty tipped-in photographs of children, all reproduced with the same dimensions and cropping as the original: *Le bambine di Carroll: foto e lettere di Lewis Carroll a Mary, Alice, Irene, Agnese.* (1974; with French and English editions in 1975).

BIOGRAPHY

Immediately after C. L. Dodgson's death on January 14, 1898, the secret that he was Lewis Carroll was out for good. Before the year was over his nephew, Stuart Dodgson Collingwood, brought out the first full-length biography of the author of the *Alice* books, *The Life and Letters of Lewis Carroll* (1898). This is still a major biography, accepted as a competent history by one who had intimate knowledge of Carroll and access to his letters and diaries.

From the time of Dodgson's death to the centenary of his birth in 1932, many useful reminiscences appeared. Particularly valuable ones are: E. Gertrude Thomson's "Lewis Carroll" (*The Gentlewoman*, 1898); Beatrice Hatch's "Lewis Carroll" (*The Strand Magazine*, 1898); Isa Bowman's book-length account of her childhood intimacy with Dodgson, *The Story of Lewis Carroll* (1899); Harry Furniss's various reminiscences (1901, 1908) rewritten for his *Some Victorian Men* (1924); Ellen Terry's remembrances in her *The Story of My Life* (1908); Henry Holiday's in his *Reminiscences of My Life* (1914); and Alice [Liddell] Hargreaves's contribution late

in her life, "Alice's Recollections of Carrollian Days, Told to her
Son Caryl Hargreaves" (*The Cornhill Magazine*, 1932).

Two full-scale biographies followed Collingwood's, Belle Moses's
Lewis Carroll (1910) and Langford Reed's *The Life of Lewis Carroll*
(1932)—the latter is notable for some information on Carroll and
Ellen Terry that Reed was able to glean from unpublished letters
and from Carroll's diary entries. Florence Becker Lennon's *Victoria
Through the Looking-Glass: The Life of Lewis Carroll* (1945) was
the next major biography to follow Collingwood's. Neither Moses's
nor Reed's lives had the impact or brilliance of Mrs. Lennon's book.
Mrs. Lennon was the first to approach Carroll's life from a psychoanalytic perspective—an approach to Carroll and his works that
became fashionable and often critically profitable through the
1950s and 1960s. Her fully documented scholarly study does miss
the mark at times and did contain some factual errors when it first
appeared, but it has always been accepted as engaging and provocative. The errors dropped out in a revised edition (*The Life of Lewis
Carroll*, 1962) that was later reprinted with minor revisions (1972).
Alexander L. Taylor's critical biography, *The White Knight* (1952),
although a bit odd, is still another work that offers useful insights.

There is general agreement that Derek Hudson's *Lewis Carroll*
(1954) is the most reliable biography available. It is a carefully
studied, well written, judicious life that was distinguished from its
predecessors in this century because Hudson was the first since Collingwood to draw upon Carroll's diaries (which were published in
1953). In 1976 Hudson's already standard biography was repub-
lished in a revised, copiously illustrated edition. Despite claims that
Hudson has brought the biography up to date, the text remains virtually identical to the 1954 edition, and Hudson has ignored much
of the best writing about Carroll that has been published in recent
years. The book's copious illustrations, however, are a joy. The
world of Lewis Carroll comes alive in the new edition through
reproductions of letters and drawings and through a generous offering of remarkable photographs taken by Carroll.

Another lavishly illustrated biography appeared the same year as
Hudson's revised biography; it is John Pudney's *Lewis Carroll and
His World* (1976). This is a brief but reasonably good introduction
to Carroll's life. Another sound introduction to Carroll, although
lacking the artwork to make the world come alive, is a monograph
by Roger Lancelyn Green, *Lewis Carroll* (1960). A reliable biography written for adolescents worthy of note is James P. Wood's
The Snark was a Boojum: The Life of Lewis Carroll (1966). This

biography also merits attention of collectors since it is admirably illustrated in Tenniel-like fashion by David Levine.

A widely noticed biography, written by the leading French authority on Lewis Carroll, is Jean Gattégno's *Lewis Carroll: Une vie* (1974), which appeared in English translation as *Lewis Carroll: Fragments of a Looking-Glass* (1976). Rather than a conventional biography, Gattégno has produced a series of thirty-seven brief and diverse essays on aspects of Carroll's life. Gattégno reasons that we can gradually and subconsciously come to understand the Carroll/Dodgson dual personality by reading about selected aspects of Carroll's life and work. Gattégno arranges his entries alphabetically, starting with Alice and running through Zeno of Elea. His approach does succeed in cleverly eliciting a sense of the complex life behind the pseudonym, and for this Gattégno's is a valuable study. It is also valuable for bringing together into unified essays much material which was previously available only through book-hopping and index-crawling. Gattégno, however, does not add substantially to our knowledge of Carroll. He has not scoured unpublished sources and turned up any revelations.

The most recent full-length study, Anne Clark's *Lewis Carroll: A Biography* (1979) is rich in fresh, small details. Hers is an assiduously prepared, carefully researched life, the first to draw upon *The Letters of Lewis Carroll*. Mrs. Clark has read all the unpublished sources—the family papers, diaries and records in Oxford and elsewhere—and has produced the best account of Carroll's early years leading up to his settling in Oxford as well as his early years there. She is very good on Dodgson's family, especially his father, and on the religious climate in which Carroll lived. She has read all that could be expected and makes many sensible judgments about key events and questions in Carroll's life: he probably wanted to marry Alice Liddell; if he was somewhat taken with Ellen Terry, who can blame him; he did not give up photography because of any scandal—the pressure of diminishing time no doubt was the cause; etc. Hers is not an easy book to read, however: her prose can be a bit turgid, her internal organization a bit questionable and ineffective, her literary criticism a bit weak; but for the specialist, someone with a good overview of Carroll's life and interested in the finer points, this is a fine biography.

The Diaries of Lewis Carroll and *The Letters of Lewis Carroll* with their useful introductory material and superlative notes are the principal sources of biographical information on Dodgson. The publication of the collected edition of letters and the announced future volumes of letters arranged by subject—e.g., Carroll and Macmillan, Carroll and his illustrators, etc.—as well as the announced edition of unedited diaries should inspire a reassessment of Dodgson's life in the next decade. Morton N. Cohen, editor of Carroll's letters, is presently at work on what will be the first of a new generation of biographies.

There have been some recent revelations that help paint a fuller portrait of Dodgson. The appearance of the suppressed "Wasp in a Wig" episode of *Through the Looking-Glass* and the photographs of nude children are important, as is the seeming proof that Dodgson wished to marry Alice Liddell. (For the proof see not only Anne Clark's biography but Morton Cohen's "Who Censored Lewis Carroll?" [*The Times Saturday Review*, January 23, 1982]). There have been other useful though lesser disclosures that help us to understand Carroll's life and the nature of his imagination better. Morton N. Cohen in "Hark the Snark" (*Lewis Carroll Observed*, 1976) has given us a fuller understanding of the events that surrounded the composition of *The Hunting of the Snark* than we had previously. Drawing from previously unpublished letters, Cohen has also given us accounts of Carroll's relationship with his publisher, "Lewis Carroll and the House of Macmillan (*Browning Institute Studies*, 7, 1979) and of his relationship with Ellen Terry, "The Actress and the Don: Ellen Terry and Lewis Carroll" (*Lewis Carroll: A Celebration*, 1982). Cohen has written about Carroll's fascination with a primitive version of the mimeograph, "The electric pen" (*Illustrated London News*, Christmas Number 1976). Cohen and Roger Lancelyn Green have told us about Carroll's loss of consciousness and possible epilepsy (*BNYPL*,1969). Joseph Sigman and Richard Slobodin have revealed a bit about the history of stuttering in Carroll's family in "Stammering in the Dodgson Family: An Unpublished Letter by 'Lewis Carroll'" (*VN* 1976). Carroll's medical history in general has been thoroughly reviewed by Selwyn Goodacre, a British physician, in "The Illnesses of Lewis Carroll" (*The Practitioner*, 1972).

A brief example of interpretative biography by Donald Rackin also deserves mention here. In "Blessed Rage: Lewis Carroll and the Modern Quest for Order" (in *Lewis Carroll: A Celebration*, 1982), Rackin looks at Dodgson's obsession for order in his life and works and sees it in part as a response to the lost visions of cosmic order characteristic of much Victorian thought, especially in post-Darwinian England. Rackin finds that "in his rather singular comic approach to the modern problem of finding new metaphysical order in an intellectual environment hostile to such order, hostile even to the search itself, Lewis Carroll ushers in our age." Finally, no survey of biographical studies of Lewis Carroll is complete without mention of Phyllis Greenacre's provocative *Swift and Carroll: A Psychoanalytic Study of Two Lives* (1955). This biography by an eminent Freudian psychoanalyst is perhaps the most frequently cited of all biographical studies of Carroll.

STUDIES OF SPECIAL ASPECTS AND INDIVIDUAL WORKS

Appreciations

Lewis Carroll's years of greatest artistic creativity were 1862 to 1876. In 1862 he made the now famous boat ride up the Thames during which he first told the story of Alice's adventures; in 1865–1866 he published *Alice's Adventures in Wonderland* and in 1871–1872 its sequel, *Through the Looking-Glass and what Alice found there*; in 1874 he heard the line "For the Snark *was* a Boojum, you see," which served as the inspiration for *The Hunting of the Snark*, published as a book in 1876. The hundredth anniversary of these events and the one-hundred and fiftieth anniversary of Dodgson's 1832 birth created, in effect, twenty years of celebrations for Carroll's special genius. There is no doubt that the publicity surrounding the centenaries in 1962, 1965, 1966, 1972, and 1976, and the sesquicentenary in 1982 has contributed to the recent upsurge of interest in Carroll's life and art.

The first wave of appreciations of and general publicity for Carroll appeared immediately after his death. Another appeared in 1932, the one-hundredth anniversary of Carroll's birth. Walter De La Mare's brief book, *Lewis Carroll*, was published in 1932; it is an extended essay on Carroll's nonsense with appreciations of diverse aspects of Dodgson's life and works, including a sensitive appreciation of the atmosphere of the *Alices*. Harry Morgan Ayres's short, diverse, and still useful *Carroll's Alice* (1936) grew out of a lecture given by Ayres in association with the centenary exhibitions at Columbia University. The Nonsense edition of Carroll's complete works had its inspiration in the 1932 centenary and it in turn was the reason for a brief but insightful appreciation in the form of a review by Virginia Woolf (rpt. in *The Moment and Other Essays*, 1948). Three perceptive appreciations of Carroll and his *Alice*, centennial essays, that appeared in the 1960s are W. H. Auden's "To-

day's 'Wonder-World' Needs Alice" (*New York Times Magazine,*
1962); Martin Gardner's "A Child's Garden of Bewilderment"
(*Saturday Review,* 1965); and Harry Levin's "Wonderland
Revisted" (*Kenyon Review,* 1965). All three essays tell us as much
about our own response to the *Alices* as they tell us about the nature
and complexity of the works. Auden's essay is notable, among other
reasons, because Auden comments on Americans' response to the
Alices; Gardner's is notable for suggesting that "*Alice* is no longer a
children's book" and that modern adult readers recognize the subtle humor, social satire and philosophical depth in the *Alices;* and
Levin's is distinguished by its critical emphasis on the nature of
Carroll's nonsense.

Critical Anthologies

Most of the critical discussions of Carroll's work that appeared
through the centenary of the *Alices* dealt, not surprisingly, primarily with the *Alice* books and the life of their enigmatic author.
Robert Phillips brought together the best of this commentary, what
he considered to be "the most interesting, if not always the most illuminating"interpretations of the *Alices* up to 1971 in *Aspects of
Alice* (1971). This anthology of thirty-nine essays is subdivided into
sections: 1) Personal and Biographical; 2) As Victorian and
Children's Literature; 3) Comparisons with Other Writers; 4)
Philosophical and Others; 5) Church and Chess; 6) Language, and
Parody, and Satire; 7) Freudian Interpretations (a particularly
strong section); 8) Jungian and Mythic; and 9) Psychedelic.

A change in Carroll criticism occurred in the 1970s as popular
awareness of Carroll as a multi-faceted genius and prolific author
increased. Critical interest in the *Alices* remained high, but the full
range of Carroll's talents received increased attention. This is
reflected in the several anthologies of new critical essays that have
appeared in recent years. The first of these comprehensive anthologies, *Lewis Carroll,* appeared in France (in French) in 1971 as part
of the distinguished series of Cahiers de l'Herne. Henri Parisot collected essays on such topics as animal language in the *Sylvie and
Bruno* books (by Raymond Queneau), language and Humpty
Dumpty (by Hélène Cixous), Carroll's photographs (by Brassaï), and
even similarities between *Moby-Dick* and *The Hunting of the Snark*
(by Marcel Marnat). Although the twenty-one new essays (there are

also some translations from English) are what Ezra Pound liked to call "work of second intensity," as a whole the collection is stimulating, valuable, and once again demonstrates that interest in Carroll in Europe parallels, and at time exceeds, our own. There are plans to bring out a new edition of *Lewis Carroll*, with a new introduction by Jean Gattégno, in 1982.

The two best articles in Parisot's *Lewis Carroll*—Jean Gattégno's assessment of Carroll's achievements, aptly titled in English "Assessing Lewis Carroll," in which Gattégno uses language as a key for deciphering and assimilating the diverse views that have been taken of Carroll's work, and Ernest Coumet's "The Game of Logic: A Game of Universes," a mature attempt at authenticating the Carroll/Dodgson duality in the logic books through a discussion of the notion in logic of a universe of discourse—appear in English translation in a second comprehensive anthology, the previously cited *Lewis Carroll Observed* (1976), edited by Edward Guiliano. For Carroll's sesquicentenary Guiliano edited another anthology of fifteen new essays on Carroll's life and art, *Lewis Carroll: A Celebration* (1982). The articles in these anthologies, many by established Carroll scholars, are discussed elsewhere in this essay. Reviewers have found these anthologies valuable for bringing together a wealth of new insights on a wide range of Carroll's endeavors.

Although the previously cited Norton Critical Edition of *Alice in Wonderland* (1971) contains no new writing aside from a sound and pleasing introduction by Donald Gray, it does contain a somewhat useful assortment of biographical background and critical essays covering a wide range of Carroll's talents and works, as well as reliable texts of the *Alices* and *The Hunting of the Snark*. In the decade since it appeared, however, this edition has become increasingly dated. Keeping abreast of Carroll criticism has become like living in the Red Queen's domain where "it takes all the running you can do, to keep in the same place." The Norton Critical Edition lacks much of the best scholarship and criticism published on Lewis Carroll here and abroad because many important studies only appeared in the 1970s and 1980s. This is true also of the collected criticism in Donald Rackin's *Alice's Adventures in Wonderland: A Critical Handbook* (1969), a volume that is now out of print. What will soon be in print, however, is a special issue of *English Language Notes* devoted to Carroll on the occasion of the sesquicentenary of his birth. This collection of essays is also scheduled to be distributed in hardcover by the University Press of Virginia.

Surveys of *Alice* Criticism

During the period of centenary celebrations beginning in the 1960s, several scholars attempted to survey and evaluate the bulk of *Alice* criticism. Donald Rackin was the first. In "The Critical Interpretations of *Alice in Wonderland*: A Survey and Suggested Reading" (Diss. University of Illinois, 1964), he discusses interpretations of *Alice in Wonderland* only, and argues for a reinterpretation of the book as an organic whole. He finds that all the various approaches that have been taken fail to explain its impact on the modern reader; furthermore, he finds that almost every analysis of *Alice in Wonderland* involves the critical error of treating the two *Alice* books as one work.

This is true, and as a result *Alice* has not received the close textual and unified readings that have been given to many other Victorian novels. Rackin has emerged as one of the shrewdest and most sensitive critics of *Alice in Wonderland* and its leading exponent as self-contained fiction.

Often ignoring that *Through the Looking-Glass* appeared seven years after *Alice* and has a more threatening tone and pervading sense of structured existence and closure, critics have treated the two *Alice* books as a single work because Carroll's use of language, his fantastic humanoids, his humor—his distinctive thumbprint as it were—all are in evidence on every page of the two dream visions. A consideration of the books' similarities and differences helps critics to come to a better understanding and appreciation of each work. Jane Page therefore decided to survey the critical commentary on both books for her "Enduring Alice" (Diss. University of Washington, 1970). She makes a point of the obvious, that there is a diversity of critical opinion and no pattern of critical style in *Alice* criticism. Her study is a soldier-like march along the road of *Alice* criticism. It is a competent introduction, but the reader is better introduced to the scope and riches of *Alice* commentary by Robert Phillips's *Aspects of Alice*.

Phillips's very valuable book, noted earlier, contains a good many seminal studies published before 1971, but like the Norton Critical Edition it is already dated. And like Rackin and Page, Phillips has confined himself to surveying critical studies which appeared in English. This limitation helps to explain the weakness of his section on "Language, and Parody, and Satire," and the almost complete absence of sophisticated discussions of Carroll's nonsense; these topics are favorites of European critics.

The *Alice* Books as Children's Literature

Discussions of the *Alice* books as children's literature have been essentially variations on the same theme, the accepted notion that *Alice* represents nothing less than a revolution in children's literature and occupies a pivotal position in the history of the genre. This belief continues to be advanced in all contemporary critical histories of children's literature, and the few serious studies of *Alice* as children's literature published in the past two decades have added little to it.

In an excellent study, "The Literary Reputation of Lewis Carroll in England and America in the Nineteenth Century" (Diss. Case Western Reserve University, 1962), Dorothy Mathews reaffirms the widely accepted view that Carroll is the writer most responsible for changing the literary fare for children from literature heavily laden with lessons toward lesson-free imaginative literature. Elsie Leach echoes this in an article, "'Alice in Wonderland' in Perspective" (*VN*, 1964), and declares that when the *Alices* are seen as mid-nineteenth-century children's literature, the reaction against didacticism that is evident in so many of the episodes is the books' most startling feature. Carroll's approach, Leach also recognizes, was novel in that he did not insist upon appealing to the reason of his readers. Donald Rackin, in "Corrective Laughter: Carroll's *Alice* as Popular Children's Literature of the Nineteenth Century" (*JPC*, 1967), sees Carroll taking a more radical stance and using satire to attack the pious, homiletic conventions prevalent in nineteenth-century children's literature. Speaking in more psychoanalytic terms, Raveena Helson, in "The Psychological Origins of Fantasy for Children in Mid-Victorian England" (*ChildL*, 1974), similarly sees the publication of *Alice* as a revolution because it introduced the pursuit of pleasure for its own sake to children's literature.

Almost all the published studies of the *Alices* as children's literature focus on what distinguishes these books from their predecessors. In his article, Rackin judiciously demonstrates that *Alice in Wonderland* is more the final flowering of a revolt in children's literature than the budding. Phyllis Reinstein has made this the subject of a dissertation, "Alice in Context: A Study of Children's Literature and the Dominant Culture in Eighteenth and Nineteenth Centuries" (Diss. Yale University, 1973). Looking for similarities rather than differences, she demonstrates that *Alice* is indeed revolutionary in many ways, but it also is clearly dependent upon the books and the age that preceded it.

Psychoanalytic Approaches to the *Alice* Books

Psychoanalytic interpretations of the *Alices* have been surveyed briefly but usefully by Paula Johnson, "Alice Among the Analysts" (*Hartford Studies in Literature*, 1972). Looking only at Freudian critics, she finds that they are unanimous in viewing art as "a non-destructive means of catharsis for the unacceptable," and that the *Alice* books are clearly a regression to a primitive state of the psyche. She does not find any of the readings of the *Alices* completely satisfactory and urges no further Freudian analyses but calls for psychoanalytic studies of the nature and values of "reader-centered response" to the books. As most critics before and after her, Johnson finds William Empson's "Alice in Wonderland: The Child as Swain" (*Some Versions of Pastoral*, 1935) and Phyllis Greenacre's biographical study with its perceptive comments on Carroll's literary works (*Swift and Carroll*, 1955) to be the best of the psychoanalytic studies.

Johnson fails to mention Kenneth Burke's excremental vision of *Alice*, "The Thinking of the Body: Comments on the Imagery of Catharsis in Literature" (*Psychoanalytic Review*, 1963), but this study is a disappointment and best forgotten. Burke adds little of value to our understanding of the cathartic element in *Alice*. Earlier Freudian studies still valuable for their tractarian unravelings of text are Paul Schilder's "Psychoanalytic Remarks on *Alice in Wonderland* and Lewis Carroll" (*Journal of Nervous and Mental Diseases*, 1938), John Skinner's "Lewis Carroll's Adventures in Wonderland" (*AI*, 1947), Martin Grotjahn's "About the Symbolization of *Alice's Adventures in Wonderland* (*AI*, 1947), and Géza Róheim's comments on Carroll and his *Alices* in *Magic and Schizophrenia* (1955). All the essays mentioned in this paragraph are reprinted in *Aspects of Alice*. In "Alice in Analysis" (*Telegraph Sunday Magazine*, 1978), Morton N. Cohen briefly surveys and rebukes Freudian critics and looks to other reasons for understanding the enduring quality or the *Alice* books.

Francis Martens looks at the implications of the mirror in *Through the Looking-Glass* in what is the first Rogerian psychotherapeutic reading of a work by Carroll, "Sage comme une image/Perinde as cadaver" (*Revue de Psychologie et des Sciences de l'éducation*, 1972). His article (in French) is illuminating and provides yet another profitable mode of thinking about the dream logic in the second *Alice* book. Martens studies Carroll's art, like many of the psychoanalysts, not as an end but as a means for understanding our world as well as his own scientific discipline.

While Freudian critics seem to have had their biggest say in the 1930s, 1940s, and 1950s, the Jungians stepped forward in the 1960s. Jung himself mentions Carroll for the first time in his last published work, *Man and His Symbols* (1964), citing Alice's dream of growing infinitely small or large as a classic example of an infantile motif. Archetypal elements in parts of *Through the Looking-Glass* have been noted by Ernest Earnest who analyzes these elements in "The Walrus and the Carpenter," and notes parallels between Carroll's poem and T. S. Eliot's *The Waste Land* (*CEA Critic*, 1963), and by Sidney Halpern who discusses the archetypal myth upon which "Jabberwocky" is based in "The Mother-Killer" (*Psychoanalytic Review*, 1965). Halpern, not the first to suggest a mythic structure for the poem (one was suggested as early as 1871), associates the poem with a specific myth: the Sumerian religious reenactments of the replacement of the matriarchy by filiarchal forces in the form of Enlil slaying the monster Tiamat.

Often cited as the most brilliant reading of *Alice in Wonderland* since Empson's seminal study is Donald Rackin's "Alice's Journey to the End of Night" (*PMLA*, 1966). Rackin also finds mythic elements in *Alice*. He sees the quest motif, Alice's quest for meaning and escape, serving the reader as a metaphorical search for meaning in our lawless universe. "Alice's dogged quest for Wonderland's meaning in terms of her aboveground world is doomed to failure. Her only escape is in flight from Wonderland's complete anarchy . . . [and] is a symbolic rejection of mad sanity in favor of the sane madness of ordinary existence."

Judith Bloomingdale's "Alice as Anima: The Image of Woman in Carroll's Classic" is the first purely Jungian reading of the *Alice* books (in *Aspects of Alice*, ed. Robert Phillips, 1971). She argues that circumstances led Carroll "to personify his inner image of woman in Alice." Bloomingdale is right in claiming that an anima impulse did exist noticeably in Carroll, but, in my judgment, the Alice of the *Alice* books is not his anima figure. Jeffrey Stern, in "Lewis Carroll the Pre-Raphaelite" (in *Lewis Carroll Observed*, 1976), rightly identifies it as the recurrent image in drawings and photographs Carroll created and collected, an image made more conscious through Carroll's appreciation of Pre-Raphaelite art. Carroll's anima figure appears in some of his drawings of Alice for *Alice's Adventures Under Ground*, but nowhere in his writings.

More Criticism of the *Alices*

It is appropriate at this point to mention two articles that deal with Alice as woman. In "Alice in Wonderland: A Curious Child" (*VS*, 1973), Nina Auerbach finds that Alice does not possess Wordsworthian innocence and is not the Victorian idealization of both child and woman; she is less passive, more savage and cruel. According to Auerbach, reading *Alice in Wonderland* one witnesses the tracing of a female psyche. Judith Little, in "Liberated Alice: Dodgson's Female Hero as Domestic Rebel" (*WS*, 1976), finds Alice's two adventures "are almost a compendium of feminist issues." In the Alice books there is "a literally 'underground' image of a woman resisting the 'system.'" In her adventures Alice resists the role of social "queen," and mother, and discovers the paternalistic knight's fallibility.

Several other critics have questioned Alice's innocence. Robert Pattison looks at Alice in *The Child Figure in English Literature* (1978) and suggests that Carroll could not "tolerate the idea of children as part of the world of sin, and in *Alice in Wonderland*, the heroine stands resolutely apart from the machinery of Original Sin." To Pattison, Alice remains innocent even though Wonderland itself "is the world after The Fall . . . a world of death where living creatures are perverted from their natural functions." Terry Otten finds it difficult to accept Alice's innocence "in light of her raw assertions of power and her dominant will." She has moved beyond the unearned innocence of Blakean childhood and "reflects a postlapsarian state by her very protestations of innocence." According to Otten, in "After Innocence: Alice in the Garden" (in *Lewis Carroll: A Celebration*, 1982), the Alice of both books "exists in opposing realities, a fallen—and so, divided character. James Suchan's "Alice's Journey from Alien to Artist" (*ChildL*, 1978) covers some of the same ground as Otten, and is useful. A rich study of the child in Victorian literature as well as of Victorian children that is at least tangentially related to the previous five essays is Jan B. Gordon's "The *Alice* Books and Metaphors of Victorian Childhood" (in *Aspects of Alice*, 1971).

The question of the *Alices*' genre has recently interested several critics. In "Toward a Definition of *Alice's* Genre: The Folktale and Fairy-Tale Connections" (in *Lewis Carroll: A Celebration*, 1982), Nina Demurova, a Russian critic and translator, looks with stunning perception at the *Alices* in the context of the tradition of fairy tales in the nineteenth century, noting the changes and reinterpretations evidenced in Carroll's work, and at his use of folklore and nursery rhymes. She proceeds in her discussion from the assumption that Carroll's work developed within the framework of late Romanticism, varying in a few major points from the classical pattern of early nineteenth-century Romantic writing. Anne K. Mellor in *English Romantic Irony* (1980) sees Carroll as a romantic ironist, psychologically and historically different, however, from such preceding romantic ironists as Byron, Keats, and Carlyle. Like them, though, Carroll conceived the ontological universe as uncontrolled flux. But unlike the others, according to Mellor, "the Victorian don was frightened by this vision." The result was that Dodgson in his life and in his works "tried desperately to deny the chaotic flow of life by transforming all human realities into a structured game whose rules he alone understood and that he alone would win." The *Alice* books are Carroll's most famous attempts "to force a system of his own making upon the chaos of the universe."

Roger Henkle sees Carroll as a modernist, at least when one tries to fit the *Alices* into established literary genres. In "Carroll's Narratives Underground: 'Modernism' and Form" (in *Lewis Carroll: A Celebration*, 1982), Henkle argues that the *Alice* books do not integrate well into the development of the novel, and they do not sit easily in such special categories as fantasy or childern's literature. He finds that "they more closely resemble what we have come to call modernist fiction than nineteenth-century social-realist fiction." He goes on to build a strong case for *Alice in Wonderland* and *Through the Looking-Glass* as forerunners of the modernist novel. He finds the *Alices* to be an Oxford don's version of the fairy tale. "Its unique combination of formal elements, its mixing of genres, results less from attempts to graft modes of literature together or to work toward some variation on the novel of his time than from the need to accomodate highly volatile emotional and conceptual material."

To close this subsection, one more valuable essay needs to be noted briefly, Lionel Morton's "Memory in the *Alice* Books" (*NCF*, 1978). This is a useful reading of the *Alices*, demonstrating that there is an undercurrent of nostalgia in the books, often most observable in Alice's "dream-rushes" in these dream visions. Although nostalgia does not advance plot in the *Alices*, the current of memory which comes to their surfaces expresses "an essential part of the meaning which his creations had for Carroll."

Through the Looking-Glass

One of Carroll's child-friends may have struck the proper note when she told him that "*Through the Looking-Glass* is more stupid than *Alice's Adventures*." Regardless of which *Alice* book a reader prefers, there is little doubt that the other is a masterpiece as well. *Through the Looking-Glass* is a rare, highly successful sequel; nevertheless, *Alice* has enjoyed greater popularity and greater critical attention through the years. For the most part, *Through the Looking-Glass* is discussed with *Alice*, often in a subordinate position, in critical essays on the *Alice* books. There are, however, a few exceptions to this rule, and they appear to be growing. Francis Martens's previously cited psychotherapeutic reading is one exception, so too are numerous notes that have appeared. A major exception is Robert M. Polhemus's excellent, forty-eight page chapter on "Carroll's *Through the Looking-Glass* (1871): The Comedy of Regression" in *Comic Faith: The Great Tradition from Austen to Joyce* (1980). Polhemus sees *Through the Looking-Glass* bearing directly on historical modernism, on twentieth-century modes of comedy. "On the whole, Carroll's humor, language, vision, and characters seem even more resonant in it than they do in *Alice's Adventures in Wonderland* and even more central to the great modern comic tradition. . . . It is less sentimental than *Wonderland*, less escapist, more critical of both solipsism and social authority." Polhemus is thorough in his analysis of Carroll's comic triumph, and his sweeping study includes separate sections on the Child; Dream and Fantasy; Language; and Play, Nonsense, and Games: Comic Diversions. It should be noted that the discovery of the suppressed "wasp in a wig" episode to *Through the Looking-Glass* has begun to generate critical discussion. Robert Dupree's "The White Knight's Whiskers and the Wasp's Wig in *Through the Looking-Glass*" (in *Lewis Carroll: A Celebration*, 1982) is a sound part-whole analysis, which Dupree concludes by stating that he "would most emphatically welcome the restoration of Carroll's Wasp in a wig."

The Hunting of the Snark

The Hunting of the Snark's striking modernity has been noticed by several critics. Robert Martin Adams remarks in his excellent, brief discussion of the poem in *Nil: Episodes in Literary Conquest of Void During The Nineteenth Century* (1966), that it is taken as a much more serious piece of humor today than it ever was by the

Victorians. Since its publication, the *Snark* has invited scores of allegorical interpretations. Martin Gardner records many of these in his valuable compendium of *Snark* commentary, *The Annotated Snark* (1962; rev. most recently in 1981). In his Introduction Gardner offers his own reading. He sees the Snark as a modern poem about existential agony, about being and not being—a characteristic concern voiced in much modern literature. Robert Martin Adams endorses Gardner's reading and remarks that the quest motif in the poem can be seen as all quests in one. Professor Adams also notes other modern features of the *Snark*. He finds its metaphorical action represents a great social paradox of our time—the pattern of self-defeating success. He further suggests that the poem has the ability to release the suggestive power of the void, and this is one of its pioneering distinctions as literature.

Michael Holquist, in an article devoted exclusively to the *Snark's* modernity, "What is a Boojum? Nonsense and Modernism" (*YFS*, 1969), approaches the poem differently, through its structure. Holquist finds that *The Hunting of the Snark* is among the first works to exemplify what he considers is perhaps the most distinctive feature of modern literature, the attempt to insure through structure that the work could be perceived only for what it is and not something else—a built-in resistance to interpretations fastened on systems outside the fictive world. In "'Hear the Tolling of Bells': Lewis Carroll's *The Hunting of the Snark*" (in *Miscellanea Americana*, 1974), German critic Kuno Schulmann finds that the *Snark*, like many modern poems, does not communicate with the reader but provokes the reader. We find answers to the poem's conundrums not through content but through construction and especially through sensitivity to the linguistic and aesthetic autonomy Carroll constructs.

Edward Guiliano finds that the *Snark* shares many similarities with the *Alice* books. "Dreams, death, probings into the nature of being, reminders of the inescapability of time, and a quest motif figure in all three works. Moreover, just as one senses terror lurking beneath the surface of the *Alice* books, one senses terror and despair throughout the overtly humorous *Snark*. "This tension," Guiliano writes in "A Time for Humor: Lewis Carroll, Laughter and Despair, and *The Hunting of the Snark*" (in *Lewis Carroll: A Celebration*, 1982), "between the comic tone and the under-lying anxieties is perhaps the poem's most distinguishing and fascinating characteristic." He sees the humor in the poem partly as Dodgson's means for controlling his universe. He notes that "the Bellman is a character almost totally neglected by modern critics of the *Snark*," and that the centrality of this main character "indicates the centrality of the time in the poem."

Morton Cohen has written two background essays on the *Snark*, "The Wonderful Day Gertrude met the Snark" (*The Times*, 1974) and the previously cited "Hark the Snark (in *Lewis Carroll Observed*, 1976) which deserve special mention. He sheds new light on the poem's genesis, comments on the nature of contemporary views of the poem, and in the latter article reprints contemporary reviews of the poem. Taken together his essays provide a sound and provocative discussion of perhaps Carroll's most elusive work. An additional essay of some merit devoted exclusively to the *Snark* is Brian Sibley's "End Game" (*Jabberwocky*, 1976). Sibley argues that the game the crew is playing is really the game of not recognizing the game which is being played. *The Hunting of the Snark* is also treated at length in almost all serious discussions of Carroll's nonsense.

The *Sylvie and Bruno* Books

The *Sylvie and Bruno* books, as I remarked earlier, are just now beginning to attract serious critical attention. While there are no claims that these books rival the *Alice* books in overall quality, every critic who has turned to them has found much of interest and merit. In a probing and comprehensive discussion, "The *Sylvie and Bruno* Books as Victorian Novel" (in *Lewis Carroll Observed*, 1976), Edmund Miller argues that the reality and nonsense in the continuous novel are not easily separable, and by moving from one world to the other through dream we learn about the nature of life as Carroll wants us to perceive it. Miller also points out that structurally the novel is not much different from many Victorian novels. Ruth Berman, in the pamphlet *Patterns of Unification in Sylvie and Bruno* (1974), finds the fantasy in both books is superior to their realism, and, like Miller, finds the two seemingly contrasting realms too closely unified thematically and structurally to separate. Brian Sibley has taken a fresh look at "The Poems to *Sylvie and Bruno*" (*Jabberwocky*, 1975), and discovers that they contain some of Carroll's best verse and represent an important stage in his development as a poet.

French critics frequently cite the *Sylvie and Bruno* books. They generally agree with Jean Gattégno who, in his brilliant but erratic book-length study of Carroll's world view, *Lewis Carroll* (1970), finds two areas in the books that are as interesting as anything Carroll wrote: language and logic. Gattégno analyzes Carroll's use of language and reprints his findings while adding new insights in his Preface to the books' first French translation (1972; in English in revised form as *Sylvie and Bruno, or the Inside and the Outside*" [in *Lewis Carroll: A Celebration*, 1982]). Gattégno compares Bruno's language with Alice's and finds Bruno's distinct from adult's language and an expression of freedom resembling that of a dream. Gattégno finds the intellectual world of *Sylvie and Bruno* regressive: while Alice moves to adult language and views, the characters in *Sylvie and Bruno* have a way of thinking which is like a child of seven or less. The language-orientated French critics of the 1970s not only have analyzed language in the *Sylvie and Bruno* books, and of course in the *Alices*, but as I have previously mentioned, Raymond Queneau even analyzes the nine sentences and eighteen different words of dog language Carroll created in Chapter XIII of *Sylvie and Bruno* (in *Lewis Carroll*, ed. Henri Parisot, 1971; also in English translation by Don Serwin, "Concerning Some Imaginary Animal Languages, Particularly Dog Language in *Sylvie and Bruno* [*Jabberwocky*, 1977]).

In a rich essay, "Lewis Carroll, the *Sylvie and Bruno* Books, and the Nineties" (in *Lewis Carroll: A Celebration*, 1982), Jan B. Gordon integrates various concerns in Carroll's life in *fin-de-siècle* England and in his art—from the *Alice* books to his photographs, and primarily to the *Sylvie and Bruno* books. Gordon sees Carroll preoccupied with three themes in the *Sylvie and Bruno* books: "the relationship of child to man; the relationship of the literal language of necessary text to metaphoric language; and the relationship of the earth to heaven." Gordon's insights into Carroll's preoccupation with texts and textuality is particularly fresh.

Nonsense

Language, nonsense, comedy, games, escape, logic, and philosophy; these are interrelated dimensions of Carroll's art that have keenly interested contemporary literary critics, linguists, and philosophers. The Germans have emerged as the people most interested in nonsense as genre and in Carroll's nonsense in particular. Annemarie Schöne's *Englische Nonsense und Grusel-Balladen* (1970), Rolf Hildebrandt's *Nonsense-Aspekte der englischen Kinderliteratur* (1970), Dieter Petzold's *Formen und Funktionen der englischen Nonsense-Dichtung im 19. Jahrhundert* (1972), and Klaus Teichert's *Lewis Carroll—Studien zum literarischen Unsinn* (1974) include extensive, and in the case of Reichert, exclusive, discussions of Carroll's art and nineteenth-century British humor. Reinbert Tabbert is another German authority who has published extensively on Carroll's nonsense, notably "Zum literarischen Nonsense: Versuch einer Orientierung" (*DU*, 1975) and "Humpty Dumpty oder die Kunst Lewis Carrolls" (*LWU*, 1973). These Germans have approached Carroll's art through a variety of entrances—linguistic, logical, sociological, historical, aesthetic, psychological. With the exception of Shöne's simplistic introductory account, all the German discussions are sophisticated and valuable. They display a fascination with how Carroll uses nonsense to escape from a world that was and is too rational and too realistic.

The Germans' interest in Carroll's nonsense is currently without parallel elsewhere in the world. There have been no book-length studies of Carroll's nonsense published in English since Elizabeth Sewell's *The Field of Nonsense* in 1952. There is, however, Richard Kelly's comprehensive bio-critical introduction, *Lewis Carroll* (1977). "The principal aim of this book," Kelly writes, "is to demonstrate Lewis Carroll's mastery of the art of nonsense, a genre which his works practically define." Kelly's discussions of Carroll's major and minor poetry are useful. Also, Lisa Ede has devoted her dissertation to "The Nonsense Literature of Edward Lear and Lewis Carroll" (Diss. Ohio State University, 1976). She finds their nonsense to be subversive. Even though Carroll establishes structural devices in his imaginative works, such as the "rule of three" in the *Snark*, which provide the reader with a sense of control and safety, the terms of his nonsense literature ultimately are reformed to reveal the nightmare of logic and surrealistic logic of dreams. All the German discussions treat Lear and Carroll as well, but the most useful comparison of the two appears in a short passage in Peter Heath's Introduction to *The Philosopher's Alice* (1974). Heath rightly points out that "Carroll's fame as a nonsense writer is so firmly established that it is probably too late to persuade anyone that, apart from a few isolated instances such as the *Jabberwock* poem, he is not strictly a writer of nonsense at all." The term nonsense is regularly misused to mean anything that fails to make sense. Carroll makes too much sense. His proper genre is the absurd, which rigidly adheres, after it has ceased to be sensible to do so, to "the ordinary conventions of logic, linguistic usage, motive and behavior." The true nonsense-writer, like Lear, neglects or defies these conventions.

Psychoanalyst Phyllis Greenacre has also looked at the meaning of nonsense as it applies to the study of Carroll's art, and to a lesser extent as it applies to Lear's and also to Kafka's in "On Nonsense" (in *Psychoanalysis—A General Psychology*, eds. R. M. Lowenstein, et al., 1966). In developing her own understanding of the concept she reviews what various critics have meant when using the term, and she scrutinizes the meanings and implications of *sense* and *senseless*. Carroll and Lear, she finds, do not come very close to creating absolute nonsense, which almost by definition is incapable of being reproduced or represented. In her readings of Carroll's work she focuses on nonsense and its relation to aggression and anxiety. Greenacre sees Carroll communicating nonsense as a defense against destructive forces in his life, as a way of transcending his purely personal experiences, his pains and pressures of life. Her diverse findings—which are not easily conveyed in abstract—are often brilliant.

Still another approach to Carroll's nonsense is taken by Elizabeth Sewell. Starting with her study of Carroll's and Lear nonsense, *The Field of Nonsense* (1952), she argued that nonsense is an intellectual game with its own rules, and is really a function of "the mind's force toward order," the establishment of some sort of order to fight and overcome the tendency toward disorder. Her most recent refinements and applications of well-known theory appear in her essay "The Nonsense System in Lewis Carroll's Work and in Today's World" (in *Lewis Carroll Observed*, 1976). When viewed as a system of mental relations, Sewell finds Carroll's logic closely resembles certain real-life systems in today's society—professional sport, business, the Roman Catholic Church, the law, politics, and education. For Sewell, Carroll's nonsense resembles games: an enclosed field of operations, limited in space and time, governed by rules. Victory or mere survival depends on manipulative skill, detachment, mastery, and, according to Sewell, ultimately leads to nightmare.

Play

Led by Elizabeth Sewell, the play aspect of Carroll's art has developed into a distinct area of Carroll scholarship. The centrality of a play and game impulse in Carroll's work is obvious even to the most casual adult reader. All his literary works are filled with puzzles, games, anagrams, playful parodies and riddles, logical queries, and an overall sense of a game-like contest with his reader. There has been one book-length investigation of this area: Kathleen Blake's *Play, Games, and Sport: The Literary Works of Lewis Carroll* (1974).

Play, the literary presentation of a psychic impulse in Carroll, is the focus of Blake's investigation. She begins by establishing a psychological model of play and traces the progression from play through games to sport. Her model, her theory of play, is aimed at making "a new kind of sense of what Carroll wrote" and can be epitomized as follows: "Play—spontaneous disinterested, nonutilitarian—is characterized by a fundamental urge to mastery through incorporation of experience to the ego rather than adjustment or accomodation of the ego to experience." Carroll endorses the innocence of play and games in his works until games become sport—in the sense of cat chasing mouse—and this presents him with a problem.

Simpler notions of escape and a probing for alternative adult lifestyles similar to play are perhaps more acceptable explanations of this impulse in Carroll's work. Such a theory is argued most eloquently by Roger B. Henkle in his essay "The Mad-Hatter's World" (*VQR*, 1973; reworked in his book *Comedy and Culture: England 1820–1900*, 1980). Wayne De La Roche also touches on this in his dissertation, "Privacy and Community in the Writing of Lewis Carroll" (Diss. Columbia University, 1975), as does Peter Coveney in an impressive section of his book *The Image of Childhood* (1967; a revised edition of *Poor Monkey: The Child in Literature*, 1957), which treats, as do most of these discussions, dream fantasy as part of escape. Two additional discussions of Carroll's fantasy, one by Barbara Hardy in *Tellers and Listeners* (1975) and the other by Eric Rabkin in *The Fantastic in Literature* (1976) are disappointing in their simplicity and naivity, especially from two such generally astute readers.

Carroll's own game theory as presented in *The Principles of Parliamentary Representation* should be mentioned briefly at this point. Duncan Black in a series of articles—"The Central Argument in Lewis Carroll's 'The Principles of Parliamentary Representation'" (*Papers on Non-Marketing Decision Making*, 1967); "Lewis Carroll and the Theory of Games" (*American Economic Review*, 1969); "Evaluating Carroll's Theory of Parliamentary Representation" (*Jabberwocky*, 1970) and "Lewis Carroll and the Cambridge School of P. R.; Arthur Cohen and Edith Denman" (*Public Choice*, 1970)— has demonstrated the sophistication of the theory postulated by Carroll, and has single-handedly rescued *The Principles of Parliamentary Representation* from obscurity and established it as an important and elegant contribution to political science. Fran Abeles in "The Mathematical-Political Papers of C. L. Dodgson" (in *Lewis*

Carroll: A Celebration, 1982) looks further into Carroll's insights into parliamentary representation as well as at his papers on committee procedures, the ranking process and elections, including a pamphlet on lawn tennis tournaments. She finds his work remarkable both politically and mathematically.

Humor

The nonsense, humor, play, and escape elements of Carroll's writing are also treated in a series of studies of his humor. Both Roger B. Henkle and Donald J. Gray have considered Carroll's writing in the context of Victorian humor. In "Spitting Blood and Writing Comic: Mid-Century British Humor" (*Mosaic*, 1976), Henkle finds Carroll rests comfortably within the peculiar tradition of Hood and Gilbert. Gray, in a long essay on "The Uses of Victorian Laughter" (*VS*, 1966), sees Carroll along with Lear, Calverley, and Gilbert as practitioners of a subtle humor with skillfull rhymes which marks a significant change in the nature of popular Victorian humor from the first half of the century. These men refined techniques and manners and produced humor that tended to turn inward to find the sources of its laughter in private absurdity rather than in public follies.

While many Carroll critics have pointed out the liberating aspects of his art and how these elements provided a means of escape for Dodgson, James Kincaid notes in "Alice's Invasion of Wonderland" (*PMLA*, 1973) that Alice does not only reject the horrifying chaos of meaninglessness at the end of each *Alice* book, but also the liberating chaos of comedy as well. French critic Henri Laporte similarly has found in *Alice au pays des merveilles: Structures Logiques et Représentations du Désir* (1973) that logic in Wonderland is repressive and only leads to false liberation.

Donald Rackin, focusing on the nature of laughter in *Alice in Wonderland*, finds it is complex and depends heavily on much that cannot ordinarily be called "funny," that might indeed be better called "horrifying" ("Laughing and Grief: What's So Funny About *Alice in Wonderland?*" in *Lewis Carroll Observed*, 1976). Alice's dream, like most dreams, dynamically fuses childish and adult states of mind into a horror-comedy. Rackin finds our adult side identifies primarily with the narrator and laughs at what our child side, which identifies with Alice, finds positively frightening. Alvin Kibel in his wide-ranging "Logic and Satire in *Alice in Wonderland*" (*ASch*, 1974) similarly considers reader response and posits that Carroll discovered an intellectual legitimacy in the childish view, making it available to both childish and adult intelligences. Charles Matthews, in his reasonably good study of "Satire in the *Alice* Books" (*Criticism*, 1970), looks at the two principal types of nonsense Alice encounters, linguistic and logical, and finds that their inherent satire is less directed at institutions than at individual human foibles. Following along somewhat similar lines as the last two essays and still useful is Peter Alexander's brief *Logic and Humour of Lewis Carroll* (1951).

Language

"When I use a word," Humpty Dumpty, one of the founding fathers of semantics, said, "it means just what I choose it to mean— neither more nor less." E. Muskat-Tabakowska has reported on Carroll's "amazingly sharp insight into general semantics." In "General Semantics behind the Looking-Glass" (*ETC: A Review of General Semantics*, 1970), she notes how some of the formal principles of semantics developed after Carroll, such as those presented by Korzybski, show close relationships with some of the features in Carroll's books. Carroll's knowledge of language and how he uses it in his comic writing is thoroughly analyzed in Robert Sutherland's excellent though now somewhat dated book, *Language and Lewis Carroll* (1970). This comprehensive overview serves the beginning and advanced student of Carroll's language equally well. Some of what Sutherland reports had been presented earlier by Patricia Meyer Spacks in her well-known article "Logic and Language in *Through the Looking-Glass*" (*ETC: A Review of General Semantics*, 1961). Spacks identifies language as a theme underlying virtually all the book's episodes and discusses the main linguistic devices Carroll employs.

Several other commentators have produced valuable linguistic studies of Carroll's art. Jacqueline Flescher has investigated "The Language of Nonsense in Alice," the interactions of language and references, and order and disorder (*YFS*, 1969). She finds conversation and argument as the essential vehicles for nonsense in the book. French critic Gilles Deleuze, in his book *Logique du Sens* (1969), investigates Carroll's use of languages, especially in paradox. Alwin Baum has attempted to demonstrate how conventional language is regularly subverted by Carroll's characters and how their reversal of the normal sign-functions serves to liberate the individual's *parole* at the expense of nullifying communication; his argument appears in "Toward a Pragmatics of Paradox: A Structural Approach to the Absurd *Récit*" (Diss. University of California, Davis, 1973). Neilson Graham has looked at the insanity in Wonderland from a linguistic perspective in "Sanity, Madness and Alice" (*Ariel*, 1973), and Charles Stickney has made a study of word distortion in *Alice*, "The Distorted Word: Word Distortion in Modern British and American Literature" (Diss. City University of New York, 1973). Carroll's own speech disorder, J. De Keyser argues in "The Stuttering of Lewis Carroll" (in *Neurolinguistic Approaches to Stuttering*, eds. Yvan Lebrun and Richard Hoops, 1973), seems to have led through blendings of synonyms to Carroll's celebrated portmanteau-words. Insights into Carroll and language are also particularly rich in two previously cited works: Jean Gattégno's *Lewis Carroll* (1970), and Robert M. Polhemus's chapter on *Through the Looking-Glass* in *Comic Faith* (1980).

Philosophy, Logic and Mathematics

In addition to linguists, Carroll has continued to attract a healthy following of logicians, mathematicians, and philosophers. Peter Heath's *The Philosopher's Alice* is designed for such an audience. This second-generation annotated edition of the *Alices* (1974) is keyed to aspects of logic, philosophy and the study of language. As Heath affirms in his Introduction, and demonstrates through his annotations, the *Alice* books "are works of unsleeping rationality, whose frolics are governed throughout, not by a formal theory of any kind, but by close attention to the logical principles, and sometimes by a surprising insight into abstract questions of philosophy." With its annotations, appendix, and introduction, *The Philosopher's Alice* is quite valuable, as all annotated editions are to some degree, as a reference book. Heath has thoroughly researched, assimilated, pondered, and presented information that previously had been difficult to come by. One of the works he draws heavily upon deserves mention: Warren Shibles's long chapter of philosophical commentary on *Alice in Wonderland*, which appeared in *Wittgenstein, Language and Philosophy* (1969).

Dodgson the mathematician and logician is as much in evidence in Lewis Carroll's imaginative works as Carroll the creative writer is in evidence in the academic work of Dodgson. In 1885 this many-faceted genius's principal academic interest shifted from mathematics to logic. In 1887 he began giving lectures on logic to young girls at the Oxford High School and published *A Game of Logic*. And from that time until his death he was at work on a logic textbook. The first of three proposed volumes, *Symbolic Logic, Part I*, appeared in 1896, and today examples from it still are routinely included in new textbooks on logic. Logicians continue to invoke Carroll's name frequently when discussing inference and the debate over "What the Tortoise said to Achilles," which Carroll inaugurated in *Mind* in 1894. J. F. Thomson treats it in "What Achilles Should have Said to the Tortoise" (*Ratio*, 1960) and so does William A. Wisdom in "Lewis Carroll's Infinite Regress" (*Mind*, 1974). And philosophers in recent years have coupled Carroll's name with Ludwig Wittgenstein's. In an article devoted to "Wittgenstein, Nonsense and Lewis Carroll" (*MR*, 1965), George Pitcher argues that Carroll exerted a profound influence on the later Wittgenstein, and that there exist some extraordinary and illuminating parallels between their treatments of nonsense.

There has been one attempt to determine the sense and significance of Carroll's (and here again I should write Dodgson's) contribution to logic at the precise moment in the history of logic in which he was working. The French philosopher Ernest Coumet has provided this overview in an essay contained in a French translation of selections from Carroll's logic books, *Logique sans peine* (1966). Coumet has also published another important article, already cited, on Carroll/Dodgson and the notion of "universe of discourse" (in *Lewis Carroll*, ed. Henri Parisot, 1971; in English in *Lewis Carroll Observed*, 1976).

I mentioned earlier that William W. Bartley, III, spent eighteen years reconstructing *Symbolic Logic, Part II Advanced*, and his definitive edition of the text Dodgson was working on when he died appeared in 1977. In two articles published in the 1970s—"Lewis Carroll's Lost Book on Logic" (*Scientific American*, 1972) and "Lewis Carroll as Logician" (*TLS*, 1973)—as well as in the Introduction to his edition, Bartley made substantial claims for the new material. He claimed that it confirms the opinions of Bertrand Russell and Eric Temple Bell that Carroll "had in him the stuff of a great mathematical logician," and that the new material contains work one might expect a first-class logician to be doing in the 1890s. Although the final results are still not in, the publication of *Symbolic Logic, Part II* seemingly proves some of Bartley's assertions. Carroll's work on logic falls into two parts: method and formulation of problems (paradoxes). Logicians, as I suggested earlier, can now make a juster estimate than before of Carroll's achievements, and they have been finding that they are by no means meager. He is now firmly established as a master technician, extraordinary puzzle maker, and probing thinker. Carroll's work with sorities and his method of trees are certainly remarkable. We know that Carroll intended his symbolic logic texts to be widely read since he signed them with his pen name rather than C. L. Dodgson; appropriately, they are filled with all sorts of marvelous creatures and lively Carrollian stories.

We also know from Fran Abeles in her previously cited essay "The Mathematical-Political Papers of C.L. Dodgson" (in *Lewis Carroll: A Celebration*, 1982) that in his work on logic and mathematics, especially in his odd little pamphlets, such as those on elections and committees, on tournaments, and on general elections, Dodgson showed a continuation, though in a different form, of the brilliance and creativity so evident in the *Alices* and the *Snark*. Indeed, in his pamphlets "Dodgson showed a grasp on the intuitive level, of ideas that did not begin to be formalized until the 1920s. The work is all the more unusual because of the integrity of its development, with many political, mathematical, and personal interconnections."

Edward Wakeling's pamphlet, *The Logic of Lewis Carroll* (1977) should be noted in this section as a good introduction to "Carroll's contribution to logic, his logical discoveries and his endeavours to teach the subject to children." Similarly, Warren Weaver's "Lewis Carroll, Mathematician" (*Scientific American*, 1956) is still a reasonable introduction to this related aspect of Carrollian interest and achievement, as is of course Martin Gardner's *The Annotated Alice* (1960).

Influences and Affinities

A considerable body of literature has grown up around Carroll's literary influences and affinities. No full study has yet been made of these matters, but Jeffrey Stern in "Approaches to Lewis Carroll" (Diss. University of York, 1973) does look at such formative influences upon Carroll's art as Dickens and the Pre-Raphaelites; at various affinities Carroll's art shares with the art of Laurence Sterne, Cervantes and George MacDonald; and at writers whom Carroll influenced such as the Surrealists, James Joyce, T. S. Eliot, and Vladimir Nabokov. Literary influences are difficult to prove and affinities are often curiously provoking, but they are deserving of study since, as T. S. Eliot remarked, "no poet, no artist of any art has complete meaning alone."

I have already cited discussions of the formative influences children's literature has upon Carroll, and I have mentioned some of the comparative discussions of the art of Lear and Carroll. The remaining list of possible formative influences and of Carroll's literary influences and affinities is so stunningly rich and diverse that all I can do is draw attention to this material, alphabetically by author, so that future work may take a meaningful direction.

Carroll's influences and affinities extend to the literatures of many non-English-speaking countries. Irmgard Z. Anderson has recorded Fernando Arrabal's debt to Carroll, citing the unmistakable correspondence between the ideas an actions in *Through the Looking-Glass* and *Pique-nique en campagne*. Artaud and Carroll have been compared in print several times. Gilles Deleuze, in "Le Schizophrène et le mot" (*Critique* 1968) and in English in *Textual Strategies, Perspectives in Post-Structuralist Criticism* (ed. Josué Harari, 1979), finds similarities between Carroll and Artaud, but in relation to language sees them as essentially dissimilar. Carroll is the master of surfaces, and read to be known and not explored, where the "logique du sens" holds. Artaud is the master of the depths of language. He explores the "infra-sens." Josette Hector, in "La métaphysiologique de Lewis Carroll" (*Synthèses*, 1970), compares and contrasts Carroll's, Artaud's, and Mallarmé's perceptions of time.

Oz, that American turn-of-the-century dream world, is compared with Wonderland at least twice: once at some length by Osmond Beckwith in "The Oddness of Oz" (*ChildL*, 1976) and once briefly but perceptively by Martin Gardner in the previously cited "A Child's Garden of Bewilderment" (*Sat. R*, 1965). If Oz evokes wonderland in readers' minds, it is not alone. To read *Don Quixote* and *Alice in Wonderland* "with the other in mind is to turn up analogues almost constantly," according to Mary Fuertes Boynton in "An Oxford Don Quixote" (*Hispania*, 1964). John Hinz previously and effectively had demonstrated the parallels between these classics in "Alice Meets the Don" (*South Atlantic Quarterly*, 1953; rpt. in *Aspects of Alice*), and numerous other writers have alluded to *Don Quixote* as a precursor along the fantasy road leading to the *Alices*. Luis López-Celpecho sees parallels between the *Alice* books and another work of Spanish literature, Cortázar's *Historias de cronopios y de famas*. In "C. de Carroll y de Cortázar" (*Cuadernos Hispanon-americanos*, 1968) López-Celpecho points out that both Carroll and Cortázar treat madness in their works, are fascinated with mirrors, and treat words like a feast. While Carroll introduces Alice, a normal human being, Cortázar introduces inhuman imps.

The inimitable one, Dickens, has been repeatedly cited as an influence upon Carroll. Kathleen Tillotson has suggested, in "Lewis Carroll and the Kitten on the Hearth" (*English*, 1954), that the opening chapter of *Through the Looking-Glass* is a parody of the opening of Dickens' *The Cricket on the Hearth*. Jeffrey Stern in his previously cited dissertation starts from this correspondence and points out many more parallels and influences. Jean Gattégno has also shown Dickens' influence on Carroll and has compared how justice is rendered in *Pickwick* and *Alice* in "D'un Procès à L'Autre, ou de *Pickwick* à *Alice*" (*EA*, 1970). Richard Arnoldi has looked specifically at *Through the Looking-Glass* and *Our Mutual Friend*, which Carroll was reading while composing his second *Alice* book. He identifies echoes and other "Parallels between *Our Mutual Friend* and the *Alice* books" (*ChildL*, 1972). In his Preface to *Lewis Carroll: A Celebration* (1982), Edward Guiliano notes that Carroll's impact today on the popular culture, like Dickens', is extensive, and that the profound impact of Carroll's art, like Dickens', is especially noticeable in the areas of language and character.

Elizabeth Sewell has looked at "Lewis Carroll and T. S. Eliot as Nonsense Poets" (*T. S. Eliot*, ed. Neville Braybrooke, 1958), and Ernest Earnest sees more Carroll–Eliot correspondences between "The Walrus and the Carpenter" (*CEA Critic*, 1963) and Eliot's *The Waste Land*. In "Some Observations on the Biography and Work of Lewis Carroll and Nikolai Gogol" (*FMLS*, 1975), Edmund Little writes that "these two authors who made merry with the norms and conventions of the waking world" are "realists . . . with a better claim than Dostoyevsky to this honour!" Carroll's "logical organization of the absurd" is compared with yet another continental artist by Mario Praz in "Two Masters of the Absurd: Granville and Carroll" (in *The Artist and Writer in France*, ed. Francis Haskell, et al., 1974).

The remarkable parallels between the *Alices* and classic works in other literatures is seen in American literature in Joseph Heller's *Catch-22*. Caroline Gordon and Jeanne Richardson were the first to make this comparison in "Flies in Their Eyes? A Note on Joseph Heller's *Catch-22*" (*SoR*, 1967). Patrick Morrow took up the same subject in "Yossarian in Wonderland: Bureaucracy, the *Alice* Books, and *Catch-22*" (*NDQ*, 1975). Terry Otten compares and contrasts *Alice* with a classic work of literature in German, Herman Hesse's *Steppenwolf*. In "Steppenwolf and Alice—In and Out of

Wonderland" (*StHum*, 1974), Otten writes that both Alice and Steppenwolf "journey into made Wonderlands similarly depicted through the use of terrors, sudden evaporation of scenes, disregard of time and space, disappearance of characters, association of savagery and cruelty, images of childhood and lost innocence, and various other common elements." Even more significant, according to Otten, is that both Alice's and Steppenwolf's flights "become a measure of their humanity, a means by which their 'beingness' is defined."

It is not two works but two men who are compared and contrasted in Derek Hudson's "Lewis Carroll and G. M. Hopkins: Clergymen on a Victorian See-saw" (*DR*, 1970). Hudson finds that the most interesting comparison between the two men is that they both "welcomed the challenge of the complicated, and both were absorbed in the study of words." Another man whose name is sometimes linked with Carroll's is Kafka. Phyllis Greenacre and Elizabeth Sewell have often made the connection, and a Rumanian critic, Monica Pillat, finds in "Ipoteze asupra semnificatiilor operei lui Lewiş Carroll" (*ViR*, 1968) that among the similarities between Carroll and Kafka is that in their works there is the impossibility of escape from the cosmos.

Joyce is one of the most significant names associated with Carroll's, and several critics have affirmed that Carroll was one of Joyce's predecessors along an important road in literary history. James Atherton was the first to analyze the Joyce-Carroll connection. In his *The Books at the Wake: A Study of Literary Allusions in James Joyce's "Finnegans Wake"* (1960), Atherton especially points out allusions and parallel techniques in Joyce's modernist text with elements in Carroll's life and art. In 1957 the French critic Michel Butor pointed out parallels between Carroll's use of language and Joyce's, especially in *Finnegans Wake* ("Equisse D'un Seuil Pour Finnegan," rpt. in *Répertoire*, 1960). Recently Ann McGarrity Buki, in "Lewis Carroll in *Finnegans Wake*" (in *Lewis Carroll: A Celebration*, 1982), has made a full and revealing study of the pervasiveness of Carrollian elements in Joyce's work. John A. Rea has reported usefully on "A Bit of Lewis Carroll in *Ulysses*" (*JJQ*, 1977). By identifying a Carrollian source in *Ulysses*, Rea is able to demonstrate that Joyce knew Carroll's work prior to 1927, the date Joyce acknowledged.

It was George MacDonald and his family who first urged their friend C. L. Dodgson to publish *Alice's Adventures Under Ground*, and in all of the biographies of Lewis Carroll his fellow children's writer, who undoubtedly influenced his friend, is mentioned and sometimes discussed. R. Shaberman, in "Lewis Carroll and George MacDonald" (*Jabberwocky*, 1976), has made the fullest comparative study of the two friends and authors. In addition to a biographical discussion, Shaberman looks at MacDonald's influence upon Carroll's art and shows how "certain passages in *Phantastes* undoubtedly influenced the *Alice* books," and how the two men's fairy tales share "certain common elements of symbolism and association." Robert Lee Wolff, in "An 1862 Alice: 'Cross Purposes' or, *Which Dreamed it?*" (*HLB*, 1975), has also shown how MacDonald in "Cross Purposes," with a heroine named Alice, was independently working the same vein of fantasy as Carroll.

In *The Hunting of the Snark*, the Bellman evokes his now famous rule-of-three, "What I tell you three times is true." We have been told at least four times that the *Snark* bears striking similarities to Herman Melville's *Moby-Dick*. W. H. Auden noted it in *The Enchafed Flood* (1950); Robert Martin Adams discussed it in *Nil: Episodes in the Literary Conquest of Void during the Nineteenth Century* (1966); but the first direct and extended comparison of the two masterpieces was by Marcel Marnat in "Du serquin au cachalot blanc" (in *Lewis Carroll*, ed. Henri Parisot, 1971). Marnat wonders if the *Snark* was a passionate parody of *Moby-Dick* or merely a teasing echo, dimly caught—with no formal parallelism in mind, a game just for the fun of it. Harold Beaver in "Whale or Boojum: An Agony" (in *Lewis Carroll Observed*, 1976) has made the fullest study of the "majestic prose saga and the inconsequential-sounding ballad." In a complex study, Beaver finds *Moby-Dick* the *Snark*'s closest analogue; they both need no external clues nor allegorial key and are both symbolically self-contained.

While parallels between *Moby-Dick* and the *Snark* may come as a surprise to some readers, parallels and other connections between the *Alice* books and Vladimir Nabokov's *Lolita* probably will not. Nabokov's first published work was a translation of *Alice* into Russian, and he thought of Lewis Carroll as the first Humbert Humbert. There are more than a few direct allusions to the *Alices* in *Lolita*, and not surprisingly they have been pointed out and discussed by several readers. Alfred Appel, Jr., in *The Annotated Lolita* (1970) discusses Nabokov's interest in Carroll and points out some allusions and parallels to Carroll's life and work in *Lolita*. Jeffrey Stern takes up the Carroll–Nabokov connection in his previously cited dissertation. And there have been two article-length studies. James Joyce in "Lolita in Humberland" (*SNNTS*, 1974) demonstrates that allusions in *Lolita* to the *Alice* books "have structural and thematic purpose, and thus important consequences for understanding the novel." Elizabeth Prioleau in "Humbert Humbert through the *Looking-Glass*" (*TCL*, 1975) identifies similarities between *Lolita* and *Through the Looking-Glass*. "Seen together, Humbert's whole narration has a 'Looking-Glass work' perspective: time and space move backward, doubles proliferate, language fractures into new combinations." At the same time, within Humbert's story itself, there is a concurrent dramatization of Humbert's struggle to penetrate the looking-glass.

Carroll spent most of his adult life at Oxford, from his matriculation in 1850 to his death in 1897. No doubt Carroll knew Walter Pater, who was at Oxford during most of these same years and subject to many of the same routines, influences, and colleagues. The names of Carroll and Pater, however, have remained conspicuously unconnected with but one major exception, David George Aivaz's "A Study of Correspondences in the Writings of Walter Pater and Lewis Carroll" (Diss. Harvard University, 1962). Although Carroll and Pater differ widely in subjects, genres, purposes, and audiences, several notions in Carroll's writing are, according to Aivaz, strikingly similar to notions and motifs in Pater's writing. "These notions and motifs derive from the writers' basic assumptions about nature, the inner nature of man and animals, and the force of 'passion' which, in their view, inexorably drives all living things." Aivaz further argues that Pater's and Carroll's own sense of terror at their view of the natural world and the natural man underlies everything they wrote. Carroll may have also seen various Pre-Raphaelites at Oxford, but it was in London that he met and became friendly with various of these poets and painters. In his dissertation and later in "Lewis Carroll the Pre-Raphaelite: 'Fainting in Coils'" (in *Lewis Carroll Observed*, 1976), Jeffrey Stern has stunningly demonstrated Carroll's involvement with these contemporaries, especially the Rossettis and Arthur Hughes, and the profound impact they had upon his art, including how Alice is visualized.

In our Wonderland world it seems at times that nothing is without affinity to Carroll's universe. Eileen Z. Cohen, in "Alex in Wonderland, or *Portnoy's Complaint*" (*TCL*, 1971), has demonstrated that Philip Roth's *Portnoy's Complaint* has a great deal in common with *Alice in Wonderland*. Alex's literal world is topsy-turvy, and his real world is what other men fantasize. His life is "one in which he can find no truth consistent with the conventions of his particular situation, just as Alice can find no logic in Wonderland in terms of the conventions of the world above ground." Both Alice and Alex "must wonder through their nightmare visions to discover who they are."

In his dissertation and most effectively in "Lewis Carroll the Surrealist" (*Lewis Carroll: A Celebration*, 1982), Jeffrey Stern has made a valuable comprehensive study of an important literary affinity. His convincing juxtapositions and analyses enable us to see Carroll's art in new light. As with his "Lewis Carroll the Pre-Raphaelite," Stern sets visualizations of Carroll's characters and events alongside paintings and drawings from another movement and demonstrates irrefutable similarities. The catalog of similarities between Carroll and the Surrealists, Stern has shown us, is rich. In his dissertation, in a useful discussion of Laurence Sterne and Carroll, he has also demonstrated that Carroll's art points back to the eighteenth century as well as ahead to the twentieth. The focus, of course, is on the nonsense of *Tristram Shandy*, which, in turn, leads back to *Don Quixote*.

It must be stated, I suppose, that in the 1930s H. M. and D. C. Partridge published a monograph, *The Most Remarkable Echo in the World* (1933), in which they state definitely that Samuel Clemens and not Lewis Carroll wrote the *Alices*. They do point out some remarkable similarities between the work of the two authors. Their monograph inspired George Lanning to review their claims tongue-in-check in "Did Mark Twain Write 'Alice's Adventures in Wonderland'?" (in *Carrousel for Bibliophiles*, ed. W. Targ, 1947; rpt. in *Aspects of Alice*). More revealing similarities with still another author, Boris Vian, are identified and discussed by Jennifer R. Walters in "The Disquieting Worlds of Lewis Carroll and Boris Vian" (*RLC*, 1972). Carroll and Vian exploit the system of verbal structure and logic that rational man lives in, and show, "with terrifying clarity, how fully words control sense and how easily they can distort it." I have already mentioned Warren Shibles's *Wittgenstein, Language and Philosophy* (1969) which contains a chapter on *Alice* and also George Pitcher's study of the affinities between these two logicians. In "Wittgenstein, Nonsense and Lewis Carroll" (*MR*, 1965) Pitcher demonstrates that absurdities exposed in the *Tractatus* and *Philosophical Investigations* were exploited by Carroll for comic effect. Wordsworth is yet another figure commentators have regularly connected with Carroll. There is a rather direct connection in *Through the Looking-Glass* in Carroll's parody of the "Ode on Immortality." This and other allusions are often noted, and it is Horace Gregory who perhaps has written most profitably "On

Lewis Carroll's *Alice* and Her White Knight and Wordsworth's 'Ode on Immortality'" (in *The Shield of Achilles: Essays on Beliefs in Poetry*, 1944; rpt. in *Aspects of Alice*). To conclude, let me give Alice the last word in this review essasy. It is all, as she might say, "curiouser and curiouser."

Index

311

Alice's innocence, 290; genre studies of 290–291; and Romanticism, 291; as forerunner of modernist novel, 291; nostalgia in, 291; and twentieth-century modes of comedy, 292; laughter in, 229–300; logic, philosophy and language in, 301; mentioned, 264, 267

Tillotson, Kathleen, 305

Times Literary Supplement, 244

Times (London): editorial attacks on commercial morality in 1840s and 1850s, 72; Dickens faithful reader of, 73, 76 n.22; contemporary awareness of *Little Dorrit* in, 74; mentioned, 69, 70, 71, 73, 94, 95, 100, 101, 114, 116

Tipperary Joint Stock Bank scandal, 68–69

Todd, Janet, 233

"To Fausta" (Arnold), 36

Tour in 1867 (Dodgson), 269

Tractarians: influence on William Morris, 247

Tractatus (Wittgenstein), 309

Trade in Lunacy, The (Parry-Jones), 99

Transactions of the Brontë Society, 8

Transcendentalism, Romantic: in Carlyle's philosophy of history, 82

Treatment of the Borderline Adolescent, The (Masterson), 123

Trilling, Lionel, 7, 45

Tristram Shandy (Sterne), 309

Trollope, Anthony, 9, 10, 15

Trollopian, The, 8

T. S. Eliot (Braybrooke), 305

Tupper, Martin, 3

Turner case, 101, 104, 137 n.23

Turpin, John, 245

"Twin Sisters, The" (Collins): and *Cinderella* story, 120

Two Tales by Charlotte Brontë, "The Secret" & "Lily Hart" (Holtz), 222

Types of the Folktale, The (Aarne and Thompson), 119

Ulysses (Joyce), 306

Under the Greenwood Tree (Hardy), 149

Unknown Lewis Carroll (Diversions and Digressions), The (Dover rpt.), 269

Unquiet Soul, A Biograhy of Charlotte Brontë (Peters), 224

Useful and Instructive Poetry (Dodgson), 269

Uses of Enchantment, The (Bettelheim), 122

Vallon, Annette, 17

Vanity Fair, (Thackeray): as novel of "felt" as opposed to "recovered" past, 78–79

Verity, Charles, 100

Vian, Boris, 309

Victims of Convention (Kennard), 232

Victoria and Albert Museum, 12

Victorian Aftermath, The (Wingfield-Stratford), 6

Victorian Bibliography, 2, 7, 14

Victorian Family, Structures and Stresses, The (Wohl), 228

Victorian Fiction: A Guide to Research, 263

Victorian Frame of Mind, The (Houghton), 11

Victorian Multiplot Novel: Studies in Dialogical Form, The (Garret), 256

Victorian Poetry, 9

Victorian Poetry: A Guide to Research, 263

Victorian scholarship: review of, 1941 to present, 1–21; early stages to 1940, 1–6; growth in 1940s, 6–8; appearance of research journals and research projects, 8–9; interest in Victorian periodicals, 10–11; rehabilitation of Victorian painting, 12; and vicissitudes of critical reputations, 15–16; notable controversies in, 17–18; appraisal of current status of, 18–20

Victorian Studies, 8, 263

Victorian Studies Centre, 9

Victorian Sunset, The (Wingfield-Stratford), 6

Victoria Through the Looking-Glass: The Life of Lewis Carroll (Lennon), 280

Viljoen, Helen Gill, 4

Villette (Brontë): attacked by Harriet Martineau for overvaluing love, 225; studies of, 229, 230, 231, 232, 237, 238, 239, 240; mother motif in, 229; sexual fulfillment in, 231; figure of the Nun in, 231–233; Matthew Arnold's reaction to, 234

"Voice From a Madhouse: By One

Contents of Previous Volumes

Volume 5 (1976)

Volume 6 (1977)

Volume 7 (1978)